INLAND WATERWAYS OF THE NETHE

Published by
Imray Laurie Norie & Wilson Ltd
Wych House The Broadway St Ives Cambridgeshire PE27 5BT England
☎ +44(0)1480 462114 *Fax* +44(0)1480 496109
Email ilnw@imray.com www.imray.com
2007

1st edition 2007

A catalogue record for this book is available from the British Library.

ISBN 978 085288 976 3

CAUTION
Every effort has been made to ensure the accuracy of this book. It contains selected information and thus is not definitive and does not include all known information on the subject in hand; this is particularly relevant to the plans, which should not be used for navigation. The authors believe that their selection is a useful aid to prudent navigation, but the safety of a vessel depends ultimately on the judgement of the navigator, who should assess all information, published or unpublished.

PLANS
The plans in this guide are not to be used for navigation. They are designed to support the text and should at all times be used with navigational charts.

CORRECTIONAL SUPPLEMENTS
This pilot book will be amended at intervals by the issue of correctional supplements. These are published on the internet at our web site www.imray.com and may be downloaded free of charge. Printed copies are also available on request from the publishers at the above address.

Printed and bound by Star Standard Industries, Singapore

INLAND WATERWAYS OF THE NETHERLANDS

Louise Busby and David Broad

Imray Laurie Norie & Wilson

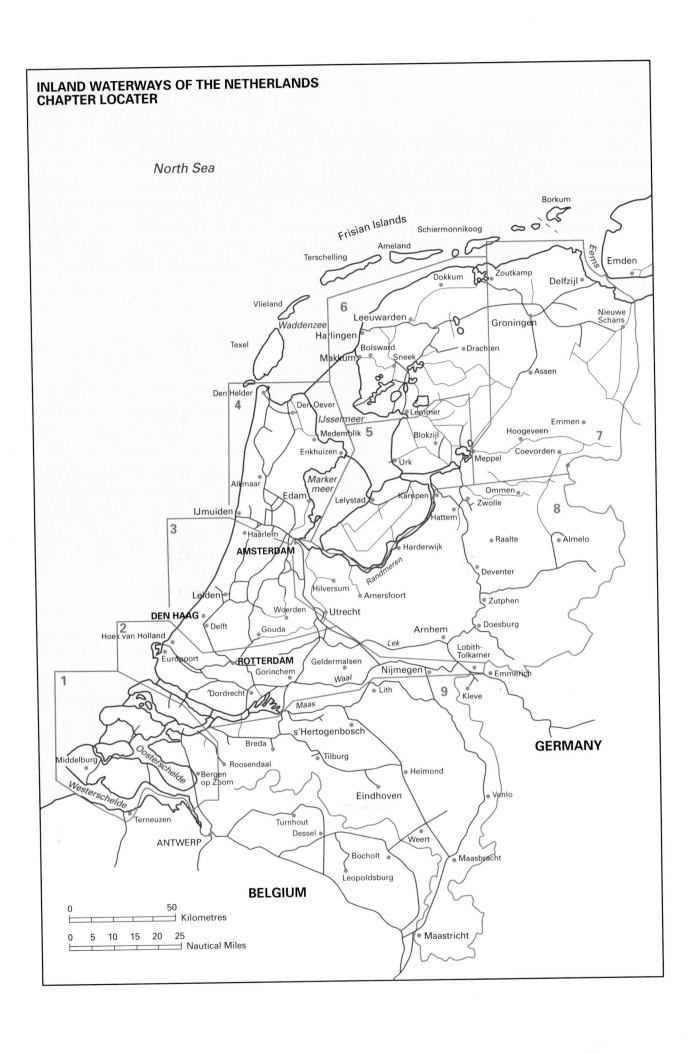

INLAND WATERWAYS OF THE NETHERLANDS
CHAPTER LOCATER

North Sea

Borkum

Frisian Islands Schiermonnikoog

Ameland

Terschelling

Vlieland

6

Leeuwarden

Dokkum   Zoutkamp

Delfzijl

Emden

Eems

Nieuwe
Schans

Harlingen

Groningen

Texel

Makkum   Bolsward

Sneek   Drachten

Waddenzee

Den Helder

Den Oever

Assen

4

IJsselmeer

Lemmer

Medemblik   **5**

Blokzijl

Emmen

Hoogeveen

Enkhuizen

Urk

Coevorden

Meppel

7

Alkmaar

Marker meer

Edam   Lelystad

Kampen

Ommen

IJmuiden

Zwolle

Hattem

8

3

Haarlem

Harderwijk

Raalte   Almelo

AMSTERDAM

Randmeren

Deventer

Hilversum

Leiden

Amersfoort

Zutphen

Woerden

DEN HAAG

Utrecht

Arnhem

Doesburg

2

Delft

Gouda

Lek

Lobith-
Tolkamer

Hoek van Holland

Geldermalsen

Nijmegen

Emmerich

Europoort

ROTTERDAM

Gorinchem

Waal

Lith

9

Kleve

Dordrecht

Maas

GERMANY

s'Hertogenbosch

Breda

Tilburg

Middelburg

Roosendaal

Helmond

Bergen
op Zoom

Venlo

Oosterschelde

Eindhoven

1

Westerschelde

Terneuzen

Turnhout

Dessel

Weert

Maasbracht

ANTWERP

Bocholt

Leopoldsburg

BELGIUM

0		50	

Kilometres

0 5 10 15 20 25

Nautical Miles

Maastricht

Contents

Foreword

The Netherlands is a wonderful country for family sailing. It also very suitable for those who like to potter, and for those who have limited holiday time and prefer not to risk being gale bound for much of it. At the same time I know a number of experienced cruising people, with more time available, who spend five months there every year.

There is a well-established standard British tour, which comprises visits to Middelburg, Veere, Goes, Zierikzee and Willemstad. These places can be very crowded during the Dutch school holiday season and this sometimes deters sailors from a return visit. There is so much more!

This new pilot guide is unprecedented in that it covers the whole of the inland cruising area rather than just the fixed mast routes. I hope it will encourage more sailors to discover for themselves how satisfying an exploration of the lakes, rivers and canals can be. There is a particular affinity between the Dutch people and the British which ensures a warm welcome and, apart from a very few remote places, there is no language barrier.

For those who do not own a boat, there are plenty of opportunities to hire both yachts and motorboats locally to extend your cruising horizons. So, no excuses. With the information in this book you can follow your dreams!

Stuart Bradley
June 2007

For fifteen years Stuart Bradley was the Editor of the *Cruising Association Handbook for The Netherlands and Belgium*. He is also the author of *An Introduction to Cruising in The Netherlands* published by the CA. During the last 30 years he has cruised extensively from Brittany to Estonia.

KEY TO SYMBOLS ON PLANS

⚓	Yacht harbour, marina
⛵	Yacht berths without facilities
⚓	Anchorage
Ⓥ	Visitors' moorings
ⓘ	Harbour office
⊖	Custom office
⌂	Tower
⋇	Windmill
ⵌ	Water tap
⛽	Fuel station
A	Chandler
➤	Public slipway
⬛	Pumpout
—	Moorings
⊕	Church
⊠	Castle
⌘	Water tower
•-•-	Underwater pipeline
WC	Toilets
⊡	Showers
⊙	Launderette
VVV	Tourist office

Introduction

An untapped opportunity

The Netherlands offer some of the finest inland cruising in Europe, devoid of many of the locks and fixed bridges that punctuate progress elsewhere and away from the sea conditions that many people wish to avoid when cruising. Until now, many of these waters have not been described in the English language, with detailed information only available in Dutch and occasionally German. Most English-speaking skippers have kept to the 'mast-up' routes or have confined their boating to certain areas close to the coast or where they have gathered information and so have seldom exploited these opportunities to the full.

With the high costs of using and keeping boats in southern Britain, and with the costs of diesel fuel for leisure ever-rising, it is most likely that more and more English-speaking boat crews will want to spend time taking full advantage of what Holland has to offer, and even to base their boat there for one or more seasons, and this book aims to combine navigational information with details of both where to go and what to do. Provided that skipper, boat and crew are well-prepared and briefed, boating in the Netherlands will be a memorable experience. As Dutch is not even the second language of most international visitors, it is anticipated that visiting

In a 'box' you normally moor bow-to a landing stage and tie lines to piles aft

skippers from other countries in Northern Europe and Scandinavia (and indeed from all over the world) might also wish to take advantage of this book.

It is assumed that the skipper and crew have previously acquired a range of general boating skills and experience, but it is recognised that the Netherlands may be the first inland cruising experience of boat crews based in coastal marinas. In this case, general preparation by taking advice and reading-up on techniques used in navigating locks and bridges is suggested, and some practice manoeuvring in confined spaces would be helpful. It might, for example, be the first time the helmsman and crew have come across the need to moor inside a 'box' of mooring stakes where access to and from the shore has to be across the bow or stern, or to moor bow-on to a bank and be secured by shorelines and aft anchors. There are many other sources of general information and publications covering a wide range of boating aspects (with the Royal Yachting Association and the Cruising Association the major ones) and they include general guidance

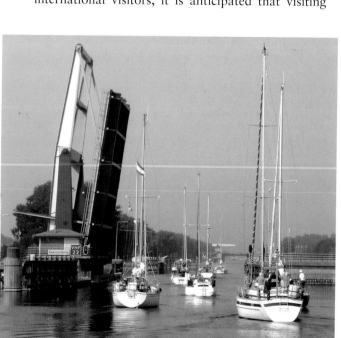

English-speaking boaters have been mainly restricted to mast-up routes due to lack of information

A barge displays a blue board to signify you should pass starboard-to-starboard

about cruising abroad, international signals and regulations to help the whole process be as well-planned and organised as possible. Some of the major considerations, and those specific to the Netherlands, are mentioned below.

Certain documentation and personal skills certificates are needed and these are listed and described below. The international systems of buoyage are followed and most of the signs and lights conform to the European CEVNI codes, so a handy list of these can be useful at first as reminders. For example, a blue board or flag hung on the oncoming vessel's starboard side asks that you pass starboard-to-starboard for navigational reasons, instead of the normal practice of 'driving on the right' common on all waterways around Europe, including the UK. Ferries are numerous and varied in their types and operation, and may leave cables trailing across the navigation channel or swing bank-to-bank from an anchor in mid-stream, so care is needed in their vicinity.

It is also assumed when making coastal passages for arrival and return that the skipper has a maritime Almanac, such as that from Imray/CA or Reeds (the former having more coverage of the Dutch inland waterways accessible to the coast) together with the offshore charts, and uses them for navigation. This book is designed to dovetail into their use and avoids repeating the same information for that reason. If your boat has been brought across in fine weather or transported for you from the British inland waterways, or hired/chartered in the Netherlands (which are all very good and valid ways of enjoying the experience) then some consideration might be necessary to ensure that the equipment and contents are well-secured and appropriate for the conditions sometimes experienced on the larger and more commercial waterways. In either case, approach the large 'inland seas' with initial caution in windy weather above Force 5/6 as they can be more akin to open seas if you stray from shelter, being generally shallow in nature.

It is also assumed that the boat itself has been prepared mechanically, electronically and domestically for inland cruising with a suitable range of spares and basic tools including oil and fuel filters,

fan belts etc and that full equipment lists and manuals are kept aboard for ease of reference should the need for assistance be required.

Also that a set of signal flags and the Dutch courtesy flag is kept on board. Many experienced British skippers swap their defaced or blue ensigns when abroad for the standard 'red duster' as it is confusing enough to the hosts that we do not use our national flag for an ensign, let alone a defaced red or blue variety!

Navigational charts and equipment

A copy of the Dutch waterway regulations is a legal requirement on board and must be produced upon request. The *ANWB Almanak 1* is a convenient way of complying with this requirement but, being totally in Dutch, is not much practical help to the English-speaking yachtsman. *Wateralmanak 2* on the other hand is a useful reference document - a detailed guide to understanding and using it is given at the end of this book.

ANWB/VVV charts of the Dutch inland waterways, or *Waterkaarten* are normally valid for two years, referenced A to R they are considered vital for cruising safely. Current editions of these Waterkaarts are very accurate and easy to use once you have become familiar with them, but beware of older out of date 'gifts' from other boating colleagues as the waterways and road networks have changed considerably over the years. Beware also of using a larger scale chart when a more detailed one of the area is available – such as for the Biesbosch. They exist for a very good reason and are necessary for safe navigation. Note also that depths and bridge heights are in decimetres, the latter being the cause of consternation at the first bridge if you were assuming it meant metres! The charts are marked with latitude and longitude scales and could be referenced in with a Yeoman plotter suitable for navigation, for example, but GPS positioning on them is not normally needed in view of the many adjacent landmarks and good buoyage in open water. A portion of the range is published in time for each cruising season, which is the best time to buy them. There are also electronic versions of the same charts with their own viewing software from ANWB.

All bridges and locks have a reference number which can be used in conjunction with the index in the back of *ANWB Wateralmanak 2* to be directed to the relevant pages of the guide, a constant requirement of navigation. There is a subset of these details in the *ANWB Staande Mast* route almanac for those boats with masts that are limited to that part of the Netherlands with only opening bridges. Summary details of bridge and lock service times are given in this guide and where operation is described as 'throughout the day' this means from at least 0900 to 1700 and often earlier and/or later. A new series of charts, called *Schipper Vaaratlas*, were first published in 2006 and cover the whole of the Netherlands in four parts. These combine chart

Even in the Netherlands there can be deep locks

pages with harbour information and are a viable alternative to ANWB charts. They also include the Dutch waterway regulations so you do not need to carry *ANWB Wateralmanak 1*.

For the areas near the coast, the *1800* series of charts by the Dutch Hydrographic office provide good and detailed information. These cover the area from the Nieuwe Waterweg and the Westerschelde and such popular cruising locations as the Delta area of Zeeland and the IJsselmeer. The sandy shallow shores of the Netherlands, like the East Coast of England on the other side of the North Sea, are constantly changing and so these should be of recent edition and kept up to date with Notices to Mariners which are available, just like the UKHO, on the Dutch Hydrographic website www.hydro.nl. These are produced in Dutch and English or for users of the Imray/CA *Almanac* regular digests of NTM changes are published on the CA website. Dedicated chart plotters, where fitted, often have electronic coverage of Dutch inland waterways close to the coast (such as C-Map, ARCS etc) and there are other providers (Max, Navionics) that can provide additional coverage inland. Unfortunately the Belgian/Dutch electronic charting supplier widely used by commercial barges, Tresco, do not currently service the leisure market, as these are excellent, but they say that they might one day. In the meantime the ANWB electronic charts fit the bill.

Certain inland waterways of the southern Netherlands are under the influence of tidal flow and so a copy of the Hydrografisch Bureau *Waterstanden*

Stromen HP 33 is well worth having and, for a change, it is provided with a full English section! It is published annually with all of the tide times for the Dutch ports, but the tidal flow atlases at the back are valid until they next re-engineer that part of the system and can save time and trouble when navigating the tidal rivers and meers. All of these publications are available from Imray outlets and sample and reference copies are available for use at the CA Library at Limehouse Dock in London, together with many pilot guides and cruising logs describing their members' experience in the Netherlands.

Handheld VHF radios are permitted in the Netherlands, and are a very useful addition to the fixed set for monitoring multiple channels, but they must be licensed and may only be used on low power. Channel 31 is sometimes used as a marina channel in the Netherlands, and as this is not available on International and UK sets, it might be beneficial to buy your handheld in Holland or to have one set modified if intending to cruise there extensively. The lack of any VHF whatsoever to communicate with bridge keepers on the common channels (often 18, 20 and 22) would be a serious disadvantage and restrict movement in areas in which VHF communication is required by regulation such as in the vicinity of port areas.

A mobile phone on a reasonable business/ international tariff (or with a local SIM) is also vital for contacting marinas, locks and bridges when VHF communication is difficult or just impossible. The railway bridge keepers (Spoorbruggen) seem to be inhibited by a policy of not having VHF and some rural area bridges are only opened after telephoning keepers living nearby.

Radar with a screen viewable by the helmsman is very helpful in bad weather and poor visibility and most advisable for navigating the Great Rivers and assessing the movements of neighbouring commercial craft. It is also the best 'rear view mirror' there is for watching for the arrival of fast-following craft, a common cause of incident and worry. The lack of a radar reflector in these circumstances would be foolhardy and having one fitted is a requirement on the busier commercial waterways.

The vessel is assumed to have at least one well-adjusted and calibrated depth gauge and forward-looking sonar for larger vessels is sometimes fitted.

A log for measuring water speed and retractable paddle wheel/impeller for weed clearance can help monitor progress safely and should be capable of reading kilometers/hour as well as knots.

On board laptops with wi-fi (wireless or *draadloos* Internet) capability and back up communication by GPRS card (such as Vodafone Connect) are a godsend when monitoring weather and enquiring about local restaurants, services and things to do. A chargeable wi-fi connection available from Enertel has been installed in many Dutch marinas and capacity can be bought by minutes or longer (20 minutes for €2 in 2006) so that it can be expended as you travel, but free wi-fi from neighbouring cafés, bars and other sources is often abroad on the ether for free use by visitors. It may also provide communication with home and the management of bank accounts etc needed to keep the cruise going! However, users are advised to have Windows security or firewall protection in place, no files shared for access, and virus and Windows software up-to-date for peace of mind when logging into wi-fi networks.

A good pair of binoculars is required for the bridge to read lock and bridge information and monitor other craft along with somewhere to keep them safely.

An organised skipper will need a suitable log book to prepare a daily voyage log the night before, detailing the bridges, locks with their VHF channels, call-signs, telephone numbers, clearances and other characteristics such as their almanac reference numbers, as well as speed limits and potential stopping places to make the passage run smoothly. It is also worth noting when you will need to call one major bridge control centre in order that others are operated remotely. For motor-sailing the display of an inverted cone is necessary and the absence of one will be noticed and frowned upon, and may get you into trouble for fraudulently seeking priority. Often sailing, but not tacking, is perfectly possible on many waterways provided you have an engine readily available or the use of sails as well as the engine if you display the cone.

Ideal boat type and specification for cruising in the Netherlands

Such is the variety of cruising grounds, lakes, rivers and canals, that the Dutch use almost all types of boats from the modest 'sloop' or open day-boat to the large domestic barge conversion, and so the lack of any particular type of boat should not put potential visitors off visiting, provided that you choose your waterways with care. Skippers with boats less than 20m long, 5m in beam, 3.5m of air draught and of 2m draught should find little difficulty in navigating the waterways featured in this guide. Where the maximum possible dimensions are close to these limits, this is noted in the waterways details. However, for those with the luxury of planning ahead and choosing their ideal boat, there are certain criteria for taking best advantage of cruising the inland waterways of the Netherlands, but there is also the matter of getting over the North Sea or English Channel in the first place. Some of these aspects are more obvious than others so all are listed for completeness.

Ideally, vessels will have a semi-displacement hull to create little wash when cruising at a displacement speed of 3.5 to 8 knots and with draught of not much more than a metre. The greater the draught than a metre and the more it approaches two metres the more care that will have to be taken and the more waterways will have to be avoided. Masted deep keel sailing yachts and fast planing hulled motorboats are at a serious disadvantage in view of

their instability and vulnerability to cross winds and wake. Simple single-engine boats are widely used and perfectly adequate but, in view of the need to manoeuvre in tight places and share waterways in locks with commercial vessels that leave their screws turning, twin engines and a bow thruster makes for a happy helmsman, particularly if the propellers are geared to achieve the slow inland and moderate coastal speeds.

When cruising in fresh water there is the need for insect screens and lotion but, also, with the lack of sea breezes inland and shelter generally, very hot weather can occur and local boats all have good forward window blinds, black-out lining on curtains and sun canopies or methods of sheltering the crew whilst allowing shade and ventilation beneath. An oscillating fan can keep the crew sane and move stale air about and the ideal resource is air-conditioning, which sounds a luxury until a continental heat-wave is experienced first hand with insect swarms preventing the windows being opened. Refrigerators need to be of good capacity and well ventilated at the rear, which is the cause of many of them failing to keep up in hot weather. Many of the larger boats have water-cooling for fridges, which is also used for their air conditioning as hot ambient air alone is often insufficient.

A large water tank capacity is very helpful to buffer supply with 500 litres plus being preferred and, for those boats fitted with fresh water toilet flushing to avoid inlet odours, a bypass valve to use river water is advisable to avoid over-taxing the supply.

From 2009 holding tanks become obligatory for all Dutch boats based on the inland waterways, after which time all yacht harbours and municipal moorings will have to provide pump-out facilities (at very low cost or free) and already this is compulsory on many British waterways. In the meantime there is a sufficient network of pump-out facilities for current use. A good capacity (150 litres plus) holding tank is therefore advisable now, and should be fitted with standard deck fitting for suction and also a sea discharge for when in tidal waterways in the meantime. As an alternative, a sealed chemical toilet can be used and emptied in the more infrequent facilities provided for this purpose.

Vessels longer than about 15 metres are subjected to a host of additional regulations and those from 12 metres start to be excluded from some moorings and, whilst this can be normally stretched with negotiation to around 13 metres and grown to include overhanging anchors and davits etc, boats longer than 42 feet (12.8 metres) nominal LOA can be restricted in where they can stop. The smaller venues also sometimes exclude boats over 10 metres but there is then normally some space for larger boats elsewhere. Mooring boxes of 3.5 to 4 metres wide is a common size, with fewer up to 4.5metres and anything over that can be a problem with even the smaller locks becoming impassable with beams of over 5 metres.

This book is written for waterways capable of passing vessels with 3.5 metres of air draught (bridge

A folding radar arch is useful at low bridges

height) or less, but waterways with small barges normally have around 6 metres and others often have fixed bridges of 4 or 5 metres. Therefore folding VHF aerials will often suffice and then lowering radar arches the next stage, keeping the canopy removal or windscreen lowering as a last resort. A detailed and exact list of air draught heights at all stages of boat disassembly (in metric and imperial) together with beam, draught and tank capacities kept on the bridge can be reassuring and save unnecessary worry. A telescopic height gauge/flag pole mounted on the pulpit with the top inch or two a spring and marks showing configurations for all of the relevant settings allows bridges to be approached safely, and beats the taped boat hook method for elegance and convenience any time!

Simple disc rope cutters work well on prop shafts on inland waterways and, accompanied by large and easily-accessed raw inlet water filters, keep props and engines relatively clear of weed and fouling.

Hulls should be well protected with good-sized ball bow and cylindrical side fenders with alternative narrower fenders for the narrower locks, mooring boxes and waterways. These may be fitted with carbine clips or looped for retention and be pulled up on deck when in open water or strong winds, but are normally kept swinging alongside for convenience so fender socks to avoid abrasion are a good option. Further half-submersible fenders are handy at those sea locks that give just a floating timber to moor against. Fender baskets or alternative storage are essential in view of the numbers and varieties needed. Strong but manageable sized ropes of at least the boat length should be available at each bow cleat and stern quarter but be stowed safely so as not to fall overboard and foul the propellers.

A type of boarding ladder or device for access to the bow of the vessel when in a typical Dutch mooring box is very useful. We are very fortunate in that our normal boarding ladder doubles up for this purpose when hooked on the pulpit, but there are

special designs that clip on to common anchor types for this use. A lock and chain will protect these from acquisition by those less fortunate.

The boat's bow anchor and chain will be brought into use on occasions, but the typical Norfolk Broads-type conical mud-weight and 3-4 metres of rope stored in its bucket can provide a better alternative to anchoring in open meers in still weather to avoid bringing aboard fathoms of muddy chain from the silt below. In this case, an anchor winch with the additional windlass can be helpful to retrieve it when it gets stuck in the mud! A folding anchor ball will complete that arrangement when displayed forward or aloft. Some mooring pins and a lump hammer will be needed for remote and rural moorings.

Last of all, an inflatable RIB on stout davits not only provides a means of carrying a dinghy with small motor readily available for investigating those smaller waterways, but also acts as a very handy repository for excess fenders, bikes and all of the things that get in the way at locks and when underway generally.

For security, a boat alarm and number of lockable security cables for protecting bikes, outboards dinghies and locker contents make for peace of mind.

The authors' boat is *Lady Martina*, an older style 1989 Broom Ocean 42, that conforms to the above criteria and has been extensively improved and fitted out over many years and thousands of miles of inland and coastal cruising to incorporate all of the facilities mentioned. At nearly 13 metres, it is at the upper end of that size recommendation, which is a personal choice, but it also has the space for comfortable longer-term cruising and the accommodation of guests, which, if the owner is to maintain family and social relationships, is another consideration. Its twin heads, large double fridges and washing machine are particularly appreciated, as is its slightly older and more spacious design. Further details of its specification and daily cruising log are viewable to all on our website www.ladymartina.com.

Documentation and paperwork

Again organisations such as the RYA and CA have a range of guides that fully prepare the reader for an overseas boating visit with the former having a boating checklist for foreign cruises and the latter having one particularly written for Cruising in the Netherlands. In common with all of the usual foreign cruising venues, you will need to have aboard details of the Boat Registration, which should either be a full Part 1 entry with the Registrar of Shipping or the alternative simpler Small Ships Registry scheme run in the UK by the RYA. In either case, the registration number on the vessel sides, together with the name of the vessel and Port of Registry aft should be clearly visible. The Ship's Radio Licence (listing all of the sets including hand-helds, radar and distress beacons) and any other licences or certificates, (such as that for the Safety Scheme, marine gas safety checks, annual fire extinguisher inspections etc. if you have them – useful but not compulsory for visiting boats in Holland at the moment) should be to hand, together with the original sales invoice or certified proof from the builder that VAT was paid upon first construction or entry into EC waters. For the boat, its insurance certificate or policy document (not a copy) is also vital that states the cruising range applicable and time abroad covered and is clearly valid in both respects. This will include third party as well as the normal risks.

As personal qualification, the responsible crew member will need a personal licence certificate for operating a VHF set (valid or updated for DSC) and an International Certificate of Competence if the vessel is either over 15m or capable of speeds greater than 20km/h. This will have to be endorsed for inland waterways use, which means having taken a CEVNI exam as well as a practical assessment (such as Day Skipper Practical). The older ICC's used to be valid for both offshore or inland, but the latter has been left off renewals and needs the above test for it to be issued. All of these personal qualifications and certificates are available from attending and completing RYA courses at approved establishments. We recommend that you have these qualifications and certificates anyway and would point out the good fortune of British-based skippers in having this scheme, as the Dutch and German domestic qualification schemes are much more onerous and expensive.

For other personal use, you will need passports for all crew members and a new-style driving licence card will fulfil ID needs as well as giving the opportunity to hire a car or scooter locally. Holland is part of the EEC reciprocal health care scheme and so you will need to get an EHIC (European Health Insurance Card) for each crew member, information is available by phone ☎ (0845 606 2030) or on the web at www.dh.gov.uk. It is as well to have vaccination certificates, details of any illnesses, conditions, or medicines with ample prescriptions for drugs and pills to supplement the ships normally fully-stocked first aid supplies. A note of any eye test prescription will be useful if you need replacement glasses or contact lens supplies. You may also wish to attend to Travel insurance in which case have details available.

The whole lot are best kept in a plastic multi-pouch wallet, with individual items in clear view slip folders, indexed and available to hand at the bridge in case of demand (when you are occasionally boarded it often occurs when underway and you need to retain control of the vessel) and for safekeeping in case of some emergency that requires leaving the boat.

Registration and immigration procedure

The good news is that there is no universal or national need to pay for using your vessel on the Dutch inland waterways, though there are a variety of local tolls and fees levied at various places. Boat

You can post your *Schengen* form in the reception at Seaport Marina IJmuiden

registration for foreign visitors to the Netherlands is not required provided you are on a short visit and your boat is registered in your home country. For vessels either over 15m or capable of speeds greater than 20km/hr and kept in the Netherlands, registration involves visiting a main post office, filling in a form with details of your boat and paying a fee (€30 in 2006). This process is not strictly enforced, particularly if you are not hurrying about above these speeds drawing attention to yourself.

Visitors arriving from the UK are required to fill in a *Schengen* form on arrival in the Netherlands, giving details of crew on board including passport numbers. This procedure followed the European convention of the same name when other EEC members (but not the Europhobic British) agreed a treaty for free movement of citizens between EEC countries. Although at one time this was only lightly enforced and widely ignored, with increasing awareness of terrorism and immigration the Dutch authorities have generally increased their attention and would expect this requirement to be properly undertaken. Once submitted, keep two copies on board for further inspection. Copies of the forms can be obtained upon entry at Vlissingen and IJmuiden, or better still can be downloaded from the RYA website and completed prior to arrival. Apart from this, provided that you are not carrying amounts of alcohol and tobacco that are in excess of the very generous EEC limits, or have firearms or signalling pistols aboard, you need not fly a 'Q' flag or clear customs.

If you have dogs on board, they are generally welcome in the Netherlands ports and venues and subjected to no arrival procedure. It will be getting back to the UK that will be your problem. You will need to have had your dog chipped and vaccinated before going and then given a vets inspection less than 48 hours and more than 24 hours before your return on a ferry as UK authorities will not let it back on your own vessel.

De-masting

As this guide covers all waterways down to an air draught of 3.5m, sailing yachts would need to de-mast to enjoy much of them. Many of the yacht harbours have mast cranes and are quite used to undertaking this work, as well as being able to offer indoor/outdoor storage facilities. Harbours that offer this facility are indicated in the *Almanak* by the symbol of an M next to a crane and information that follows being the typical price, maximum weight or length.

Fuel

Petrol (benzine) and diesel is available widely in the Netherlands, often from a fuel barge or by tanker delivery. Costs vary and so prices should be checked for 150 litres and above and compared for deals before fuelling. By law, red diesel (gasoil) is not available to leisure boaters and can only be used to fuel ferries and commercial craft but it is often available on the same barges as white, which provides a mutual temptation for vendor and skipper alike. The white is more expensive but not so much so as in Britain where the fuel taxation is very high. Red diesel when bought in the Netherlands is therefore very cheap indeed and you may come across areas where the regulations are commonly flouted, but both parties break the law and risk fines and worse if it is taken on board 'without a ticket'. Particularly, the skipper with totally full tanks of red diesel can hardly argue that he has brought it from overseas so you have been warned!

Since the taxation laws were changed in 2007, red diesel is no longer available in Belgium and is being phased out in the UK. In the future inland boaters will have to content themselves with merely using less fuel than their sea-going cousins, as consumption at conservative inland speeds is much lower for most boats.

Gas

Gas bottles are widely available at chandlers or boatyards, but these are often camping gaz butane in the smaller sizes or propane bottles provided by Shell, Esso or local suppliers. These have different regulators to normal UK installations and are also covered by similar contractual arrangements to Calor's proprietary policy and so cannot be used as a direct replacement. For boats visiting the Netherlands with blue Calor Butane or red Calor

Gas bottles are in plentiful supply but are not compatible with all installations

Propane for a short period, by far the easiest solution is to take sufficient gas for the duration of your stay. If you are planning an extended cruise or keeping your boat in the Netherlands, the ideal solution is to convert half your installation to the continental fittings with a change-over valve so that either brand of gas bottle can be exchanged. Butane is not so widely available as propane and since it is only really suitable for use in warm climates it is not recommended. There are some freelance suppliers who may offer a re-fill service for Calor bottles, but beware as this is illegal under Calor contractual terms and be sure that they know what they are doing as this can be very dangerous if the cylinders are overfilled such that liquefied gas reaches the outlet. Good Dutch chandlers sell the gas bottle conversion kits so you could complete the switch on arrival if you find yourself without supplies.

Domestic equipment

Given that electrical capacity is often very low at Dutch moorings (4 and 6 amps is common, 10 amps a treat and 16 amps unusual, except where chargeable at the going rate of €0.50 per two kilowatt hours) motor boats and the larger cruising sailing yachts are advised to adopt equipment that maximises and stores what is freely available without overloading the supply. Often the cabinets for re-setting trips are also locked. This is compounded by the problems of replenishing gas mentioned above, as that too has to be conserved.

The first very valuable aid to smoothing over the consumption is a combined battery charger/AC inverter, that adds to the available shore power (rather than replacing it) by supplemental inversion of domestic battery amps when needed at peak times (such as the Victron Energy Multi-Plus with battery monitor and control) that can be set to shore capacity on arrival. By then taking a steady trickle of power in replenishment, it is possible to use kettles, hairdryers, immersion heaters and even washing machines and air-conditioning units, and all of the major domestic needs of the crew can be catered for by the power of 4 amps delivered 24 hours a day. In the absence of this, a generator will be needed frequently with consequent expense, noise and servicing. Good-sized domestic battery banks of modern and efficient capacity and performance are worth the installation cost to back these up. Many Dutch boats with lower power consumption needs also use modern solar panel arrays to provide power of up to 100watts when moored at free and remote locations, but these do not yet seem capable of providing the needs of visiting boats.

Another very simple way to manage power supply limitations is to adopt the use of special low wattage electric toasters, kettles, vacuum cleaners and other appliances that take 600–800watt (3 amps) instead of the 2–3Kwatt (8–12amps) ones used at home, and to review the size of the boat's immersion heating element, which are often over-specified for continental power availability. These appliances are widely and cheaply available at caravan and camping stores and are as modern and effective (albeit slower) as any others.

For early and late season warmth and reducing condensation, low wattage heated towel rails are cheap and easy to install and the odd low-wattage fan or convection heater can help with those chilly Dutch mornings and evenings and take the strain off the diesel cabin heater.

Flat screen TVs save cupboard space and can be put away in drawers etc when not in use and, by taking your satellite TV box and setting up a portable dish aerial, you will be copying the Dutch boats in receiving good reception wherever you stay.

Personal Care

As most of the waterways are fresh water with lush vegetation, the fitting of fly-screens to the boat is also essential for the welfare of any crew prone to *muggen* as the Dutch gnats are known. The customary precaution of avoiding windows open with lights on proves insufficient for these varieties as they are adept at following the warm carbon dioxide trails us poor human mortals leave for them. The local Autan *muggenverjager* lotion in 100ml sizes seems to keep them at bay for as long as its application lasts and spraying of sleeping quarters before retiring can help control the problem.

Given the strong sunlight, with its reflection from the water and decks, and hours spent inland cruising, good polarised sunglasses reduce this glare effectively. Sun cream is always a priority for prolonged exposure or those with sensitive skin, together with plentiful water or soft drinks to maintain hydration when it is hot or breezy.

Many harbours are well-served by public transport

Transport

Travel by train is easy, cheap and reliable when compared to Britain and provides an excellent way of getting about for crew changes or just for visiting venues. Tickets are paid for in train terminals, but often only by coin or local bank card. Buses, branded 'Connexion' are paid for by *Strippenkaart* tickets bought in newsagents, vending machines, at terminals and other places and are used by inserting into the bus machine on entry; less economic versions are also normally available to buy on the bus. They typically have fifteen partially punched segments and journeys take 2–3 units per person. You find out how many units are needed for the journey and then fold the ticket at the relevant place and push it into the machine and it demonstrates that you have paid by printing on it. You can repeat the process on the same *Strippenkaart* for second and further passengers.

Bicycles are almost essential for shopping, sightseeing and investigating the area when you have moored and, as the Netherlands is generally very flat, they are the most convenient, easy to use and the most common form of transport. The Dutch use them extensively and have very well developed networks of cycle-ways, signals and priorities for them and trains are adapted to carry them without difficulty. To those who think that they are no longer mobile enough or able to cycle, the winter before is the time to learn or practice the habit and attention is drawn to the elderly Dutch cyclists who use them for the whole of their active life. Being without a bicycle in some places means losing time, having to further stress your feet by walking or face not seeing the place at all. A pair of good folding bikes aboard is considered essential to get the most out of the experience, but thankfully the large robust Dutch 'sit up and beg' bikes can be hired from most venues given the time and money to find and return them. If you arrive without, do not worry as the best place to buy a bike is in the Netherlands with shops like Halfords specialising in bicycles and all of the accessories that the Dutch find useful. Folding varieties range from the expensive all-aluminium models to cheaper ones made entirely of steel. The middle-range compromise has alloy frames and steel

Bikes are the most common form of transport in the Netherlands

wheels which normally represents the best value. Pairs of huge pannier bags and heavy duty all-over rain capes will help you blend in! A spare innertube, repair kit and pump will act as good insurance and simple lights need to be fitted along with a bell, a legal requirement. If you have a good place to store those large comfortable full-sized non-folding Dutch models and do not mind lifting them on and off the boat, another strategy would be to buy a couple of second-hand bikes at the start of an extended stay and sell them on afterwards; but a pair of folding ones pack away a lot better.

The last suggestion may seem to be bizarre but the use of a TomTom™ personal navigator (used extensively in Britain in cars but made in Holland and used there on bikes and for walking as well) is most helpful as it has Dutch and English maps as standard and special settings for walking and cycling journey plans. It is no coincidence that they are sold in all of the cycle and ANWB shops and, fitting in the palm of you hand, they take you straight to the attractions when the points of interest are downloaded into them. Also, when you zero the unit at the boat before leaving, it is a very good way of making sure that you can wander or cycle off and find your way back! Otherwise, when touring around, you would need detailed street maps for every place.

A folding bike stows easily on the boat

Many locks collect their modest dues in the traditional fashion - a clog on the end of a fishing rod

Cash and Credit Cards

The Netherlands personal finance system currently presents a particular problem to the British boating tourist. Their custom and practice varies from the norm in that they have a well-developed domestic low-cost banking system that does not easily link into the international banking networks and so the locals pay by Dutch cash cards for the larger items and a form of prepaid card called *Chipknip* for the smaller ones. This system, much beloved by the prudent Dutch consumer who is loathe to pay charges, is under pressure from the EEC who consider it anti-competitive due its exclusion of foreign banks. Until this situation changes, English VISA credit or Switch cards are very seldom useable for normal purchases apart from 'high-ticket' items and restaurant/hotel bills in the tourist areas, and even then often incur a surcharge. Even supermarkets, fuel bowsers and harbours do not accept credit cards in general. Mastercard/Eurocard is very slightly more acceptable, but UK visitors should ensure that they have plenty of cash in Euros; notes for purchases and €0.50 and €1 coins for electricity and water at moorings and a range of coins for bridge and lock fees (*geld*). The old tradition of lowering a wooden clog on a rod and string still prevails and has even enjoyed a revival since opportunistic bridge-keepers seek gratuities in the same way!

For obtaining cash outside the UK, beware the insidious extra 2.75% foreign charge that is levied by almost all of the UK banks and not always shown on statements. Prior selection of a bank that does not

levy this charge (at time of writing only Nationwide) will allow replenishing wallets in Euros from ATMs with cash cards at no charge and favourable exchange rates up to a maximum of €375 per day. The same charge applies to transactions with a credit card, except those made with Nationwide or Liverpool Victoria VISA cards or the Post Office Mastercard.

When the Dutch use their *Chipknip* cards, they can re-charge them with cash by the use of their cash cards and special terminals, but there is no way (unlike UK Oyster cards, for example) of replenishing them at shops and post offices with cash. If you do want to be able to use *Chipknip* and do not have a Dutch bank account, there are places for tourists (such as Rotterdam Central Station) where you can buy €20 (and sometimes €50) pre-paid cards, costing the face value plus €2–3, and this can be useful to keep in reserve for when you do not have the correct cash or change. They last until the end of the following year, but there is no facility to re-charge them.

Facilities

All harbours featured in this guide have onsite showers and toilets available unless it is stated that facilities are limited, and many have washing and even drying machines. This information can be easily ascertained by checking *ANWB Wateralmanak 2*, looking in the second alphabetical index for the town or village concerned. Yacht harbours and marinas are listed alphabetically within each town section and the same names have been used in this book to describe them. Available facilities are shown in symbol format so no language skills are required. Explanation of the symbols is given in English on page 29 (2007 edition), or in Dutch on the inside front cover. Similarly the phone numbers and contact details for each harbour are given in the same section, and as these can change regularly they are not repeated here.

Most harbours have good facilities, sometimes including washing machine and dryer

VVV offices come in all shapes and sizes

ANWB, VVV and local information

The ANWB is a membership organisation, which supports land and water-based recreation with a wide range of maps, charts, guides and other resources. These include a good range of navigational charts for the inland waterways that are the main source of information for local and visiting boaters. Their range of publications is sold in ANWB shops along with equipment and clothing of use to the outdoor enthusiast. They also have some publications free to members such as the Vaarkaart Nederland (a complete folded map of the Dutch waterways with locations of harbours and suggested routes) and an extensive discount scheme. Sadly, foreign nationals without a permanent Dutch address cannot join, but if you are a member of the UK AA (Automobile Association) or another affiliated motoring organisation in other countries they offer reciprocal benefits upon production of your membership card and number. Unfortunately this does not apply to the RAC and so that might influence your choice if you are preparing to visit.

The VVV is the Netherlands tourism authority and their offices provide a wide range of documentation and advice on leisure facilities and attractions, and often organise walking tours and sell tickets for events. The two services are sometimes combined in one office which is normally situated either near the town's railway station or in the market square or town hall (Stadhuis). The small VVV offices may open late, close early and sometimes for lunch and on Mondays as well, so make it an early priority to visit them. In addition to these many harbourmasters keep leaflets, maps and guides and are a useful source of information on most topics.

The problem for English-speaking visitors is that, whilst the Dutch grasp of spoken English is often very good (from exposure to UK/US films and TV), few can write in English and so often printed information is only available in Dutch or German. However, it is well worth asking as sometimes sheets

in English are produced from behind the desk having been written by local staff.

Increasingly the internet reveals some of the best information and is well worth using before visiting and a very useful facility to have on board. The website accompanying this publication www.inlandwaterwaysofthenetherlands.com has a wide and constantly updated range of links; and additional information has been signposted for ease of access, taking the reader to the English language page where available.

Harbours and yacht clubs

Formal moorings in the Netherlands generally take one of three forms. Firstly, the commercial yacht harbour or marina, which normally offers extensive and good quality services and facilities in return for a comparatively higher mooring rate. Electricity and water for visitors can be metered or unmetered, but there is always full-time staff and every assistance available.

The second alternative is the private club haven, normally preceded by the initials WV, WSV or VVW, which mean much the same thing as watersports club. They lease their facilities (often from the local water or land-based government authorities) and run them for the benefit of their members and (in view of the above by rules imposed) for visitors as well. Some have their berths full with waiting lists and do not have the ability or inclination to welcome visitors formally and many of these are in out of the way areas reached by car by the berth-holders and not often attractive for visiting boats, but even these have spaces made vacant by their own boats cruising and can be approached if circumstances require.

Those maintaining a range of berths specially for visitors have the numbers and types listed in the *ANWB Wateralmanak 2* as such, but in each case there may be mooring boxes temporarily vacant for the same reason. Many use the convention of displaying green 'free' (*Vry* or *Vrij*) and red

Some of the smallest yacht clubs have only a handful of boats

'occupied' or 'busy' (*Bezet*) tabs in the boxes to show availability and often have the beam and length marked on plates on the posts or landing stages (*steigers*). Beware the sign *Vrij Houden* which means 'keep this free'.

The management of these clubs varies enormously depending upon their ethos, numbers of visiting boats and location. Some have professional or seasonal harbourmasters, others have their offices manned by duty club members in rotation, or it can be combinations of the two. Whether they are saving money to keep their own berthing costs down or maximising income from visitors, they choose an approach that suits them, but it means that you never quite know what language skills and experience will greet you! They all share an ethos of welcome and hospitality however, as the visiting fees are vital and they are very much part of the boating fraternity and become visitors themselves elsewhere when on board. Existence of facilities and how much or whether they will be charged for varies so much that this book makes a point of giving details where known, as it can make all the difference to whether or not they are the place for you.

The third alternative is a harbour run by the town, often called a *Gemeente* (Municipal) or *Passanten* (visitors) haven. These also vary enormously from free unserviced moorings to very friendly harbours with dedicated harbourmasters and ample facilities. In many cases these will be closest to the town's amenities and the most suitable for visiting boats.

Principal venues

When preparing the regional chapter summaries, the following judgements and designations have been made:

Principal venues – Places recommended as being pleasant to visit with comfortable moorings incorporating good facilities and where there are interesting things to see and do. Normally, these are labelled in bold letters on overview maps and have harbour plans and facilities described. We envisage that visitors will want to include these places in their itinerary and even stay for several days if time permits.

Other stopping places – Other venues mentioned in the text and described in less detail and noted on the overview maps in standard lettering. These vary from attractive smaller places worth considering to others which could be useful as safe and comfortable overnight stops.

A further category are certain other venues which we have chosen not to feature because they either offer little of interest to visiting boats, or the moorings are poorly serviced/situated or remote and mainly used by locals with cars as somewhere to keep their boat. It is realised that tastes and priorities vary and so any such choice might be subjective, but we have tried to incorporate the views of others when making these selections.

Some notes on the culture and society of the Netherlands

By addressing this subject, we inevitably run the risk of creating misunderstandings and offence as the Dutch, far from being stereotypical as with every nation's peoples, are a collection of individuals with diverse characteristics, tastes and views. However, we feel that it can be helpful to prepare the English-speaking visitor as to what to expect and how to best understand the people of this fine boating nation and are aware that many people who claim to understand the Dutch have limited their experience of them to international cities and tourist resorts rather than those of the Dutch heartland, where things are quite different.

Though small in geographical terms, the Netherlands is full of waterways, big and small, and they take the visitor from the North Sea and the boundaries of Belgium and Germany to the coastline of their inland seas and on through cities, towns and villages so that all types of Dutch people are encountered. They share a historical communal struggle to hold back the sea and a heritage of creating whole new areas of land to enlarge the country so that they can genuinely be regarded as being responsible for their own nation's shape and landscape. In recent times, this has involved building huge drainage structures on water and large motorways and transport systems on land, making the inland waterways by far the most attractive way of seeing the traditional landscape and meeting its people.

Still in use as working footwear

Whilst the professional, urban and young Dutch people will generally speak English; older or less 'international' ones may not and even those that do, generally have fewer written language skills. This means that signs and information in English on the waterways are quite rare and so learning the meaning of the main Dutch notices and signs will be worthwhile for the visitor. Until recently, the principal first foreign language taught in schools was German and, for this reason and because of the proximity of that country and the large number of Germans arriving as tourists, you must expect German to be far more common as a language in leaflets and on signs.

The Dutch have a very complicated relationship with the Germans; the close proximity of that country and the result of wars and conflicts have taken their toll, but they also depend very much upon German technology and money for their economic well-being and so older antagonisms are waning but re-surface from time to time. In general, English-speaking people are always most welcome, particularly as British boats are still a rarity in many places, and the Dutch people like to practice their English where they have it, but still much appreciate us learning a few words and phrases of their language and showing them respect in this regard.

First and foremost, the Dutch are very patriotic, celebrate Royal and national events enthusiastically with copious orange flags and routinely wear orange in their daily life. They love their country and its traditions and try hard to avoid it being diluted by foreign influence. There are places, like Spakenburg, where national dress is still worn by many and, on special occasions, by all and, yes, many of them do wear traditional wooden clogs, particularly as workwear (where they fulfil the role of work boots with toecaps for protection) and elsewhere for keeping by the back door and slipping on when they go out in the garden or to the local shop.

The Dutch are a direct and engaging people, which contrasts with English reticence and reserve. They use a vocabulary of fewer words and nuances, which leads to a direct form of communication which, if misunderstood, can seem to be brusque. They enjoy the company of large groups of friends and family members and typically form circles in restaurants, open places etc and will chat, drink and socialise loudly. In these situations, their demeanour and body language may seen unwelcome to strangers but, once you are known to them or introduce yourselves, this closeness is extended to you and they will do anything they can to help. This also leads to Dutch boaters sometimes being reluctant to allow you to moor alongside and to avoid doing so with you unless they know you but, by gentle persistence, you will end up the best of friends.

The Dutch habit in shops, markets and paying booths is also a direct one, often diving in to get served or interceding in other transactions and so do not be surprised if your tentative approach leaves you in the background. If any aspect of your behaviour or situation is incorrect or unwelcome,

they will be very forward in putting you straight or asking you to move, alter your moorings etc. appearing to be 'pushy'. You should therefore not worry about doing so equally in return, for they will not think the worse of you for doing so and would be blissfully unaware otherwise.

Dutch houses, boats and cars are often beautifully kept with lots of attention and care lavished upon them and many rituals performed daily with plants etc and ornaments displayed and cared for. Show the least interest in them and you risk being taken in and shown around to their obvious pride and pleasure! However, property is regarded as very personal (they often fence or divide off a section of the pavement outside for example) and so do not fall into the trap of touching or trespassing or they will react adversely. In boating terms, this might be touching their ropes or moving their dinghy etc and so it is always best to approach them wherever possible and clearly state the problem.

Often benches or pairs of chairs are left outside houses and the occupants will sit on them in the evening sun, interacting with neighbours and passers-by. Houses are most often adorned with the names of the occupying family on a name-plate. The Dutch want to know who is about, what they are doing and what is going on and so curtains are left open and eye contact maintained with passers-by in a way that the reserved English would find nosey but is quite normal to them. A mutual greeting by wave or word is all that is required. Your boat, if different to the norm, will attract interest and, if you are eating on deck, prepare to be greeted with '*Eet smakelijk*', meaning 'good tasting', the Dutch for '*bon appetit*', for which there is not a satisfactory English term for we would have averted our gaze and scurried by!

A large number of the Dutch communities are very religious, contrasting with what has become a very secular English culture of late and so expect Sundays to be respected more and hours for shopping and businesses to contrast with those in Britain. Hours are routinely taken for lunch and Mondays often continue the inactivity of the weekend, but there are late shopping evenings to be enjoyed. Dutch markets start and finish at all times, with traders often scheduled to be at more than one location during the day.

In conclusion, the peoples of the Netherlands are first and foremost Dutch, keen to maintain their language, customs and culture and may at first seem cold to strangers or anyone doing things differently, but engage them, ask for help, or help in return and they reveal themselves as a caring and friendly people. Show interest in their language, history or culture and then avoid being embarrassed when they treat you like close friends and neighbours as a result and will not stop offering you things and doing things for you!

River outflows and tides affecting navigation
Understanding the inland waterways of the Netherlands

The terrible tidal surge and floods of 1953 which ravaged the shores of England's East Coast and lead to fatalities in such places as Canvey Island in Essex were tragic for the English communities that were affected but, in the low-lying polders and lands of Holland they were a national disaster. Apart from the 1800 people that were drowned and tens of thousands that were displaced from their homes and farms, a very large proportion of the country was inundated, its lands lost to agricultural production for years and its infrastructure destroyed. The nation was deeply shocked and there developed a national resolve and urgency, whatever the cost, to try and remove any possibility of it occurring again. At great cost and sacrifice, and with all haste, a programme of works was started with its first results in the forms of flood barriers such as that on the Hollandse IJssel in the late 1950s and huge new dams, with the first arriving in Zandkreek and the Veerse Gat in the early 1960s. Further works carried on until the great surge barrier was built across the Oosterschelde in the late 1980s.

As a direct result of all this the sea was held back and various inland lakes and estuaries either isolated from the sea with stagnant salt water, changed from salt to fresh water or, increasingly, left with tidal flows but given protection from exceptional events in the same way as the Thames Barrier in England. Other books have carefully described this procession of events and many of them have been left hopelessly out of date as further work left areas of sea drained as land, made tideless and fresh instead of salty, and other predictions of future works were cancelled or amended! Visiting mariners who had cruised these waters over this period kept updating their knowledge and views of the country, which was physically growing before their eyes with each visit!

We have not repeated this chronology fully as this book has concerned itself with the way the Netherlands are today rather than with how it once was for the whole waterways system is complicated enough to the newcomer in any case! We were thus determined not to fall into the same trap of this book being a treatise on the drainage of the country. However, though we hoped that the national waterways structure had stabilised so that we could write the definitive work, we have found out during our latest visits that changes are still being made and suggested. Nevertheless, with reference to our schematic 'River Outflows and Tides of the Dutch Rivers' (on page 15) we hope that we can eliminate much of the confusion that exists amongst boaters new to this phenomenon, and explain how the Dutch water engineers reconcile the problems of protecting the country from the twin perils of inundation from the sea and from the flood waters of the great rivers of Europe that flow to the sea through Holland as their 'Delta' and what effect their management has on the navigation.

The recent problem has been that those great schemes, conceived with single purpose and in haste, inevitably overlooked the longer term consequences for the fisheries and the natural flora and fauna of the area and also, provided longer term engineering problems as hostages to fortune. They did, however, also create Europe's greatest resource of inland water space that was ripe for boating tourism and enjoyment by readers of this book. Now, in this new 'green' age of ours, they are trying to rectify the former without prejudicing the latter and the outcome remains to be seen.

The problems and opportunities of drainage; of reclamation or 'polderisation' were not new to the Dutch, as they had been draining and protecting reclaimed lands since before the 15th century. The ancient method was to build clusters of houses, barns and farms on raised mounds called *werfs*, which are still visible in the older landscapes today such as on Marken 'island'. Then they were joined together with dykes of raised land to enclose an area, which was in turn drained to form some of the ancient polders and this process continued in cells like honeycomb until they had large extents of drained and polderised lands, often several metres below sea level making them vulnerable to surges and inundations. They soon learnt that the peaty land thus drained shrank as it dried out and sunk further, and then could not be re-hydrated and this latter problem has now led to calls for areas of North Holland, in particular, to be allowed to re-flood in the same way as many of England's coasts have been increasingly left to a process tactfully called 'managed retreat'.

The next problem is what to do with the inland estuaries and lakes now cut off from replenishment and formed of stagnant salt water, where gradual death of sea life and concentration through evaporation and local deposition form them into veritable 'dead seas'. The Veerse Meer, one of the first cut off in this way, is stuck in this situation as it

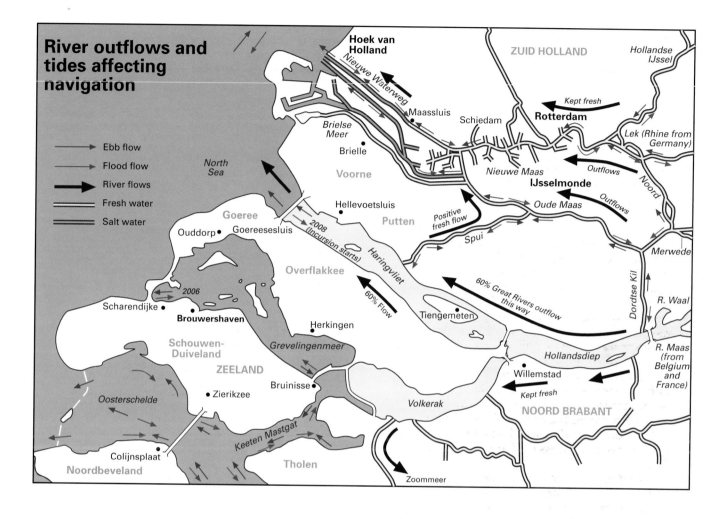

River outflows and tides affecting navigation

Legend:
- Ebb flow
- Flood flow
- River flows
- Fresh water
- Salt water

Hoek van Holland

ZUID HOLLAND

Hollandse IJssel

Nieuwe Waterweg

Maassluis

Schiedam

Kept fresh

Rotterdam

Brielse Meer

Brielle

Voorne

North Sea

Lek (Rhine from Germany)

Nieuwe Maas

Outflows

Noord

IJsselmonde

Outflows

Hellevoetsluis

Putten

Oude Maas

Positive fresh flow

Goeree

2008 (Incursion starts)

Ouddorp

Goereesesluis

Spui

Merwede

Overflakkee

Haringvliet

Dordtse Kil

R. Waal

2006

60% Flow

Tiengemeten

60% Great Rivers outflow this way

Scharendijke

Brouwershaven

Herkingen

Schouwen-Duiveland

Grevelingenmeer

Hollandsdiep

R. Maas (from Belgium and France)

ZEELAND

Bruinisse

Willemstad

Zierikzee

Volkerak

Kept fresh

Oosterschelde

NOORD BRABANT

Keeten Mastgat

Tholen

Colijnsplaat

Noordbeveland

Zoommeer

---

is surrounded by flat river-less land with no hope of changing to fresh water and its proximity to the same stretch of sea at each end means that opening it up for salt water replenishment would result in unacceptable level changes. Most visitors and some locals do not realise that this problem has been solved in the Grevelingenmeer. The former stagnant salt water in this inland lake is now constantly replenished as sea water flow is allowed in at its extreme northwest and southeast ends. The former opening is direct to the sea, which has earlier flood tides than the latter where the flood tide reaches much later along the Oosterschelde. They can therefore maintain a small flow along it and back of around half a knot without significant level changes and that has cleared the water and, not only led to a return of healthy sea life but also re-enforced the deep sea diving activities at Scharendijk.

The tideless freshwater lake of the Haringvliet is now top of the agenda of the conservationists as they rue the lack of tides and bird life, in particular, that once graced this estuary. There are many traditional Dutchmen who also feel that Holland is the poorer for losing its tidal ebbs and flows and the landscape

duller with its dykes and ditches replacing the sea estuaries, and this lobby feels that the flood prevention measures went too far. Currently, the Haringvliet acts as the water control point for this whole part of the continent, with its dam and sluices passing around 60% of the whole of the collective output of the major rivers from this part of Northern Europe: The Rhine (called the Lek by the time it arrives); the Maas originally from France and thence from Belgium; and the huge Waal used as the main navigation from Germany. It backs up the fresh water to provide navigable levels in Germany, diverts some of the flow back along the Spui to keep the waters around Rotterdam fresh for water extraction and only opens at low water twice a day to allow an out-rush of excess fresh water and then closes before the sea can return. In 2000, the landmark political decision was made to start letting sea water back in the Haringvliet during the year 2008, which has been hugely controversial given the current dependence upon the fresh water thus provided and many locals are very unhappy about it, even given this long period to allow the development of alternative infrastructure. The eventual effect on the water, its tides and levels has yet to be seen, but already the low-lying island of Tiengemeten in the Haringvliet has been de-populated and prepared for reclassification as a wetland nature reserve and the Dutch do not let the sea win back land easily.

As another, unrelated, development intended to lessen the effect of winter flood level changes and to provide a safer depth for navigation, the River Maas is due to experience an increased normal water level of some 30cm (1 foot) over the next eight years or so. This timescale (and a reduction from the figure formerly initially proposed of 50cms) has been agreed to enable mooring stages to be adjusted

For present boating our schematic and the current tide tables are what we have to work with. Working southwest to northeast, the Oosterschelde (and the Westerschelde beyond it) are fully tidal with the huge barrier at Neeltje Jans Island (with its Delta project Expo centre) ready to close it off and cap the levels inland in the event of large tides. The estuary rises and falls, and the flow floods and ebbs right up past the Keeten Mastgat and up to the tidal part of Bruinisse. The Westerschelde is a totally open tidal estuary and thus outside the scope of this inland waterways book though it might be the point of arrival of many visitors via Vlissingen. Next the Grevelingenmeer is enclosed salt water as described above with no navigation to the sea but has that half knot ebb and flow of refreshing salt water which has only a minor effect on navigation but provides a splendid boating lake of islands and anchorages.

When locking into the Volkerak, you have that seemingly pointless lock and delay where the level does not seem to change, but the sidewards gushing of water jets reveal that it is something of an isolation chamber where the removal of salt water is vital to the freshwater ecosystem back from the Volkerak to the lovely Biesbosch region. Just enough fresh river water is fed into the Volkerak to maintain it, and the Schelde-Rijnverbinding, fresh and its level changes only in the region of a few inches. Now in the low-lying drained area the locks point upwards towards the sea. Inward and on to the Hollands Diep as the linear water lake that feeds the Grevelingenmeer under an open bridge and we are now in the main stream of river water discharge. 60% of the river flow moves through here and conditions are affected by rainfall upstream in three countries, as well as the dramatic venting of fresh water out to sea at low tide outside through the Grevelingenmeer. From a boating point of view there is therefore a flow in aggregate from the south as the Spui and Dordtse Kil are fed with fresh water and then a surge of flow seawards with a propogation delay when the sluices are opened. On top of this is a slight tidal influence from the distant sea via the Oude Maas and the Nieuwe Waterweg. Assuming normal river conditions and the absence of drought and downpours, the venting is probably the only flow that can be counted on or avoided, but in any case is not significant given the width of the waterway.

For vessels leaving Holland or arriving from the North Sea it is best to avoid those low water surges as the lock channel to seaward then crosses the sluices path in order to avoid shoal areas. In strong northwesterly winds this will make for even more wind against tide as it ebbs after half tide. Arriving at just before high water always seems to be a good rule wherever you go! From then on both the Spui and Dordtse Kil have fairly predictable tidal influences in normal river conditions. At times of low flows, they cannot maintain large net positive flows seaward through these water courses and note the following extract from the tidal publication; 'During extremely high Rhine discharges of 6000 cubic metres at Lobith, the Haringvliet sluices are fully opened. In that case it is impossible to keep the discharge through the Nieuwe Waterweg at a constant level. During sluicing, strong currents may occur in the vicinity of the Haringvliet sluices'. That warning makes the link to the Nieuwe Waterweg, the main navigation from Rotterdam to the sea. Always subject to the tidal influence of the North Sea with its predicted tidal times and flows, the positive influence currently of the additional fresh water along the Spui and Oude Maas keeps the water around Rotterdam fresh but the vast hectares of Europort – the world's largest cargo-handling area – are salt as is a varying amount of the river navigation in between. Tucked alongside the latter with its access channel running peacefully alongside and under the dykes of the massive navigation, is the tranquil haven of the Brielse Meer and the lovely old port of Brielle, now bathed in fresh water and haven to wildlife and leisure boater alike.

It is worth re-reading this chapter and studying the schematic of the tidal flows and fresh/salt water regimes to full understand how the system functions in order to best predict the flows and behaviour of these tidal inland navigations of the Southern Netherlands and Great Rivers. In that way, they can be used as a considerable benefit rather than being seen as a problem. However, with the inevitable variations of nature and the fact that tidal predictions are just that; it will be necessary to make the appropriate allowances for 'current' conditions.

International waterway signs

LOCK SIGNALS

No entry

Opening soon

Enter now

Lock not in operation

SOUNDS

– – Attention
· I am turning to starboard
·· I am turning to port
··· I am going astern
···· I am incapable of manoeuvring
····· Danger of collision
– – – – (repeated) Distress signal
––––· I am turning round to starboard
––––·· I am turning round to port

WARNING SIGNS

or red lights No entry

No overtaking

No passing

No long-term mooring

No anchoring

No mooring

No turning

Do not cause wash

Pleasure craft forbidden

Rowing boats forbidden

Motor boats forbidden

Mandatory direction sign

Stop

Speed limit (km/h)

Sound horn

Danger

Major waterway ahead

Height (m)

Depth (m)

Width (m)

Keep away from bank (m)

Keep out of port and tributary

Prohibited

With Caution

VHF 11 Must contact waterways staff by radio

Channel is 40m from the (right) bank

Cross to left-hand side

Cross to right-hand side

Keep on right-hand side

Keep on left-hand side

Head for left-hand side

Head for right-hand side

Keep within limits

Port Entry

OTHER SIGNS

or green lights Entry allowed

Electricity cable

Weir

Ferry

Side turning

Turning place

Anchoring place

Mooring place (long term)

Advisory direction sign

End of prohibited area

Mooring place

Junctions or crossings of secondary waterways

Priority waterway ahead (junction or crossing)

Keep within limits

BRIDGES

Signal marks or lights

Passage allowed from both directions

Passage allowed for you forbidden from the other side = one way only

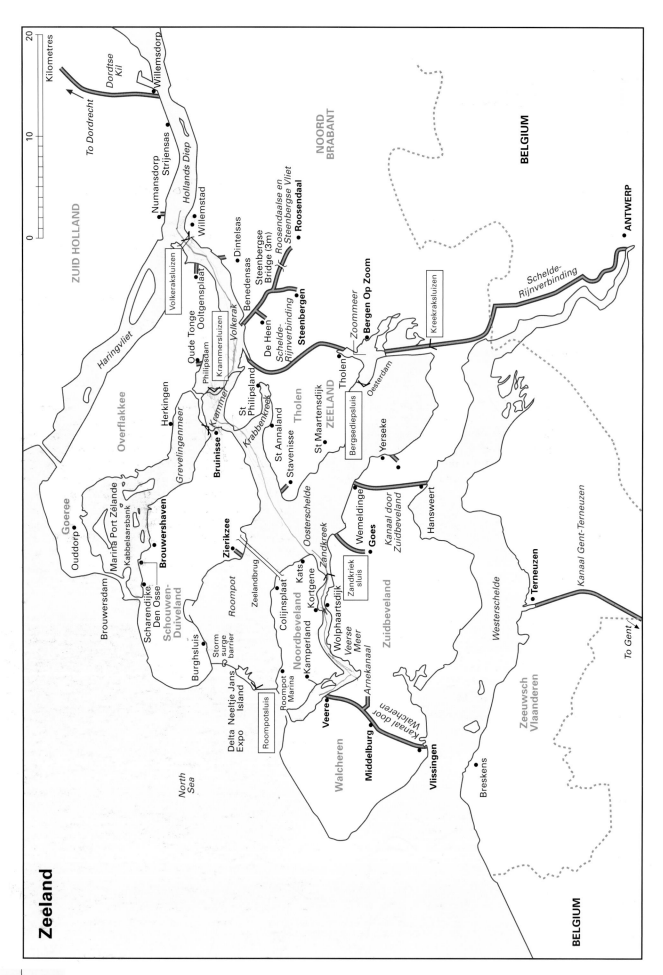

Zeeland

1 Zeeland

Waterways	Principal venues	Other stopping places
Kanaal door Walcheren	Vlissingen, Middelburg	
Kanaal door de oude Arne (Arnekanaal)		
Veerse Meer	Veere	Kortgene, Wolphaartsdijk
Oosterschelde	Zierikzee, Goes	Colijnsplaat, Burghsluis, St Annaland, Yerseke
Kanaal door Zuid-Beveland		Wemeldinge
Kanaal Gent-Terneuzen	Terneuzen	
Grevelingenmeer	Bruinisse, Brouwershaven	Scharendijke, Kabbelaarsbank, Ouddorp, Herkingen
Volkerak		Oude Tonge, Ooltgensplaat
Schelde-Rijnverbinding and the Zoommeer	Bergen Op Zoom	Tholen
Roosendaalse en Steenbergse Vliet	Steenbergen	De Heen

Zeeland (pronounced 'Zay-lont') is one of the most-visited cruising grounds in the Netherlands, especially for British boaters, who arrive here via Vlissingen and can happily spend a two-week holiday without venturing beyond the region. It is an area well-equipped for boating and in many of the towns, and even villages, you will find large marinas and excellent chandlers. Yet more amenities lie in isolated and coastal areas where the Dutch especially enjoy holidaying in their own country, taking part in water sports and outdoor pursuits, be that walking and cycling or kite-surfing and water-skiing. The region has changed enormously over the past 40 years: formerly an estuary dotted with large islands, these are now largely enclosed by dams and linked together by efficient road networks. Much effort has been put into preserving and enhancing the natural environment and this, together with good accessibility, puts it amongst the most popular leisure regions in the country. Compared to the more densely populated conurbations, Zeeland enjoys fresh air and lots of open space, making it a natural magnet for those looking for a change of scene. The Dutch are known throughout the world as accomplished drainage and hydraulic engineers and the exhibitions showcasing the work that has been undertaken in this region, including the flagship Delta Expo (located on Neeltje Jans island at the mouth of the Oosterschelde), are well worth visiting.

This chapter describes the inland waterways of the Zeeland region from Vlissingen in the southwest to the locks at the eastern end of the Volkerak.

The large tidal estuary of the Westerschelde (meaning the Western Schelde estuary and pronounced 'Vesta-skelda'), which runs west-east from Vlissingen to Antwerp, is excluded as it is not defined as an inland waterway by the regulatory body. However, harbours on the Westerschelde that form the gateway to one of the canals have been included as these can be important landing points. Also excluded is the Haringvliet, which falls within the South Holland province, but is dealt with in Chapter 2: Great Rivers, as it is in open connection with the fresh waters of the Hollands Diep and the Amer, with its level being determined by the flow from the rivers Maas and Waal. The Roosendaalse & Steenbergse Vliet is included in this chapter for convenience, although falling within the Noord Brabant province, as it can only be accessed via the Volkerak and offers no onward passage to the rest of that region.

A typical Zeeland scene - boats jostle for position at the Zandkreek lock

Kanaal door Walcheren

The Canal through Walcheren (pronounced 'kanarl door volkeren') is a 14.5km stretch from Vlissingen on the Westerschelde to Veere on the Veerse Meer and bisects the Walcheren region, one of the former islands that now make up the province of Zeeland. There are no height restrictions on this canal as all bridges open.

Canal entry is via the Vlissingen sea lock which operates 24 hours but has waterline planks so rig fenders as low as possible. The stretch between Vlissingen and Middelburg is 7km long and contains all of the five bridges on the canal. The bridges operate throughout the day and whilst they should open according to a fixed timetable the best way to transit this section is by joining one of the convoys. The Kanaal door de oude Arne (or Arnekanaal) branches east to Arnemuiden 1km northeast of Middelburg. At the north end of the canal are the Veere locks that operate throughout the day. Even a smooth transit between Vlissingen and Middelburg takes 90 minutes and during rush hour times the delays can make the journey much longer. The onward section to the Veere lock is obstacle free and takes another hour.

Length 14.5km
Maximum permitted draught 3.7m (4.5m between Vlissingen and the Arnekanaal)
Speed limit
Vessels over 30m^2: 8km/h (4.3 kn)
Vessels of 20–30m^2: 12km/h (6.5 kn)
Vessels less than 20m^2:15km/h (8.1 kn)
Locks
Sluis Vlissingen operates 24 hours, VHF 18
Sluis Veere operates throughout the day, VHF 18
Bridges
5 opening. Operate throughout the day, VHF 22. Convoys from Keersluisbrug (north-going) at H+5 and from Stationsbrug (south-going) at H+41.
Middelburg Spijkerbrug : Operates throughout the day at H+30 (but only mornings and evenings on Sundays and holidays).

VLISSINGEN

Where to stop

The most central mooring in Vlissingen (pronounced 'Flissinga') is the recently restored Michiel de Ruyterhaven yacht harbour in the old Visserhaven. The entrance lies a mile west of the Buitenhaven where the ferries depart for Breskens and is conspicuous by the public observation tower just to the east. The marina is tidal and there is a gauge at the port side of the entrance showing depth of water over the sill. Beware of the many pilot boats which leave from the adjacent dock. There is no canal access from here, but it is convenient for a visit to the town and has all facilities including wi-fi. The best stopping place if you are intending to continue on the Kanaal door Walcheren is the VVW Schelde. Enter the Buitenhaven, keeping a good look out for ferries and other shipping which uses this entrance, and turn to port for the Vlissingen sea locks. Continue round to the first bridge on the canal and the small harbour is to starboard just before the

bridge. *Schengen* forms are available here and once completed can be left at the clubhouse for forwarding to Customs. There is a small chandlery nearby but the town centre is a half-hour walk. Security was improved in 2006 with gate access and this location is much more private than the de Ruyterhaven, which is in the centre of the tourist area surrounded by cafés and attractions.

Facilities Ashore

Fuel Diesel at VVW Schelde (cards accepted)
Chandlers v.d. Gruiter, on Edisonweg – opposite VVW Schelde
Supermarket & Shops Albert Heijn on Aagje Dekenstraat or Gildeweg.
ATMs Plenty in the town
Cycle hire At rail station

What to see

No book on the Netherlands would be complete without mention of the British visitors' favourite port of entry and this former herring-trading centre is still an active fishing port and naval shipyard. The VVV office is on the Oude Markt and one of their most popular attractions is the 19th-century arsenal building that has been converted into the maritime attraction 'Het Arsenaal'. Here you can enjoy a naval review, the shipwreck simulator or lose the children on a treasure island. The 65m tower gives a good view of Walcheren and the Westerschelde. The town's local history museum was revamped as 'MuZEEum' and rehoused on Nieuwendijk in 2002

Sluis Vlissingen - note the floating planks at the water-line

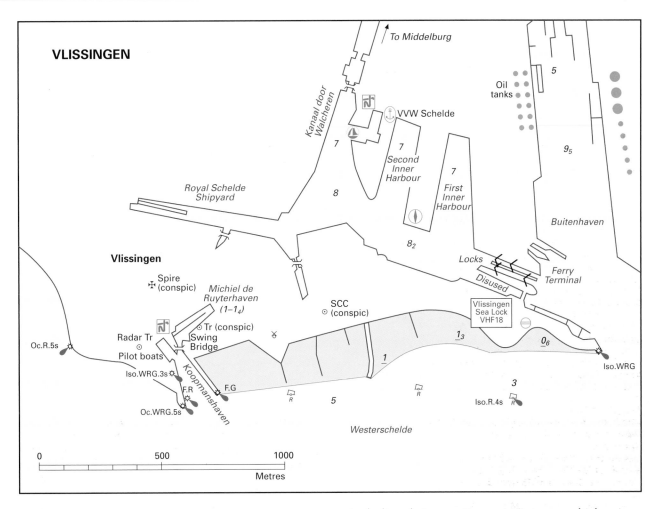

VLISSINGEN

To Middelburg

Kanaal door Walcheren

VVW Schelde

Oil tanks

5

7

Second Inner Harbour

7

First Inner Harbour

7

8

9₅

Royal Schelde Shipyard

Buitenhaven

8₂

Locks

Disused

Ferry Terminal

Vlissingen

Vlissingen Sea Lock VHF18

Spire (conspic)

Michiel de Ruyterhaven (1–1₄)

SCC (conspic)

Tr (conspic)

1₃

0₆

Oc.R.5s

Radar Tr

Swing Bridge

Pilot boats

1

Iso.WRG

Iso.WRG.3s

Koopmanshaven

F.G

3

F.R

R

R

Iso.R.4s

R

Oc.WRG.5s

5

Westerschelde

0   500   1000
Metres

Entrance to the Michael de Ruyterhaven with Het Arsenal tower and the boulevard walk

and nominated for European Museum of the Year in 2004. For a completely different type of attraction, reptiles and insects are featured at Reptielenzoo Iguana on Bellamypark. As well as being the sixth largest port in the Netherlands, Vlissingen is a popular beach resort and the boulevard walk along the seafront is a good way to check the weather.

Restaurant tip

In the season the harbourmaster at VVW Schelde runs the onsite bar/restaurant and most visitors take advantage of its convenience and value. De Ruyterhaven is surrounded by bars and restaurants,

including their own Brasserie Evertson which enjoys a view of the Westerschelde.

Connections

The railway station is only 0.5km from VVW Schelde, for all destinations via Roosendaal, as is the terminal for the Breskens pedestrian and cycle ferry.

Michael de Ruyterhaven from the south *Patrick Roach*

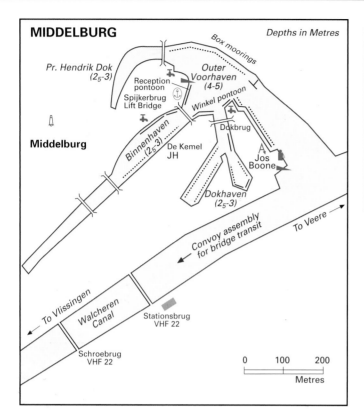

MIDDELBURG

Depths in Metres

Box moorings

Pr. Hendrik Dok (2₅-3)

Reception pontoon

Spijkerbrug Lift Bridge

Outer Voorhaven (4-5)

Winkel pontoon

Binnenhaven (2₅-3)

Middelburg

De Kemel JH

Dokbrug

A Jos Boone

Dokhaven (2₅-3)

Convoy assembly for bridge transit

To Veere

To Vlissingen

Walcheren Canal

Stationsbrug VHF 22

Schroebrug VHF 22

0   100   200
Metres

Binnenhaven mooring boxes beyond Spijkerbrug

Facilities ashore

Fuel & Chandlers Jos Boone – well-stocked floating emporium with visitor moorings – port side as your turn off the main canal. Diesel and petrol (cards accepted)

Supermarket & Shops Albert Heijn on Kalverstraat Konmar on Pottenbakkerssingel
Excellent selection of smaller stores in the town centre

ATMs A variety in the market square

Cycle hire At rail station

MIDDELBURG

Where to stop

Middelburg (pronounced 'Middelburkh') is the most common stopping point on the canal and WV Arne is often the first port of call for British boaters. It is well set up to receive them and the helpful harbour staff not only speak good English, but will also forward your *Schengen* forms for fulfilling immigration obligations. As you turn off the main canal there are box moorings on both sides (those to port being nicely shaded by trees in hot weather and least disturbed by road noise) but report first to the reception pontoon next to the Harbour Office ahead to your left. This is also the waiting pontoon for the historic Spijkerbrug which gives access to the Binnenhaven, where there are further boxes and alongside berths (closest to the town). For short stays of up to two hours there is a shopping pontoon (winkelponton) in the outer basin and you can also stay here overnight by arrangement if you want to leave early in the morning. Berths in the Dokhaven, accessed via the lifting Dokbrug, are sometimes allocated to visitors, and this is a good place to leave a boat unattended or to lay up afloat for the winter. Yacht crews who are pushed for space aboard sometimes make use of the harbour-side Hotel Princenjagt, where a more comfortable bed for the night and facilities can be had at a modest cost.

The well-stocked floating chandlers, Jos Boone, is the largest in the region and if you don't want to stay in Middelburg overnight they have their own visitors berths for filling up with fuel or shopping. They stock a wide range of products including an extensive supply of Vetus parts and accessories.

What to see

Middelburg thrived during Holland's Golden Age when warehouses of the Dutch East India Company lined the canals. Most of these are now converted into chic apartments, restaurants and office buildings having largely escaped damage during the second world war. The 15th-century town hall, which forms the focal point of the market square, befits the town's status as Zeeland's provincial capital, although it had to be rebuilt along with the abbey and its tower following a retaliatory bombing raid in 1940.

The Tourist Shop on the Markt has taken over the functions of the VVV in Middelburg, whilst the ANWB on Nieuwe Burg is a good place to buy waterway charts and other guides. The nearby Zeeuws Museum, housed in the restored buildings of

Middelburg's Outer Voorhaven from southeast   *Patrick Roach*

the 14th-century abbey, has topical exhibitions as well as their fixed collection. Climbing the 207 steps of abbey tower 'Lange Jan' provides a birds-eye view of the town and the adjacent waterways. For younger crew members the Miniatuur Walcheren model village makes a non-nautical diversion, whilst the old canals which encircle the town make an enlightening tour by dinghy or trip-boat (hourly departures from near the Konmar supermarket).

An excellent market every Thursday is the ideal place to stock up on fresh produce or local fish, and the extensive range of town centre shops includes many familiar favourites.

Restaurant tip

There are numerous cafés and bars around the market square, as well as others nearer the moorings. The harbour's own Clubhuis 'De Kemel' serves as a friendly home from home and offers excellent food with a Flemish theme. Wi-fi and an internet terminal are also available here.

View from 'Lange Jan' tower over Damplein

Connections

Trains to Amsterdam take about two and a half hours from here. Bus services to Vlissingen, Goes and Zierikzee.

Kanaal door de oude Arne (Arnekanaal)

This short canal branches southeast to Arnemuiden (pronounced 'Arner-mowder') 1 km northeast of Middelburg on the Kanaal door Walcheren.

Length 3km
Maximum permitted draught 2.2m
Speed limit 10km/h (5.4kn)
Bridges 2 opening. Operated remotely and open throughout the day, VHF 22. The rail bridge opens as timetables permit on request throughout the day

ARNEMUIDEN

Limited moorings, with water and electricity only, are available at Knolle boatyard for boats up to 12m. The village is home to one of the oldest shipyards in the Netherlands, which still restores and maintains historic wooden boats and can alternatively form a pleasant excursion by bike from Middelburg.

Veerse Meer

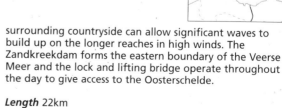

A tideless salt water lake, the Veerse Meer (pronounced 'Fearsa Mere') is popular with local sailors and there are peaceful moorings dotted amongst the islands. Regulations for use of these moorings are displayed on tourist information boards at various locations, or you can check at the VVV office in Veere before embarking. Red and green spar buoys mark the 1.5m contour and some of the island approaches can be shallow. There can be confusing direction of buoyage changes marking the channels between the islands, but these are marked by red/green buoys. Although tideless, the open nature of the surrounding countryside can allow significant waves to build up on the longer reaches in high winds. The Zandkreekdam forms the eastern boundary of the Veerse Meer and the lock and lifting bridge operate throughout the day to give access to the Oosterschelde.

Length 22km
Minimum depth in main channel 3m
Speed limit 15km/h (8.1kn)
Lock Sluis Kats at Zandkreekdam operates throughout the day, VHF 18.

VEERE

Where to stop

Marina Veere lies at the northern end of the Kanaal door Walcheren or you can find a spot in the picturesque, but busy town harbour, almost immediately to port as you turn northwest out of the canal. Here, Jachtclub Veere has a popular bar and wi-fi internet. Continuing northwest from Veere you arrive at the large harbour of Oostwatering (pronounced 'Oastvarterinkh'). Also run by WV Arne, this can offer an alternative berth for a visit to Veere, now a 1.5km bike ride away,

Facilities Ashore

Chandlers & Repairs Jachtwerf Flipper sells boat
　　spares and can undertake most repair work
Shops Good selection of small shops in the town

What to see

The attractive town of Veere (pronounced 'Feara') was named after the ferry which departed from this spot for the village of Campen, and was sited on land belonging to a local Lord. After Campen was washed away by a tidal wave in the 14th century, Veere became a town in its own right and the marriage of the Lord's son to a Scottish princess facilitated a lively trade in wool between the two countries. At one point Veere held a monopoly over imports, and in return the Scottish enjoyed a number of local privileges, including two properties on the quayside. The Gothic facades remind us that this

The Power Horse Competition comes to Veere over the last weekend in August

tiny village was once a prosperous trading centre, but since the construction of the Veerse Dam in 1961, even the fishing boats can no longer trade and it relies on watersports and tourism for its industry.

There is a VVV on Oudestraat and the Grote Kerk, which has over the centuries been used as a warehouse, barracks, workhouse, military hospital and exhibition space, still offers a good view of the town and meer from the top of the tower. The Scots Houses on the quayside, marked out by their ornate gables and indicative names, house a collection of artefacts from the era of their prominence. A Power Horse competition over the last weekend in August and a town fair that takes place at the same time draws good crowds and traditionally dressed competitors.

Restaurant tip

The Campveerse Toren on the quayside is a very exclusive eating place but there are plenty of alternatives, including De Peperboom on Kapellestraat, a bistro with plenty of history and a decidedly Dutch flavour.

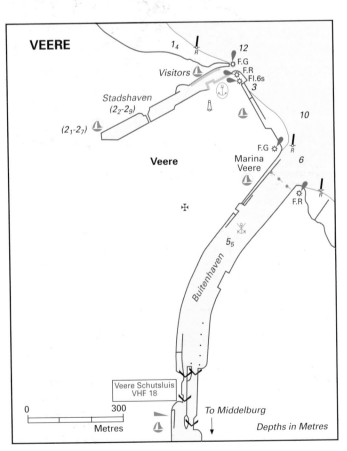

VEERE

Visitors
Stadshaven
(2₂-2₉)
(2₁-2₇)
Veere
Marina Veere
Buitenhaven
Veere Schutsluis VHF 18
0   300
Metres
To Middelburg
Depths in Metres

VEERE TO THE ZANDKREEKSLUIS

Opposite Veere, on the north coast of the meer, the large municipal yacht harbour of Kamperland ('Komperlont') lies at the entrance to the 1km long harbour canal. At the head of the canal there are some temporary moorings in the old agricultural harbour which once shipped products grown on the polders to the mainland. The village is dominated by bungalow parks which are busy with visitors in the summer months, when a foot and cycle ferry links the town with Veere.

Further east on the Veerse Meer, but about 5km west of the Zandkreekdam, lie harbours at Kortgene (pronounced 'Kortkhena'), on the north bank, and

Wolphaartsdijk ('Volp-arts-dike') on the south. Both offer good marina facilities with plenty of space for visitors and a launderette. Delta Marina in Kortgene boasts a Volvo service centre, chandlery and on-site restaurant amongst its attractions and is close to the small town. Kortgene has always had town rights but before the fixed bridges, the ferry to Wolphaartsdijk was the only link between Noord Beveland and the rest of Zeeland. Today a foot and cycle ferry continues the tradition. There are several yacht clubs on the Wolphaartsdijk side including the oddly located Royal Yacht Club of Belgium, but the village is 4km away.

Oosterschelde

The Eastern Schelde estuary (pronounced 'Oasta-skelda') has been the only part of the Delta region which remains tidal salt water with the storm surge barrier closing only in times of extreme high water. There is no speed limit in the main buoyed channels, but outside these areas a speed limit of 20km/h (10.8kn) applies. This is a tidal estuary and care must be taken to anticipate water level changes and currents for safe and efficient navigation. The Roompotsluis is used by fishing boats and these have priority in the lock. Boats with VHF are required to keep a listening watch on Channel 68.

Locks
Sluis Kats at Zandkreekdam operates throughout the day, VHF 18
Roompotsluis and fixed bridge (18.1m at HW) at western entrance operates 24 hrs during the week and throughout the day at weekends, VHF 18. Krammersluizen at Philipsdam operate throughout the day, VHF 22
Sas van Goes operates throughout the day, VHF 18
Bergse Diepesluis at Oesterdam operates throughout the day, VHF 18
Bridges
1 fixed (at Roompotsluis, see above), 1 opening Zeelandbrug (min. 11m when closed) opens twice per hour throughout the day

A water-filled model at the Delta Expo explains the working of the barrier

ZANDKREEKDAM TO THE BARRIER

The Zandkreek buoyed channel leads from the Zandkreekdam at the boundary with the Veerse Meer into the main channel of the Oosterschelde and 3km north of here Marina Kats can be found on the western side. This small marina and boatyard is popular for maintenance work, but the nearby village offers little to attract visitors. Continuing northwest the impressive Zeeland bridge spans the waterway connecting the two former islands of Noord Beveland and Schouwen-Duiveland. There are buoyed passages on the south and north side with a minimum clearance of 11.8m. At the northern end is a lifting section which opens for brief periods at set times during the day, full details of which are given in the *Almanak*, under 'Zeelandbrug'.

Two kilometres west of the bridge lies the large tidal marina at Colijnsplaat. The town, with its 16th-century corn mill, is nearby and there are Fisherman's days on the second weekend in August to celebrate the large and still active fleet. The Oosterschelde is accessible from the North Sea via the Roompot lock on the south side of the barrier, although there is no longer a customs/immigration post here. The nearby Roompot marina lies on the south side of the estuary: keep the red/green buoy to port on approach and follow the buoyed channel into the harbour. This is home to a large camping and watersports centre with its own shops and restaurants and a weekly programme of entertainments for visitors. To the north of the lock

Zierikzee's Nieuwe Haven from west   *Patrick Roach*

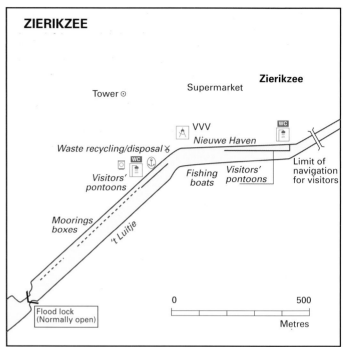

ZIERIKZEE

approach channel another buoyed channel winds north into the shelter of Neeltje Jans island (pronounced 'nail-tye yonce'), where Roompot marina also provide a pontoon in season for visiting the Delta Expo but there are no facilities apart from a possible toilet if open. An artificial island built as part of the construction of the storm surge barrier, Neeltje Jans was named after the Roman goddess of the sea once worshipped in this region. Follow the buoyed channel carefully as there are shallow areas to both sides. The extensive visitor centre provides models and films to explain the history and working of the Delta project whilst the water-themed outdoor attractions keep children and the young-at-heart entertained. On the north side of the estuary on the Schouwen coast the small harbour at Burghsluis is 3km from the popular resort of Burgh-Haamstede, and it is about 6km along the dam to the Delta Expo.

ZIERIKZEE

Where to stop
A popular stop is the tidal fishing port of Zierikzee (pronounced 'Zeer-ik-zay'), approached along the harbour canal. The floodgate normally stands open, except in very high water conditions (NAP+1.9m), and beyond it are the box moorings of WV Zierikzee and municipal harbour 't Luitje. At the windmill a bend to starboard brings you into the Nieuwe Haven, where further pontoon moorings are available beyond the fishing boats nearer the town centre. The traditional town is a magnet for summer visitors and it is advisable to arrive early to secure a good spot, although the harbourmasters are adept at rafting boats and normally find room. The facilities have been impressively modernised and as well as wi-fi, there are disposal facilities for all types of waste next to the harbour office.

Facilities Ashore
Fuel & Chandlers 't Loefje on Nieuwe Haven also run the diesel berth
Supermarket & Shops Nearest on Appelmarkt and Albert Heijn on Lange Nobelstraat
Good selection of small shops in the town
ATMs Several on Havenpark

What to see
At the east end of the Nieuwe haven, the 15th-century north and south gates stand guard over the entrance to the old harbour which forms the town's museum haven. In the centre, the 16th-century prison, called the Gravensteen, which continued to fulfil this role until 1923, is now the maritime museum, but you can still visit the old wooden cells in the basement. Preserved as it was when the last prisoner was released you can still see the names of former inmates carved in the oak walls. The former town hall on Meelstraat is home to the municipal

The Museumhaven lies shelter by the 15th-century harbour gates museum which, as well as historical artefacts, houses an exhibition on the 1953 floods. Next to the church the St Lievens Monstertoren, intended when building began in 1454 to be at least 130m high, offers a trip to the top of the 62m tower for an imposing view of the surrounding area. The VVV office is on the quay at the Nieuwe Haven and the weekly Thursday market on the Havenplein offers all necessities. Harbour days are held over the last weekend in August, when fishing boats take visitors on trips round the Oosterschelde for the Mussel Princess to receive the first catch of the season. Music, stalls and mussel cooking competitions contribute to the carnival atmosphere.

Restaurant tip

Plenty of good bars and restaurants on the Nieuwe Haven and in the town centre. Markzicht on Havenplein seems universally popular and many make a feature of fresh mussels in season.

ZEELANDBRUG TO THE KRAMMERSLUIZEN

Continuing eastwards back under the Zeeland bridge, the channels of the northern arm of the Oosterschelde, known as the Keeten, the Mastgat, the Zijpe and finally the Krammer, lead to Philipsdam and the Krammersluizen. Four kilometres west of here on the east coast of Duiveland lies the town of Bruinisse and the lock entrance to the Grevelingenmeer. The Vissershaven and Reparatiehaven are no longer accessible to leisure boats, who must lock through to the yacht havens on the Grevelingenmeer. See Grevelingenmeer section for details of Bruinisse. A small port of refuge, called a vluchthaven, lies south east of the town for yachts caught in poor weather or out of hours.

The Krammersluizen act as the barrier between the salt water Oosterschelde and the fresh water Volkerak. To protect the habitat and wildlife the locks have to exchange the fresh water for salt and vice-versa to ensure that there is no contamination between the different eco-systems. This means there can often be a long delay during which nothing appears to be happening whilst this takes place.

Returning southwest from the Krammersluizen on the south side is the entrance to the buoyed Krabbenkreek channel. Claimed to be one of the prettiest in Zeeland, the Krabbenkreek runs for 3km to the harbour at St Annaland, from where trip-boats continue the passage upstream to St Philipsland. In St Annaland itself, the regional museum in Bierenstraat is a reminder of Zeeland's industrial past with its exhibits illustrating the production of madder, a red dye .

At the western tip of the island of Tholen, the harbour canal of Stavenisse emerges into the Oosterschelde. The narrow channel is tidal and, along with the harbour itself, can have less than half a metre of water at low water springs so should be navigated with care.

SOUTH EAST OOSTERSCHELDE

At the eastern end of the southern arm of the Oosterschelde lies the Bergsediepsluis giving access to the Zoommeer and the Schelde-Rijnverbinding canal which passes north-south through it. This is the smallest lock in Zeeland, taking only three boats at a time, and long queues can build up in busy periods. Details of the Zoommeer and the Schelde-Rijnverbinding are given later in this chapter. West of the Bergsediepsluis across the Oosterschelde, a buoyed channel picks a route through the shallows to the mussel and oyster capital of Yerseke. The main yacht harbour lies in the Prinses Beatrixhaven and is entered by turning to starboard after the red/green buoy.

This small port holds the only mussel auction in the world and comes to life with its annual mussel festival on the third Saturday in August. Free mussels and boat trips round the estuary are part of the long-standing tradition. The VVV office on Kerkplein also houses a small exhibition of the history of the town.

Continuing west from Yerseke the entrance to the Kanaal door Zuid-Beveland on the south side is 0.5km east of the large yacht harbour, constructed in a closed-off arm of the canal.

GOES

One kilometre to the east of the Zandkreek, lies the red and green buoys marking the entry to the Goessche Sas channel. The lock operates throughout the day to give access to the harbour canal which winds 5km through Zuid Beveland to the regional centre of Goes (pronounced 'Khoose'). A large yacht harbour lies immediately to starboard on passing through the lock, but is mainly used by local boats.

Where to stop

The Wilhelminabrug crosses the canal after 2.5km and is opened as if by magic by the lock-keeper. In the centre of the town the Ringbrug is operated by the harbourmaster who then cycles back to open St Maartens brug. Opinion is strictly divided between

Goes Havenkanaal from southwest   *Patrick Roach*

those who favour the tree hung harbour of WV De Werf with its miniature lighthouse, 'honesty bar' clubhouse and leafy out-of-town ambience (suitable for boats up to 12m only); and those who prefer to be cheek by jowel in the municipal town centre moorings, where you are on view to curious passers-by and a noisy disco entertains into the small hours at weekends. Both offer 2.2m depth, all the usual facilities and nearby access to the town and its attractions.

Facilities Ashore

Fuel, Repairs & Pump-out Jachtwerf Goes, just north of the Ringbrug
Supermarket & Shops Albert Heijn on Kolveniershof
  Wide selection of other shops in the town
ATMs Several in Market square
Cycle hire At rail station

What to see

This attractive town is another popular stop for UK boats and flotillas, and the harbourmaster offers a warm welcome and good English. The town is the regional centre for North and South Beveland and the busy Tuesday market, as well as the large range of shops, brings in a lively trade. The Museum De Bevelanden housed in a former orphanage on Singelstraat, has a recently updated presentation of historic artefacts from the region. Within walking distance of the town centre just north of the Ringbrug, the Hollandsche Hoeve leisure park offers a huge range of activities, from traditional Dutch crafts in the Ambachtscentrum, to the well-equipped water park, as well as walks in the botanical gardens and a mini-golf course. Teenagers might prefer a trip to Zeelandhallen karting, one of the largest indoor circuits in Europe.

For a day out-of-town take the Goes – Borsele museum steam train and stop for lunch and a walk round the Berkenhof Butterfly garden at

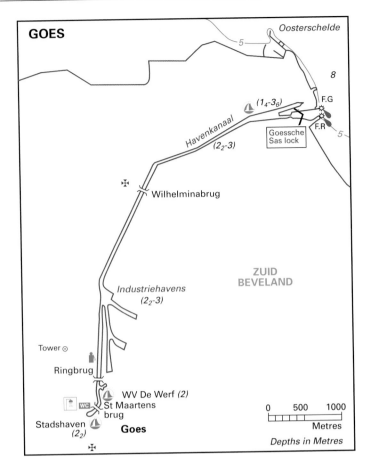

Kwadendamme. Station Hoedekenskerke is the end of the line and there is time to visit 'ye olde sweet shop' and the artesan clogmaker before the return train departs. First train leaves at 1100 from near the main station, but arrive early to see the locomotive being prepared and visit the old goods shed café.

Kanaal door Zuid Beveland

The canal through South Beveland ('Kanarl door Zoud-bay-fer-lant') connects Hansweert on the Westerschelde with Wemeldinge on the Oosterschelde. It is a much used through route for commercial traffic and the normal regulations for busy commercial waterways apply. There are locks at the southern end which are operated 24 hours. The two lifting bridges have a minimum clearance in the closed position of 7.5m, but can be operated remotely three times per hour during the day at times given below and in the *Almanak*; call Sluis Hansweert to request. Be aware that there is an open connection from the canal to the Oosterschelde, making it a tidal waterway with varying depth. Those travelling from north to south should check before starting the likely state of the tide in the Westerschelde when they eventually lock out. Yachts particularly will want to ensure the current will be with them for their onward passage.

Maximum permitted draught 4.75m
Speed limit 20km/h (10.8kn)
Lock Sluis Hansweert operates 24 hours, VHF 22
Bridges 2 lifting (7.5m when closed) operates throughout the day and opens at H+22 and H+57, VHF 22

WEMELDINGE

There are no stopping places along the canal, but at Wemeldinge ('Vaymal-dinkher') there is a large harbour in the old canal lock complex, accessed via the Oosterschelde. The direction of buoyage in this section of the Oosterschelde is from west to east, so the green buoy to the north of the east pierhead, which marks an underwater obstruction, should be kept to port if approaching from the canal. JH Wemeldinge is to port as you enter the harbour and offers all facilities including launderette, restaurant, bakery, chandlery and servicing.

Kanaal Gent-Terneuzen

In the small part of the Netherlands situated on the opposite (south) side of the large Westerschelde estuary, the Kanaal Gent-Terneuzen ('Kanarl Khent-Turn-ooser') links the Belgian city of Gent (pronounced 'Khent' and spelt Ghent in Walloon) to the Westerschelde at Terneuzen. The canal crosses the Dutch/Belgian border at the town of Zelzate, about 1km north of the Zelzate bridge. This guide covers only the Dutch part of the canal, and readers are referred to *Inland Waterways of Belgium* or *The Cruising Almanac* (both published by Imray) for their onward journey.

The entrance to the canal from the Westerschelde is via one of the Terneuzen locks. The Oostsluis (east lock) is designated as the yacht lock, but leisure boats are sometimes put through the Middensluis (middle lock) or Westsluis (west lock) with commercial vessels. In this case instructions will be given over the loudspeaker or on VHF 3. Leisure boats are not required to call the harbour but should listen out on VHF 3 and may use this channel to request passage through the locks.

Length 14km
Depth 13.5m
Speed limit 16km/h (8.6kn)
Locks Oostsluis, VHF 18 and Middensluis/Westsluis, VHF 6 operate 24 hours for three hours either side of high water.
Bridges 2 opening. Sluiskil and Sas van Gent bridges both have opening sections for the central and west spans, with a clearance in the closed position of 7m. The fixed eastern span of the bridge has a clearance of 6.5m. The bridge can be swung on request to Havendienst Terneuzen, VHF 11, at all times except the rush hour closing times (Mon–Fri 0740–0800 and 1640–1700). Southgoing vessels that do not require the bridge to be opened should use the west span, and northgoing vessels the east span. There are fixed height gauges on the bridge to indicate current headroom.

TERNEUZEN

Where to stop

Outside the sea locks, WV Neusen and JH Terneuzen are situated in the Oude Veerhaven, to the east of the lock entrances. Strong tides run past the entrance and it is dangerous for yachts to enter on the ebb

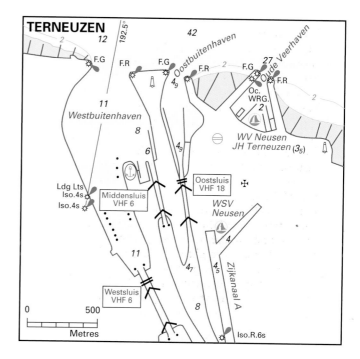

Terneuzen *Patrick Roach*

without powerful engines. The approach channel is narrow and care should be taken not to be driven onto the harbour moles, particularly on the east side where there are drying mudbanks extending up to 20m from the pierhead. Ideally, vessels should enter at slack water, which occurs HW+0030 or LW+0045. WV Neusen has further moorings inside the sea locks in Zijkanaal A, as does Vermeulen's Jachtwerf. Aricom Yacht Services 2km upstream specialise in maintenance and repair of Grand Banks. There are mooring places with water and electricity north of the Sas van Gent bridge should you wish to stop along the canal.

Facilities Ashore

Chandlers, Repairs & Servicing Vermeulen's Jachtwerf in Zijkanaal A
Supermarket & Shops Nearest on Schuttershofweg Good selection of other shops in the town
ATMs Several in town

What to see

The town, originally called Ter Nose on account of its nose-shaped headland, is surrounded by industrial areas but at its heart there is still some of the traditional town. There is extensive shopping in the town centre and a weekly market on Wednesdays. For a step back in time, visit Terneuzen's School Museum on Vissteeg where

Locking through the amply proportioned Middensluis

educational equipment, school photos and toys are displayed. The museum is part of Oud Terneuzen, a collection of craft shops, bars and restaurants situated in a network of 'olde-worlde' lanes. Music festivals and harbour days are held on summer weekends and the lock complex, the Poortal van Vlaanderen, runs guided tours throughout the summer, consisting of a video presentation, tour of the lookout tower and a boat trip round the harbour. Youngsters might prefer Scheldorado, a 'sub-tropical swimming paradise'.

Grevelingenmeer

Like the Veerse Meer, the Grevelingenmeer (pronounced 'Khrayfa-linkha-mere') is a salt water lake, closed off from the sea at its western end by the Brouwersdam, and separated from its freshwater tributaries to the east by the Grevelingendam. Although nominally tideless, flow through the Flakkeesespuissluis cycles the water in the meer and creates a small current. A single lock at Bruinisse gives access to the meer which has found new life as a watersports venue and now houses numerous first class facilities. Most of these are concentrated at the two ends of the meer, with much of the central region defined as a nature reserve. The lock operates continuously throughout the day, but it is one of the busiest in the country and long delays and plenty of shouting should be expected during summer weekends.

Red and green spar buoys mark the 1.5m contour and navigation is not permitted in the nature reserve areas. Mooring pontoons with toilets and rubbish bins are provided on the small watersports islands of Ossehoek, Archipel and Mosselbank and there are public moorings on the larger islands; on all sites visitors are allowed a maximum stay of three days. Permits for use of the public moorings are available at modest seasonal or weekly rates

from yacht havens, VVV offices and the De Punt visitors' centre. A contemporary exhibition, De Punt, telling the history of the meer and the reasons for damming up the estuary lies at the north end of the Brouwersdam, and has its own public mooring pontoons.

Speed limit 15km/h (8.1kn)
Lock Grevelingensluis operates throughout the day, VHF 20

BRUINISSE

Where to stop

As you leave the lock you find yourself in the first of Bruinisse's (pronounced 'brown-isser') two harbours, the smaller but cheaper WSV Bru, with usual facilities and next door to a handy mussel and fish shop. Beyond this is the larger, more commercial marina of JH Bruinisse. A launderette, supermarket, restaurant and chandlery are all at your disposal, along with fuel and service facilities. Wi-fi is

Bruinisse from the northwest; JH Bruinisse in the foreground, WSV Bru
and the Grevelingensluis beyond *Patrick Roach*

One of the watersports islands on the Grevelingenmeer *Patrick Roach*

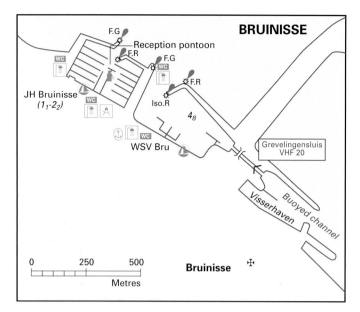

BRUINISSE

F.G
Reception pontoon
F.R
F.G
WC
WC
F.R
JH Bruinisse
(1₁-2₂)
WC
Iso.R
4₈
WC
WSV Bru
Grevelingensluis
VHF 20

Visserhaven
Buoyed channel

Bruinisse

0   250   500
Metres

What to see

Once a busy fishing port, a small fleet still trades from the tidal harbour on the Oosterschelde side of the lock and a trademark giant mussel keeps watch over the village. The Fisherman's Museum on Oudestraat gives the visitor an insight into the lives of earlier residents complete with mussel cooking demonstrations every Wednesday. The museum is also home to the VVV service and next door to the Oudheidkamer, where further historic artefacts are on display. For golfers, a well-respected course lies just northwest of the marina. Mussels are everywhere in Bruinisse and as well as the shop by the yacht club, there is a larger mussel and fish shop/café in the Visserhaven, De Zeebanket. The town is en fete during the summer on Fisherman's Days that are held on a weekend in mid-July.

Restaurant tip

De Meeuw, just under the road bridge, serves a wide range of fish and seafood specialities, whilst further into town De Vrienden van Bru on Oudestraat is a friendly spot popular with locals. If you happen to be stuck at the vluchthaven or want to push the boat out, the Brasserie De Vluchthaven is known for its €49 lobster menu, with real Oosterschelde lobster.

expected to be added shortly, followed by several hundred more berths in the coming years. Both harbours are a short walk back to the village which stands south-east of the lock. Conveniently situated at the entrance to the meer, many boats make an overnight stop here before embarking for a few days stay on the islands. The area is particularly popular with older people or families with young children, and gets extremely busy in high season.

Facilities Ashore

Fuel, Chandlers, Repairs & Servicing JH Bruinisse
Supermarket & Shops Albert Heijn on Dreef. Good selection of other shops in the town. Specialist mussel and fish shops at WSV Bru & Visserhaven
ATMs Several in town including Nieuwstraat
Cycle hire From the bungalow park next to JH Bruinisse

BROUWERSHAVEN

Where to stop

Towards the western end of the Grevelingenmeer, 6km to the east of the Brouwersdam, stands the large marina and town centre moorings of Brouwershaven (pronounced 'brow-ers-harfen'). The entrance lies southwest of Dwars in den Weg island and it is important to follow the buoyed channel to avoid the end of an underwater obstruction. The old floodgates still stand in the entrance with 2 metres depth over the sill and harbour lights control vessels entering and leaving. The harbourmaster greets you via a two-way loudspeaker system or VHF 31 from his office near the lock. A reply can be called out which is picked up by the harbourmaster; occasionally it is necessary to wave the red ensign to get a welcome in English. There are box moorings in the marina basin and the Oude Haven, although the latter are only really suitable for smaller boats. A limited number of alongside berths lie at the eastern end of the Oude Haven. Fuel is available from the diesel berth, at the southern end of the marina basin.

An alternative stop or a pleasant 2km cycle northwest along the Grevelingenmeer, is the yacht harbour and holiday village of Den Osse (pronounced 'den osser'). Formerly the base for the construction of the Brouwersdam, the harbour has been converted into the large WSV Den Osse marina where ample space can be found. Already celebrating its 25th anniversary the yacht harbour is well-established and boasts a launderette, café and chandlery as well as 5 metre depth, a legacy of its former use. Visitors to the bungalow park share the adjacent large supermarket and attractive beach complete with its pavilion café.

Bruinisse is the mussel capital of Zeeland

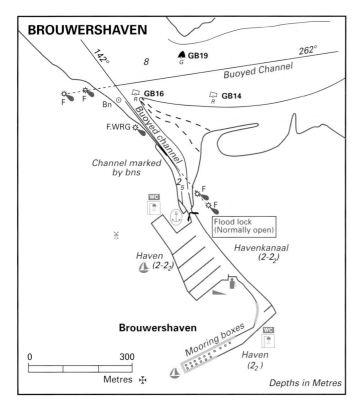

BROUWERSHAVEN

GB19

Buoyed Channel

142°   8   262°

GB16   GB14

Bn   R   R

F   F

F.WRG

Buoyed channel

Channel marked
by bns

2₅

F

WC

F

F

Flood lock
(Normally open)

Haven
(2-2₂)

Havenkanaal
(2-2₂)

Brouwershaven

Mooring boxes

WC

Haven
(2₂)

0   300

Metres

Depths in Metres

Facilities Ashore

Fuel, Pump-out & Chandlers At southern end of
marina basin

Supermarket & Shops Small supermarket on the
market square along with fish shop and diving
specialist

ATMs Several on market square

Cycle hire From van der Hoek, south of market
square on Zuiddijkstraat

What to see

Originally an important beer-trading port, hence the
name, Brouwershaven now concentrates mainly on
its boating and leisure industry. On Haven Zuidzijde
the Brouws Maritime Museum is open Sunday to
Friday and recounts Brouwershaven's rich maritime
history, including a brief phase as the country's
principal harbour after the silting up of Rotterdam's
tidal inlets. The Clubhouse 't Roefje lies at the east
end of Haven Noordzijde. The still, clear waters of
the Grevelingenmeer make it popular with divers
and Dolphins Dive Centre on the market square as
well as home to the VVV service point is the place to
stock up with necessary equipment. An annual fair
with music and market stalls is held in July.

Restaurant tip

't Zwarte Schaap on the harbour is very popular
with boaters.

BROUWERSDAM

Just south of the dam itself on the north coast of
Schouwen-Duiveland, the large yacht harbour of
Scharendijke lies close to the modern town. There is
a chandlers and extensive service facilities, but it is

mainly known as home to a popular diving centre
from where divers can explore some nearby deep
wreck dives. Former and occasional work harbours
along the dam itself have been converted into public
harbours all with a minimum depth of 2.2m and
again these are subject to a maximum three-day stay
and require the seasonal or weekly permit. All the
harbours have easy access to the popular beaches on
the seaward side.

At Kabbelaarsbank, a man-made island halfway
along the dam, lies the substantial and very
commercial Marina Port Zélande. Holiday
bungalows and a watersports centre accompany the
450 berth marina which is popular with large
motorboats. A common venue for large cruises in
company, amongst its endless list of attractions are a
comprehensive service centre, 40-ton boatlift, fuel
and wi-fi. Extensive facilities for watersports, shops,
cafés and restaurants are shared between the whole
complex and a steam train links the site with the
visitors centre at De Punt.

At the north end of the dam, on the south coast of
Goeree, lie the marina and town harbour of
Ouddorp. The single row of buildings by the
harbour is an outpost of the town, which lies 2km
away on the other side of the main road. The tiny
yacht club bar, open to members and visitors, has an
unimpeded view over the meer and makes a good
stop for a lazy lunch on a sunny day.

HERKINGEN

Back at the east end of the Grevelingenmeer,
opposite Bruinisse, a relatively narrow and shallow
buoyed channel (40m wide and 2m deep) leads to
the large marinas at Herkingen. To starboard
Marina Herkingen has every possible facility
including chandlery, servicing, boat lift, restaurant
and wi-fi. The adjacent small town was one of the
worst hit in the 1953 floods and is now protected by
the highest dykes.

The harbour office at Brouwershaven stands guard over the
entrance next to the open flood lock.

Volkerak

Separated from the Grevelingenmeer by the Philipsdam, the Volkerak is a tideless fresh water lake which is a protected nature area and boats are only permitted to navigate in the designated areas. Red and green spar buoys mark the 1.5m contour and leisure boats are advised to keep out of the main channel, which is heavily used by commercial traffic during the week. An area to the east is designated for waterskiing.

The Krammersluizen (on the Philipsdam at the west end) is a large complex of three locks, the most northerly of which is designated as a yacht lock which operates all day during the summer. A fixed bridge crosses the east side of the lock with a clearance of around 18.3m, the exact height being given on a matrix board. Yachts with higher masts can use the main lock which has a lifting bridge, call on VHF 22 to request. Yachts with VHF should keep a listening watch on VHF 68 when approaching from the Osterschelde. One kilometre to the east of the lock on the north side is the entrance to the Oude Tonge buoyed channel. Speed limit in the channel is 6km/h and maximum permitted draught is 2m. There is a flood lock halfway along the channel which normally stands open with a depth over the sill of 2.2m. At the head of the channel is the yacht club of WV Oude Tonge with all usual facilities.

The Volkeraksluizen (at the east end) also has a yacht lock as the most northerly of the four in the complex which operates continuously and can get very busy during high season. A fixed bridge with an air draught of 18m lies over the yacht lock and yachts with higher masts may use the commercial lock. Leisure boats are advised to listen out on VHF 7 (north of lock) and VHF 25 (south of lock) but are requested not to contact the lock unless they require passage through the commercial lock or at night between 2200 and 0600 when VHF 18 should be used. One kilometre west of the Volkeraksluizen, on the north side, is the entrance to the Ooltgensplaat harbour canal, which is buoyed but unlit. A flood lock stands open in the entrance and at the head of the channel stands WV Ooltgensplaat.

The entrance to the Schelde-Rijnverbinding canal lies on the south side of the Volkerak, 1km to the west of the Benedensas. (See the next section for details on the Schelde-Rijnverbinding). The Benedensas is the entrance to the Roosendaalse and Steenbergse Vliet, a waterway which is also described later in this chapter. Five kilometres west of the Volkeraksluizen on the south side is the Dintelsas entrance to the river Dintel which is described in Chapter 9: South East Netherlands.

Length 20km
Maximum permitted draught 2m (at Krammersluizen)
Speed limit 20km/h (10.8kn)
Locks Krammersluizen and lifting bridge (18m under fixed span) operate throughout the day, VHF 22.
Volkeraksluizen and lifting bridge (18m under fixed span) operate 24 hours, VHF 18.

Schelde-Rijnverbinding and the Zoommeer

The Schelde-Rijn link canal (pronounced 'skelt-rine-furbindinkh') runs from the Belgian border north of Antwerp through Zuid Beveland, into the Zoommeer and on through Noord Brabant to the south side of the Volkerak. It is a waterway busy with commercial traffic and there are no stopping places en route apart from those at Tholen and Bergen Op Zoom.

The southern section of the canal has fixed bridges with minimum air draught of 9.1m and, at the north side of Zuid Beveland, boats must lock through the Kreekraksluizen before crossing the eastern end of the Oosterschelde in a dammed channel. There is a small waiting pontoon on the south side of the locks, on the east side and boats must call the lock either on VHF or use the reporting station provided. Leisure boats using the canal should keep to the starboard side and out of the main channel where possible. Yachts using the canal must have a motor available capable of at least 6 km/h.

At the Zoommeer the waterway opens out and there are turnings to port and starboard as well as the continuation of the canal ahead. The Bergse Diep channel lies to starboard and gives access to Bergen Op Zoom, whilst the Tholense Gat to port leads to the Bergsediepsluis and on to the Oosterschelde. In the Zoommeer the 1.5m contour is marked by spar buoys and the area between these and the shore is not navigable. Parts of the meer are marked out for water-skiing and jet-skis and the speed limit only applies in the approach area to the lock. Continuing north the canal runs through Noord Brabant, with a second turn to port for the harbour of Tholen. Beyond Tholen, fixed bridges have an air draught of 9.85m.

Length Zandvlietsluis (Belgium) – Bergse Diep 19km; Bergse Diep – Volkerak 18km
Maximum permitted draught 4m (2m in Bergsediepsluis)
Speed limit 20km/h (10.8kn)
Locks Kreekkraksluizen operates 24 hours, VHF 20. Berg Petterssluis stands open but the accompanying lift bridge (4.2m when closed) operates throughout the day except 1100–1500 at weekends, VHF 22.
Bergsediepsluis operates throughout the day, VHF 18.
Bridges Belgian border to Kreekraksluizen, 1 fixed 9.1m; Tholen to Volkerak, 2 fixed 9.85m

BERGEN OP ZOOM

Where to Stop
At the end of the Bergse Diep channel two fixed lights on the end of the harbour moles show the way into the outer harbour and on to the Berg Peterssluis. The lock is no longer in operation and the accompanying bridge (4.2m when closed) operates throughout the day during the week (see above). Entry to the Theodorushaven is controlled by lights which must be followed by leisure craft as well as commercial vessels. WV De Schelde lies to starboard (depth 2.2m) at the end of the Theodorushaven canal. The harbour is surrounded by commercial boatyards and busy industrial units, but the security is good and there is an on-site bar/restaurant. A new marina is being planned which will lie in less industrial surroundings in the Binnenschelde, but this is not likely to be ready before 2010.

Facilities Ashore
Fuel At WV De Schelde
Chandlers & repairs Bruijs jachtbouw on Havendijk
Supermarket & Shops Albert Heijn on Vlaszak near Grote Markt
Extensive shopping in centre and weekly market on Thursday
ATMs Plenty in town

What to see
The centre of town is about 1.5km away and if you don't fancy the 15-minute walk you can hire bikes from the harbourmaster. Bergen Op Zoom (pronounced 'berkhen-op-zohme') is renowned for withstanding two Spanish sieges and latterly for its asparagus. Approach the town via Lievevrouwestraat and you will pass under the last of the town's medieval gateways. The marquises palace, the Markiezenhof on Steenbergsestraat, was built in the 15th and 16th centuries and, now restored, remains one of the best examples of its type in western Europe. The second

floor houses the municipal museum including a scale model of the town's star-shaped fortifications. The last remains of the real thing are to the northeast of the town with an attractive park opposite. Every year a major outdoor theatre performance is held in the Grote Markt, but tickets sell like hot stroopwafels so you would need to book ahead.

Restaurant tip
The onsite clubhouse wins for convenience but there is a wide choice in the town centre.

THOLEN
A buoyed channel runs from the Tholense Gat through the Nieuwe Haven or from the Schelde-Rijnverbining at green buoy NH11, avoiding the Vluchthaven. WSV De Kogge lies immediately outside the old harbour entrance, and boats longer than 15m may berth inside the municipal harbour after consultation with the harbourmaster (depth 2.4m). The large marina area is bordered by residential apartments and waterside restaurants, giving it a pleasant ambience.

Although St Maartensdijk is officially the 'capital' of the island of Tholen, the town of Tholen is the largest on the island with 6,000 residents. The heart of the town is protected by its star-shaped fortifications, now a greenbelt and a nice spot for a walk. It contains a good selection of shops and cafés. For some active outdoor entertainment make your way back to Speelmansplaten Outdoor Boats and Fun on the Oesterdam where you can hire a pedalo.

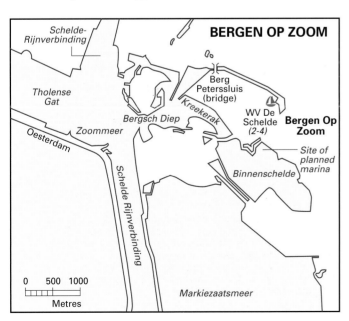

Relax on a terrace in Bergen Op Zoom's Grote Markt

Roosendaalse en Steenbergse Vliet

One kilometre east of the Schelde-Rijnverbinding junction with the Volkerak, the Roosendaalse and Steenbergse Vliet is accessed via the Benedensas. Although strictly part of the West Brabant province, this waterway is described here as no onward connections to the rest of that province are possible. Red and green buoys mark the safe entrance to the 1km-long channel. Before the lock in the port arm there are moorings at WSV Volkerak and after it at JH De Vliet, where diesel is also available. This waterway is not covered by either the 1800 series or the ANWB charts and links to alternative charts are given on www.inlandwaterwaysofthenetherlands.com. The lock normally stands open except sometimes during warm summers when there is heavy algae bloom. The buoyed and signposted channel winds through pleasant countryside and makes a change to the open waters of the Zeeland region.

Speed limit Volkerak to Benedensas 8km/h (4.3kn)
Benedensas to Steenbergse bridge 9km/h (4.9kn)
Maximum permitted draught 2.4m
Lock Benedenas normally stands open. When closed, locking possible throughout the day with a break for lunch on weekdays only (1300-1400).
Bridge 1 opening at Benedensas. Normally stands open except when requested by pedestrians.

DE HEEN

From Benedensas the river continues eastwards, with a turning to starboard after 2.5km leading to the JH De Schapenput at De Heen. The harbour has all the usual facilities including launderette and grocery store, and the small village is a popular camping and chalet holiday venue. The Vos Mill is still in use for grain and cattle feed and when operating it is open for visitors.

STEENBERGEN

Where to stop

Continuing on the Vliet for 3.5km brings you to another turning to starboard which leads 2.5km to JH Steenbergen (pronounced 'stain-berkher') in the centre of the town. Permanent berths in the old harbour (depth 2.8m) are freed up for summer visitors and are only a short walk from the town centre amenities. Continuing a further 3km on the Vliet would bring you to the Steenbergse bridge with a fixed air draught of 3m.

Facilities Ashore

Fuel By Benedensas at JH De Vliet
Repairs & servicing The boat-building harbourmaster also runs Jachtbouw Brabant
Supermarket & Shops Albert Heijn on Lindenburghlaan. Weekly market on Wednesday afternoon
ATMs Two near market square

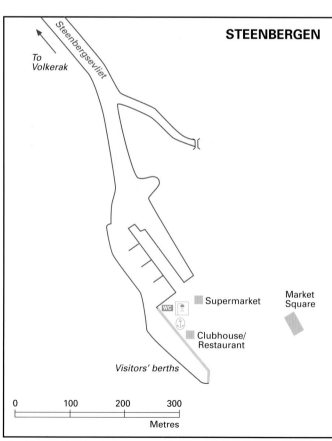

What to see

Although the VVV office in the town hall on Kaaistraat could think of no attractions to recommend to visitors the 'Old Gaffers' make a bi-annual pilgrimage and certainly enjoy it. There is a good selection of shops in the town centre with late night opening on Fridays and a weekly market on Wednesday afternoon. Once encircled by star-shaped fortifications, parts of the canal remain to the northeast of the harbour but most have been filled in to make way for progress. Students of wartime history will know that Guy Gibson of Dambusters fame is buried in Steenbergen, having crashed here in 1944 whilst checking anti-aircraft positions, over a year after that historic raid. Gibsonstraat, northwest of the harbour, marks the spot where he died, along with his navigator JB Warwick and there is a memorial to the Dambusters in the town park.

Restaurant tip

The quayside Z 'Onder Zeil has been in the harbourmaster's family for 20 years and is now run by his son. Good food in an authentic nautical atmosphere with regular special events that are popular with the waterborne clientele.

A typically well stocked fish stall at the Wednesday market

Cruising in Zeeland

From the content of this chapter it is clear that there is a lot more to Zeeland than the well-trodden paths of the 'Staande Mast' routes. The opportunity can be taken to explore the venues to the east or to lay up on the islands in the Grevelingenmeer, as well as those on the Veerse Meer. Choosing passage times that avoid the queues at locks and bridges is a good plan, as is choosing low season periods in June and September to visit. There are far less busy areas of the inland waterways of the Netherlands to visit in July and August as the later chapters of this book

will reveal. Many Dutch yachtsmen leave their centrally-located and well-serviced home berths to cruise to Zeeland and the coast in the summer and this makes it an ideal time to visit those areas.

Having said all this, many readers will still be restricted by their logistics to the most easily accessible areas but by careful planning and use of the detail we have provided, this can still be made into an enjoyable first visit to this land of sheltered inland cruising opportunities.

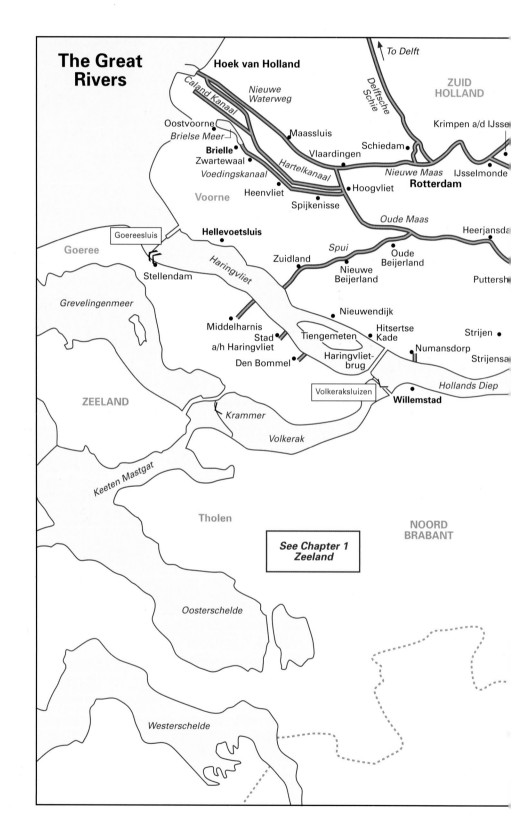

The Great Rivers

To Delft

ZUID HOLLAND

Hoek van Holland

Caland Kanaal

Nieuwe Waterweg

Delftsche Schie

Krimpen a/d IJsse

Oostvoorne

Brielse Meer

Maassluis

Schiedam

Brielle

Zwartewaal

Vlaardingen

Nieuwe Maas

IJsselmonde

Hartelkanaal

Voedingskanaal

Heenvliet

Hoogvliet

Rotterdam

Voorne

Spijkenisse

Oude Maas

Goereesluis

Hellevoetsluis

Heerjansda

Goeree

Haringvliet

Zuidland

Spui

Oude Beijerland

Stellendam

Nieuwe Beijerland

Puttersh

Grevelingenmeer

Nieuwendijk

Middelharnis

Stad a/h Haringvliet

Tiengemeten

Hitsertse Kade

Strijen

Numansdorp

Strijensa

Den Bommel

Haringvliet-brug

ZEELAND

Volkeraksluizen

Willemstad

Hollands Diep

Krammer

Volkerak

Keeten Mastgat

Tholen

NOORD BRABANT

See Chapter 1
Zeeland

Oosterschelde

Westerschelde

2 Great Rivers

including the Haringvliet and the Biesbosch

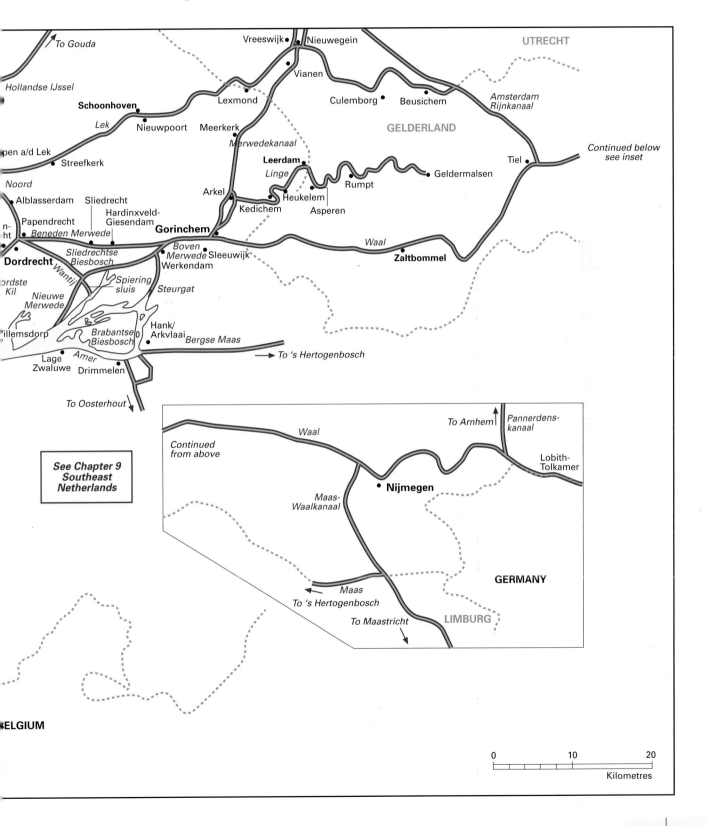

Waterways	Principal venues	Other stopping places
Haringvliet	Hellevoetsluis	Stellendam, Middelharnis
Spui		Oud-Beijerland
Oude Maas	Dordrecht	Heerjansdam
Brielse Meer	Brielle	Oostvorne
Nieuwe Waterweg/Nieuwe Maas	Rotterdam	Maassluis, Vlaardingen, Schiedam
Europoort and the Hartelkanaal		
Hollands Diep	Willemstad	Numansdorp
Dordtse Kil		
Noord		Alblasserdam
Amer		Lage Zwaluwe, Drimmelen
Nieuwe Merwede		
Biesbosch, Dordtse		
Biesbosch, Brabantse		Werkendam, Hank/Aarkvlaai
Biesbosch, Sliedrechtse		
Merwede (Boven & Beneden)	Gorinchem	Papendrecht, Sliedrecht, Hardinxveld-Giessendam, Sleeuwijk
Waal	Zaltbommel, Nijmegen	Tiel, Tolkamer
Maas-Waalkanaal		
Merwedekanaal bezuiden de Lek		Meerkerk, Vianen
Linge	Leerdam	Arkel, Kedichem, Heukelem, Asperen, Rumpt, Geldermalsen
Lek	Schoonhoven	Krimpen a/d Lek, Streefkerk, Nieuwpoort, Vreeswijk, Culemborg, Beusichem

This chapter, the only one in the book that is not based on provincial boundaries, has been designed to address the special navigational influences of these waterways. We start at Stellendam and work our way along the Great Rivers, made up of the Maas from France via Belgium, the huge Waal, the main navigation from Germany, and the Lek (a continuation of the Rijn), which converge in a corridor bordered by Rotterdam in the north and the Haringvliet in the south. Much of this chapter concerns itself with the settlements on the banks of these important rivers whose flood banks and dykes act as the second half of the Netherlands flood management system – against the threat from within of inland flooding. Readers are referred to the introductory chapter and the chart River Outflows and Tides of the Dutch Rivers to fully understand the additional tidal and drainage influences on navigation.

Although the Lek is included here until it crosses the Amsterdam-Rijnkanaal, its continuation, the Nederrijn is dealt with in Chapter 8: Central

Netherlands, as this forms part of a popular cruising route linking the Vecht and the Gelderse IJssel. To the south, from the Haringvliet ports and sluices we continue along the fresh water Hollands Diep, stopping at the popular port of Willemstad and the major waterways junction and historical inland port of Dordrecht: the latter demonstrating, with the sea port of Rotterdam, the huge importance of waterborne freight to this area which continues to the present day.

Away from this commercial activity, the very special ecology of the Biesbosch provides respite and contrast with its leisure lakes and nature areas, as does the charming river navigation of the ancient Linge. For those using the Waal as a through route with its congestion and fast flows, safe harbours are detailed as far as the historical port of Nijmegen and Tolkamer, close to the German border.

Haringvliet

Separated from the North Sea by the Haringvlietdam, the Haringvliet is fed by the upstream river flow. Its level is controlled by sluices which result in a weak tidal flow. The Haringvliet has been fresh water since its closure from the sea which has proved useful as a reservoir for water supplies, but has now been considered to have been detrimental to the environment. Consequently, a decision has been taken to reopen the sluices in normal weather conditions from 2008 to allow tidal water back into the Haringvliet.

Speed limit 20km/h except in the vicinity of the shores and islands, 9km/h
Depth Spar buoys mark the 2m depth line and there is minimum depth of NAP+0.25m throughout the buoyed channels.
Lock Goereese sluis and lifting bridges operate 24 hours (except in winds of Force 6 or above). VHF 20.
Bridge Haringvliet bridge at east end has east and west going passages marked at both ends of the bridge with a minimum clearance at HW of 9.4m and an opening span at the northern end which operates throughout the day from 0900 except 1600-1800. Height gauges on each pillar show the actual clearance according to the tidal conditions.

STELLENDAM

The Goereese Sluis gives access through the Haringvlietdam from the sea and the first available stopping point is the large and well-equipped Marina Stellendam. Here all facilities are provided including a comprehensive chandlers and popular harbourside restaurant. Fuel, yacht services, pump-out and launderette are all provided on the site, which is some 3km remote from the small village.

Next to the lock, the Haringvliet Expo is a smaller version of that on the Oosterschelde, but gives an interesting insight into the increasingly important role played by the Haringvliet sluices in the control of river levels all the way back to Germany. The visit commences with an introductory film in English explaining the effect of the 1953 floods and the 14-year construction of the Haringvliet dam, which was completed in 1970. The highlight of the exhibition is a guided tour to the inner workings of the barrier and, when weather permits, a windy walk back along the top of the dam.

Since the closure of the dam Stellendam has become one of the largest fishing ports in the area and a busy auction takes place every Friday.

HELLEVOETSLUIS

Where to stop
Hellevoetsluis has become a major boating centre and there is no shortage of places to moor. To the west of the town, several marinas are clustered in the large and modern Heliushaven, including Marina Cape Helius, WSV Helius and WV Hellevoetsluis. Best facilities are at Marina Cape Helius but rates are slightly cheaper at the yacht club moorings.

Hellevoetsluis from the southwest; Heliushaven in the foreground with the Groote Dok and Voornsekanaal beyond   *Patrick Roach*

Visit the Noord Hinder lightship in the Koopvaardijhaven at Hellevoetsluis

The entrance to the main harbour is identifiable by the white lighthouse which stands to the west of the entrance. There are municipal moorings in the Haaven, prior to the bridge, and also in the Koopvaardijhaven, in the entrance to the Kanaal door Voorne, although these are exposed to the south and uncomfortable in strong winds. Havendienst Hellevoetsluis can be called on VHF 74 for bridge details and moorings. Beyond the Haaven swing bridge (which opens roughly every hour during the day – see *Almanak* under Hellevoetsluis for exact times) moorings in the Groote Dok are provided by WV Hellevoetsluis and Marina Hellevoetsluis. These lie within the town's fortification canal and are the most central for all amenities.

The eastern most entrance is the old Kanaal door Voorne, which is no longer navigable for most of its length. To starboard immediately inside the entrance lies the Tramhaven, where a range of service companies are located. Beyond the lock and opening bridge (also opens roughly every hour during the day – see *Almanak* for exact times) there are a few moorings available for boats up to 12m at WV Waterman and at WV Haringvliet. Further upstream a visitors pontoon is available by the new shopping centre alongside the canal.

Facilities ashore
Fuel In the Heliushaven
Chandlers At Marina Hellevoetsluis in the Groote Dok
Supermarket, Shops & ATMs In the centre, to the north of the Groote Dok
Cycle hire At WSV Helius
VVV office Oostzanddijk

What to see
As one of the Netherlands' fortified towns, Hellevoetsluis (pronounced 'hella-foot-slous') has a distinguished history and was also the home port of the Dutch navy for a period at the end of the 16th century. A walk around the fortified walls takes in many of the interesting sites, starting at the 17th-century corn mill De Hoop, which is open to visitors at weekends. At the north end of the Groote Dok,

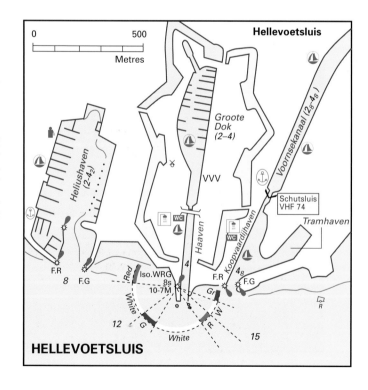

the Jan Blanken Dry dock was the first brick-built dry dock in the Netherlands; and in the Koopvaardijhaven, the restored North Hinder lightship is also open to visitors.

The VVV office houses a well-presented introduction to the town's attractions, which also include the National Fire-fighting Museum and the Museum 'Gesigt van 't Dok' which recounts historic moments in the town's nautical history.

MIDDELHARNIS

Middelharnis lies on the south side of the Haringvliet, with municipal moorings at the end of the long harbour canal. A footbridge is operated by pedestrians and red lights show when the bridge is about to close. The bridge opens again automatically after use.

Speed limit 7km/h
Lock and bridge Often stands open or operates throughout the day on the hour. VHF 12

Visitors may take any space which does not display the sign Vrij houden (Keep free). Two water berths are located on either side of the canal near the southern end, and there are rubbish and chemical toilet disposal facilities nearby. Jachtwerf Peeman on the east bank has a fuel berth (cards accepted) and a very small shop selling a few items of chandlery. The harbour has a cosy ambience and is protected by the long canal.

An important fishing port until the end of the 19th century, Middelharnis is now a sleepy village which relies on visitors for its main industry. A good selection of restaurants line the quayside and the pedestrianised shopping centre, D'n Diek, has special late night Friday opening in the summer with entertainments and events. For everyday requirements, there is an ATM at the head of the moorings opposite the VVV office, and a Plus supermarket on Westdijk.

EASTERN HARINGVLIET

A number of further stopping opportunities exist around the eastern end of the Haringvliet, which are of limited interest to visiting boaters. The first of these is at Stad aan het Haringvliet which, despite its name, is a very small village with a large marina outside the flood lock into the old harbour. Next along the south coast is Den Bommel, which has a small yacht club with usual facilities. Beware of the eastern harbour mole which lies partly under water.

On the north bank there are free moorings at the very small Nieuwendijk harbour, but again skippers should be aware of covered harbour moles on both sides. Further east at Hitserse Kade the small harbour is home to WV De Hitsert, which has limited space for visitors up to 12.5m. It is not permitted to make use of the small harbours on the island of Tiengemeten and in any case it is intended that this island will revert to a wetland nature reserve when the estuary becomes tidal in 2008.

Spui

The Spui is an old branch of the Oude Maas, which connects the Haringvliet (from a position on its north bank opposite Middelharnis) to the Oude Maas north of Oud-Beijerland. It runs close to the small settlement of Nieuw Beijerland and along the northern edge of the original town at Oud-Beijerland. The water is tidal and partly buoyed along its whole length and, because it is narrow and quite winding, has little commercial traffic making it a peaceful spot for leisure boaters. The tidal direction and strength detailed in *Wateralmanak 2* is influenced by the water run off from the Rijn and the Maas, the tidal movement of the sea and the manipulation of the Haringvliet sluices. Generally the Haringvliet is kept at a level to force a flow of fresh water north towards Rotterdam to assist in keeping it a fresh water port.

Length 15.4km
Speed limit 20km/h
Depth Minimum depths along the length of the river are at HW NAP+0.6m, and at LW NAP-0.06m (~3m)
Locks and bridges None

OUD-BEIJERLAND

Modern harbours are available at Zuidland and Nieuw Beijerland but the nicest stop is the old harbour at Oud-Beijerland which still has some character. The lock stands open except in extreme high water conditions and the depth over the sill (NAP-2m) is given by a tide gauge. Moorings are managed by Watersportcentrum Kats and WSV Het Spui; the usual facilities are available including a reasonably-sized chandlers and some service facilities. A lot of residential development is underway around the harbour which might be more attractive once it is finished. A good selection of shops, bars and restaurants are available nearby.

Oude Maas

This deep tidal river connects the Beneden Merwede at Dordrecht with the Nieuwe Maas at Vlaardingen and forms an alternative to the main commercial route, via the Noord and Nieuwe Maas. This original watercourse travels through attractive countryside, but the waterway itself is not always quiet as it is heavily used by barge and sea-going traffic. Vessels are advised to stay just outside the main channel, but not close to the banks. Current can be up to 2.5knots, and details of direction and flow at various states of the tide are given in the *Almanak*. Boats fitted with VHF are required to keep a listening watch on VHF 4/79 (see riverside boards for details).

At the western end two junctions give access to the Hartelkanaal (which continues via the Calandkanaal through Europoort to the sea) and to the Voedingskanaal to the Brielse Meer (see below). At its eastern end the junction with the Dordtse Kil at km 980 leads south to the Hollands Diep, whilst the Oude Maas continues northeast to form a three-way junction with the Beneden Merwede and the Noord at Dordrecht.

Moorings at Hoogvliet south of the Brielse Meer junction are not recommended for visitors with only 0.8m depth at LW, and nearby moorings at Spijkenisse should also be avoided for the same reason. On the south bank at km 983.5 a very small harbour at Puttershoek is situated in a new cut to the east of the town with very basic facilities and space for boats up to just 10m.

Length 30km
Bridges 4 opening. Botlekbrug (6.8m when closed) and Spijkenisserbrug (11.4m when closed) open 24 hours (Spijkenisserbrug only at H+30) with breaks for the morning and evening rush hour on weekdays (0630-0830 and 1600-1800). Dordrecht road (10.5m when closed) and rail (9.7m when closed) bridges have opening sections on the east side which open at 0616 and then every two hours from 0916 with additional times at weekends and holidays.

HEERJANSDAM/BARENDRECHT

East of km 987 Marina Barendrecht lies 1km from the small town of Heerjansdam. It is run by the same company as City Marina Rotterdam and offers 2.5m depth and a good range of facilities to visitors, including wi-fi.

DORDRECHT

Where to stop

Beyond the junction with the Dordtse Kil, the Oude Maas continues northeast to its junction with the Beneden Merwede and the Noord. Dordrecht is blessed with a number of marinas- but visitors tend to gravitate towards the Royal Dordrecht rowing and sailing club (KDR&ZV) in the Nieuwe Haven which is accessed just north of the road and rail bridges and is contactable on VHF 31. If crossing the channel remember to keep a sharp look out for barge traffic which cannot manoeuvre easily. The Engelenburger lift bridge crosses the entrance and

opens on request (VHF 74) throughout the day on the hour and half-hour with breaks for lunch and dinner (1200–1230 and 1800–1830). WSV Maartensgat offers a cheaper alternative for boats up to 12m with the Mazelaars bridge opened on request (VHF 74) by the harbourmaster.

Alternatively, you may find space in WSV Drechtstad (again only up to 12m) in the Wijnhaven. Access is via the Boombrug opened in request (VHF 74). The Wolwevershaven is a commercial harbour, sometimes used by the brown fleet and historic yachts. The Leuvehaven is provided as a waiting pontoon for yachts awaiting bridge opening. It is not permitted to overnight here.

Fuel is available from bunker boats along the Oude Maas as well as in the Nieuwe Haven.

Facilities Ashore
Fuel In the Nieuwe Haven and from bunker boats along the Oude Maas
Chandlers Gebr. Moret Watersport is 15 minutes by bike
Supermarket & Shops Albert Heijn on Voorstraat
ATMs In the centre
Cycle hire & VVV office Near train station

DORDRECHT

A Boombrug
B Damiatebrug
C Lange IJzerenbrug
D Engelenburgerbrug
E Mazelaarsbrug
F Kalkhavenbrug

Grote Kerk overlooks the Nieuwe Haven and you get a good view from the top of the tower

What to see

Dordrecht is an important river centre at the junction of the Rijn, the Noord and the Merwede and from the top of the Grote Kerk tower, you can have a commanding view of the area. For an insight into life in previous centuries visit Museum Simon van Gijn on the Nieuwe Haven, where an 18th-century residence and its contents are on display in situ. Close by, the private Resistance Museum is maintained independently to honour those who fought and suffered during the second world war. Few of the exhibits are interpreted in English but the passion of the volunteer guides makes up for its deficiencies. The town centre is blessed with all amenities, and tours by boat or horse-drawn carriage can give an illuminating overview. From the ferry terminal near the Grote Hoofdpoort, the river bus can take you, amongst other places, to the popular recreation area of the Sliedrechtse Biesbosch. Only the VVV office is somewhat distant, situated near the train station on the far side of town.

Restaurant tip

If you like fish then you can't beat De Stroper (The Poacher) on Wijnbrug but do book especially at weekends.

Brielse Meer

The Brielse Meer is a narrow inland lake some 14km long which varies in breadth between 200 and 700m. A wide buoyed channel runs the length of the mere with a minimum depth of 2.5m. It is a popular water sports area for those who live and work in the region and there are numerous clubs and facilities, but it is considered too small for serious sailing. The entrance to the Brielse Meer is at km 1003 on the Oude Maas, just south of the eastern end of the Hartelkanaal, where the Voornesluis gives access to the Voedingskanaal. The centre of activity is the old fortified town of Brielle, but there are many moorings on the lake's shores, around islands at the western end near Oostvoorne and around Middenplaat island to the east of Brielle. There are also harbours at Hairt Hille, Heenvliet and Zwarte Waal but these are not recommended for visitors. Boats longer than 14m are requested not to use the harbours and creek moorings or those belonging to the Recreatieschap Voorne-Putten-Rozenburg, except for moorings specially designated for boats of this size. Mooring is restricted to three days in the same place, with no return within five days.

Lock Voornesluis operates throughout the day.
Bridges 1 opening, 1 fixed (10m). Hartelbrug (10.9m when closed) operates throughout the day on request at the Voornesluis or for east-bound vessels, by a bell to the west of the bridge. Brielsebrug (min clearance 10m).

BRIELLE

Where to stop

Visitors moorings are on the starboard fork at the end of the harbour entrance canal where token-operated electricity and water are provided. These are managed by Maritiem Centre Brielle, whose harbourmaster has an office on the south quay. Tokens are available here, and out of hours at Café Dixi, Eetcafe 't Swarte Schaep and Watersport Op Hoop, which are all within sight of the moorings. The facilities block is behind the harbour office and is accessed and charged via an electronic SEP-key. Bike hire is also available from the office. The moorings do get very busy in summer but the harbourmaster will accept bookings if you phone in advance ☎ 0181 412536.

Jachthaven De Meeuw has a limited number of spaces for boats up to 10m in the Havenbatterij and WSV Brielle has some space for boats up to 14m in the Molen Haven.

Facilities ashore

Chandlers Watersport Op Hoop is by the moorings
Repairs & Services Neptune Jachtreparatie can fix most problems ☎ 06 1090 1659
Supermarket & ATMs Albert Heijn on Slagveld at the far end of the Zuid Spuihaven
Cycle hire From harbour office
VVV office In the market square

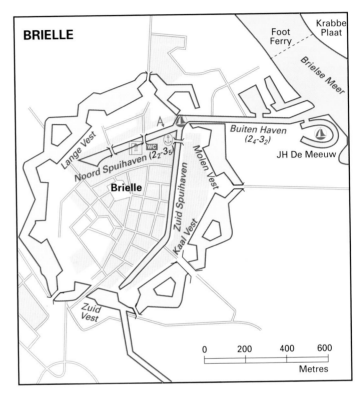

What to see

Brielle (pronounced 'breeler') was formerly a port at the mouth of the Maas and its star-shaped fortifications are still very much intact. The old centre is close by with an ample selection of shops and restaurants and, at the centre, the Historisch Museum Den Brielle is a good place to find out about the town's turbulent past. It owes its fame to the taking of the town from the Spanish by Dutch rebels called the *Watergeuzen* (Sea Beggars), led by William of Orange in 1572, and a costumed parade on 1 April each year enthusiastically commemorates the event.

Restaurant tip

Café Dixi is a friendly watering hole for a casual lunch, but for something a bit more special try De Zalm on Voorstraat or the Hoofdwacht in the market square.

Connections

There is no rail station in Brielle, but there are bus services to Rotterdam and Hellevoetsluis.

OOSTVORNE

At the head of the mere JH Geijsman is a large marina complex with a wide range of facilities including wi-fi, and is a good base for exploring the nearby beaches and dunes.

Nieuwe Waterweg/Nieuwe Maas

The Nieuwe Waterweg, opened in 1872, forms the continuation of the Nieuwe Maas from its confluence with the Oude Maas to the sea at Maasmond (Mouth of the Maas). The Maasmond entrance is formed by the 3km long Noorderdam on the north side and the man-made Europoort to the south. This is one of the busiest ports in Europe and leisure boats entering the inland waterways at this point should exercise caution, maintain a listening watch on VHF (area boundaries, channels and call signs shown on the 1809 series of charts), stay to the starboard side of the channel and keep a sharp lookout. A reliable engine and a radar reflector are essential; yachts are permitted to sail but not to tack. Once inside the harbour walls, the channel splits into two, the north side forming the Nieuwe Waterweg, and the south side leading to the Europoort. Leisure boats are prohibited in the dock areas of the Europoort, but there is a route via the Calandkanaal and the Hartelkanaal to the Oude Maas. Tides up to 5km/h can run in the Nieuwe Waterweg and skippers should make use of the Dutch tidal atlas, Waterstanden en Stromen, or the tidal advice in the *Almanak*.

At km 1013 the waterway changes its name to the Nieuwe Maas, and the Oude Maas joins the waterway from the south. The Nieuwe Maas continues east through Rotterdam to join the Lek, whilst the Oude Maas takes a roughly parallel path to the south as far as Dordrecht, continuing west as the Merwede to join the Waal. The Noord joins these two parallel routes at Dordrecht and it is a combination of these waterways which forms the main through route from the German border to the Hook of Holland - from east to west, the Waal, the Boven Merwede, the Beneden Merwede, the Noord, the Nieuwe Maas and the Nieuwe Waterweg.

JH IJsselmonde on the south bank at the junction of the Nieuwe Maas with the Hollandse IJssel is of little interest to visitors.

Length 46km
Speed limit None, but avoid making dangerous wash
Bridges 1 fixed (10.3m), 2 opening. Erasmusbrug (11.3m when closed - see Rotterdam for details) and van Brienenoordbrug at IJsselmonde (23.8m when closed) opens only on request with three hours notice on ☎ 078 681 9950.

Hoek van Holland approaching from seaward. The northern channel (shown here on the left) is bound for Rotterdam, whilst the southern channel leads to Europort and the Calandkanaal   *Patrick Roach*

Maassluis from the southeast   *Patrick Roach*

MAASSLUIS

A flood lock normally stands open in the outer harbour, and rail and road bridges cross the inner harbour beyond. Minimum depth in the outer harbour is 3.8m at LW, and 3m in the inner harbour. The bridges operate throughout the day, except Sundays and holidays when there is only a single opening (2035–2055, Easter to October only). Havendienst Maassluis can be called on VHF 68.

As the first port along the Nieuwe Waterweg you would expect more of a harbour at Maassluis, but the town seems to have only just realised the potential and plan to develop a Museumhaven and more visitors' facilities. At present moorings are available in the Binnenhaven after consultation with the harbourmaster and there is no charge for a stay of up to 48 hours. Harbour facilities are basic with the possibility of power but not much else. De Haas boatyard on Govert van Wijnkade provides service facilities.

Beyond the Binnenhaven, the town's Monsterse sluis is not navigable but forms a focal point, with shops and cafés clustered along the narrow canals behind. West of the small residential town, a huge storm surge barrier stands ready near the Nieuwe Oranjekanaal. The two white gates are supported by giant lattice arms and more about the construction and the working of the barrier can be learnt at the free Keringhuis exhibition at Maeslantkering, 20 minutes bike ride along the Nieuwe Waterweg from Maassluis.

VLAARDINGEN

East of the Oude Maas junction and the waterside Delta Hotel the entrance to Vlaardingen's buitenhaven opens to port. Berths here are affected by wash from the main river, but the Oude Haven, accessed via two lifting bridges and a lock offers comfortable berths in the centre of the largish town. Deltabrug and Delflandse lock operate throughout the day with a break for lunch (1200-1300). The rail bridge which follows has slightly more restricted hours, and must be requested an hour in advance

☎ 010 434 4700 or VHF 20. The remaining bridges and locks give access to the Vlaardingervaart which connects with Delft, but is restricted in headroom to 1.9m. Fuel available from Van der Linden Watersport in the Oude haven.

The former fishing village has been overshadowed by international industrial development but the Fisherman's museum on Westhavenkade remains to tell of former times. A herring and beer festival makes the beginning of September a good time to visit.

SCHIEDAM

There are several yacht clubs in the Spuihaven west of km 1007 on the north bank, including Jachtclub Schiedam, WSV Volharding, and WV De Nieuwe Waterweg. Moorings are open to the main river, but the entrance has a minimum depth at low water of 2.5m. East of km 1007 is the entrance to the Voorhaven which leads to the Buitensluis. This gives access to the town centre canals of the Buitenhaven and the Nieuwe Haven where there are several mooring places. Pass through the Buitensluis and turn to port at the junction to pass under the Hoofdbrug for the Nieuwe Haven moorings of WV De Nieuwe Haven with basic facilities and space for boats up to 19m. Opposite, sailmaker Mak Zeilmakerij also has a small chandlers.

Alternatively, continue on along the Buitenhaven under a further two opening bridges to short-stay shopping moorings in the Lange Haven or turn to port immediately south of the Beurssluis under a further lifting bridge which gives access to the Korte Haven, where WV De Schie has spaces for visitors up to 12m. Beyond the Beurssluis and a further lifting bridge lies the municipal yacht harbour, the Florijn Haven, on the Doeleplein. There is a modern facilities block with security gate access and the harbourmaster can be contacted on VHF 22. These moorings are close to the historic centre which is enclosed by the semi-circular Buitenhaven canal.

Locks Buitensluis and Koninginnebrug (VHF 22) and Beurssluis and Beursbrug operate throughout the day with a break for lunch (1200-1300; 1200-1500 on Saturdays; 1200-1900 on Sundays and holidays).
Bridges Nieuwe Haven: Hoofdbrug operates throughout the day Monday-Saturday only with a break for lunch on weekdays (1200-1300)
Buiten/Lange Haven: Koemarkt, Appelmarkt and Ooievaars bridges operate the same hours as the Buitensluis.

Although part of the Rotterdam conurbation, Schiedam retains an attractive historic centre ringed with canals. The grain mills which stand along the Noordvest canal are the last of 19 which were used for milling grain used in the town's 400 distilleries. Today, five companies maintain the tradition, and their recipes for jonge (young) and oude (old) jenever gin remain a closely-guarded secret; even at the town's Jenever Museum on Lange Haven. If you want to see still more of the waterways there are whisper-boat tours around the central canals which depart three times daily from the Museum-Molen De Nieuwe Palmboom, which itself is open to visitors.

Schiedam to Delft

From the Florijn Haven the canal continues north as the Schiedamse Schie, which connects with the Delftse Schie to Delft.

Bridges 6 fixed (min 3.6m), 5 opening. Proveniers, Branders, Delfland, 's Graveland, Rol (VHF 22) and Oost-Abts bridges operate throughout the day with a break for lunch (1200-1300; 1200-1500 on Saturdays; 1200-1900 on Sundays and holidays).

Rotterdam to Delft

West of km 1002 the Parkhaven and Parksluizen form the entrance to the Delfshavense Schie, which joins the Delftse Schie and continues on to Delft. All bridges on this route are opening and operate throughout the day, some with rushhour breaks. There are cheap moorings at the Delfshaven with basic facilities.

The route to the north of Rotterdam which connects the Delfshavense Schie, via the Schie-Schiekanaal and the Noorderkanaal to the Rotte, is restricted to fixed air draught of 2.4m.

Lock Grote Parksluis and lift bridges operate throughout the day Monday-Saturday, VHF 22. Kleine Parksluis and fixed bridges (min 3.75m) operate throughout the day Monday-Saturday and mornings and evenings on Sundays (0700-1000 and 1700-2200)
Bridges 7 opening. Operate throughout the day except rush hours (0715-0830 and 1600-1730), with the exception of the rail bridge (7m when closed) which opens only on request with three hours notice ☎ 010 436 5405, and then only Monday-Saturday between 1120-1124. For onward passage see details in Chapter 3, Holland South.

Delfshaven was built by the city of Delft in the 14th century at the end of a new canal which linked it to the Maas. It was one of the few parts of Rotterdam which was not destroyed during the war and the café-lined canals are a quieter alternative to the city centre. The Museum De Dubbelde Palmboom has a varied collection including the history of the Pilgrim Fathers who embarked from here in 1620 for England and the New World. Complete the experience with a visit to the Bar-Restaurant De Pilgrim, where you can sample the pilgrim's beer.

ROTTERDAM

For vessels continuing upstream, the Nieuwe Willemsbrug has a fixed clearance of 10.3m and this route should be used by boats lower than this, even if they are coming from the City Marina. Yachts which require greater headroom may make use of the lifting bridge in the Koningshaven.

Bridges Erasmusbrug (clearance under fixed section 11.3m) opens during the day at 1000, 1100, 1330, 1530 and 1900. Night service (2030–0700) can be requested with one hour's notice ☎ 010 485 7900 or VHF 18. Koninginne bridge (3.7m when closed) opens only on request (☎ 010 485 7900 or VHF 18). The rail bridge normally stands open (raised clearance of 45m, 7m when closed).

Where to stop

Just west of km 1001 and the Erasmus bridge, the entrance to the Veerhaven is on the north bank

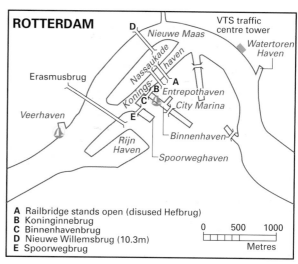

ROTTERDAM

A Railbridge stands open (disused Hefbrug)
B Koninginnebrug
C Binnenhavenbrug
D Nieuwe Willemsbrug (10.3m)
E Spoorwegbrug

0   500   1000
Metres

where municipal moorings and the Royal Rowing and Sailing Club De Maas can be found. The harbourmaster works only part time so you just find a suitable space and he will come to see you when he is next on duty. The moorings are open to the main river and can be affected by wash, especially as the harbour is used by the frequent high-speed water taxis. There are good facilities including a free wi-fi network close to the harbour office and the location is very convenient for the city centre attractions as well as local shops and restaurants. Although it is part of the historic maritime quarter between the Euromast and the Erasmus bridge, the harbour's immediate neighbours are mainly office buildings, making it very quiet at night.

The harbour office building at the Veerhaven has a lively history - originally the headquarters of the water police it was removed during the war for safekeeping and bought back by the city council only recently for a nominal €1.

The southern side of the Erasmus bridge leads into the Koningshaven, where the second turning to starboard gives access to the Binnenhaven and the Entrepothaven. This is home to City Marina Rotterdam where they always have space to

Rotterdam's Erasmus bridge from the southwest. The Veerhaven is on the left   *Patrick Roach*

welcome visitors, but also accept bookings which could be useful for larger boats or groups. Request the Binnenhavenbrug on VHF 18 throughout the day except rush hours (as for Koninginne bridge above). The marina boasts an exceptionally well-serviced facilities block and wi-fi to the pontoons. Fuel will also be available from 2007. The harbour office also houses a small chandlers with a limited selection of charts and accessories, and can be contacted on VHF 77. Plans to expand the marina in 2008 will provide even more capacity and facilities, including berths suitable for fixed mast vessels in the Rijnhaven to the west of the Erasmus bridge.

An adjacent waterside shopping and restaurant complex opened in June 2006 and provides a selection of bars, café-restaurants and shops as well as a large Konmar supermarket. Nearby tram, metro and bus stops provide an easy journey to the city centre and all attractions.

Facilities ashore

Fuel At City Marina from 2007 (cards accepted)
Chandlers Small selection at City Marina harbour office
Supermarket & Shops Konmar supermarket at the City Marina complex & Albert Heijn on Vuurplaat.
ATMs At the City Marina shopping complex
VVV office On Coolsingel (city centre)

What to see

Boasting the largest port in Europe, if not the world, Rotterdam is dominated by its harbour, with more than 30,000 deep sea vessels and millions of containers passing through every year. For boaters there is plenty of maritime heritage of interest, with outdoor exhibitions of both inland and sea-going vessels sited in the Oude Haven and the Leuvehaven, where you will also find the Maritiem Museum. Also in the Oude Haven is the 11-storey Witte Huis, one of the only buildings in this area to survive the 1940 bombardments. Next door, the Mariners Museum, tells the history of the Marine Corps and if you

Be close to the city centre attractions in Rotterdam's Veerhaven

Take a vertigo-inducing trip to the top of the 185m high Euromast for a panoramic view of the city

haven't seen enough of the harbour on your way in, you can take one of the Spido boat tours which show some or all of the port areas between Rotterdam and the sea.

Next door to the Veerhaven, the Euromast is the focal point of the Museum Park, and was originally financed and built in 1960 largely through contributions from rich Rotterdam port barons. The Space Tower, which brought the total height to 185m, was added in 1970. The view from the top stretches for 30km and after lunching in the Michelin-starred Panorama Restaurant, you could abseil or rope-slide down if you dared. Also in the park you will find National Museums of Art and Architecture.

For those interested in wartime history, the OorlogsVerzetsMuseum is a private collection housed on Veerlaan, south of the river, for which the City Marina is most convenient. The founder suffered great hardship from his wartime experiences (about which he has since written a book available in English) and established the museum in memory of these events and the displays are now adopted and sponsored by the city.

Restaurant tip

The Seaman's Café at the Maritime Hotel is known for its good value daily specials and is frequented by genuine seamen. Take a water taxi from the Veerhaven to the Golden Wok floating Chinese restaurant, or at the City Marina visit the City Palace on Laan op Zuid for their fixed price menu of unlimited speciality dishes. Bar-restaurant De Pilgrim in the Delfshaven makes a welcome break from the hustle of the city.

Europoort and the Hartelkanaal

The southern fork of the Nieuwe Waterweg at Maasmond leads into the Europoort area. Continuing straight on leads to the Calandkanaal, whilst the turn to starboard into the Beerkanaal and dock areas is prohibited to leisure traffic. Vessels are required to keep to the starboard side of the channel and stay out of harbour areas. A radar reflector is required and sailing is prohibited. The Calandbrug crosses the waterway at its eastern end, just before the Rozenburgse locks, which link the canal to the Hartelkanaal. Open to the Oude Maas at its eastern end, the Hartelkanaal is subject to tidal influence.

The Hartel storm barrier is also part of the Keringhuis exhibition at Maassluis.

Locks Rozenburgsluis and lifting bridges operate 24 hours. Grote Hartelsluis stands open except in flood conditions – see Hartelbrug below.
Bridges 2 opening. Calandbrug (10.5m under fixed span) operates 24 hours. Hartelbrug storm barrier and bridge (10.3m under fixed spans) opens only on request with 2 hours notice ☎ 0181 21 41 15.

Hollands Diep

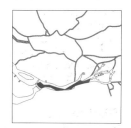

The freshwater Hollands Diep is the continuation of the Amer river from its confluence with the Nieuwe Merwede to the Haringvliet at the Haringvliet bridge. It is a wide waterway with heavy commercial traffic and forms part of the north-south route between Zeeland and Dordrecht. South of the Haringvliet bridge at the western end, the Volkerak dam and locks form the link with Zeeland. Leisure vessels are not permitted to use the Zuid Hollandsch Diep, south of Sassenplaat island; vessels bound for the harbour at Roode Vaart must approach from the east.

West of the Moerdijk bridges the waterway joins with the Dordtse Kil and leads north. Several harbours lie near this junction which could provide a berth in an emergency, but are of very little interest to visitors. These are at Klundert/Noordschans, Strijensas, Roodevaart, Moerdijk and Willemsdorp.

Depth The water level can be controlled by sluicing and in normal conditions varies only 0.2m, with a minimum of NAP+0.46m
Bridges 3 fixed (minimum clearance 9.6m) east of Dordtse Kil junction

WILLEMSTAD

Where to stop

For moorings in Willemstad you have a choice of the large and well-equipped yacht harbours or the traditional town quay. Both have their attractions and their supporters but can be busy in high season, so you may not be spoilt for choice. The harbour office is to port on entering and the staff use a tannoy to determine your requirements. The yacht harbour has good shower and laundry facilities, and a little more privacy. Boats on the town quay need to be self-contained (only water and power are available), but their crews need only to step ashore to be in the historic centre. Short stay pontoons are available to starboard as you enter the old harbour for visits to the supermarket - head inland from the

Willemstad from the west. The new marina is in the unused basin in the foreground   *Patrick Roach*

windmill on the quay. Fuel is available at the entrance to the yacht harbour and an excellent chandlers is on the town quay.

A large new marina, De Batterij, has been opened to the west of the harbour entrance with the first berths available from April 2006, which should help to relieve some of the congestion during busy holiday periods.

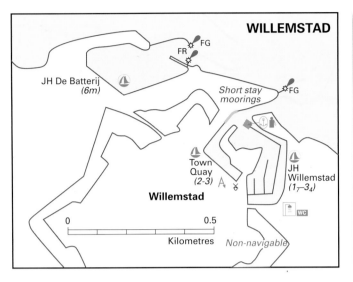

The Festival of the Fortress Towns in full swing at Willemstad

Facilities ashore

Fuel At the yacht harbours
Chandlers Yachting Willemstad on the Benedenkade
Supermarket, Shops & ATMs Small supermarket on Achterstraat and selection of shops on Voorstraat
VVV office Opposite the old harbour

What to see

Star-shaped fortifications define the character of Willemstad (pronounced 'villem-stad') which was named after its founder, William of Orange, and once every ten years it hosts the festival of the Fortress Towns. The inner ring makes a good walk along the battlements and round the bastions, whilst the outer ring offers an easy cycle ride along a tree-lined canal. The old town hall houses the tourist office as well as a small historical collection and the mill, the Oranjemolen, still turns on special occasions. Willemstad is a popular tourist spot and offers a small selection of enticing shopping opportunities for those so inclined. Of particular interest is the chandlers on the town quay which has an excellent selection of nautical equipment, clothing and accessories.

Restaurant tip

You don't have to look far for good restaurants in Willemstad and most visitors enjoy the quayside Wapen van Willemstad or the Restaurant Bellevue, which also offers free wi-fi.

NUMANSDORP

Opposite Willemstad on the north bank of the Hollands Diep, lies the small harbour of Numansdorp. Several yacht clubs lie to the west of the village in the old Veerhaven including Marina Numansdorp with fuel and good facilities, but the moorings nearest the town lie in the Dorpshaven. Beware of the covered mole on the west side of the entrance to the harbour and then proceed past the open flood lock along the narrow harbour canal (depth 2.2m). Stop either at boxes belonging to WV Numansdorp or at the municipal quayside moorings at the head of the canal, where coin-operated electricity and water are available.

The modern village has the usual high street of shops and services but the Schippershuis restaurant on the quay looks the most appealing destination.

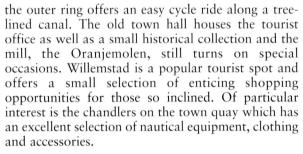

The town quay at Willemstad with the Oranjemolen at the eastern end

Dordtse Kil

The Dordtse Kil joins the Hollands Diep west of the Moerdijk bridges to the Oude Maas, southwest of Dordrecht. It is very busy with commercial traffic both day and night, sometimes carrying ships up to 25,000 tons. Leisure boats are advised to keep to the starboard side of the channel and keep a sharp lookout behind them for following vessels. Strong tides can run, which are north-going on the ebb and south-going on the flood, despite the small range of tidal heights. Vessels fitted with VHF are required to keep a listening watch on channel 4.

On the west bank, overnighting at the harbour at 's Gravendeel is reserved exclusively for local residents, but visitors can be permitted a short daytime stay on request from the harbourmaster. There are no other suitable stopping places on this stretch - for Dordrecht, see Oude Maas.

Length 9.9km
Speed limit 20km/h
Depth Minimum 8m

Noord

This short waterway connects the Beneden Merwede at Dordrecht to the junction of the Lek and Nieuwe Maas at Slikkerveer and forms part of the main commercial route from the German border to the Hook of Holland. It is a wide and busy waterway with an unattractive landscape. The hurrying barges create a lot of wash which is reflected by the many quays and the Noord is also part of the fast ferry route between Dordrecht and Rotterdam, which travels at up to 55km/h (30 knots). Leisure traffic should keep to the starboard side and keep a sharp look out behind them. The three-way junctions at each end are particularly busy and vessels should cross these with extreme caution.

The little used Rietbaan channel, home to several ship scrapyards, offers a useful short cut with a minimum of 2.5m depth at LW. It also gives access, via the Stooppot channel at its southern end, to the moorings of WSV Zwijndrecht.

Length 9km
Speed limit 20km/h except in the Rietbaan, 9km/h
Bridges 1 opening. Alblasserdam (11.5m when closed) is operated remotely and can be requested on VHF 22 Verkeerscentrale Noordtunnel. There are two or three openings per hour and yachts are normally grouped together or with commercial vessels.

Visit the famous Kinderdijk windmills from the yacht harbour at Alblasserdam

ALBLASSERDAM

Just north of the bridge, on the east bank, lies the entrance to the harbours at Alblasserdam. A lifting bridge stands open in the harbour entrance and beyond it are the adjacent yacht clubs of WV Alblasserdam and WSV d'Alblasserwaerdt (depth 2.5m). WV Alblasserdam, immediately to starboard past the bridge, has space for boats up to 14m and has showers available whilst WSV d'Alblasserwaerdt can only accommodate boats up to 12m and has limited facilities. Both are close to the high street which has a good selection of local shops and café/restaurants. The town is part of the Alblasserwaard, a polder below sea level which was drained by the Kinderdijk mills until 1950, and a visit here is the main reason for a stop at Alblasserdam. Today their sails turn only on Windmill days (every Saturday in July and August) but the mills can be visited and boat tours operate daily from May to September. The visitor centre is located at the north end of the dykes but cycle paths run near to the windmills and this is the best way to cover the extensive polder.

Amer

The Amer forms the continuation of the Bergse Maas to its junction with the Nieuwe Merwede, where it becomes the Hollands Diep. Although part of the North Brabant province, the harbours on its southern shore relate strongly to the Brabantse Biesbosch to the north, which are considered in this chapter along with the Sliedrechtse Biesbosch, north of the Nieuwe Merwede, and the Dordtse Biesbosch, to the west. It is a wide and open waterway, with little commercial traffic, which makes it a nice river for sailing marred only by the occasional thoughtless soul who decides to make a wash for the jetskiers. The unlimited speed areas are marked in purple on the ANWB charts and these are heavily used, especially at weekends in fine weather.

Length 10km
Speed limit 20km/h (where applicable) except for stretch north of Drimmelen, 9km/h
Depth Minimum draught is NAP+0.15m
Bridges None, except at entrance to Lage Zwaluwe

LAGE ZWALUWE

At Lage Zwaluwe (pronounced 'larkher **zvarl**-ovay') Watersport Crezée has moorings both sides of the 4.5m fixed bridge. In the outer harbour are spaces for boats up to 3m draught. Fuel and a large chandlers are also to be found here and whilst these berths are convenient, there is a constant stream of power boats and jetskiers who zoom in and out until they run out of petrol. Telephone reservations are taken but you can also stop at the fuel berth and ask in the chandlers to be directed to a berth. For boats that can clear the bridge there is a large inner harbour which is slightly nearer the small town and rather more peaceful. A municipal quay, also beyond the bridge, is available free for up to three hours for shopping. A bakery is nearby and further east along the main street a greengrocer, and eventually a supermarket, Chinese restaurant and two takeaways. One of these, Aspendos, will deliver pizza or a host of Turkish delicacies to your boat until the small hours of the morning ☎ 0168 482389. You will also find a selection of 13 bars and cafés around the town if you look hard enough. Harbour open days are held the first weekend of April.

Lage Zwaluwe is a convenient base for visiting the Brabantse Biesbosch or there are cycle routes along the dyke to Drimmelen. For something completely different check out the Boerengolf (Farmer's golf), a typically Dutch recreation involving a clog on a stick.

DRIMMELEN

At Drimmelen (pronounced 'derimmeler') visitors make for the new harbour, which is the more easterly of the two entrances. There is a fuel berth and harbourmaster sited just inside the entrance from where you can take a berth in Biesbosch Marina Drimmelen. All new facilities are available, operated by electronic SEP key. If you prefer to try one of the yacht clubs, WSV Biesbosch has all the pontoons hard to starboard on entering, whilst WSV Drimmelen is to be found in the southern harbour, accessed via the open channel. For technical accessories Zijlmans Watersport on Havenkade is a Vetus stockist and there is a modest floating chandlers in the old harbour.

The marina area is a hive of activity and nearly swamps the adjacent old harbour and village with its numerous cafés and restaurants. The Biesbosch visitors' centre is at its west end, but it is a poor imitation of the one in the Sliedrechtse Biesbosch and has none of the Biesbosch ambience. Limited VVV information is also available here. The old harbour no longer has places for visitors but if you want to get away from the madding crowds walk or cycle round to the far side where Café/Restaurant 't Voske has a large terrace overlooking the Amer. In 1944–45 it was a start and end point for the 'Line Crossers', resistance workers who brought downed pilots across the Biesbosch from Werkendam into the unoccupied Brabant province.

Café 't Voske enjoys a view of the Amer and the Biesbosch

Nieuwe Merwede

The Nieuwe Merwede forms a link between the Hollands Diep at its junction with the Amer and the Merwede east of Dordrecht. In places up to half a kilometre wide, it is a busy commercial route and leisure vessels are advised to navigate outside the main channel where there is still a minimum of 1.5m depth. Shallower patches between km 979–978 are marked. Tidal differences are currently small, averaging not more than 0.3m, but there is nearly always a slight ebb current, which can be greater when the Haringvliet sluices are open (2–3 knots), making it most suitable for downstream navigation. The whole area is bordered by the Biesbosch National Park, making it a pleasant route despite the heavy traffic. At km 970 the Ottersluis gives access into the Wantij to Dordrecht and to the Sliedrechtse Biesbosch.

Length 20km
Speed limit 20km/h (where applicable)

Biesbosch, Dordtse

The Biesbosch is made up of a network of wide and narrow creeks interspersed with reed beds and marshland, and forms one of the largest freshwater tidal areas in Europe. Its origins lie in the St Elizabeth's Flood of 1421 when 16 villages were engulfed and what had been land changed overnight into an inland sea. Gradually silt was deposited by the great rivers and in combination with the tidal incursions sandbanks emerged. Rushes, or biesem, grew here, giving the area its name, the Biesbosch (Rush-woods). Over time, rushes were followed by reed, and subsequently willow and the new landscape created its own industry. Duck hunting and fishing prevailed at first and then gradually areas were colonised back into land for agriculture.

The Nieuwe Merwede canal was completed in 1870 and this divided the area into two parts. Today the main area is the Brabantse Biesbosch, to the south east of the Nieuwe Merwede, with the smaller but still popular Sliedrechtse Biesbosch lying between the Beneden Merwede and the Nieuwe Merwede.

The only navigable part of the Dordtse Biesbosch is the Zuid Martensgat as far as Prinsesheuvel, which leaves the Hollands Diep just east of Willemsdorp and the Dordtse Kil. The channel is very shallow in places and even in moderate winds significant waves develop from the Hollands Diep.

Biesbosch, Brabantse

The Spijkerboor and Steurgat channels form the principal navigable channel through the Brabantse Biesbosch linking the Amer at Geertruidenberg with the Nieuwe Merwede at Werkendam. Another important route leads from the Noordergat van de Vissen in the west of the area along the Gat van Van Kampen, Gat van de Noorderklip and the Ruigt to join the Steurgat. At the north end of the Steurgat, the Biesbosch lock west of Werkendam controls the exit onto the Nieuwe Merwede. Further west the Spiering lock gives access onto the Gat van de Hardenhoek and connects with the Noordergat van de Vissen. This forms the most direct route from the Sliedrechtse Biesbosch, with a minimum depth of 1.3m. Regulations require that visitors do not disturb the peace and tranquility of the area and that the natural habitats are protected.

The southern side of the Biesbosch is open to the Amer and there is a small tidal variation of around 0.2m. Heights are given relative to HW and depths relative to LW, but many of the shoal patches are not marked and careful and cautious navigation with an up to date copy of the detailed ANWB Biesbosch Waterkaart is essential if grounding is to be avoided. The planned partial opening of the Haringvliet sluices in 2008 will lead to an increased tidal variation of up to 0.8m. Parts of the area have recently been developed as water storage reservoirs and there are further plans to significantly alter the extent and format of the navigable waterways, the details of which are not yet known.

There are overnight mooring stages laid throughout the area (no facilities) and boats may also anchor in the wider channels for up to 3 days in one place. At the southern end of the Gat van de Hardenhoek, the Biesbosch Museum has temporary moorings for visitors.

A new recreation area, called Recreatiepark Aakvlaai, has been established in the southeast corner of the Biesbosch,

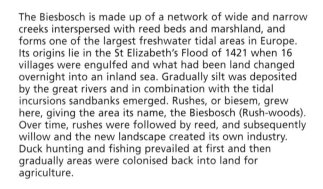

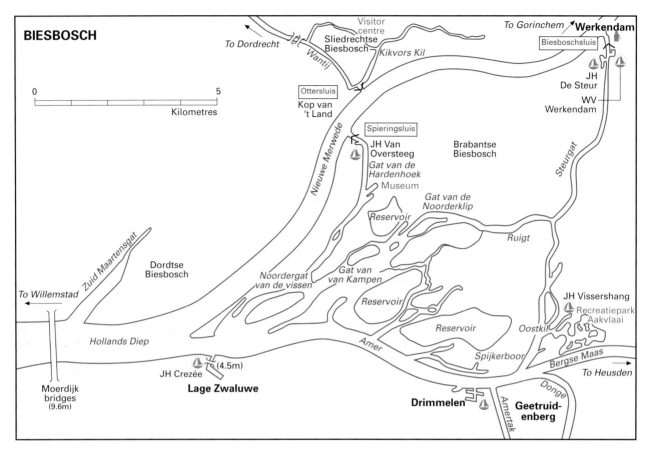

BIESBOSCH

accessible via the Spijkerboor and Oostkil channels. Here there are numerous moorings places, beach areas and wooded islands where boats may stay for up to three days. These are marked in detail on the Biesbosch Waterkaart. Two cautions for those swimming from boats: check the depth before diving in and beware of sharp shells on the bottom - swimming shoes are recommended.

Speed limit 9km/h in the principal channels, otherwise 6km/h
Depth In principal channels, minimum of 1.5m.
Locks Biesboschsluis and lifting bridge operates throughout the day (from 1000 on Sundays). Spieringsluis and lifting bridge operates throughout the day with a break for lunch (1300-1400)

WERKENDAM

Just south of the Biesboschsluis, WSV Werkendam is a large harbour on the east bank. Visitors should report on the hammerhead opposite the clubhouse and the harbourmaster will allocate you a berth. There is plenty of space in boxes for boats up to 5m beam, but telephone reservations are welcome. The small town has a good shopping street and two supermarkets but it is a good 20-minute walk away so hire one of the bikes from the harbour (only €1/day). Fuel is available from a bunker station just north of the lock.

In Werkendam (pronounced 'verek-endam') Hotel-restaurant Gasterij de Notaris at Hoogstraat 38 doubles up as the VVV information point, but their principal recommendation is to visit the Biesbosch. Next door to the harbour Restaurant De Waterman scores for convenience and has a sheltered terrace.

Also regarded as part of Werkendam is the Jachthaven-Café van Oversteg, just south of the Spieringsluis. The boxes and boat lift can accommodate boats up to 4m beam and draught is limited to 1.4m (a little more on the outer berths). There is normally more space at weekends when resident boats are out and the harbourmaster will come out in a dory as you arrive to allocate you a berth. This is a convenient stop inside the Biesbosch and specialises in hiring out rowing boats and canoes if you want to explore the remoter parts of this natural wilderness. Boats caught out by the shallow draught can have propeller shafts and rudders repaired here (☎ 0183 501633 and speak to André). There is no village or shops nearby but next door the Restaurant Brabantse Biesbosch is a very nice place to be stranded for the evening.

HANK/AARKVLAAI

In the Aarkvlaai area of the Biesbosch JH Vissershang, which predates the new development, has a large population of permanent berthholders in a wooded backwater off the Oostkil channel. Visitors stop on the hammerhead on Pontoon 2 and report to the harbour office at the east end. Water and electricity (14A) is unmetered and many of the residents are small day or weekend boats so it is very quiet in the evening. The surrounding Aarkvlaai area still has a rather artificial feel and you can walk or cycle around the area, but avert your gaze from the pylons and power station which are just across the river. Hank village is 2km away where you will find a baker and a chemist.

Biesbosch, Sliedrechtse

This section of the Biesbosch lies between the Beneden Merwede and the Nieuwe Merwede and is bordered to the west by the Dordrecht-Sliedrecht railway line. It forms the northern section of the Biesbosch National Park and is characteristic of the area's history. There is an open connection with the sea from here via the Oude Maas and the Nieuwe Waterweg, giving the area an unusual range of flora and fauna.

The main waterway through this area is the Wantij, which connects the Beneden Merwede at Dordrecht to the Nieuwe Merwede, via the Ottersluis at Kop van 't Land. There is a second route from the Ottersluis, northeast along the Kikvors Kil (depth 1.5m) to another locked access onto the Beneden Merwede at the Helsluis. A narrow channel, the Moldiep, runs north west off the Kikvors Kil to give access to the Biesbosch visitors' centre, where temporary and overnight moorings are available.

The waterways of the Biesbosch are popular with leisure boats, especially at weekends in good weather, and there can often be a long wait for the lock, with boats moving between the Sliedrechtse and the Brabantse Biesbosch.

There are several harbours available along the Wantij but it is nicer to make for the visitor centre or one of the mooring pontoons nearby.

Length (Wantij) 7km
Depth Minimum depth NAP+0.1m
Locks Ottersluis and lifting bridge operates throughout the day with a break for lunch (1300-1400). Sill depth of 1.8m at LW. Helsluis operates the same hours and has a sill depth of 2.35m at LW.
Bridges 4 opening The Wantij rail bridge and the nearby cycle bridge (4.4m when closed) are opened on request, and require three hours notice on ☎ 078 613 2421 or VHF 71 'Post Dordrecht'. Details for Prins Hendrik and Wantij road bridges are given in the Dordrecht section of the *Almanak*. The Prins Hendrik bridge (3.6m when closed) opens only for vessels with non-folding masts and operates throughout the day with breaks for lunch and dinner (1200-1230 and 1800-1830). The Wantij road bridge (5.5m when closed) operates throughout the day Mon-Sat and for a period in the morning and evening on Sundays and holidays.

Merwede (Boven & Beneden)

The Merwede connects the Waal at Gorinchem with the Oude Maas and the Noord at Dordrecht, and consists of the Boven (Upper) and Beneden (Lower) Merwede. Between Dordrecht and Sliedrecht the tide continues to affect the current, but above Sliedrecht the downstream current has a greater effect and is normally 3.5-5.5km/h (2-3 knots). The Kanaal van Steenenhoek is an alternative route for small vessels, but is restricted in headroom to 2.9m. It is possible to anchor in peace in the Avelingerdiep at km 958 with a depth of 2.5m.

A fuel berth and chandlers is at km 964 and leisure vessels can lie on the inside of the barge. Two more chandlers are Bouwmeester Watersport and Klop Watersport, both near the entrance to the Peulensluis at km 965.

Length 23km
Speed limit 20km/h
Bridges 3 opening on request only (12m when closed). Merwedebrug at Papendrecht (12.6m when closed) opens at set times on request with 3 hours notice on VHF 71 Post Dordrecht or ☎ 0800 023 6200. Baanhoek rail bridge (12.1m when closed) has the same arrangement and can be called on VHF 71 Post Dordrecht (or Post Werkendam for westbound vessels) or ☎ 078 613 2421. Gorinchem bridge (12.5m when closed) requires 24 hours notice and is also contactable on VHF 71 Post Dordrecht or ☎ 0800 023 6200

PAPENDRECHT

WV Papendrecht has the usual facilities in a yacht harbour at the head of the commercial harbour. A restored cell on Veerdam depicts its former use as the military police barracks with picture postcards of Old Papendrecht providing the historical perspective.

SLIEDRECHT

WV Sliedrecht is at the east end of the haven accessed via the entrance canal near km 970, and has the usual basic facilities. Sliedrecht is known as the home of the National Dredging Museum, which is the only one of its kind in the world. Models of historic and contemporary dredging vessels are supplemented by model ships, historical artefacts and some curious dredged-up objects. In a separate hut a collection of steam engines are demonstrated.

HARDINXVELD-GIESSENDAM

Vessels with less than 5m air draught can lock in at the Peulensluis and stay at WV De Snap. Cycle along the dyke road by the permit-only Giessen river for 10 minutes and you should come to the 'Copper Knob' museum - a substantial 17th-century farmhouse which is furnished in traditional period style. The former stables are home to topical exhibitions and the museum garden and tearoom complete the visit.

SLEEUWIJK

The secluded harbour of Sleeuwijk Yachting is popular with large motorboats and features diesel and a restaurant amongst its facilities. In quiet, leafy surroundings you can take one of the regular ferries to Gorinchem and Woudrichem.

GORINCHEM

Where to stop

The most central moorings are those in the Lingehaven which are accessed via the Lingesluis (length 30m, width 4.4m, depth 1.7m). This operates throughout the day with a break for lunch (1300–1400). Coin-operated electric (€1/2kWh) and water (€1/100 ltrs) are provided as are newly built facilities. The helpful harbourmaster operates the lock and has a good stock of information as well as free tokens for use of the pump-out. Next to the harbour, Bouwmeester Watersport is a small but well-stocked chandlers. A fixed bridge restricts passage through the harbour to 2.85m but for boats en route to or from the Linge there are further moorings under the same management just south of the Korenbrug (air draught 3.6m).

Alternatively, stop at WV De Merwede, in the Voorhaven. This is convenient for access to the Boven Merwede and next to the lock into the Merwedekanaal. Good facilities including wi-fi, and a small clubhouse which serves food Wednesday – Sunday in the season. North of the Grote Merwedesluis the small Gorcumse Roei- en zeilvereniging has a few places for visitors and is the closest harbour to the train station.

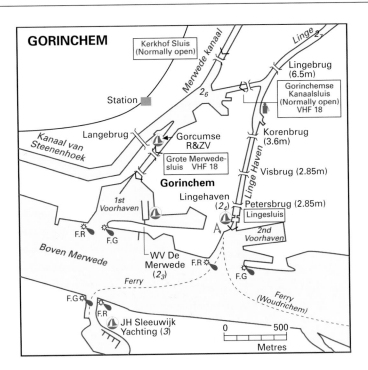

Gorinchem is a good base for excursions to nearby attractions

Lingehaven moorings are close to the town centre

Facilities ashore

Fuel (diesel only) Jachtwerf de Goesting, between Korenbrug & Lingebrug.
Chandlers Bouwmeester Watersport at the Lingehaven
Supermarket, Shops & ATMs Large selection near the Lingehaven and a small supermarket on Westwagenstraat
Cycle & 'Step' hire From Lingehaven
VVV office Stadhuis on Grote Markt

What to see

Gorinchem (pronounced 'khorekum') is an important waterway junction at the old confluence of the Waal and the Maas and the remains of its star-shaped ramparts are still intact. Transformed into an esplanade these offer a 7km walk around the town with good views of the 16th-century water gate and across the river to Loevestein castle. The local history museum is housed on the Grote Markt in the former Stadhuis and, as well as a fixed collection, has regularly changing exhibitions. The St Janstoren has leant to one side since its early 16th-century construction but is currently undergoing refurbishment so that may be about to change. Ferries from Buiten de Waterpoort leave regularly for the 'Fortified Triangle' which as well as Gorinchem consists of Woudrichem, Slot Loevestein and Fort Vuren.

A weekly market is held on Monday mornings.

Restaurant tip

De Hoofdwacht in the Grote Markt is popular for special occasions but there are a wide variety of other options in the same square.

Connections

Trains go every half-hour to Dordrecht and Geldermalsen from the station just west of the centre. The walk from WV De Merwede takes 25 minutes.

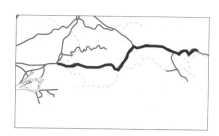

Waal

The Waal (pronounced 'vwarl') forms the continuation of the Boven Rijn and runs from the junction with the Pannerdenskanaal to Gorinchem where it joins the Boven Merwede, and forms part of the main commercial route across the country. Vessels should follow the usual requirements of having a reliable engine, maintaining a minimum of 6km/h, keeping to the starboard side of the waterway and, where necessary, crossing swiftly at right angles to the traffic.

Particular caution is advised around the river bends in the vicinity of the road and railway bridges at Nijmegen where very strong flows, even in the summer months, create hazards. All commercial traffic, whether laden or not, will display a blue board and stick close to the insides of the bends: the upstream traffic furthest inside for better progress, and the downstream traffic just outside it for better control. Leisure vessels are advised not to go close to the walls on the outside of these bends, particularly at times of high winds against the current, when there are always large waves from wash being reflected back to create troubled water. Apart from accessing the Passantenhaven at Nijmegen, these areas should be avoided.

Length 85km
Speed limit 20km/h where applicable.
Depth Average minimum of NAP+1.8m (Exact figures given daily on Radio 5 or by answerphone 026 362 9000)
Bridges 6 fixed (min 14m)

ZALTBOMMEL

Where to stop

The harbour at Zaltbommel lies just downstream of the road and rail bridges and the current flows strongly across the entrance. Once inside the harbour, the visitors' moorings are immediately in front of you and have good-sized pontoons, reflecting the variation in water level which is possible here. Although sheltered by the harbour moles there is still quite a strong wash at times from passing barges. A toilet and shower are provided in a small kiosk on the pontoon and there is unmetered electricity and coin-operated water available (€0.50/100ltrs). Turn to starboard and then follow the harbour to port and you will find the moorings of WV De Golfbreker where there is limited space for smaller boats. These are more sheltered and have the usual basic facilities.

Facilities ashore

Fuel Bunker boat on the main river just outside the harbour entrance
Supermarket Konmar right next to the west entrance to the harbour. Albert Heijn on Markt and good selection of shops around the town.
ATMs Several on Markt
Cycle hire At the train station

If flood water reaches the boy's hand it's time to call for the bill

What to see

Lying on the borders of Brabant, Holland and Gelderland, Zaltbommel was a regular battleground for rival lords, but its fortifications now serve mainly against flooding. On the quay, statues of two young boys indicate with their hands the level of the defences. The preserved walls are laid out as park and much of the town centre retains its original character with the shopping and leisure facilities concentrated into a few central streets. The local history museum is housed in an elaborately decorated castle-style house belonging to a Marten van Rossum, famous as a 15th-century plunderer in the service of the Duke of Gelre. St Maartenskerk is notable for its tall tower, completed in 1500, which was originally even higher until the steeple was twice destroyed by lightning. You can climb the tower on weekend afternoons or enjoy organ concerts on Saturdays at 1500 or 2000.

Restaurant tip

Near to the east entrance to the yacht harbour, the Waterpoort is the focal point for cafés and restaurants. Overlooking the Waal with a sunny terrace is the Grand Café Restaurant De Verdraagzeimheid, but inside the gate the Bistro De Waterpoort has a cosier atmosphere. IJssalon Fresco is also not to be missed with their 18 flavours of Italian ice cream.

Connections

A train station east of the town has direct services to Utrecht and 's Hertogenbosch

TIEL

Just west of the junction with the Amsterdam-Rijnkanaal lies the Tielse WV De Waal (depth 1.9m). The harbour is open to the river and the berths nearest the entrance do suffer from an amount of wash. Vessels are advised to give the upstream bank a wide berth on entering and beware of the projecting groynes on the south side of the river. There is a reporting pontoon between the two basins and a voluntary harbourmaster is on duty to allocate you a berth with larger boats normally going in the easternmost of the two basins. Coin-operated water (€0.50/500ltrs) and electricity (€0.50/2kWh) are available as are adequate basic facilities.

The centre of the town is a five-minute walk away and although it was a former Hanseatic town there is little of the former heritage visible today. At the centre of the fruit-growing region a procession, the Fruitcorso, celebrates the end of the fruit-picking season every second Saturday in September.

A tourist information point is available at the local history museum and annual events include a Jazz festival over the first weekend in July.

NIJMEGEN

Where to stop

A visitors' harbour is provided in the Lindenberghaven just downstream of the Waal road bridge where the entrance is marked by a flashing green light and is close to trip boat berths. The top of the breakwater which protects the berths from current and wash is marked by triangular markers, and it can be covered during winter flood conditions. Yachts are warned to beware of a strong current across the harbour entrance. The harbourmaster is

Scenes from Nijmegen's past depicted inside the Museum De Stratemakerstoren

contactable on VHF 12 but it is not necessary to call. Moorings are close to the city centre and have unmetered water and electricity, but a maximum stay of two days is specified. Payment is by parking meter which takes Chipknip or credit cards.

What to see

Nijmegen (pronounced 'nigh-may-kher') claims to be the oldest city in the Netherlands, and is also the only one to be built on a series of hills. It was an early Roman settlement and a castle was built by Emperor Charlemagne on a site overlooking the harbour. The Valkhof park stands here today and as well as seeing the remains of the Roman chapel, in 2006 a temporary replica of one of the towers had been erected which gave visitors a panoramic view of the town. The nearby Museum Het Valkhof houses one of the country's largest collections of Roman artefacts and artworks. At the foot of the hill on the quayside, the Museum De Stratemakerstoren has been established in the underground passageways of a 16th-century tower which was part of the city wall. Hidden from view until 1987 by factories and housing, the stone walls of the original fortification were found intact and have now been illustrated with scenes depicting the city's turbulent history. Next door on the quayside you can also visit a shrine

The visitors' moorings at Nijmegen are in the shadow of the infamous bridge

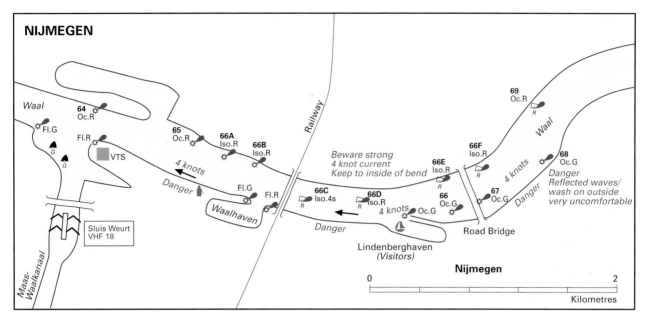

NIJMEGEN

to the Dutch people's favourite mode of transport: the National Fiets (Cycle) Museum, Velorama, has more than 250 examples of bikes through the years.

To many visitors Nijmegen will be known as part of the Battle of Arnhem and the visitors' moorings stand in the shadow of the infamous bridge. A monument to the liberation of the city stands in the Valkhof park and others around the town remember the fallen. A bus journey away is the National Bevrijdings (Liberation) Museum which devotes a major part of its exhibition to Operation Market Garden and is located at the site of one of the Airborne landings. Take Bus 5 from the Central Station.

As a major city Nijmegen has all the shopping amenities you would expect with a pedestrianised centre close by and a weekly market near St Stevens church on Monday mornings. The church and its tower are also open to visitors and there are guided walks of the city on Wednesday afternoons starting from the Valkhof museum. The Wandelvierdaagse, or Nijmegen Marches, are an international four-day walking event held in the third week of July which attracts up to 50,000 participants of 30 nationalities and more than a million spectators.

Restaurant tip

The Belvedere is sited in a former watch tower of the old curtain wall and the terrace offers a fine view over the Waal. There are also café/restaurants and bars overlooking the embankment as a popular venue for warm days and evenings.

Connections

A train station is to the west of the centre for services to 's Hertogenbosch, Arnhem and Roermond.

TOLKAMER

The last stopping point before the German border is at the large lakeside harbour of JH de Bijland. A fixed bridge over the entrance has an air draught of 9.5m above mean (summer) river level. Fuel is available from a bunker boat just to port beyond the bridge and the harbour, which lies ahead to starboard. All facilities are available including chandlers, servicing and a restaurant.

Maas-Waalkanaal

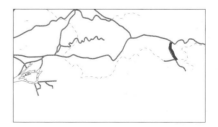

The Maas-Waalkanaal joins the Waal at Nijmegen to the Maas at Molenhoek, and runs just west of the city of Nijmegen. The lock at Heumen normally stands open and there are traffic lights controlling passage through the single channel. It is difficult to sail on the canal due to the high trees, the shallow banks and the heavy commercial traffic.

Length 13.4km
Speed limit 20km/h
Locks Sluis Weurt operates 24 hours Monday to Saturday and throughout the day on Sunday. Sluis Heumen stands open.
Bridges 6 fixed (min 8.5m)

Merwedekanaal bezuiden de Lek

The Merwedekanaal is dealt with in two parts; that part north of the Lek is covered in Chapter 8: Central Netherlands, whilst this section covers the part south of the Lek from Gorinchem to Vianen. It is an attractive tree-lined canal for much of its length with reed-fringed banks and isolated dwellings dotted here and there. Near the towns the occasional concrete factory blots the landscape but does not make it an unpleasant cruise.

The waterway leaves the Boven Merwede at Gorinchem's 1st Voorhaven at km 955.5 and passes through the Grote Merwedesluis where it joins the low air-draught Kanaal van Steenenhoek. A short section to starboard joins the waterway to the canalised Linge via the Gorinchemsekanaal lock which normally stands open. Leisure vessels with an air draught of less than 5m are recommended to take this alternative route via the canalised Linge and the normally open Arkel lock. This route continues as the 'Verbindingskanaal tussen Merwedekanaal en Linge' and rejoins the Merwedekanaal south of the Arkel rail bridge. (See Linge, below).

Vessels over 5m air draught can take the Merwedekanaal route through the Kerkhof sluis (also normally open) and on past a popular barge mooring area south of the A15 bridge. Bolgerijense bridge south of km 4, marked on the *ANWB Waterkaart K* (2005/06) as an opening bridge in reconstruction is now a fixed bridge with a headroom of 7.3m.

Length 24km
Speed limit 12km/h
Maximum permitted draught 2.8m
Locks Grote Merwedesluis (VHF 18) and Grote Sluis at Vianen (VHF 22) operate throughout the day (from 1000 on Sundays.)
Bridges
Merwedekanaal: 4 fixed (7.2m), 7 lifting. Concordia, Rijkstraatweg, Bazel, Meerkerk and Zwaanskuiken bridges operate throughout the day (from 1000 on Sundays), VHF 22. The opening rail bridge north of Arkel has a maximum air draught when open of 7.5m and opens throughout the day at H+12 and H+42.
Gekanalised Linge & Verbindingskanaal: 3 fixed (min. 6.4m), 2 opening. Gorinchemsekanaalsluis (4m when closed, 6.5m when open) operates throughout the day Monday-Saturday but is closed on Sundays, VHF 18. Schotdeurense bridge operates throughout the day (from 1000 on Sundays), VHF 22.

MEERKERK

A good stretch of unserviced moorings are available along the canal between the town and the Meekerksebrug. Those with better quay heading are at the western end near the island. A maximum stay of 3 days applies in July and August.

VIANEN

Just south of the Grote Sluis a closed off canal arm branches to the west and provides a large visitors' harbour, with unmetered water and electricity. Moorings are provided free by the town for a maximum stay of three days and there is detailed tourist information and a map of the town on the information board at the north end of the moorings (where the water berth and rubbish bins can also be found). Not surprisingly these places are popular with visiting motor boaters, but rafting seems to be accepted and there is a good amount of space. A few more spaces are available on the main canal, north of the Juliana bridge, which lies to the south of the Grote Sluis and not within it, as shown on the *ANWB Waterkaart K* (2005/06).

The historic town centre is a short walk away and the centre of activity is the Voorstraat, a wide street with a good selection of shopping opportunities. Towards the southern end you will find the Stedelijk Museum, which houses a fixed collection of glass, silver and ceramics from the 15th to the 20th century, as well as temporary exhibitions on particular themes. The museum is also a VVV agent and provides information about the surrounding area. The town revisits its historic past with a series of summer events, which include National Sleepbootdagen (Tug boat days), and an annual Horse Fair at which the medieval sport of Ringsteken (similar to jousting) is practised.

North of the Lekpoort a foot and cycle ferry crosses the Lek, and those wishing to venture further afield can make an interesting excursion to the old canal town of Vreeswijk. (See Section on the Lek for details.)

For a traditional Dutch restaurant, try De Graaf van Brederode at the north end of the Voorstraat, but to dine with the locals visit the China Wok on weekends or holidays and enjoy their good value walk-up buffet. Also nearby on Prinses Julianastraat you will find Pizzeria Moma Mia which offers a full selection of traditional Italian pizzas amongst their extensive menu.

Linge

The Linge (pronounced 'Linkher') is an attractive waterway especially in the Spring when the trees are full of blossom. However, navigation for most vessels is only possible as far as Geldermalsen and there are no connecting waterways so boats must return the same way. Although locked off from tidal waterways levels can vary as it is used as a flood relief channel for the Waal, and after periods of heavy rain the sluices at Tiel divert excess water this way. The trip from Gorinchem to Geldermalsen can be done in one day's cruise of about 5 hours, but a stop half way at Leerdam breaks the journey nicely. The area is mainly agricultural and many of the farms offer milk, cheese or ice cream, as well as fruit products for sale.

Entry to the waterway can be via Gorinchem or via the Merwedekanaal north of Arkel.

From Gorinchem, vessels use the Grote Merwedesluis (as above) and then take the connecting canal to starboard through the open Gorinchemsekanaal lock. A lifting bridge over this lock has an air draught of 4m when closed, and 6.5m when raised and can be requested on VHF 18. From here the canalised Linge continues north, with three fixed bridges (minimum 6.4m), to join the Linge east of Arkel. A second route through Gorinchem via the Linge Haven is restricted to 2.85m air draught.

From the north the fixed bridge over the connecting canal between the Merwedekanaal and the Linge has a minimum air draught of 5m. This bridge lies at the southern end of the flood lock (normally stands open) and passage through the lock and bridges is controlled by automatic traffic lights, where vessels may need to wait for opposing traffic. The Schotdeurensebrug is operated remotely from the Grote Merwedesluis in Gorinchem and can be requested on VHF 22.

Navigation beyond Geldermalsen is only advisable for vessels less than 8m in length, 3m wide and 0.8m draught. Fixed bridges at Buren have an air draught of 4m and there are no good mooring places, but it is possible for a few boats to moor on the starboard side before the first bridge.

Length 35km
Speed limit Below Asperen lock 9km/h; above Asperen 7.5km/h
Depth Canalised Linge, 2.1m; below Asperen 2.25m; above Asperen 1.8m.
Locks Asperen locks normally stand open. The west lock is for leisure traffic and is controlled by automatic traffic lights.
Bridges 9 fixed (minimum 4.94m)

ARKEL

Both sides of the Schutsluis there are moorings on the west bank which are permissible for overnight mooring after 1700. These are free, but have no facilities; those to the south of the bridge have better quay heading and are more private. One hundred metres east into the Linge lies the good sized harbour of WV De Gors. There is a reception pontoon outside the harbour office and clubhouse, where the water hose is also situated, and from here the harbourmaster will direct you to a berth. Visitors normally moor along the river frontage just east of the clubhouse and there is unmetered electricity available at all moorings. Good basic facilities including disposal for batteries, oil etc and information is provided on local boat engineers who can assist if necessary. The nearby modern village is within walking distance and has a handful of local shops and restaurants. This would make a very acceptable stop in a quiet location and, if you didn't want to cruise the Linge, you could make a cycle tour along all or part of it with the aid of the regularly spaced foot and cycle ferries that cross to the opposite bank.

A little further upstream, just next to the foot ferry to Spijk, there is a good, free but unserviced mooring for 4 boats next to a tiny café that serves tea in pots.

KEDICHEM

On the south bank, a large inlet at Vogelswerf is closed from January to July for tern breeding, but after 1 July is accessible for free 48-hour moorings. A very rural and peaceful spot, the garden café De Uitspanning is nearby and it is a short walk to the Lingebos, a woodland recreation park where you can swim, walk and visit the Pancake House. Moorings at the Hotel/Restaurant Cosmopolitie are no longer in use as the business is undergoing refurbishment into a residential home. Just upstream WV De Gantel is only for day boats and does not take visitors.

HEUKELEM

Here moorings are available at the JH De Wiel for boats up to 13.5m with good basic facilities including cycle hire. Adjacent on both banks are 48-hour moorings provided by the local river recreation authority who collect a small mooring fee. Those on the south (village) side are on floating pontoons but have no services, whilst on the northern bank the moorings are against slightly run down fixed stages on a flood meadow, but have electricity (6A €1.50/night), rubbish bins and toilets available. Overrun by Canada geese in Spring these are only suitable for summer river levels.

A foot and cycle ferry crosses the river at this point and in the village there is a baker, café and supermarket. The ferry operator has a range of information about local attractions which include a visit to Leerdam or the Herberg-Restaurant De Lingehoeve at Oosterwijk, where you can dine in an authentic country farmhouse. At weekends you can visit the local brewery (marked Fabriek on the *ANWB Waterkaart*) and sample their beers.

LEERDAM

Where to stop

Good moorings at WV De Oude Horn with all usual facilities including launderette and pump-out. A reporting pontoon is on the river frontage and visitors' moorings are along the quay to starboard. Free moorings are available for up to 3 hours during the day on the town quay, or overnight after 1700.

Facilities ashore

Supermarket & Shops Netto Rama on Markt, Albert Heijn on Hoogenhoek, or Edah on Westwal. Plenty of other good shops in the town.
ATMs Next to VVV office on Dr Reilinghplein
Cycle & Canoe hire From De Blauwe Hoed restaurant next to the bridge
VVV office In the library on Dr Reilinghplein

What to see

Leerdam is 'glass town' and visitors arrive by the coach load to do the sights. Next to the harbour, Glas Centrum holds demonstrations of glass-blowing throughout the day and you can ask for the handout and explanation in English. A glassware gift shop and café round off an informative visit. Just west of the centre lies Royal Leerdam Kristal where you can visit the Kristal Winkel or take a tour of the production facility (by arrangement only). Further along Lingedijk the National Glasmuseum displays their extensive collection in temporary exhibitions. In all there are 14 galleries many of which are concentrated on the Zuidwal near the harbour where you can admire or buy glassware made locally.

The town has a good selection of individual shops in the pedestrianised centre as well as three supermarkets within walking distance of the harbour. A weekly market is held every Thursday.

For a cycle excursion you can visit Schoonrewoerd where the NatuurCentrum Schaapskooi has displays and information about the surrounding area and the environment. Local fruit and fruit products are also on sale here. Nearby on Overheicop, the farmer's wife at Kaasboerderij (Cheese farm) Bikker has no English but a nice selection of farmer's cheeses and other home-made products in their farm shop. The cheese-making tour and the café are mainly opened for groups but might be in business on Saturdays and holidays.

Restaurant tip

You can walk across town to the Two Chez Royal but you won't improve on the popular terrace restaurant De Blauwe Hoed, next to the yacht harbour by the bridge.

Connections

Trains from the station just to the north of the town go to Dordrecht or Geldermalsen.

ASPEREN

A little upstream of Leerdam at Asperen there are 48-hour moorings provided by the river recreation authority for a small charge with toilets and rubbish bins available. Located on a well-kept riverside garden opposite a flood meadow these are very quiet and peaceful. The small old village has only a baker and a post office, but directions are given on the information board to a supermarket a 10-minute walk away. The Restaurant De Oude Asperen is your only dining option here.

Across the lock Fort Asperen is part of the preserved defences of the Nieuwe Hollandse Waterlinie. Ordered by King William I in 1815 this is an 85km long system of forts, sluices and dykes which can flood an area 5km wide with a shallow layer of water. This made it impassable to soldiers, wagons and horses but too shallow to navigate by boat and runs from Muiden to the Biesbosch, protecting the land to the west. Last time it was put on alert was in 1939 at the outbreak of the second world war but it has never been tested in battle. The fort is open to visitors and also houses contemporary art exhibitions.

RUMPT

De Twee Gazellen is a very nice restaurant and if you want to dine there you can use their bankside mooring. Three-course and surprise menus start at €32 and they have a terrace for open-air dining in fine weather. The very pretty, sleepy village also has a tea-garden.

GELDERMALSEN

The head of the navigation for vessels over 8m, there is a comfortable yacht harbour at WV Achter 't Veer. Space for boats up to 15m with all usual facilities including diesel. Further moorings are provided by the river recreation authority beyond the bridge, but these are next to a car park and not very appealing.

The large town is not of historical significance but there is a convenient supermarket right next to the harbour and a selection of shops and restaurants nearby. Trains from here run to Dordrecht, Utrecht and 's Hertogenbosch.

A visit to the Glas Centrum is a must in Leerdam

Lek

The Lek runs from the junction with the Rijn and the Amsterdam-Rijnkanaal at Wijk bij Duurstede to the junction with the Noord at Krimpen a/d Lek, where it becomes the Nieuwe Maas. A tidal river, it is wide and meandering, with very few bridges. Regular ferries provide the only crossing points and natural beaches have been encouraged in small bays which are much enjoyed by the local population, as are jet-skiing and water-skiing in the unrestricted areas. Where the shores are shallow the main channel is marked with red and green buoys, with red on the north bank and green on the south. Some of the inlets are used as temporary anchorages but skippers should be aware of the possibility of surges from passing barges.

Between the bridges at Vianen, junctions on the north bank connect the waterway with the Merwedekanaal benoorden de Lek (north of the Lek) and the Lekkanaal. Both of these join the Amsterdam-Rijnkanaal south of Utrecht, with the Lekkanaal providing the quicker, but busier route, and are described in Chapter 8: Central Netherlands.

East of Vianen, the Hagestein weir complex controls water flow in the downstream section and diverts water into the IJssel which in turn feeds the IJsselmeer. The weir gates are normally closed and the water flow used to generate electricity, but in times of above average river levels the weir is opened. The adjacent lock forms the main route when the weir is closed and traffic lights and buoyage indicate which passage to take. When the weir is open boats can pass underneath the semi-circular gates which have an average air draught over their span of 14.9m. Air draught at the lock is unrestricted and can be used by high-masted yachts.

Ferries cross the river at regular intervals with those at Culemborg and Beusichem being suspended on a cable. These are anchored in the middle of the river and marked by black and yellow buoys.

Length 61km
Speed limit 20km/h where applicable
Locks Sluis Hagestein VHF 18. Lock operates 24 hours except weekend nights.
Bridges 3 fixed (13m). Two road bridges at Vianen (minimum 13.3m clearance) and Culemborg rail bridge (13m).

KRIMPEN A/D LEK TO STREEFKERK

One of the two small harbours just east of the junction with the Noord might make a useful stop if you want to cross on the ferry and visit the Kinderdijk windmills which turn on Saturdays throughout the summer. WV De Lek is the larger of the two and has slightly more extensive facilities, but WV Smit has the attraction of being marginally nearer the town and ferry.

WV Lekkerkerk lies 2km east of the small town and has usual facilities but there is little to warrant a stop here. Spaces for boats up to 12m on pontoon moorings are protected from the main river by a wave break.

At Streefkerk, JH Liesveld is a well-equipped marina on the edge of the small town, with good service facilities and on-site restaurant. This could make a useful overnight stop if you are looking for a serviced environment.

SCHOONHOVEN

Where to stop

If you like to be in the town centre there are limited free moorings in the Voorhaven, outside the flood lock (which normally stands open). Those on the south side are managed by WV De Zilvervloot but visitors can stop for free on the north bank as a guest of the town. No facilities and beware of the tidal variation of just over 1m as well as strong surges when barges pass close by. Inside the flood lock there are only moorings for very small boats.

A more straightforward option is the yacht harbour and campsite of 't Wilgerak, which lies on the eastern boundary of the small town. Here there are good basic facilities including a nice playground for small children. Boats up to 14m can be accommodated and fuel is available.

Facilities ashore

Fuel At JH 't Wilgerak
Supermarket & Shops Albert Heijn on Van Goedhartweg. A fish van calls at the Waagplein on Friday evenings serving fresh and fried products.
ATMs Rabobank on Haven
Cycle hire Nearest is in the neighbouring village of Bergambacht
VVV office On Stadhuisstraat

What to see

Schoonhoven (pronounced 'scone-hoven') is known throughout the Netherlands as a centre for gold and silver craftsmen. The main street is lined with tempting jewellery boutiques and at the far end the Gold, Silver & Clock museum shows an exclusive collection, including many rare pieces made in the town. The former water tower, built in 1901, houses workshops and galleries for contemporary

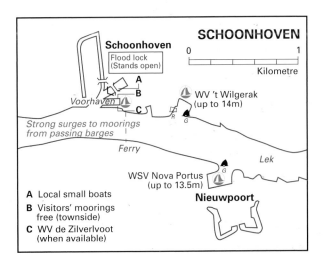

Visit the old water tower to see silversmiths at work and exhibitions of their art

NIEUWPOORT TO VIANEN

Just east of Schoonhoven, Nieuwpoort is one of the best preserved fortified towns in the Netherlands, with its centrepiece town hall straddling the haven canal. Little changed since the 17th century, this is a popular trip out for coffee or lunch at Eetcafe De Dam. WSV Nova Portus is a small harbour with space for boats up to 13.5m with coin-operated water and electricity and the usual basic facilities, but again beware of wash and suction from passing barges. The city walls, also largely intact, were built to defend against the French but serve to this day to protect the town from flooding. Cycle or walk southwest past the Gelkenes industrial estate to Ooievaarsdorp Het Liesvelt, where up to 10 pairs of nesting storks are comfortably housed on purpose-built platforms. The informative visitors centre tells all about the habits of these migratory birds which have been successfully reintroduced throughout this region.

Unserviced moorings are possible on the municipal quay at Ameide but can suffer heavily from wash. If you do find yourself stranded here, Restaurant 't Wapen van Ameide holds special events in a party tent on the quay and offers free wi-fi at their café-restaurant on Benedendamsestraat.

The tiny harbour next to the campsite at Lexmond has been allowed to silt up and, with only 0.8m draught at low water, can no longer accept visitors. West of Vianen, JH Keizerskroon is next door to an extensive camping site and the popular bar-restaurant Paviljoen Klein Scheveningen but their substantial pontoons are open to wash from the river.

VIANEN

The large harbour of WSV De Peiler is sheltered in a large gravel pit on the south bank of the river to the west of Vianen. There is plenty of space for visitors and the good facilities include launderette and cycle hire. Call VHF 31 for a berth. There are further unserviced moorings (maximum stay 48 hours) on the inside of the lock waiting pontoon to the north of the Grote Sluis on the Merwedekanaal, which are useful for an overnight stop and a visit to the town if you are intending to continue on the Lek. For those turning onto the Merwedekanaal there are comfortable berths with water and electricity at the visitors' harbour south of the lock. See Merwedekanaal section for details, and a description of the town.

VREESWIJK (NIEUWEGEIN)

JH ZV De Lek on the north bank is a small harbour on the edge of a built-up suburban area. Limited space for boats up to 10m with basic facilities and diesel. A ferry crosses from the entrance to the Vianen side.

The old canal town of Vreeswijk has been absorbed into the modern conurbation of Nieuwegein, but some of its old character still remains. Its position at the junction of the Lek and

craftsmen. National Silver Day is held annually at the beginning of June on Whit Monday (known in Dutch as 2e Pinksterdag) with a wide range of activities and exhibitions.

From the Voorhaven, turn left through the Veerpoort (Ferry gate) to reach the old town centre. This is the only remaining example of the town's five original gates, thanks to its status as part of the town's flood defences. The star-shaped form of the fortifications can still be seen in the Grote Gracht canal, which together with the neighbouring town park make a peaceful spot for a walk. A relaxing cycle ride east to Willige Langerak becomes quickly very rural, and beyond the deer farm and the fields of goats you will find a family-run nature museum and next door an extensive clog shop.

Restaurant tip

Eethuys De Waag has a commanding view along the Haven canal that runs down the middle of the main street. Near the carillon tower, the newly opened Eetcafe Bizar is a fashionable choice, but if you want to watch barges sail into the sunset then opt for Hotel/Restaurant Belvedere, on the Lek near the harbour entrance.

the Merwede made it an important stopping place for barges and it was also a harbour for the city of Utrecht. The Dorpsstraat is lined with small white lift bridges and the pretty houses and the old lock are nice to see.

CULEMBORG

Just north of the railway bridge and ferry the entrance to JH De Helling is on the south bank. There can be a strong current across the entrance when the upstream weirs are open and boats mooring near the entrance are advised to more with their bow facing the river. Further into the harbour, visitors normally moor on the quay along the west side, where there is electricity (€0.50/kWh) but not water. When places are available, boats can moor in a box where there is also water. The harbour gets very busy in summer and the harbourmaster advises booking ahead, but always finds places for everyone who arrives. The small chandlers next to the harbour has a limited range, and does not stock charts.

Culemborg is a picturesque combination of three walled fortress towns which have been situated on the banks of the Lek since the 13th century. A weekly market has been held on Tuesday morning since the 16th century and persists to this day, making good use of the wide pedestrianised square, where you can also see two 18th-century pumps. The town was spared serious damage in the second world war with most of the population evacuated in May 1940. Jewish residents, including businessmen and shopkeepers, did not fare so well, with most being sent to concentration camps, never to return.

The Museum Elisabeth-Weeshuis is housed in a former orphanage and some of the displays depict this original use. Other exhibitions display valuable collections of gold and silver church goods from the town's numerous faiths. The museum also acts as VVV information point but this extends only to a town walk and history of the town, both only in Dutch.

For special occasions the Restaurant Op De Haven is popular but if you want to venture a little further afield, Ander Maal on Havendijk is also recommended. The tired exterior hides a tastefully decorated conservatory overlooking a small canal. A nice place for lunch is the Willemien Eetwaar on the Markt, where you can also browse the delicatessen and buy culinary gifts.

BEUSICHEM

Here a small harbour is located next to a popular campsite and although mainly used by small boats there are a few spaces for boats up to 15m, immediately to starboard on entering. The usual basic facilities and petrol are available (not diesel). The centre of the small town is 2km away, but next to the harbour and by the ferry is the pancake restaurant Het Veerhuys. If you cycle towards Culemborg you can buy strawberries and eggs from a road-side farm or on a fine day follow signs to De Meent, a swimming lake and landscaped recreation park.

Cruising the Great Rivers

With many of the waterways busy with commercial barges and others under the strong influence of tidal differences and flows, or by shallow water such as in the Biesbosch, there is always the need for care and respect by helmsmen. Apart from the special conditions described under the Waal section at Nijmegen, we would also add a general caution concerning the numerous projecting groynes (or kribben in Dutch) with navigation marks atop, which should be given a wide berth on account of the hazards beneath and the strong turbulence created around them. Having said that, provided the correct charts, aids and practice are employed it would be a great shame to avoid this area and miss the Brabantse Biesbosch, or the Linge, where special excursions to both can be planned and enjoyed.

Arriving from the North Sea and locking into the Haringvliet at Stellendam, avoiding low water, the positive flow can be ridden up the Spui and on to Rotterdam so that the voyage from England could be completed in 2-3 days. Alternatively, a voyage from South Holland via the Hollandse IJssel or via the Vecht or Amsterdam-Rijnkanaal to arrive at Vreeswijk on the Lek, would suit those landing via IJmuiden or coming south from the IJsselmeer.

The cruise upstream on the Lek in the summer months is a pleasant and not too onerous an experience (with minor adverse flows) before turning south on the Merwedekanaal to Gorinchem, another favourite place, from which an excursion up the Linge would be enjoyable.

Venues at Werkendam, Spieringsluis, the Amer banks at Lage Zwaluwe and Drimmelen provide well-serviced hopping-off points for lazy days in the Biesbosch, a treat in fine and sunny weather. Willemstad is on the through route for any path through the southern Netherlands and Brielle is well worth a detour when passing through the Spui, either on the way to or back from Rotterdam.

Sometimes challenging, often charming, there is much to experience and learn on the Great Rivers and the region will never be boring.

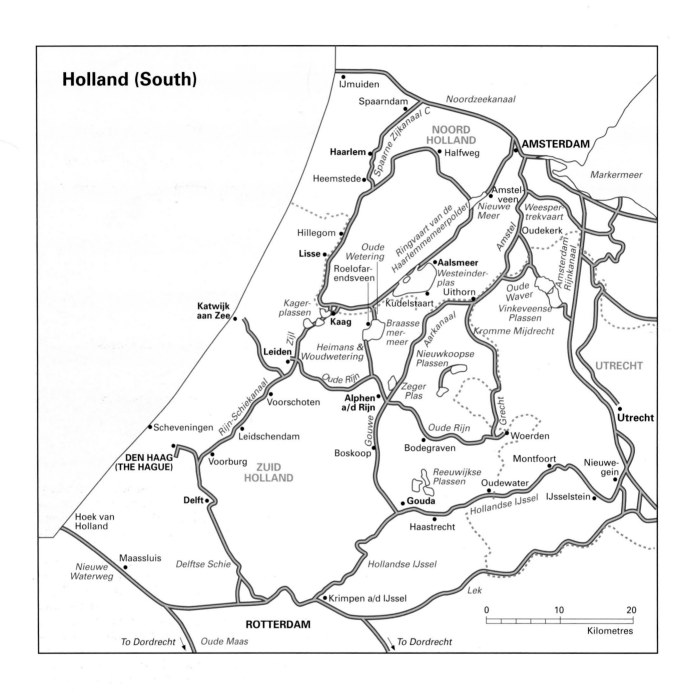

Holland (South)

IJmuiden
Spaarndam
Noordzeekanaal
Spaarne Zijkanaal C
NOORD HOLLAND
Haarlem
Halfweg
AMSTERDAM
Heemstede
Markermeer
Amstelveen
Nieuwe Meer
Weespertrekvaart
Hillegom
Ringvaart van de Haarlemmemeerpolder
Oudekerk
Lisse
Oude Wetering
Amsterdam Rijnkanaal
Roelofarendsveen
Aalsmeer
Westeinderplas
Oude Waver
Katwijk aan Zee
Kagerplassen
Uithorn
Vinkeveense Plassen
Kudelstaart
Braasse mermeer
Kaag
Kromme Mijdrecht
Zijl
Heimans & Woudwetering
Aarkanaal
UTRECHT
Leiden
Nieuwkoopse Plassen
Oude Rijn
Grecht
Voorschoten
Zeger Plas
Alphen a/d Rijn
Rijn-Schiekanaal
Utrecht
Scheveningen
Gouwe
Oude Rijn
Woerden
Leidschendam
Bodegraven
Montfoort
Nieuwegein
DEN HAAG (THE HAGUE)
Voorburg
Boskoop
ZUID HOLLAND
Reeuwijkse Plassen
Oudewater
IJsselstein
Delft
Gouda
Hollandse IJssel
Hoek van Holland
Haastrecht
Maassluis
Nieuwe Waterweg
Delftse Schie
Hollandse IJssel
Lek
Krimpen a/d IJssel

0   10   20
Kilometres

ROTTERDAM
To Dordrecht
Oude Maas
To Dordrecht

3 Holland (South)

Waterways (south to north)	Principal venues	Other stopping places
Delftse Schie	Delft	
Rijn-Schiekanaal	Den Haag (& Scheveningen)	Voorschoten, Leidschendam, Voorburg
Leiden canals	Leiden, Katwijk aan Zee	
Hollandse IJssel		Krimpen a/d IJssel, Haastrecht, Oudewater, Montfoort, IJsselstein
Gouwe		Boskoop
Gouda canals	Gouda	
Oude Rijn	Alphen a/d Rijn	Bodegraven, Woerden
Grecht		
Kromme Mijdrecht		
Aarkanaal		
Amstel		Uithoorn, Oudekerk
Vinkeveense Plassen		
Weespertrekvaart		
Heimans & Woudwetering		
Braassemermeer		Oude Wetering/Roelofarendsveen
Oude Wetering		
Zijl		
Kagerplassen	Kaag	
Ringvaart van de Haarlemmermeerpolder	Lisse, Aalsmeer	Hillegom, Heemstede, Halfweg
Nieuwe Meer		Amstelveen
Westeinderplas		Kudelstaart
Haarlem canals (Spaarne)	Haarlem	
Spaarndam canals		Spaarndam

This chapter covers all the freely navigable waterways between the Nieuwe Maas and the Noordzeekanaal, from the west coast of Holland to the Amsterdam-Rijnkanaal. Although this does not exactly coincide with the province of South Holland, these waterways form conceptual boundaries for the cruising yachtsman. This means that Haarlem and the Ringvaart van de Haarlemmermeer polder fall into this chapter, although they are strictly speaking part of the Noord Holland province, as do places such as the Vinkeveense Plassen, Woerden and Oudewater, which are in Utrecht province. Also, some waterways and towns to the south of the province, notably Rotterdam and Dordrecht, fall into the separate chapter which covers the Great Rivers. Having discussed these simplifications with Dutch friends and colleagues and assured them this does not represent a local government reorganisation, they concur that it makes more sense presented this way to waterborne visitors.

The area then covered by this chapter is distinguished by the large number of lakes, arising out of early peat extraction, and the areas of reclaimed land, much of which is given over to farmland and pasture. To the north are the major bulb-growing areas of the country and a cruise through this area in the spring time is a visual treat. Many of the smaller lakes and waterways are only navigable by those in possession of a special Rijnland permit, and in some cases these are only available to local residents or those who keep a boat in the area. These waterways have not been included in this guide, on the basis that there is already plenty of scope for visiting boaters within the publicly accessible navigations.

Although the area is densely populated, most people are concentrated in a few large conurbations with a large number of small towns and villages retaining distinct geographical boundaries and individual characters. For the visiting boater this means that many waterside stopping places are not well-known venues, but they have their own story and charm, making them well worth a stop. South Holland is therefore a region of contrasts, with the modern industrialised southwest influenced by the neighbouring port of Rotterdam with its oil and chemical plants (see Chapter 2: Great Rivers) and Den Haag (the administrative and government centre), against the traditional industries of the pottery town of Delft and the cheese centre of Gouda. It has the old towns and navigations such as those on the Oude Rijn, Grecht, Kromme Mijdrecht and Hollandse IJssel and then the polders in the central part of the region with their open landscapes and large lakes or plassen. With the museums and attractions of the large cities, the coastal port and beach resorts of Scheveningen and Katwijk aan Zee and then the old houses and buildings of such places as Oudewater and Oudekerk, there is something for everyone.

Delftse Schie

The Delftse Schie runs from Rotterdam roughly north to Delft becoming the Rijn-Schiekanaal on the southern side of the town. The transit through Rotterdam to reach the waterway is via the Delftshavense Schie which has unrestricted air draught and is described in Chapter 2: Great Rivers under Rotterdam canals. An alternative route along the Schiedamse Schie from Schiedam has a maximum air draught of 3.6m and is described in Chapter 2: Great Rivers under Schiedam canals.

Motor driven vessels are not permitted in the canals through the centre of Delft but the route to the east via the Rijn-Schiekanaal continues north. To the west of Delft, the area of small waterways is known as Westland, and a special permit is required to navigate here.

Length 9km
Speed limit 12km/h
Maximum permitted draught 2.5m
Bridges 4 lifting. Doenkade bridge (6.8m when closed) north of Overschie is operated remotely from the Hogebrug in Overschie and opens only on request throughout the day Monday to Saturday and evenings (1900-2100) on Sundays and holidays, on ☎ 010 415 3247 or VHF 22. Kandelaars cycle bridge at Zweth (4.15m when closed) and Kruithuis bridge (5.4m when closed) are operated remotely from Abtswoudsebrug in Delft on VHF 18 but only on Mondays, Saturdays, Sundays and holidays

DELFT

Where to stop

Visitors' moorings are provided in the Zuid Kolk, in the turning area north of the Abtswoudsebrug. Coin-operated electric and water are available and the harbourmaster may visit to collect the mooring fee. This quay is also sometimes used by passenger boats and you are only allowed to stay for a maximum of 24 hours, but it is close to the town centre and the only option for a stop in this historic city.

Facilities Ashore

Fuel Diesel and gas on west bank of canal north of Abtswoudse bridge
Supermarket & Shops Plenty of choice in the town centre
ATMs In town
Cycle hire NS Rijwielshop on Van Leeuwenhoeksingel
VVV office On Hippolytusbeurt

What to see

Delft (pronounced 'Deleft') found prosperity in the 13th and 14th centuries based on the cloth trade and brewing industry, but acquired an international reputation for making ceramics in the 17th century. Several shops around the market square sell the traditional Delft blue, some with on-site workshops where you can see craftsmen at work. For a more extensive visit take a trip to Koninklijke Porceleyne Fles (Royal Delft) on Rotterdamseweg, which claims

Obligatory shopping for Delft blue in the market square

to be the last remaining authentic delftware factory from the 17th century and has guided tours, a museum, painting demonstrations and factory shop.

Tours by horse-drawn tram or trip boat are a relaxing way to see the canal-lined town, which has pavement and floating cafés around every corner. The tower of the Nieuwe Kerk, dating from 1381, offers a panorama as far as Rotterdam and Den Haag. The Leger Museum, near the moorings, retraces the evolution of the Dutch army through the ages and hosts topical exhibitions as well as its permanent collection. The first King of the Netherlands, William of Orange was assassinated here in 1584 and is buried in the Nieuwe Kerk, near to a statue of his dog who died a few days later.

Restaurant tip

Delft has many restaurants to suit all tastes and budgets and a guidebook is available from the VVV with their recommended selection arranged by type of cooking.

Connections

The train station is near to the Zuid Kolk moorings and has direct services to Den Haag and Rotterdam.

Rijn-Schiekanaal

The Rijn-Schiekanaal, known alternatively as the Delftse Vliet, forms the continuation of the Delftse Schie and continues from the turning basin on the south side of Delft, around the town and then eventually northeast to Leiden. This is a busy route for leisure vessels and delays should be expected during summer weekends, with most boats heading north on Fridays and Saturdays and returning south on Sundays. There is a fuel berth on the east bank just north of the Leidschendam lock.

Length 25km
Speed limit 12km/h
Maximum permitted draught 2.5m
Lock Leidschendam and two lifting bridges operate throughout the day with breaks for the morning and evening rush hour (0730-0845 and 1630-1800) but only from 1000 on Sunday. VHF 18.
Bridges 4 fixed (min 5.6m), 14 lifting (maximum air draught when open, 5.1m – see below).
In Delft: 6 lifting, operated throughout the day, but only from 1000 on Sunday, except Reineveld bridge which is closed all day (4m air draught when closed). VHF 18.
In Rijswijk: 1 lifting – Hoornbrug opens throughout the day Mon–Fri with breaks for the morning and evening rush hour (0730–0845 and 1630–1745), all day Saturday but is closed Sunday. VHF 18.
In Voorburg: 4 lifting – Nieuwe Tol, Oude Tol, Kerk and Wijker bridges are operated throughout the day, but only from 1000 on Sunday. At certain times (0600–0900, 1700–2200 and on Sundays) a convoy system is operated.
In Leidschendam: 1 lifting – the rail bridge has a clearance under the fixed span of 4.9m, and only 5.1m when open. It opens Mon–Sat only on request with 24 hours notice ☎ 070 385 9881.
In Voorschoten: 2 lifting – Overhaal and Vlietland bridges are operated remotely from the Hooghkamer bridge on the Korte Vlietkanaal throughout the day, but only from 1000 on Sunday. VHF 22.

DEN HAAG

Where to stop

Turn to port at the Trekvliet, just south of the Nieuwe Tolbrug, where the Geestbrug opens on request on VHF 18. A small yacht club in the Binckhorsthaven, WV De Vlietstreek, offers adequate places for visitors during the summer with usual basic facilities. Many of the members take their boats elsewhere for summer berths so the clubhouse bar is unfortunately closed. The harbour is staffed evenings only so if you arrive in the day then follow the instructions on the board near the entrance and look out for the duty harbourmaster between 1830–1930. He will provide a key to the security gate and a map of the area, which you are expected to return prior to leaving.

Continuing on the Trekvliet under the opening bridge brings you to the municipal moorings of Den Haag, but these are unserviced and unsecured and not to be recommended on account of their popularity with the local tramp boat community.

Facilities Ashore

Fuel On the east bank north of the Leidschendam lock
Supermarket, Shops, ATMs Nearest are at Voorburg
Cycle hire On Keizerstraat or at the Hollands Spoor train station
VVV office Koningen Julianaplein

What to see

Home to the Dutch parliament, Den Haag (pronounced 'den harkh'), or 's Gravenhage as it is officially called, is also known as home to the International Court of Justice and the official residence of Queen Beatrix. The Binnenhof visitors' centre offers extensive tours to acquaint visitors with the official buildings. The Mauritshuis museum houses the royal painting collection, one of the finest in the world, which is displayed in the form of temporary exhibitions around a particular theme. Signature works by Rembrandt and Vermeer are amongst the large collection.

Of more general interest in Den Haag is the Madurodam, a miniature town built in 1952, which forms a microcosm of the Netherlands, complete with bulb fields and windmills. Completely renovated in the 1990s, modern additions have kept the display up to date and it is open late and illuminated on summer evenings.

The elegant seaside resort of Scheveningen is part of the Den Haag administrative district and the coastal marina offers all facilities for visiting yachtsmen. With no access to the inland waterways

In Scheveningen, stroll along the boulevard from the Kurhaus to the yacht harbour

it is not covered in this guide, but a visit from Den Haag is very easy by bus or bike and the highly developed beach pavilions are a must on a fine evening. A walk along the promenade from the Kurhaus casino to the yacht harbour can finish at one of the two well-stocked chandlers. The view of the beach from the top of a mythical dune is recreated at the Panorama Mesdag, complete with real sand. The 360° painting was completed in 1879 by locally based artist Hendrik Mesdag.

The North Sea Jazz Festival is a major event held every year in July.

Restaurant tip

Just south of the Nieuwe Tolbrug on the east bank of the Rijn-Schiekanaal, the very popular 'Chinese Muur' serves an extensive buffet of Chinese and Indonesian inspired specialities for a fixed price. Alternatively head to the old centre of Voorburg, near the junction of the railway and the canal, for a selection of restaurants and bars in a network of narrow lanes.

Connections

Railway station at Voorburg provides a service into Den Haag central in just a few minutes. Bus terminal also situated here.

VOORBURG

Unserviced canalside moorings are available just north of the Nieuwe Tolbrug in a quiet park area which are possible for an overnight stop; and a limited number north of Kerk bridge, intended for short stays for shopping only. The moorings at the Nieuwe Tolbrug are convenient for a visit to the Chinese Muur restaurant, as well as the Drievliet theme park, which lies right next door.

LEIDSCHENDAM

The municipal harbour, 100m south of the lock on the west bank, is suitable for boats up to 11m but has no facilities, such as electricity or water. The bridge is opened by the harbourmaster in the lock office. There are free moorings suitable for larger boats along the quay on the east bank south of the lock. These are close to the village centre with a good selection of local shops and a bakery and snack café on the quay are convenient for quick stops.

VOORSCHOTEN

Just south of the Vlietland bridge is the entrance to JH De Vlietopper on the east bank, which is a very friendly and pleasant yacht club of 340 boats with unmetered water and coin-operated electric (€0.50/2kWh). It is situated within a beautiful nature park which offers lots of interesting walks and cycle rides. The onsite clubhouse has all new facilities, together with canteen above serving meals and drinks. Chemical toilet disposal facilities available and pump-out at adjacent boatbuilder, Ad. Spek, which also has a small chandlers and mechanic. Stop at the reporting pontoon on the left as you enter the basin and report to the duty member in the harbour office. There are no shops nearby so get your provisions beforehand. It is a 4km cycle through the Vlietland park to the De Knip restaurant, just west of the Overhaal bridge, which has a wonderful reputation and a shady terrace. A little further west, Duivenvoorde castle is based on a 13th-century moated tower and was owned by the same family until 1960. There are guided tours of the magnificent rooms furnished in 17th-century style and an extensive collection of family heirlooms.

The large JH Vlietopper lies in an attractive recreation park and has a popular terrace bar

Leiden canals

Voorschoten to the Kagerplassen

The Nieuwe Vaart forms the continuation of the Rijn-Schiekanaal and runs to the east of Leiden to the junction with the Zijl and the Oude Rijn. This route continues north as the Zijl as far as the Kagerplassen.

Bridges 6 opening. Lamme bridge, the rail bridge, and the Kanaal cycle bridge just north of it are operated remotely from the Wilhelminabrug. Spanjaards and Zijl bridges are operated remotely from De Waard island. All operate throughout the day (from 1000 on Sundays), with a rush hour closing on weekdays for the road bridges (0700–0900 and 1600–1800). This applies to leisure vessels only and passage may still be possible with commercial vessels. VHF 22.

Oude Rijn to Leiden centre

From the junction of the Oude Rijn and the Rijn-Schiekanaal, east of Leiden, the old course of the Rijn runs through the centre of the city. It is navigable as far as the municipal visitors' harbour beyond which low bridges restrict headroom to less than 1.5m. The central canals form a network which is accessible by dinghy or low day boat and this is a popular recreation for locals.

Bridges 2 opening. Sumatra and Schrivers bridges operate throughout the day (from 1000 on Sundays) with short rush-hour stoppages, VHF 22.

LEIDEN

Where to stop

The best place to stay for a visit to Leiden is the town centre visitors' moorings at the end of the navigable section of the Oude Rijn. The moorings are well-equipped and the key to a palatial shower block can be obtained from the harbourmaster at the Schrijvers bridge, as can electricity and water tokens.

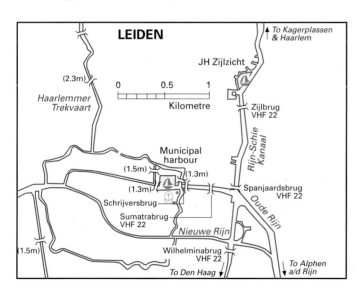

Floating cafes and small boats are common on Leiden's attractive city canals

Facilities Ashore

Supermarket & Shops Albert Heijn on Hooigracht
ATMs Plenty in the centre
Cycle hire De Rijwielshop at the train station
VVV office Stationsweg

What to see

The junction of the Nieuwe and the Oude Rijn forms the focal point of Leiden (pronounced 'Li-den') and the central canals are lined with bars and teeming with small boats; a tour by dinghy under the low bridges is a good way to see the town whilst saving your legs, but take a map as it is easy to get lost. Ashore, the Burcht formed the town's fortress but as it was rarely called into active service the circular wall and battlements are still largely intact; the short watch walk provides a wide-ranging aerial perspective. Being a university town, Leiden has been home to some eminent citizens and the museums based in the city reflect this heritage including state Ethnography and Antiquities museums, as well as the country's foremost Natural History museum. As well as their permanent displays, each hold well-presented temporary exhibitions on topical subjects.

Restaurant tip

De Poort van Leyden is well regarded and near the harbour, whilst Zout en Peper on Nieuwe Rijn is nearer the centre and offers a fixed-price mix-and-match menu.

Rijn-Schiekanaal to Katwijk aan Zee

To the south of Leiden the Korte Vlietkanaal leaves the Rijn-Schiekanaal and runs northwest to Katwijk aan Zee, partly as the Rijn, and then changing its name to the Additioneelkanaal and the Uitwateringskanaal en route. All bridges on this route are opening but several require notice in advance. Journey from the Rijn-Schiekanaal takes about an hour.

Maximum permitted draught 2.5m
Bridges 10 opening. (Maximum 4.5m air draught avoiding notice-only bridges.)

On the Korte Vlietkanaal: Hooghkamer, Hofland and Waddinger bridges operate throughout the day Monday–Friday, and Saturday mornings only (0900–1400). No service Sundays and holidays. VHF 22.

On the Oude Rijn: rail bridge (5.6m when closed) opens only on request with two hours notice to the Waddinger bridge ☎ 071 576 3652 or to the rail company in Den Haag ☎ 070 385 9881, and then only Monday–Friday 0559–0604 and 2101–2104. Stevens and Haagse Schouw bridges are operated remotely from the Schrijvers bridge in the centre of Leiden and operate throughout the day the same hours as for the Korte Vlietkanaal bridges. VHF 22. The A44 road bridge (5.4m when closed) opens only on request with 24 hours notice on ☎ 071 576 0167, and then only Monday–Friday and Saturday morning outside rush hour periods. Torenvliet bridge (5.6m when closed) also opens only on request with 24 hours notice on ☎ 071 576 3652 or VHF 22.

On the Additioneelkanaal: Sandtlaan bridge operates throughout the day Monday–Friday and Saturday mornings only (0900–1200). No service Sundays and holidays. No VHF. ☎ 071 406 2265. (See Katwijk aan de Rijn in the *ANWB Wateralmanak 2*.)

On the Uitwateringskannal: Roover (4.9m when closed) and Kon. Juliana (4.5m when closed) bridges are opened only for fixed mast yachts and must be requested before 1600 the previous day (workdays only) on ☎ 071 406 2266. (See Katwijk aan Zee in the *ANWB Wateralmanak 2*.)

KATWIJK AAN ZEE

Where to stop

The very large municipal marina is close to the sea at the mouth of the Oude Rijn which is now closed off by a flood control barrier, rebuilt after the 1953 floods. The harbour boasts excellent facilities only recently installed and receives around 13,000 visiting boats a year. Report by the pontoon in front of the harbour office to be allocated a place in a vacant box or alongside the quiet moorings on the opposite bank. The latter are without any electricity and water, but are a shorter walk to the beach, with Snackbar De Driehoek providing refreshments en route. It is a 20-minute walk to the centre of town, but you can hire bikes from the harbour office. Above the office is a comfortable terrace café and across the road a handy fish shop, and a larger one just round the corner. The large Rabobank office building next to the harbour has an ATM near the front entrance.

Climb the old lighthouse at the south end of Katwijk's boulevard

Facilities Ashore
Supermarket & Shops Dirk van de Broek on Prins Hendrikkade and many more in town centre
ATMs Rabobank opposite moorings
Cycle hire From the harbour office
VVV office On Voorstraat

What to see

The large seaside town has a local history museum depicting memories of the coastal town with reconstructions of a ships bridge and 19th-century shop interiors. Climb the old lighthouse at the far end of the boulevard during summer months for a good view of the town and the coast. A major tourist market is held on six Tuesdays from the end of June, and the town's own Bloemencorso flower parade is held in late August, when the festivities include a Herring and Shanty festival in the evening. Nearby Noordwijk is the start point of the Noordwijk-Haarlem 'Bloemencorso', a major flower parade held on the last Saturday in April. Noordwijk is also home to the European Space Agency's only visitor centre, Space Expo, which gives an insight into the progress of European space travel.

Restaurant tip

For a good value meal with a view of the sea try the monthly menu at the Hotel Savoy's Panoramic Restaurant where the river meets the sea.

Connections

The nearest train station is in Leiden.

Hollandse IJssel

The Hollandse IJssel is made up of two very different sections: from Krimpen aan den IJssel to Gouda it is a fairly wide, tidal river, occasionally with attractive banks, but mainly bordered by high dykes, whilst from Gouda to Nieuwegein it is a tideless canalised waterway, but one that retains a pleasant rural character. The southern section joins the Nieuwe Maas near its junction with the Noord and forms part of the mast-up route between Amsterdam and the south. The Waaiersluis east of Gouda forms the boundary between the two sections and south of here the waterway is numbered with kilometre posts increasing towards the sea.

Krimpen aan den IJssel to Gouda

At km 18 the Algerasluis storm surge barrier protects the upper reaches but is normally kept in the raised position when not needed. A fixed bridge (minimum 7.5m) crosses the waterway next to the flood barrier, and a lock and lifting bridge provide access for fixed-mast yachts or when the barrier is in use (including during test closures, normally 1st Thursday of the month). There are tide gauges for the fixed bridge on the starboard sides up and downstream. There is always sufficient depth in the channel (3.6m) but some areas near the banks can be shallow at low water. The current can run at up to 3km/h near IJsselmonde; less near Gouda. Mooring is not permitted in the tideway outside of designated mooring spots. There is a yacht harbour at Cappelle aan den IJssel, but it is mainly a home berth for local yachts and the nearby town is a modern residential suburb of Rotterdam. South of Gouda the Gouwe kanal joins the waterway – turning north here gives access to the Nieuwe Gouwe and the town of Gouda.

Length 21km
Maximum permitted draught 3.1m
Speed limit 20km/h where applicable
Locks Algerasluis and bridge (fixed span 7.5m at HW). Lock and lifting bridge opens Monday–Saturday at H+20 (0900–1600) and throughout the day on Sundays (1000–1800). VHF 22.

Gouda to Nieuwegein

East of Gouda the Hollandse IJssel is a narrow and winding waterway which makes a popular cross-country route for motor boaters from South Holland towards the east of the country. Although there are few yacht harbours, there are canalside municipal moorings in many of the small villages en route and these make very pleasant stopovers. West of Utrecht the waterway joins the Merwedekanaal and here you must pass through rather more industrial surroundings in order to continue your passage. The moorings at the Doorslaghefbrug were no longer in use in 2006 being part of a redevelopment area. North of the Doorslagsluis the waterway joins the Merwedekanaal and boats have a choice of continuing northeast towards Utrecht or turning southeast towards Vreeswijk and the Lek. For details of the Merwedekanaal waterway turn to Chapter 8: Central Netherlands.

Length 32km
Maximum permitted draught 1.75m
Speed limit In built up areas, 4.5km/h; otherwise, 9km/h.
Locks Waaiersluis at Gouda operates throughout the day with a break for lunch (1230–1330). Doorslagsluis at Nieuwegein normally stands open.

Bridges 10 fixed (minimum air draught 4.4m), 11 opening as follows:
In Gouda: Haastrechtse bridge (VHF 20) operates throughout the day except for rush hour periods on weekdays (0730–0845 and 1630–1800); Sundays only have a break for lunch (1230–1330 or 1300–1400).
In Haastrecht: Goverwelle bridge (VHF 20) operates throughout the day; Sundays only have a break for lunch (1230–1330 or 1300–1400). Ophaal bridge closes for lunch every day (1230–1330).
In Hekendorp: Wilhelmina van Pruisen cycle and footbridge stands open throughout the day except when closed on request by pedestrians or cyclists.
In Oudewater, Montfoort and IJsselstein: Hoenkoop (VHF 22), Cosijn, Draai, Oranje and Ophaal bridges operate throughout the day with a break for lunch (1230–1330).
In Nieuwegein: Gein and Doorslag bridges are lifting bridges with a maximum air draught of 4.9m when open. Both operate throughout the day; Saturdays and Sundays only have a break for lunch (1230–1330).
Bridge tolls payable in Oudewater.

HAASTRECHT

At Haastrecht (pronounced 'Hars-trekt') there are good free canalside moorings for a maximum stay of 3 days both sides of the bridge, which are equipped with a coin-operated water hose and rubbish bins. There are further moorings by the former draining pump station the Hooge Boezem just to the east, although these are not suitable for overnight stops.

Free moorings by the bridge in Haastrecht have a coin-operated water hose and rubbish bins provided

The village is well-equipped with a small supermarket and a range of local shops in the main square as well as a selection of bars and restaurants, including the well-regarded De IJsselborgh on Veerstraat, next to the bridge. On the main road to the south of the town the 19th-century town mayor's residence, Bisdom van Vliet, has been opened as a museum. All the original fittings and decorations are intact, just as they were when the mayor's wife left the house to the town on her death in 1923. The adjacent coach house houses a display on local trades and is also used for temporary art exhibitions. Opposite the house, the gardens lead into a large woodland park which makes a nice spot for a walk, or to the east of the village you can make your way to the stork-breeding station and maybe catch a glimpse of them on their protected nesting poles. The Hooge Boezem visitor centre, in conjunction with the VVV office opposite, gives an insight into the polderisation of the adjoining countryside.

OUDEWATER

At Oudewater (pronounced 'Owder-varter') there are free 72-hour canalside moorings both sides of the Hoenkoopse bridge, or a little further east along a pleasant grassy bank. Whilst there are no waterside facilities, the town has interesting small shops and good restaurants. Brasserie Joia has plenty of tables so you should always find room, whilst Rendezvous De Bontekoe is a little more exclusive, but well regarded for special occasions. One of the Netherlands' oldest small towns, Oudewater was

Small canals run through the centre of the old village of Oudewater

originally known for rope production, but gained notoriety in the 16th century as a place where witches were tried. They were weighed on the scales in the Heksenwaag (Witches Scales), and if they were too heavy to ride a broomstick there were not a witch. Needless to say, all the women weighed in Oudewater were acquitted, with the last trial taking place in 1729. The Heksenwaag now houses a small museum in honour of its infamous past with the nearby Touwmuseum (Rope Museum) recalling the source of the town's economic boom.

MONTFOORT

A long stretch of free canalside municipal moorings (maximum stay 3 days) are provided east of the bridge. Those at the east end are away from the road and convenient for the facilities block which houses toilets and a chemical toilet disposal facility, as well as coin-operated showers, a washing machine, and a dryer. A coin-operated water hose is nearby and there are rubbish bins available at various points.

The town does not boast much historical significance but is well-equipped with a supermarket and ATMs on the quayside and a choice of restaurants around the town. Next to the moorings an open air swimming pool is used by the early-season visitors as well as families in high summer. A good recreational stop using the pool and the shops- but choose Oudewater if you want more historical character.

Good dining choices are Het Oude Stadhuis restaurant housed in the combined town hall and gatehouse; or for an upmarket option try the Kasteel Montfoort.

IJSSELSTEIN

Northwest of IJsselstein (pronounced 'I-sull-stine') a new yacht harbour JH Marnemoende has been established, offering pontoon berths and good marina facilities. The moorings, with metered water and electricity, were in place in 2006 but the shore side facilities were still under construction. When completed these will include a chandlers, small service centre, and terrace restaurant. The same site will offer charter boats, which may help to boost facilities but might also cause congestion along this already popular waterway.

In the town centre there are municipal moorings at various points along the quayside, although most are in rather dull industrial or residential areas. The large town has a wide range of shops and services in an extensive pedestrianised centre. A municipal museum near the river presents exhibitions on regional history with depictions of the town and waterway from the 17th century onwards. From the adjacent waterway Yselvaert offers boat tours of the inner canals during summer months. On Kronenburgplantsoen, the 16th-century castle tower is open to visitors at weekends, when it is populated with authentically dressed castle dwellers. For visits further afield there is a direct bus service to Utrecht if you are not planning to go by boat.

Gouwe

The Gouwe (known as Gouwekanaal south of Gouda) connects with the Hollandse IJssel and runs north to join the Oude Rijn at Alphen aan den Rijn. Unappealing looking canalside moorings are on the west bank north of the Waddinxveen bridge. These lie in a car park and commercial area but are close to the small town for local amenities.

Length 14km
Speed limit 12km/h; except in Boskoop between the Hefbrug and the Otwegwetering, 9km/h.
Locks Julianasluis and lifting bridges operate 24 hours from Monday morning to Friday evening and throughout the day Saturdays and Sundays. VHF 18
Bridges 6 opening. Gouda rail bridges (7m air draught when closed; 34m when open) open four times a day between 0600 and 2113. Coenecoop, Waddinxveen, Boskoop and Gouwsluis road bridges operate 24 hours from Monday morning to Friday evening and throughout the day Saturdays and Sundays. VHF 18. Gouwsluis rail bridge is operated remotely on demand from the nearby road bridge.

BOSKOOP

The small, but friendly harbour lies on the Otwegwetering and is accessed by a lifting bridge (ring bell on the red and white post to request). Usual facilities including washing machine. The harbour lies some distance from the small town and in between lies an area of tiny islands which have been used for the cultivation of trees since the middle ages. Boskoop (pronounced 'bos-cope' and meaning Trees to Sell) is famous for its auction which exports shrubs and plants to all parts of the world. The Boomkwekerij (Tree cultivation) Museum on Rijerskoop consists of a reconstruction of a 19th-century nurseryman's house as well as a historic garden and unique collection of gardening books.

Gouda canals

The Nieuwe Gouwe connects the Gouwekanaal west of the town to the central town canals. Onward passage via the Kattensingel leads to the Reeuwijkse Plassen (restricted to a maximum air draught of 1.8m) and via the Turfsingel back to the Hollandse IJssel (maximum air draught 3.3m).

Speed limit 12km/h
Locks Ir. De Kock van Leeuwensluis operates throughout the day VHF 20. Mellgatsluis and fixed bridge (min 3.3m) operate throughout the day including Sundays and holidays. The fixed bridge is on the IJssel side and air draught varies with state of the tide (NAP +4.65m) Toll payable at the lock.
Bridges 3 opening. Steve Biko (H, H+20, H+40), Rabat and Potters (H, H+15, H+30, H+45) bridges operate throughout the day Monday–Saturday VHF 20. Sundays are worked in addition during July and August. Gulden, St Remeijn, Crabeth and St Joost bridges operate throughout the day.

GOUDA

Where to stop

The yacht club at Gouda is to the west of the town, accessed off the Nieuwe Gouwe prior to the town centre bridges. It is distant from the town centre but of use to yachts wanting to catch an early or late opening of the Gouwe rail bridge. The more attractive moorings are along the Kattensingel, and to a lesser extent along the Turfsingel where water,

and in some places, electricity is provided (free) to visiting boats. Further moorings even nearer the town centre are available on the Binnen Gouwe after a further three opening bridges, but boats must return the same way and these are little used. All moorings share a shower and toilet block near the Pottersbrug, where a pump-out and chemical toilet disposal facility are also available.

Facilities Ashore

Chandlers Aquarius on Spoorstraat or Macdaniel Watersport in Reeuwijk
Supermarket & Shops Albert Heijn in the Markt and many other shops in the centre
ATMs At the station and several on the way to the Markt
Cycle hire From the Rijwielshop at the train station
VVV office On the Markt

What to see

From the moorings on Gouda's (pronounced 'khow-dar') Kattensingel, the Markt is a short walk and every Thursday from late June until the end of August the spectacle of the weekly cheese market is held here. Although these days the real deals are

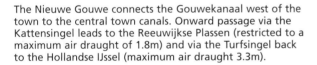

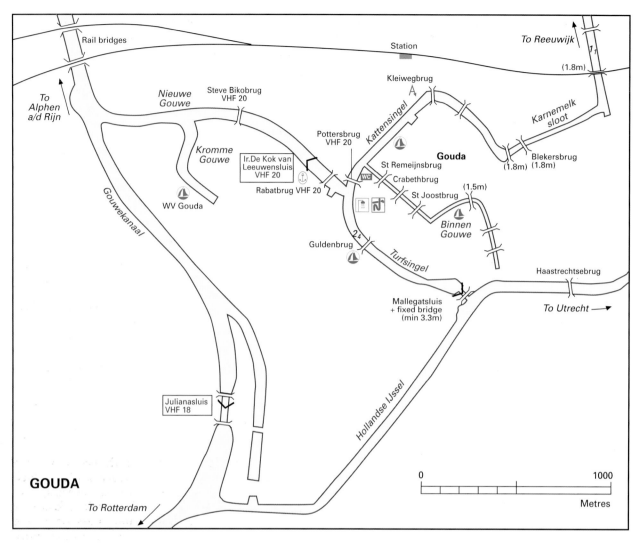

GOUDA

Visit Gouda on Cheese Market day; Thursdays from late June

done over the phone before the cheese is made, the old ritual of hand-clap trading is re-enacted in the market place for the benefit of the tourists. Of course there is plenty of chance to sample and buy cheese, as well as visit the cheese-making demonstration in De Waag (Weigh House). There is more to Gouda than cheese though and the town is also renowned for its pottery, pipes and stroopwafels.

In St Janskerk, the Goudse Glazen are an impressive collection of 70 stained glass windows, whose significance are explained by audio tours in English. Next door the Museum Het Catharina Gasthuis is housed in a former women's hospital and the courtyard gardens still offer a haven of tranquillity to those who venture beyond the unlocked door. On the Turfmarkt, the Resistance Museum includes an unusual sculpture garden with miniature replicas of war memorials from around the Netherlands.

For the energetically minded the Reeuwijkse Plassen, north of the town, offer miles of car-free cycling. Formed through peat extraction, the lakes are intensively used for a variety of watersports, but this does not seem to detract from their appeal. For those who prefer a waterborne excursion you can also go by dinghy, with a mobile bridge-keeper taking convoys of boats three times daily from the

Kleiwegbrug on the Kattensingel. There is a small toll for the bridge service and for the daily pass for the lakes, available from the Restaurant Het Wapen van Reeuwijk.

Restaurant tip

De Brunel on Hoge Gouwe has popular outdoor tables in the old stone fish market in nice weather, whilst De Zalm on the Markt claims to be the oldest restaurant in Europe. Scheeps on Westhaven also comes well recommended.

Connections

The rail station is near the moorings for crew changes or excursions.

Oude Rijn

For the purposes of this guide, the navigable part of the Oude Rijn begins at Woerden and runs west, joining the junction of the Rijn-Schiekanaal and the Zijl east of Leiden. The old course runs through the centre of Leiden, and on to Katwijk, although this town centre section is now restricted to air draught of less than 1.5m and an alternative route to Katwijk is described in the section on Leiden. The eastern section, part of which is called the Leidse Rijn and which connects with the Amsterdam-Rijnkanaal is restricted to a maximum air draught of 2m.

Length 34km
Maximum permitted draught 2.5m
Speed limit Woerden to Bodegraven 9km/h; Bodegraven to Rijn-Schiekanaal, 12km/h.
Depth 2.5m
Lock Bodegravensluis and lifting bridge operate throughout the day (from 1000 on Sundays). Toll payable.
Bridges 10 opening, as follows:

Woerden to Zwammerdam: Nieuwerbrug, Broekveld, Burg.Croles and Zwammerdam bridges operate throughout the day (from 1000 on Sundays). VHF 20. Bridge toll payable at Nieuwerbrug.

Gouwsluis to Rijn-Schiekanaal east of Leiden: Steekter bridge (4.6m when closed) is operated remotely from Gouwsluis road bridge and operates throughout the day with breaks for the morning and evening rush hours on weekdays (0700–0900 and 1615–1815). Sundays from 1000. VHF 18. Swaenswijk, Alphense, Kon. Juliana (4.4m when closed) and Albert Schweizer (5.4m when closed) bridges operate 24 hours from Monday morning to Friday evening and through the day Saturday and Sunday (from 1000 Sundays). VHF 18. Due to heavy road traffic, leisure boats may be grouped together or with a commercial vessel.

Koudekerk bridge operates throughout the day (from 1000 on Sundays). VHF 20. A4 road bridge (5.4m when closed) operates throughout the day with breaks for morning and evening rush hours on weekdays (0700–1000 and 1600–1900). Sundays from 1000. Leiderdorpse bridge operates throughout the day with breaks for morning and evening rush hours on weekdays (0700–0900 and 1600–1800). Sundays from 1000. VHF 22.

WOERDEN

Where to stop

There is a municipal harbour in the centre of town accessed via the Kwakel and Rozen bridges which operate throughout the day with an evening rush hour break (1630–1730). A single bridge keeper is based at the Kwakel bridge and cycles on to the Rozen bridge. For your departure, contact the bridge keeper to request opening ☎ 0348 416336. The moorings are heavily used by local boats but there are a few spaces for visitors to starboard as you enter the harbour, equipped with coin-operated electricity.

Alternatively pass under the Blokhuis bridge into the Grecht where the moorings of WV De Greft lie just north on the east bank. Adequate spaces for visitors up to 15m with coin-metered water (€0.50/100 ltrs) and electricity are provided. The alongside reporting pontoon on the frontage can be

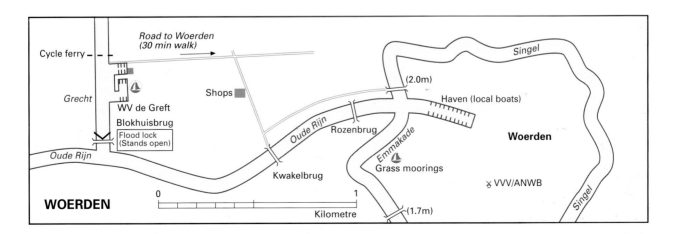

Woerden mill turns for visitors every Wednesday in the summer

used overnight if the harbourmaster has gone home. Very small clubhouse and usual basic facilities including cycle hire and pump-out are available.

What to see

It is a 10-minute bike ride (30-minute walk) to Woerden (pronounced 'vwoor-der') city centre, but there is a small local shopping centre halfway for urgent supplies. The VVV office is in the windmill which is open to visitors on Wednesday, when a weekly market is also held in the morning. The former *Stadhuis* is home to the municipal museum but the 15th-century castle is not open to visitors.

Intact star-shaped canals surround the mainly pedestrianised centre, which has a good selection of shops.

BODEGRAVEN

The yacht harbour west of the town is reserved for berthholders of WV De Oude Rijn, but there are short-term moorings for several boats in the town centre to the east of the bridge. These are close to a selection of shops and bars on the high street and the station is nearby.

ZWAMMERDAM

West of Zwammerdam free canalside moorings alongside a grassy bank (maximum stay 2 days) are opposite a gravel-loading depot and are downwind when the wind is from the southwest. Just east of the village the Restaurant Rust Even has space for four boats with coin-operated electric points.

ALPHEN AAN DE RIJN

Where to stop

Short-term town centre moorings are available just north of Alpense bridge and south of Albert Schweizer bridge. For overnight stops, the yacht harbour on the Woudwetering is the best option, although not so convenient for the town. See Heimans and Woudwetering for details.

What to see

Alphen is a bustling town with a busy weekly market every Saturday on Thorbeckeplein and a very good range of shops. It is also home to two nationally recognised attractions: Vogelpark Avifauna features over 3,000 birds including rare species, a tropical aviary, a penguin pool and flamingo pond; whilst Archeon, on the south side of town, is an archaeological theme park with zones on prehistoric life, the Romans and the Middle Ages.

Restaurant tip

The Royal Bar on Thorbeckplein offers free wi-fi.

Stop on the canal at Alphen a/d Rijn for lunch and shopping or at the yacht club for a longer stay

Grecht

The Grecht (pronounced 'Greft' due to a historical spelling anomaly) runs north from the Oude Rijn at Woerden to the settlement of Woerdense Verlaat on the edge of the Nieuwekoopse Plassen. Access to the meers and waterways of the Nieuwekoopse Plassen is restricted to vessels with a special permit, and the JH at Slikkendam deals mainly in small day boats. The waterway is quite shallow and winding, surrounded by drained polders with lots of wildlife. Just the one canalside stopping place (maximum stay 24 hours) on the starboard side where there is space for two boats. The lock at Woerdense Verlaat has a width of just 5.1m and is 30m long but there is a sharp turn to starboard as you exit. The yacht harbour of WSV De Greft lies at the southern end and is the best stopping place for a visit to Woerden. (See entry under Oude Rijn for details.)

Length 10km
Speed limit 6km/h
Maximum draught 1.5m; beam 5m
Lock Woerdense Verlaat operates throughout the day with breaks for lunch and dinner (1200–1300 and 1700–1800). From 1000 on Sundays. Toll payable.
Bridge Blockhuis bridge at the junction with the Oude Rijn operates throughout the day (Sundays from 1000). The adjacent flood lock normally stands open. Kollen bridge operates as for Woerdense Verlaat lock.

Kromme Mijdrecht

The Kromme Mijdrecht forms the continuation of the Grecht from Woerdense Verlaat to the Amstel at Amstelhoek. Kromme means winding in Dutch and this waterway lives up to its name, although it is a very attractive waterway with pasture land and fens on each side. The Overzet cycle bridge at Zomerlust stands open unless requested by cyclists, when a red light over a green flashing light indicates that the bridge is about to close. Depth of 2m in the main channel, but less near the banks. The open-standing flood lock at the northern end has a beam of 7m.

Several mooring places along the canal (no facilities) some near to leisure and recreation areas, and others in the small village of De Hoef. Kromme Mijdrecht Recreatie Centrum north of the Overzet bridge has moorings near to a small café. In De Hoef there are visitors' moorings at canalside Restaurant De Strooppot. Access to the visitors' harbour on the Kerkvaart is restricted to 2.5m air draught.

Speed limit 9km/h
Maximum permitted draught 2.1m, beam 5m (at Woerdense Verlaat)
Lock The flood lock at the northern end stands open.
Bridges 2 opening. The Overzet cycle bridge at Zomerlust stands open except when operated by cyclists. The Oude Spoorbrug De Hoef (road bridge) operates throughout the day with a break for lunch Saturdays and Sundays (1300–1400) and can be requested by push button or the phone number on the bridge. At busy times yachts are grouped together for bridging with a maximum wait time of 30 minutes.

Watch out for navigational hazards like this dredging barge and train

Aarkanaal

The Aarkanaal runs north from the Oude Rijn at Gouwsluis to Tolhuissluizen where it joins the permit-only waterway, the Drecht, and continues as the Amstel to Amsterdam. A flood barrier north of the Zeger bridge stands open. Water and fuel available near the Aardammer bridge.

Length 11km
Speed limit 12km/h
Maximum permitted draught 2.5m
Bridges 1 fixed (5.6m), 4 opening. Zeger, Aardammer, Papen and Katten bridges operate throughout the day (Sundays from 1000).

There are canalside moorings on the west bank near the Zegerplas which is a popular recreation area with facilities for small boats and windsurfing. Motor boats are not permitted and access is restricted to 2.5m air draught. On the east bank north of Zegerbrug there are moorings for visiting the Neptunus pumping engine and further places south of Aardammerbrug (for a maximum stay of 3 days).

Amstel

The Amstel forms the continuation of the Aarkanaal and runs northeast via Uithoorn and Ouderkerk aan de Amstel to the central canals of Amsterdam. The Amstelroute continues north through the city via the Rapenburgersluis to the Oosterdok and the Afgesloten IJ with opening bridges, although two (5.1m when closed) open only at night, and another is crossed by an electric tramline, restricting air draught to 7.9m.

The waterway passes through countryside and small villages and is quite quiet, being mainly used by small boats. From Ouderkerk the river is lined with trees and parks as far as the Utrechtse bridge where you approach the built-up area of Amsterdam.

There are good moorings for several boats on the east bank north of Uithoorn but these have no access to the shore. Canalside moorings are available 1 km north of Ouderkerk on the east side, and limited space exists a little further on at the popular Kleine Kalfie restaurant on the west bank. Just south of Roozenoord A10 bridges there are unappealing moorings on the port side, and south of Utrechtse bridge is Restaurant Miranda with good landing stages for customers.

South of Nes aan de Amstel is the junction with the Oude Waver and there are canalside moorings just inside the open-standing flood lock. At Ouderkerk there is a junction with the Bullewijk which runs southeast to the Vinkeveense Plassen and at Utrechtse bridge there is a junction with the Omval navigation, which continues east as the Weesper Trekvaart. In this wider basin area you will find the Scheen Service Centre, which includes a small chandlers and fuel berth. A little further on the starboard side near the Omval entrance are moorings at Weinholt Watersport yacht haven with water and electricity.

A canalside garage south of Nes aan de Amstel sells diesel, petrol and gas bottles and takes all types of credit cards.

Length 26km
Speed limit 9km/h
Maximum permitted draught 2.35m

Bridges 3 fixed (5.8m), 4 opening. Vrouwenakker, Prinses Irene, Bus and Ouderkerk bridge operate throughout the day with a break for lunch weekends and holidays (1300–1400). Restricted opening before 0900 and after 1700. VHF 20 or ☎ 0297 561378.

UITHOORN

Canalside moorings in Uithoorn (pronounced 'out-horn') just south of the junction with the Kromme Mijdrecht on the west bank. There are moorings for vessels up to 6m only at the visitors' harbour at Marktplein unless you can persuade someone otherwise. Uithoorn is a large modern village with a range of shops and a weekly market on Wednesdays. A VVV and ANWB office is also situated on the quay. A stop at Uithoorn is within 20-minutes cycling distance of the Aalsmeer Bloemenveiling.

See Aalsmeer on the Ringvaart van de Haarlemmermeerpolder for details.

OUDERKERK AAN DE AMSTEL

A picturesque old village, Ouderkerk (pronounced 'owder-kerk') is a popular day out for Amsterdammers and, with its authentic stage mill, makes a pleasant short stop. Moorings for customers alongside the exclusive 't Jagershuis hotel/restaurant and others just south of Ouderkerk bridge on the west bank provide a further 30–35m of free 72-hour canalside moorings. On the quay, Eetcafe Loetje has open and covered terraces and further along is the more upmarket Restaurant Praq, which uses its large terrace only from time to time. The rest of the village is a short walk away, but there is a post office and VVV.

At Ouderkerk aan de Amstel the junction with the Bullewijk leads to the Vinkeveense Plassen

Amstel to the Afgesloten IJ (Amstelroute)

The bridges from the Omval junction are managed by Amsterdam port authority and are listed in the ANWB *Almanak* under Amsterdam (Doorvaartroute B2). The first five bridges together with the Amstelsluis (which normally stands open) should open in sequence (VHF 22) with harbour dues payable at the Amstelsluis office. This toll is valid for the whole Amsterdam port complex and allows a stay of up to 3 days. An electric tramline over the Hogesluis bridge on the Amstel restricts air draught when open to 7.9m. After a turn to starboard into the Nieuwe Herengracht the next six bridges open in succession on VHF 20 and in some cases the same bridgekeeper has to cycle ahead. This leads to the Rapenburger flood lock which stands open during the day but its bridge has to lift.

Emerging into the Marine Haven cruise between the the Scheepvaart Museum and NEMO into the Oosterdok where a new bridge, the Oosterdoksdraaibrug (2.7m when closed) must be requested on VHF 22. The bridge operates

throughout the day or out of hours on request by telephone to the Oosterdok office. ☎ 020 6241457 South of this bridge on the west side is the Oosterdok harbour office where you should tie up to pay harbour dues when making the passage north to south. The following two bridges leading to the Afgesloten IJ, the Oosterdoks bridges, have an air draught when closed of 5.1m (NAP+4.7m). Vessels above this height can seek night-time bridge lifts available at 0220 and 0320 on VHF 22 or ☎ 020 6241457. When emerging into the IJ, keep a sharp watch for fast approaching barges and ferries and the frequent trip-boats that turn into the Oosterdok. Listen on VHF 68 in the IJ.

Maximum permitted draught 2.35m
Bridges 14 opening, of which 2 operate only at night (5.1m when closed) and one has a maximum clearance when open of 7.9m. The five opening bridges on the Amstel (VHF 22) and the six on the Nieuwe Herengracht (VHF 20) operate throughout the day except for rush hour closures on weekdays (0715–0900 and 1615–1815). From 1000 weekends and holidays.

Vinkeveense Plassen

There are three access routes to the Vinkeveenseplassen:
• from the Amstel north of Uithoorn via the Oude Waver and Winkel (max. draught 1.2m)
• from the Amstel at Ouderkerk via the Bullewijk, Waver, Winkel (max. draught of 1.2m, max. air draught 4.8m)
• from the Amsterdam-Rijnkanaal at Nieuwersluis via the Nieuwe Wetering, Angstel, Geuzensloot (max. draught 2.2m, max. air draught 3.8m)

This large lake is a popular recreation area and is bordered with luxury lakeside homes, as well as water sports businesses. For boats that can manage the low air draught it offers an interesting cross-country route from the Amstel to the Vecht, perhaps with a stopover at one of the many island moorings on the lake en route. These are provided for public use by the lake authority, but boats may only stay on any one island for up to 3 days. The route between the northern and southern halves is via the opening bridge towards the east side, with that on the west side being suitable only for very low boats. Locks give access at the northern and southern entry channels and these are very busy at weekends in high season so expect long delays heading towards the lakes on Friday evening and leaving on Sunday. There are several lakeside harbours with moorings for visitors. Fuel and all services are available at JH Omtzigt on the northern lake and JH De Wilgenhoek in the southeast corner of the southern lake.

Maximum permitted draught 2m, beam 6m, length 30m
Speed limit On the lakes 9km/h
Locks Proostdijersluis (on the Winkel) and Demmerikse sluis (on the Geuzensloot) operate throughout the day with a break for lunch (1230–1330). Toll payable.
Bridge Middenwetering bridge connects the north and south lakes on the east side and operates throughout the day with breaks for lunch and tea (1230–1330 and 1630–1730)

Weespertrekvaart

The Weespertrekvaart leaves the Amstel south of Amsterdam at the Omval junction and runs east and south to cross the Amsterdam-Rijnkanaal and join the Vecht at Weesp. The part to the east of the Amsterdam-Rijnkanaal is known as the Smal Weesp and is covered in Chapter 8: Central Netherlands, under Weesp. The first part passes through rather industrial and uninspiring surroundings before reaching the Diemer Bos woods where it becomes a more attractive and rural prospect. Before the opening of the Amsterdam-Rijnkanaal in 1952 the Weespertrekvaart, in conjunction with the Vecht, formed the main waterway between Amsterdam and the Rijn. There are little or no official stopping places along the waterway, but it offers a useful passage between Amsterdam and the Vecht for boats that can pass under the fixed bridges. The Tulip Inn, just south of the A9 bridge, has a waterside terrace but moorings only suitable for small boats. However at Driemond there are canalside moorings on the south side just west of the lock junction with the Amsterdam-Rijnkanaal, which would be suitable for a visit to the quayside grocery store and post office. Once you exit the lock, remember to keep a sharp look out for crossing traffic as the barges move deceptively quickly and create a lot of wash.

Length 9.2km
Maximum permitted draught 2.1m
Speed limit 9km/h
Bridges 7 fixed (min. 4.95m), 5 opening. Omval (3.1m when closed, 5.15m when open), Duivendrechtse (2.9m when closed, 5m when open) and Rozenburglaan (2.9m when closed, 5.6m when open) lift bridges operate throughout the day with breaks for the morning and evening rush hour on weekdays (0700–0900 and 1600–1800). Weekends and holidays from 1000. The Omval bridge is operated remotely from the Duivendrechtse bridge and can be called on VHF 22 (Omvalbrug) or by push buttons on both sides of the bridge. In Diemen: Venser and Diemer bridges are operated from the Venser bridge throughout the day as above. Diemer bridge can be requested by loud horn signal. Driemond bridge crosses an open flood lock and operates throughout the day (Sundays from 0900).

Keep a sharp watch for crossing traffic at the junction with the Amsterdam-Rijn Kanaal

Heimans and Woudwetering

The Heimanswetering leaves the Oude Rijn at Alphen aan de Rijn and runs north, becoming the Woudwetering until it flows into the Braassemermeer. With opening bridges and good depth it forms part of two of the three mast-up routes between Amsterdam and the south, linking both with the more direct night-convoy route and the longer route through Lisse and Haarlem. A small boat yard in Woubrugge has good service facilities and there is fuel at the junction with the Braassemermeer.

Length 4km
Speed limit 12k/h except through Woubrugge, 9km/h
Maximum draught 2.8m
Bridges Molenaars and Woubrugse bridges operate 24 hours from Monday morning to Friday evening and throughout the day at weekends (Sundays and holidays from 1000). Night passage is arranged in convoys between the two bridges. VHF 18.

The yacht harbour of WV Alphen aan de Rijn lies towards the southern end of the Heimanswetering and is accessed via a bridge over the entrance which is operated throughout the day with breaks for lunch and dinner (1230–1300 and 1830–1700). There is adequate space and all of the usual facilities, but it is a 15-minute cycle to the centre or even longer if you are walking.

Braassemermeer

This is a good size mere with minimum depth of 2m outside the main channel making it popular with yachts. There is fuel at the southern end at the junction with the Woudwetering.

Speed limit 12km/h
Maximum permitted draught 2.8m

The lake is popular for holiday apartments whose owners might keep a little run-around in the garage

ROELOFARENDSVEEN/OUDE WETERING
There are three marinas on the lake of which the largest is Watersportcentrum Braassemermeer that always has spaces for visitors, who should make for the north end of the marina. The approach is also close to the JH De Brasem and so you can make your choice at this juncture. This offers a convenient stopping point on the mast-up through route between Gouda and Amsterdam and provides a full range of facilities. There is a mechanic on-site, a visiting electrician and a crane for up to 4-tons, but heavier duty and mast-craning facilities are available at Woubrugge. There is no cycle hire but for those with bikes onboard there are good circular routes taking in nearby windmills. On site is the Bar/bistro Braasseme Taverne, with swimming pool, shops and banks in the village.

Oude Wetering

This short channel leaves the north side of the Braassemermeer and connects with the Ringvaart van de Haarlemmermeerpolder. Moorings along the length of the waterway through the village on the west side, for a maximum stay of 24 hours.

Speed limit 12km/h
Maximum permitted draught 2.5m

Zijl

The Zijl is a wide, but winding waterway, which runs from the junction of the Oude Rijn and the Rijn-Schiekanaal east of Leiden, north to the Kagerplassen. Details of bridge openings are given under Leiden, See Voorschoten to the Kagerplassen.

Speed limit 12km/h
Maximum permitted draught 2.5m

Zijlzicht yacht harbour is mainly occupied by the small day boats which are popular around Leiden and which have been made on site since 1994, but there are visitors spaces for smaller boats in boxes, and for larger boats along the river frontage. A peaceful and secure berth can be had here but the harbour is in the middle of a residential area some distance from the town. Facilities on site include the usual showers, launderette and small chandlers, but beyond that there is not much on offer.

Mainly sloops at the Zijlzicht marina

Kagerplassen

The Kagerplassen (meaning Kaag lakes and pronounced 'car-kher-plarzer') lie between the Ringvaart van de Haarlemmermeerpolder at Kaag and north Leiden, accessed from the south by the Zijl. The easternmost lakes are accessible only with a special permit and are not covered in this guide. However, this still leaves a large area of open waters and free moorings to be explored. The van der Wensum Service Centre has a waterside fuel berth next to the car ferry at Buitenkaag.

Speed limit 12km/h in channels wider than 6m, otherwise 6km/h. The Norremeer and Dieper Poel are designated as areas for speed boats and waterskiing and have no speed limit.

Stop at the farm for homemade products

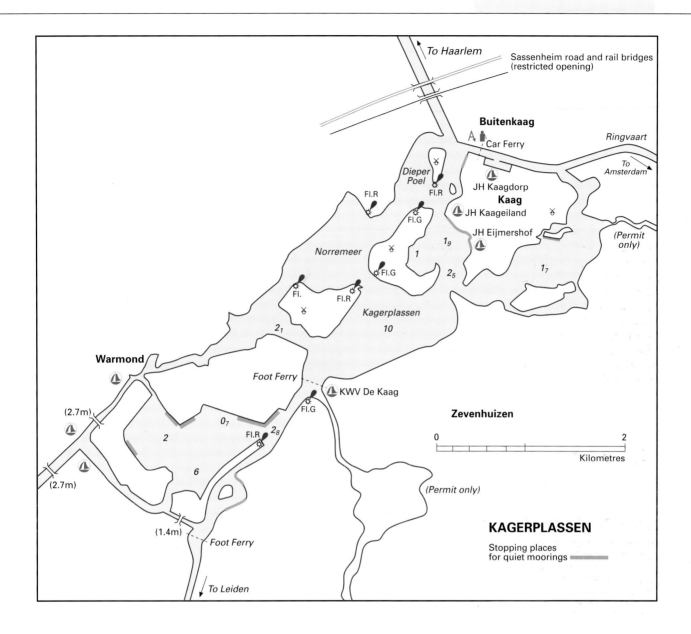

KAAG

Where to stop

The island village of Kaag (pronound 'karkh') is the focal point of the lakes but there are free mooring pontoons and lakeside harbours all around the area. At Kaag village, several yacht harbours cluster around the SW corner of the island, including JH Kaageiland for boats up to 12m. On the Ringvaart JH Kaagdorp has more space and capacity for larger boats. A 24-hour ferry connects the island with the mainland where a few shops and a small chandlers can be found.

Facilities Ashore

Fuel and small chandlers v.d. Wensum service centre near the floating bridge
Shops Few small shops in Buitenkaag and a visiting shop on Kaag twice a week
ATMs On Buitenkaag near the floating bridge

What to see

Several places on the island hire small boats and canoes, or take the dinghy and explore the smaller channels of this peaceful lake complex. On the island Kaasboerderij van Ruiten sells homemade cheese and dairy products during the season.

Restaurant tip

There are moorings with electricity for customers at the exclusive Tante Kee restaurant, close to the junction with the ringvaart, which offers high standards of catering and service from a member of the Jeunes Restaurateurs Europe, and at the lower budget Eijmershof café/restaurant, both with a splendid view of the lakes. Twee Wilgen (Two Willows) has a more laid back atmosphere with dining at the bar or in the small non-smoking restaurant.

In the centre of the lakes you can also moor at the first class Restaurant De Kaag Societeit at KWV De Kaag (Warmond).

Ringvaart van de Haarlemmermeerpolder

The Ringvaart van de Haarlemmermeerpolder forms the main drainage system for one of Holland's most important areas of reclaimed land as well as being a principal navigation for waterborne traffic. The 18,000 hectare Haarlemmermeer lake was the result of peat extraction but as early as the 17th century it became a threat to neighbouring cities during storms. The dangerous waters became known as Ship's Hell Hole and later became the site of the International Airport, Schiphol, from which that famous airport's name is derived! Three steam-powered pumps were used to drain 88 million cubic metres of water and the resulting polder land is an average 4m below sea level. The pumps at Cruquius and Halfweg have been converted into working exhibitions and are well worth a visit for the mechanically minded. The waterway is 60km long and is marked with kilometre boards starting at the junction with the Kagerplassen and travelling clockwise.

Length 60km
Speed limit 9km/h
Depth 2.5m, except between Cruquius and the Buiten Liede, 1.6m.

Kaag to the Spaarne
A busy stretch which begins with the limited opening Sassenheim bridges. Vessels with air draught greater than 4.7m must time their passage to accommodate these, but the rest of the bridges open on demand and the whole section takes about two hours. Canalside moorings on the east bank just to the north of Sassenheim bridges.

Length 16km
Bridges 7 opening. Sassenheim rail (5.13m when closed) and road (4.7m when closed) bridges open nine times per day on weekdays (three times during each of 0558–0658, 1228–1328 and 1828–1928) with weekend openings spread more evenly throughout the day. The bridges do not operate in high winds or poor visibility. Lisse bridge operates throughout the day with a break for the evening rush hour on weekdays (1700–1730) and an afternoon break on Sundays and holidays (1200–1600). VHF 18. Elsbroek bridge operates throughout the day with an afternoon break on Sundays and holidays (1200–1500) except during July and August. VHF 18. Hillegom bridge operates throughout the day with a break for the morning rush hour (0745–0830) and an afternoon break on Sundays and holidays (1130–1530). VHF 18. Bennebroek bridge operates throughout the day again with the afternoon break on Sundays and holidays (1130–1530) VHF 18. Cruquius bridge operates the same hours as Elsbroek bridge.

LISSE
WV Lisse (pronounced 'lisser') has moorings for visitors on the west bank of the Ringvaart, close to the town. If you visit in April or May a visit to the nearby Keukenhof, a 32-hectare Spring Garden, is a must. Only ten minutes by bike, the exhibition borders the famous bulb fields. At other times the Museum Zwarte Tulp (Black Tulip) gives information about the bulb-growing industry and

The Bloemencorso rolls into town on the last Saturday in April

has a collection of preserved blooms. On the last Saturday in April the Noordwijk-Haarlem flower parade, the 'Bloemencorso', passes through the town. This continues a 50-year tradition and involves a parade of some 30 or so elaborately decorated floral floats.

HILLEGOM
The Hofzicht visitors' harbour is situated off a narrow channel which leaves the west side of the Ringvaart south of the Hillegom bridge. Passage under the Hillinen bridge on request on ☎ 06 5389 3525. A small village distinguished by the Den Hartogh Ford Museum. Its collection of 185 cars by the Detroit manufacturer is the world's largest private collection of this marque.

HEEMSTEDE
West of the Cruquius bridge, WV Van Merlenhaven is based in a short canal off the north bank and has good basic facilities. South of the Schouwbroeker bridge round the corner on the Spaarne, the Heemsteedskanaal turns to port and at the end of the canal is Haven van Heemstede. A fixed bridge restricts access here to 5m and there are no facilities but it is convenient for a visit to Museum Cruquius. East of the Cruquius bridge, a pontoon outside the Cruquius Museum belongs to the owner and should only be used with permission.

Housed in one of three pumping stations completed in 1849 to drain the Haarlemmermeerpolder, the British steam engine which powered Cruquius could do the work of 160 windmills. The neogothic architecture has long been replaced by more discreet, modern equipment but the building

The 19th-century steam driven pumping station, Cruquius, is open to visitors at the junction of the Ringvaart and the Spaarne

remains to recall its history. The boilers have been cleared out to make space for an informative museum, but the original steam engine can still be seen in operation, now driven by electricity.

Spaarne to the Nieuwe Meer

Length 19km
Speed limit 9km/h
Bridges 9 fixed (5.27m), 6 opening. Schalkwijker foot and cycle bridge is operated remotely from the Cruquius bridge and opens throughout the day on the hour and half-hour with an afternoon break on Sundays and holidays (1200–1500) except in July and August. Vijfhuizen bridge operates throughout the day on the hour and half-hour (from 1000 on weekends and holidays), with an afternoon break (1200–1600) on Sundays and holidays.
Weeren, Halfweg, Lijnden and Badhoevedorp bridges operate throughout the day with a break for the evening rush hour on weekdays (1600–1800), from 1000 on weekends and holidays with an afternoon break on Sundays and holidays (1200–1600). VHF 22

HALFWEG

WSV De Swaenenburght lies on the north bank, east of the bridge and forms a convenient stop for a visit to Museum Stoomgemaal Halfweg. The pump at Halfweg is the oldest operational steam-driven pump in the world and in its day could move water at a rate of 25,000 litres a second. One of the boilers has been dismantled for visitors to look inside, whilst the other remains operational and is brought into service on twelve Pumping Days during the summer.

Nieuwe Meer to Oude Wetering

This section forms part of the mast-up route from Amsterdam to the south and yachts higher than 23m should report in advance to the Aalsmeer bridge (☎ 0297 324548) or the Nieuwe Meersluis (☎ 020 615 5115). It runs along the northwest side of the Westeinderplas, a huge open lake with a myriad of yachting facilities, details of which are given in the separate section below.

Length 19km
Bridges 5 opening. Schipol A9 road bridge (fixed span 7.9m) operates (0500–0630, 1230–1330 and 2000–2100) and morning and evening only on Sundays and holidays. See *ANWB Almanak* for exact times. VHF 22. No service in high winds or poor visibility. A second Schipol road bridge operates throughout the day at quarter or half-hour intervals depending on road traffic and the Bosrand bridge opens a quarter of an hour later.
   Aalsmeerder and Leimuider bridges operate throughout the day with breaks for the morning and evening rush hours (0700–0900 and 1600–1800) and a break for lunch (1300–1400) on Sundays and holidays. VHF 18.

Oude Wetering to Kaag

This short section completes the circular Ringvaart, and also forms part of the boundary between North and South Holland. Fuel is available at De Hanenpoel near km 56.

Length 6km
Bridges 2 opening. Wetering and Meer bridges operate throughout the day with a break for lunch (1300–1400) on Sundays and holidays except during July and August.

Nieuwe Meer

As well as being a popular sailing lake the Nieuwe Meer is the mustering point for the convoy to the Houthaven in the centre of Amsterdam which is covered in Chapter 4: Holland North.

A series of yacht harbours are situated on the east side of the Nieuwe Meer providing plenty of choices of places to stay overnight, the main purpose of which would be waiting to join the convoy to Amsterdam, or recovering after a tiring night arriving that way. The nearby suburb of Amstelveen is populated with large office buildings and busy roads, but the yacht havens maintain some sanctity, except for the noise from the busy A4 which crosses the northeast end. A variety of yacht service facilities, small chandlery and outboard motor service centre are available and clubhouses and the hotel restaurant provide somewhere to eat. Nearby bus and metro services are available to the city centre if you are not going by boat. South of the mere is the Amsterdamse Bos, a large wooded recreational area where you can hire bikes, canoes and pedalos. Also in Amstelveen is the internationally recognised COBRA modern art museum.

Stop on the Nieuwe Meer to await the night convoy to Amsterdam

Westeinderplas

The large lake of the Westeinderplas is dotted with small land strips in the northeast corner which are separated by narrow channels. Vessels should follow the buoyed channels through the larger gaps to access the facilities on the south side. The area between the islands is called the Kleine Poel and a buoyed channel marks the route into this area. Although the depth is limited in some areas of the Kleine Poel there is good depth to access the yacht harbours of the WV Nieuwe Meer and JH Dragt at the east end.

Access from the Ringvaart is possible via the Blauwe Beugel and Wijde Gat or at the west end via the Pieter Leendertsloot, depth 1.7m.

Depth Grote Poel 2.25m; Kleine Poel 1.6m in the middle and 1.25m near the banks
Speed limit 12km/h, or 6km/h within 50m of the shores. The area marked by yellow buoys for water-skiing has no speed limit, but requires a permit from the municipality of Aalsmeer.

AALSMEER

A good choice among the many harbours is WSV Nieuwe Meer which is very close to the town and has good depth and ample facilities. Stop at the reporting pontoon near the harbour entrance to be allocated a spare berth. There is also a shopping pontoon behind the clubhouse for short stays of up to 2 hours. On the south side of the channel, a slightly longer walk to the town, Dragt Watersport has a large marina complete with chandlers and a restaurant.

Facilities Ashore

Chandlers Well stocked shop at Dragt Watersport
Repairs & Servicing Several companies around the area offer a wide range of services
Supermarkets, Shops & ATMs Albert Heijn on Drie Kolommen Plein and good selection of other shops and banks nearby.
Cycle hire Waning Tweewielers on Zijdstraat
VVV Drie Kolommen Plein

What to see

Bloemenveiling Aalsmeer is the largest covered auction in the world and extends over an area the size of 250 football fields. Twenty million units are

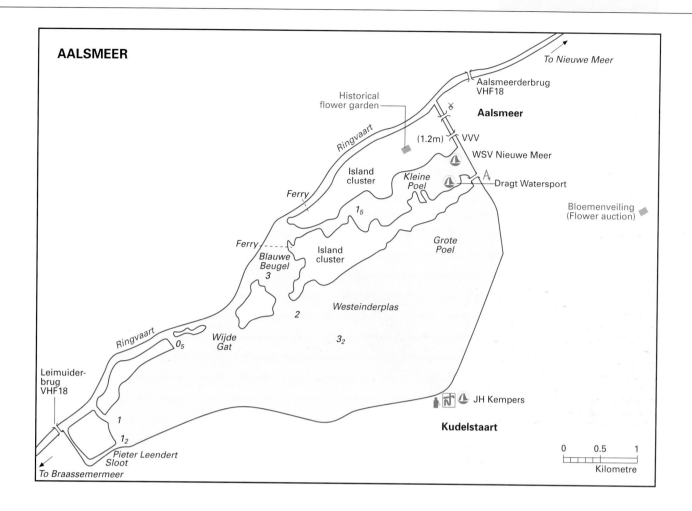

AALSMEER

traded everyday with the price decided by 'Dutch auction', where the price falls from high to low. Visitors can watch the trading halls from a gallery walkway and then see each buyer's order collated and sent to the lorries for distribution. Open Monday to Friday, 0730–1100. The auction originated on a site on the Ringvaart where the historical garden can still be visited on Uiterweg. The Aalsmeer Bloemencorso, a procession of floral floats takes place on the first Saturday in September.

KUDELSTAART

JH Kempers is a very well-equipped marina on the south side of the Westeinderplas and boasts amongst its many services wi-fi internet, fuel and pump-out. There is also a well-stocked chandlers and on-site restaurant. Cycle hire is available next door, and across the road a small shopping centre includes a supermarket, ATM and a selection of small shops.

Millions of blooms are trundled past the international buyers at the Aalsmeer flower auction

Haarlem canals

The Zuider Buiten (Southern Outer) Spaarne leaves the Ringvaart van de Haarlemmermeerpolder at Cruquius and runs north through the city, becoming the Binnen (Inner) Spaarne and then the Noorder Buiten (Northern Outer) Spaarne. Here it widens out and joins the Mooi Nel lake south of Spaarndam. A transit fee is payable at the harbour office north of the Prinsenbrug which is also where you pay for an overnight stay in the city centre moorings. There is a pump-out station here and it is a good place to fill up with water as there is a large, free hose. Fuel is also available from a bunker boat south of the Prinsenbrug.

Length 9km
Speed limit 6km/h
Bridges 8 opening. The bridges are operated in a convoy system with traffic only in one direction at a time. Boats with VHF should request passage from the harbour office (call Havendienst Haarlem,) VHF 18, giving position, direction of travel and the next bridge you wish to pass. Coming from the south, call after passing the Cruquius bridge. Convoys start promptly at the harbour office at 0900 and work up and down the bridges throughout the day. The Waarderbrug (north of the harbour office) operates from 0840. Tolls payable for passage through Haarlem or overnight stay. Stop at the harbour office north of Prinsenbrug or pay at the Melkbrug if stopping overnight coming from the south. (Shower tokens also available here.)

HAARLEM

Where to stop

Moorings are available along the canal in the town centre, some with water and electricity. These are handy for visiting the city but are alongside a busy road, making them public, noisy and dusty. The best places are north of the Gravestenenbrug on the east bank, which are rather more secluded. Showers and toilets are in the old bridge keepers house at the Gravestenenbrug and access tokens are available from the harbour office, the Melkbrug bridge-keeper and the Woltheus Cruises office opposite the Teylers Museum. Inside there is a further machine for the shower tokens.

The Teylers Museum overlooks the central moorings near the Gravestenenbrug

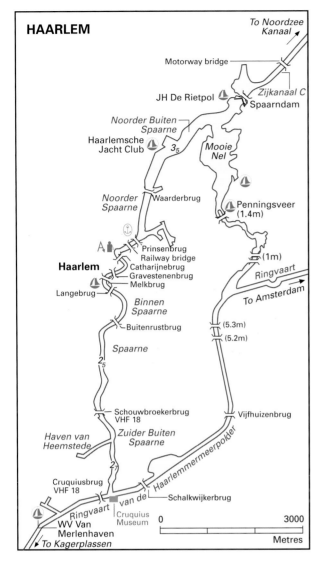

HAARLEM

To Noordzee Kanaal

Motorway bridge

JH De Rietpol

Zijkanaal C

Spaarndam

Noorder Buiten Spaarne

Haarlemsche Jacht Club

3₅

Mooie Nel

Penningsveer (1.4m)

Noorder Spaarne

Waarderbrug

(1m)

Ringvaart

To Amsterdam

Prinsenbrug

Railway bridge

Catharijnebrug

Gravestenenbrug

Melkbrug

Haarlem

Langebrug

Binnen Spaarne

Buitenrustbrug

(5.3m)

(5.2m)

Spaarne

2₅

Schouwbroekerbrug VHF 18

Vijfhuizenbrug

Haven van Heemstede

Zuider Buiten Spaarne

Haarlemmermeerpolder

2₇

Cruquiusbrug VHF 18

Schalkwijkerbrug

van de

Ringvaart

Cruquius Museum

0   3000

WV Van Merlenhaven

To Kagerplassen

Metres

What to see

The heart of the old city is the market square overlooked by Sint Bavo's Grote Kerk, completed in 1550 after 150 years of construction. The square is also home to the well-regarded Frans Hals museum of art, housed in a former almshouse. Teyler's Museum on the Spaarne waterfront has the distinction of being the first major museum to be founded in the Netherlands, established in 1778 to encourage the study of science and art and, whilst some of its collections could be described as fossils, the magnificent Oval Hall is worth a look. For an overview of the city's development, visit the low key Historisch Museum Zuid-Kennemerland and ask for the film in English, which is enlived by 3D visual aids. On the last Saturday in April, flower-bedecked floats process from Noordwijk to Haarlem for the annual Bloemencorso flower parade.

In hot weather locals flock to nearby Zandvoort, 11km from Haarlem, and one of the busiest beach resorts in the Netherlands. Here there are well-marked cycle paths through the dune parks and you can stop en-route at the ruins of Kasteel Brederode, destroyed by the Spanish in 1573. There is also a full programme of summer festivals and events including the Flower Weekend in late April, Haarlemmerhout in mid-June, and Food and Jazz events in August.

Restaurant tip

De Karmozijn on Gierstraat comes highly recommended.

Connections

Haarlem had the first train station in the Netherlands and has direct and frequent services to Amsterdam and Zandvoort.

Two kilometres north of the town, the Haarlemsche Yacht club offers a warm welcome to visitors in a more peaceful and secure lakeside location. Free showers and water, a club bar and convenient bus to the city or a 15-minute cycle, for which you can borrow one of the club's bikes. Supermarket, swimming pool and banks are a ten-minute walk away.

Facilities Ashore

Fuel Fina bunkerboat south of the rail bridge
Chandlers Van der Noord Watersport, on the Spaarne
Repairs & Servicing Good facilities at JH De Rietpol at Spaarndam or at Haarlemsche Jachtwerf, on East bank South of the Schouwbroekerbrug
Shops & ATMs Supermarket, banks and shops near to Haarlemsche YC at the end of Jan Gijzenkade
Cycle hire & VVV At rail station to north of the centre

The Haarlemmerhout Festival celebrates world music and food every year in mid-June

Spaarndam canals

North of Spaarndam lock the Spaarne becomes the Zeekanaal C until it joins the Noordzeekanaal at Buitenhuizen.

Length 3.5km
Speed limit 6km/h
Lock Spaarndam lock operates throughout the day with an afternoon break on Sundays and holidays (1130–1600). VHF 18. Toll payable at the office.
Bridges 2 opening. A9 road bridge (6.9m when closed) opens early morning, lunchtime and evening. See *Almanak* for exact times. Buitenhuizen bridge (6m when closed) is operated remotely from the Wijkertunnel and open throughout the day. The bridges do not operate in high winds or poor visibility. VHF 18.

Spaarndam has a small harbour and eco-energy centre at JH De Rietpol with good servicing facilities. Haarlemse Zeilvereniging on the east side of Mooie Nel has a few visitors places for boats up to 12m but is a long way from civilisation. Just south of the junction of Zijkanaal C with the Noodzeekanaal, the large harbour of WV IJmond has 250 berths with plenty of visitors' space. It is a popular home berth with good access to the sea and canals, close to Amsterdam and next door to the Spaarnwoude recreation resort, which boasts amongst its attractions a 200-metre covered ski run with real snow. Laundrette and diesel available on site; groceries from the nearby campsite shop.

The attractions of the quaint former fishing port of Spaarndam do not take long to enjoy. As well as an eel-smoking house, its main claim to fame is the statue by the old lock of Hans Brinker, the boy who saved his town by putting his finger in the dyke, although he is a character from an American children's book and not in any way an historical figure.

Cruising in South Holland

Similar to Zeeland in forming part of the mast-up route, South Holland boasts some locations that are quiet in the summer months. This is when many of the local boaters leave their comfortable winter berths for a summer mooring in Zeeland or Friesland, leaving the places in the cities free for visitors. In variable weather the cities of Den Haag and Leiden have much to see and do and the many lakes and lesser-visited towns and waterways await the attention of those wishing to enjoy them. With an accurate measurement of your boat's depth and air draught capability you can choose waterways in which red ensigns are seldom seen and enjoy some of the traditional and older parts of the country.

Gouda is a hub for routes proceeding along the Hollandse IJssel, and from here you can go north for Alphen aan de Rijn and Leiden, or east for Utrecht and the Vinkeveenseplassen. In the north of the region, turning south from the Noordzeekanaal returns early rewards with the provincial capital of Haarlem, followed shortly by Lisse and the Kagerplassen, possibly returning via the Ringvaart and Aalsmeer to Amsterdam. The Amstel is a delightful way of cruising south from Amsterdam and entering the small winding waterways of the Kromme Mijdrecht and the Grecht before cruising west on the Oude Rijn.

4 Holland (North)

from the Noordzeekanaal including the west coast of the IJsselmeer

Waterways	Principal venues	Other stopping places
IJmuiden harbour complex	IJmuiden	
Noordzeekanaal, including Zijkanaal A and Zijkanaal H		Beverwijk
Amsterdam canals	Amsterdam	
Nauernasche Vaart (& Zijkanaal D)		Nauerna, Krommenie
Zaan (& Zijkanaal G)	Zaanstad	Zaandam, Zaanse Schans, Zaandijk
Jisperveld (De Poel)		Wormer
Knollendam canals		East Knollendam
Alkmaardermeer		Akersloot, Uitgeest
Noordhollandsch Kanaal	Alkmaar, Den Helder	Purmerend, 't Zand
Trekvaart van Het Schouw naar Monnickendam en Edam	Monnickendam	
Kanaal Alkmaar (Omval)-Kolhorn	Broek op Langedijk	Kolhorn
Kanaal Stolpen-Schagen		Schagen
Wieringermeerpolder	Medemblik	Den Oever, Middenmeer
Waardkanaal		Nieuwesluis
Amstelmeer		
Balgzandkanaal		
Ewijcksluis, Van and the Van Ewijcksvaart		Van Ewijcksluis, Anna Paulowna
IJsselmeer	Marken, Monnickendam, Volendam, Edam, Hoorn, Enkhuizen, Medemblik	Schellingwoude, Durgerdam, Uitdam, Andijk, Schardam, Broekerhaven, Den Oever

Although the provincial boundary of Noord-Holland lies south of Haarlem, the Noordzeekanaal forms a convenient conceptual boundary, with this and the waterways north of here being considered together. The Noordzeekanaal connects to the river IJ (pronounced 'ay') and after this is named the port at its mouth, IJmuiden. As Amsterdam falls naturally into this chapter, the Amsterdam section also includes the canal route south through the city starting from the Houthaven and travelling south as far as the Nieuwe Meer (the night convoy route), which forms one of the mast-up routes. A second route south through the city via the Oosterdok and the Nieuwe Herengracht is primarily of use to vessels continuing south on the Amstel and so is described in Chapter 3: South Holland.

As there are several connecting waterways from within the province to the IJsselmeer, ports on the west coast of the IJsselmeer (east coast of Noord-Holland) are also included, with those on the east side being part of Flevoland, Overijssel or Friesland as appropriate. Historically the ports of Hoorn, Enkuizen and Medemblik fell into a region known as

West-Friesland and there are still references to these origins in some of the local customs, although they are now formally part of the Noord-Holland province.

Although as a coastal sea the Waddenzee is not a formal part of this book, it would be helpful here to make brief mention of the passage between Den Oever and Den Helder. To complete a circular route linking the IJsselmeer with the Noordhollandsch Kanaal, river boats can take advantage of a well-timed passage across the Waddenzee which ideally involves locking out of Stevinsluis (Den Oever) at slack high water and taking the following tide through Visjagersgaatje and Malzwin channels to arrive at Den Helder HW+3. For Den Helder arrival details see port entry under Noordhollandsch Kanaal.

For navigation on the IJsselmeer use *Dutch chart folio 1810* and for canal navigation and details of connecting waterways use *ANWB charts G & F. 1810.2* covers the Noordzeekanaal from IJmuiden to the Oranjesluizen.

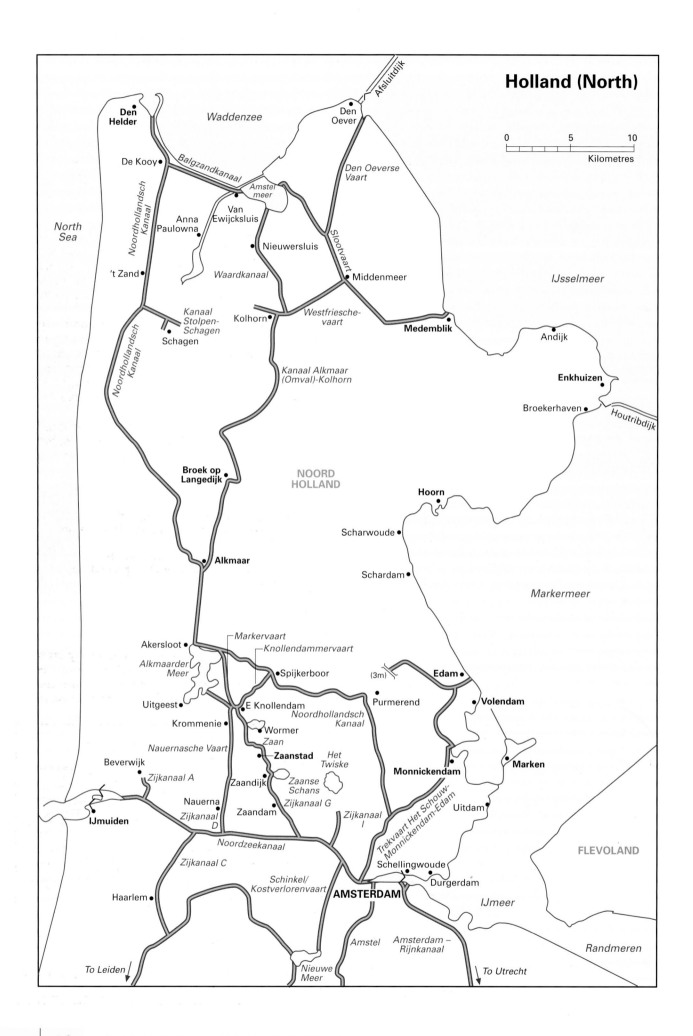

Holland (North)

Afsluitdijk

Den Helder

Waddenzee

Den Oever

De Kooy

Balgzandkanaal

Den Oeverse Vaart

Amstel meer

North Sea

Noordhollandsch Kanaal

Anna Paulowna

Van Ewijcksluis

Nieuwersluis

Slootvaart

'Zand

Waardkanaal

Middenmeer

IJsselmeer

Kanaal Stolpen-Schagen

Kolhorn

Westfriesche-vaart

Schagen

Medemblik

Andijk

Kanaal Alkmaar (Omval)-Kolhorn

Enkhuizen

Broekerhaven

Houtribdijk

Broek op Langedijk

NOORD HOLLAND

Hoorn

Scharwoude

Alkmaar

Schardam

Markermeer

Akersloot

Markervaart

Knollendammervaart

Alkmaarder Meer

Spijkerboor

(3m)

Edam

Uitgeest

E Knollendam

Noordhollandsch Kanaal

Purmerend

Volendam

Krommenie

Wormer

Zaan

Zaanstad

Het Twiske

Nauernasche Vaart

Monnickendam

Marken

Beverwijk

Zijkanaal A

Zaandijk

Zaanse Schans

Zijkanaal G

Zijkanaal I

Uitdam

Nauerna

Zaandam

Trekvaart Het Schouw-Monnickendam-Edam

IJmuiden

Zijkanaal D

Noordzeekanaal

Schellingwoude

FLEVOLAND

Zijkanaal C

Schinkel/Kostverlorenvaart

Durgerdam

Haarlem

AMSTERDAM

IJmeer

Amstel

Amsterdam – Rijnkanaal

Randmeren

To Leiden

Nieuwe Meer

To Utrecht

0   5   10
Kilometres

IJmuiden harbour complex

IJmuiden (meaning IJ mouth and pronounced 'I-mouw-der') forms an important coastal harbour and also ranks as the country's biggest fishing port and the seventh largest in Western Europe. Vesssels entering or leaving the port, or navigating within it, should seek clearance on VHF 61. The huge lock complex can accommodate ships up to 400m long, but leisure boats normally use the Kleine Sluis which is the most southerly of the four. Even this is a large lock basin and the process can take some time, with normally only one locking in each direction each hour. The customs and immigration office is situated near the leisure boat waiting pontoon, on the south side of the lock complex. Skippers arriving from the UK should report here with their *Schengen* forms, although visitors stopping at Seaport marina (see below) can fulfil obligations with forms and a posting box available in their reception. Don't forget when looking up IJmuiden in Dutch books that 'IJ' is a single letter which follows Y in the alphabet.

Locks Kleine Sluis and opening bridge (min 6m when closed) operates 24 hours. VHF 22.

IJMUIDEN

Where to stop

Seaport Marina is the first entrance to starboard as you enter the outer harbour, beyond the second set of pier head lights. Navigate carefully between the red and green buoys and do not turn too soon. This is a convenient landing point for boats crossing from the UK or coasting from the south and is accessible at all tides. The fuel berth and reception pontoon are to starboard as you enter or you can call for a berth on VHF 74, which is manned 24 hours. Mooring is in boxes with very short finger pontoons so be ready with ropes on both sides forward and aft, and a long

boat hook. Electricity is included but water is metered at €0.50/100ltrs. The marina also offers wi-fi internet, paid for by cards available at the harbour office. The pontoons are protected by security gates and out of office hours you can get an access card by paying your berthing fees at the ticket machine in reception which accepts €10 and €20 notes and gives change. There is a good range of facilities on site including supermarket, launderette, boat engineers, café-bars, and yacht club restaurant. The town itself is a 20-minute cycle ride away; bikes can be hired from the harbour office or there is a regular bus service.

There is an alternative small mooring pontoon east of the sea locks which is nearer to the town, but facilities are very limited and it is mainly used by large charter yachts.

Facilities Ashore

Fuel At Seaport Marina (cards accepted)
Chandlers Hermans Marine has a small onsite store and a megastore nearby
Repairs & Servicing Terlouw Repair is onsite
Supermarket & Shops Small onsite supermarket is open during the season
ATMs Available onsite
Cycle hire From harbour office

What to see

Just over the dune a popular beach is served by cafés and bars, and its visitors, along with those of the onsite hotel and holiday apartments share the selection of leisure facilities. If you happen to be in

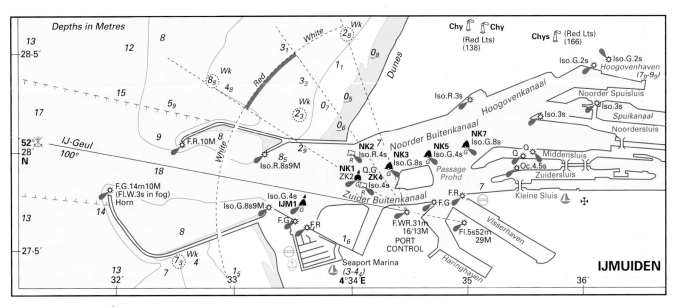

The well-serviced Marina Seaport has all necessities close at hand

port on the first Sunday of a month other than July or August, you might like to take the conducted tour to Fort Island, which lies in the middle of the inner harbour. Built on the northern bank of the canal in the 1880s, it only became an island with the construction of the huge new Noordersluis in 1930. The trip boat leaves from the Kop van de Haven restaurant, on Sluisplein, at 1200 and 1400.

Restaurant tip

The yacht club bar, The Dutch Admirals is a convenient watering hole and serves a very acceptable range of traditional Dutch fare. Its terrace bar has a relaxed ambience and a view of the harbour entrance.

Connections

DFDS ferry to Newcastle and fast hydrofoil to Amsterdam. Regular bus service to Amsterdam and Haarlem.

IJmuiden harbour complex from the east; the yacht lock is on the left with Seaport Marina beyond   *Patrick Roach*

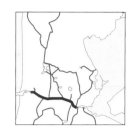

Noordzeekanaal

The Noordzeekanaal runs from the sea locks at IJmuiden to Amsterdam. It is heavily used by seagoing vessels of up to 80,000 tonnes, some of which travel at high speeds. Leisure vessels should keep to the starboard side of the channel and maintain a very sharp lookout behind them for the hydrofoil ferry, which travels at between 60–70km/h. Yachts are permitted to use their sails but not to tack. The ferry crossing at Central Station marks the end of the canal, where the waterway changes its name to the Afgesloten IJ (Locked IJ). Keep a listening watch on VHF 3 from the locks to the Afrikahaven (km 11.2) and then VHF 68 to Amsterdam.

Length 24km
Speed limit 18km/h for vessels of <4m draught
Locks Kleine Sluis (at IJmuiden) and opening bridge (min 6m when closed) operates 24 hours, VHF 22.

Several *Zijkanaals* (meaning side canal and pronounced 'zi-kanaal'), named A, B, C etc from the seaward end, open off the waterway, some of which lead onto longer waterways and some of which are just short spurs. There are yacht harbours in several of these side canals which may offer alternative berths to those at IJmuiden or Amsterdam. From west to east these are firstly, in Zijkanaal A, municipal moorings at Beverwijk. This is mainly a commercial harbour for smaller ships, but if you follow the canal to port and go beyond the loading docks the restaurant and party ship, 't Schip has some moorings nearby. Call the harbourmaster 'Havendienst Beverwijk' on VHF 71 to report and request a berth. No toilets or showers. If you arrived at the weekend you could visit the 3000 stall 'black market', the Beverwijkse Bazaar and even dance salsa on 't Schip.

Continuing east Zijkanaal C on the south side is home to a large and well-equipped harbour at WV IJmond, which is described in Chapter 3: South Holland. Slightly further east Zijkanaal D is on the north side and (as this continues as a waterway into Noord-Holland) it is described in its own

section below under Nauernasche Vaart & Zijkanaal D. The next turning of interest is also on the north bank, Zijkanaal G, and again as this leads onto a connecting waterway it is described in its own section below under Zaan & Zijkanaal G. Zijkanaal H runs alongside an open lake area, the IJ-plas, and is only navigable for a short distance before low bridges restrict headroom to 1m. At the junction with the Noordzeekanaal though, lies the large and potentially useful moorings of yacht club WV Bruynzeel, which are much cheaper than Seaport Marina. Fixed pontoons are protected from wash by a fixed wave break and basic facilities are available. Further east again, also on the north bank, is the entrance to Zijkanaal I where a further small yacht harbour, JH d'Anckerplaets, has limited space for visitors with basic facilities. A neighbouring boat yard specialises in multi-hulls.

Details of the waterway and harbours east of Zijkanaal I are described below under Amsterdam.

Look out behind for the fast ferry which plys regularly along the canal

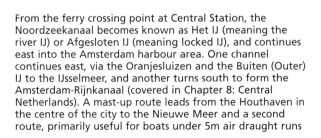

Amsterdam canals

From the ferry crossing point at Central Station, the Noordzeekanaal becomes known as Het IJ (meaning the river IJ) or Afgesloten IJ (meaning locked IJ), and continues east into the Amsterdam harbour area. One channel continues east, via the Oranjesluizen and the Buiten (Outer) IJ to the IJsselmeer, and another turns south to form the Amsterdam-Rijnkanaal (covered in Chapter 8: Central Netherlands). A mast-up route leads from the Houthaven in the centre of the city to the Nieuwe Meer and a second route, primarily useful for boats under 5m air draught runs

south through the Oosterdok to the Amstel, but the rest of the central canals are restricted to air draught of less than 3.5m. A toll is payable when entering the Amsterdam canals as described later. Fuel is available from a bunker boat in the mouth of the Amsterdam-Rijnkanaal.

Speed limit 14km/h for vessels 20–50m² (length x beam). (Temporary restriction to 12km/h likely until 2009 whilst construction work is in progress.)
Locks Oranjesluizen operate 24 hours, VHF 18.

Afgesloten IJ, the Oranjesluizen and the Amsterdam-Rijnkanaal

The lock complex lies just east of Amsterdam and connects the Amsterdam canals with the IJsselmeer. Leisure vessels proceeding towards the Oranjesluizen must use the separate buoyed leisure channels marked outside the main channel (minimum depth of 2.6m) and this is strictly enforced by the water police. Skippers should listen out on VHF 68 to the west of green buoy IJ11, and on VHF 60 to the east thereafter. West of the lock a turning to the south leads to the Amsterdam-Rijnkanaal via the Nieuwe Diep with fixed bridges (minimum 9m).

Leisure boats normally use the most northerly lock of the three in the Oranjesluizen complex; there are clear Sport signs and waiting pontoons provided. Lock entry and access is controlled by traffic lights and instructions are sometimes given over the loudspeakers. The locks operate 24 hours and skippers are advised to listen on VHF 18 but it is not necessary to call.

Houthaven to the Nieuwe Meer (otherwise known as the 'night convoy' route)

This route via the Schinkel (also called the Kostverlorenvaart) has 14 opening bridges of which rail bridges at either end (min 6m when closed) open only at night. The route is suitable for vessels with less than 6m air draught during the day, but is primarily used by yachts traversing in convoy at night and forms the most westerly passage south through Amsterdam. The convoys do not operate in poor visibility, in wind strengths above F9 or on Sundays.

The entrance to the Houthaven lies roughly opposite Zijkanaal I (west of Central Station) on the south bank of the Noordzeekanaal, and its southern end is called the Oude Houthaven. In the southwest corner of the Oude Houthaven [C, see plan], the Westkeersluis lifting bridge forms the entrance to this route. A toll is payable for

Moor at the Westkeersluis bridge to pay transit tolls for the canal passage

passage through the canal and skippers should report to the bridge control office to pay the transit dues; for the night convoy this should be by midnight at the latest. Vessels can pass through the first bridge to await the rail bridge during the evening. The rail bridge over the Westerkanaal (the first south of the lock) can open from 0100 but normally opens later at 0225. Check with the bridge operator for details. The northbound convoy has priority at the Westerkanaal bridge. The remaining bridges open as needed and the convoy takes 1.5 to 2 hours. From the other direction, the northbound convoy starts at the east end of the Nieuwe Meer [C]; skippers must report to the Nieuwe Meersluis lock office (on foot) by 2300 to pay for the transit. The first opening of the rail bridge over the Nieuwe Meersluis is at 2352 for 5 minutes. The rail bridges open only once for each convoy.

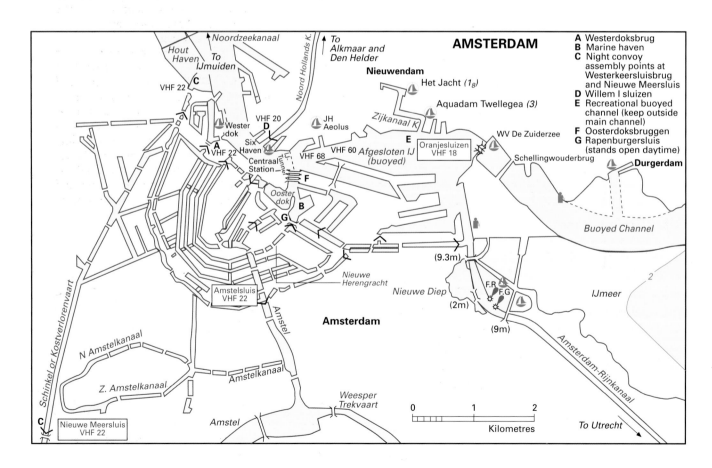

Map labels:

Noordzeekanaal
Hout Haven
To IJmuiden
To Alkmaar and Den Helder
Noord Hollands K.
AMSTERDAM
Nieuwendam
Het Jacht (1₈)
VHF 22
C
Aquadam Twellegea (3)
Wester dok
VHF 20
D
JH Aeolus
Zijkanaal K
A
VHF 22
Six Haven
Centraal Station
VHF 68
VHF 60 Afgesloten IJ (buoyed)
E
WV De Zuiderzee
Oranjesluizen VHF 18
Schellingwouderbrug
Durgerdam
F
Ooster dok
B
G
Buoyed Channel
2
(9.3m)
Nieuwe Herengracht
Nieuwe Diep
IJmeer
Amstelsluis VHF 22
Amstel
F.R
F.G
Amsterdam
(2m)
(9m)
Amsterdam-Rijnkanaal
N Amstelkanaal
Schinkel or Kostverlorenvaart
Z. Amstelkanaal
Amstelkanaal
Weesper Trekvaart
0   1   2
Kilometres
To Utrecht
C
Nieuwe Meersluis VHF 22
Amstel

A Westerdoksbrug
B Marine haven
C Night convoy assembly points at Westerkeersluisbrug and Nieuwe Meersluis
D Willem I sluizen
E Recreational buoyed channel (keep outside main channel)
F Oosterdoksbruggen
G Rapenburgersluis (stands open daytime)

Amsterdam from the northwest; Sixhaven and the Noordhollandsch Kanaal in the foreground with the Oosterdok bridges on the south side of Het IJ *Patrick Roach*

Bridges 14 opening. 12 road bridges operate throughout the day with rush hour breaks (0700–0900 and 1600–1800 during the week; or 0600–1000 and 1800–2200 weekends and holidays). Two rail bridges (min 6m when closed) open at night only. Toll payable. VHF 22.

Afgesloten IJ to the Amstel

The route from the IJ to the Amstel is via the Oosterdok and the Nieuwe Herengracht and is described in Chapter 3: South Holland with the section on the Amstel. Boats wishing to cruise the Amsterdam canals should be aware that harbour dues are payable and these can be paid at the offices at the Oosterdok, Amstelsluis, Westerkeesluis, or Nieuwe Meersluis.

AMSTERDAM

Where to stop

Most people choose the Sixhaven marina, opposite Central Station and to the east of the lock entrance to the Noordhollandsch Kanaal [D]. The harbour is protected from wash and convenient for the free 24-hour ferry to the city centre. It gets extremely busy in high season, when the harbourmaster will normally allocate you a berth by hailing or whistling from the pontoon. It is not possible to reserve berths and a space cannot be guaranteed. Boats are often rafted several deep and you need to be prepared to move to let others out. Electricity (6A) and water are free, and there are separate river water hoses (red) for boat-washing. There are showers, toilets, launderette and small yacht club bar. Subway construction is currently underway adjacent to the harbour which causes noise and dust, and work is planned to continue until 2009.

West of Sixhaven and Central Station, moorings known as the Spoorweghaven, formerly reputed to be insecure and susceptible to wash, are no longer recommended for leisure boats, but next door the entrance to the Westerdock leads to Aquadam Marina. The entrance is crossed by the Westerdok bridge which operates throughout the day except rush hour closures (0630–0930 and 1530–1830 during the week; or 0530–1030 and 1730–2230 weekends and holidays). The bridge is not manned and must be requested on VHF 22. This harbour is under new ownership and its approach to visitors is under review as we write. Its sheltered position and gated access could make it a convenient base on the city-side of the waterway. Water and electricity are available but no showers or toilets.

Alternatively a comfortable berth is just east of Sixhaven in WSV Aeolus. The entrance is next door to a lightly-used factory building marked 'Stork' and the fixed pontoons are protected by a wave break forming a narrow (8m) entrance. Mooring here is mainly in boxes (8–12 metre boats up to 4m beam) so you avoid some of the rafting and shuffling common in the Sixhaven. Three 15m by 4.5m boxes lie near the entrance and a bay to starboard allows rafting of craft up to 12/13m. Unmetered water and 4A electricity and friendly club house bar with usual

Sixhaven lies east of the Shell tower and the entrance to the Noordhollandsch Kanaal

facilities. This harbour is right next door to a large supermarket making it very convenient for stocking up with supplies and another free ferry to the city is a short walk away.

Further east in Zijkanaal K lie more harbours including Aquadam JH Twellegea with good servicing facilities and WV Het Jacht, which is a sister club to WSV Aeolus for 'overspills' by cooperative arrangement.

Facilities Ashore

Fuel Bunker boat in mouth of Amsterdam-Rijnkanaal
Chandlers Rien de Wolf on Distelweg
Repairs & Servicing JH Twellegea in Zijkanaal K
Nautical Bookshops Excellent selection at Datema and LJ Harri both on Prins Hendrikkade
Supermarket & Shops Dirk van den Broek supermarket is next door to WSV Aeolus or 15-minute walk from Sixhaven
ATMs At Dirk van den Broek and Central Station
Cycle hire At Central Station
VVV office Opposite main entrance to Central Station

What to see

As a lively cosmopolitan city with almost 24-hour nightlife, Amsterdam does not present its best side to those arriving via the Centraal Station; offering the tourist-crowded Damrak, restaurants with pictures of the food and the sex museum all within a stone's throw. This is the starting point for many of the water buses and canal tours, or you can very efficiently get round the city by buying a multi-use bus and tram ticket called a strippenkaart and hopping on one of the frequent services.

Gabled houses and boats of all sizes make a typical Amsterdam scene

NEMO is one of Amsterdam's many waterside attractions

Museums, markets and entertainment to suit all tastes are to be found. The Anne Frank House and the Dutch Resistance (Verzets) museum offer a moving insight into the war years, together with the National Monument on the Dam. The Scheepvaart museum covers nautical history and includes a full size replica of Dutch East Indiaman Amsterdam. Also on the waterfront the science and technology centre, NEMO, is filled with interactive exhibits and boasts a spectacular view from its roof. The Rijksmuseum and Het Rembrandthuis offer the works of some world-class Dutch masters, whilst the Heineken brewery tour offers a more hedonistic pleasure. If you want Holland to come to you, then you might like the Holland Experience 3D movie, on Waterlooplein next to Het Rembrandthuis. Between the National Monument and the Royal Palace on the Dam is an open square in which public music events and concerts often take place and the infamous Red Light District is centred around the Oude Kerk. After dark the buildings and bridges are beautifully illuminated, and for the best variety of gables in the world take a walk along one of the principal canals, the Herengracht, with the aid of a leaflet that describes the most famous facades and occupants.

Unlike many Dutch cities that have been designed using rectangular grids of roads, Amsterdam developed in a semi-circular shape around a series of concentric canals. The radial roads make it pedestrian and cycle-friendly and many locals use this mode of transport. Founded in 1270 where the mouth of the river Amstel flowed into the river IJ, the canals were added in the 17th century when trade was booming and the population soared. A great many houseboats and pleasure yachts line the banks of the canals and the traditional bridges are icons of this water-borne city.

Restaurant tip

Amsterdam caters for every taste and pocket but as a suggestion try Café Bern in the Nieuwmarkt whose secret recipe steak fondue at modest price attracts a keen following – but book ahead or arrive early.

Connections

International flights from Schiphol airport; train and bus hubs to all European cities via low cost and efficient service.

Nauernasche Vaart (& Zijkanaal D)

The most westerly of the canals heading north from the Noordzeekanaal is Zijkanaal D, which changes its name to the Nauernasche Vaart after the Nauerna lock. This waterway runs west of the Zaanstad conurbation and joins the Markervaart just north of Krommenie. A strong current can flow north of the Nauerna lock due to the outlet from the Duikersluis. This is a little used waterway other than for access to JH Nauerna, or from the north for visiting Krommenie, which is reflected in the limited opening times of some of the bridges.

Length 9km
Speed limit 9km/h
Locks Schermersluis and lifting bridge (at Nauerna) operate 0900-1630 with a break for lunch (1200-1300). Toll payable.
Bridges 6 opening. Nauernasche bridge operates throughout the day with a break for lunch at weekends only (1200-1300). Request service via intercom, VHF 20 or ☎ 075 681 6521. Toll payable.
Vrouwenverdriet, Rient Laan jr and Vaart bridges operate 0900-1630 with a break for lunch (1200-1300). Rient Laan jr and Vaart bridge must be requested via intercom or telephone (number as Nauernasche bridge).
Krommenie rail and road bridges operate 0900-1630 and open at H+15 and H+45 with a break for lunch (1200-1300).

Just south of the Nauerna lock, JH Nauerna lies on the west bank and offers extensive mooring opportunities and a wide range of facilities, within striking distance of both IJmuiden and Amsterdam.

KROMMENIE

Canalside moorings are available in Krommenie, north and south of the Vaart bridge and there is good shopping and a train station nearby. The high street is notable for some nice examples of typical Zaanse wooden buildings; richly decorated merchants houses and a so-called barn church, where services of a non-approved faith used to be held.

Zaan (& Zijkanaal G)

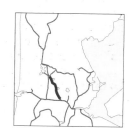

The next canal which leads into Noord-Holland from the Noordzeekanaal is Zijkanaal G, which changes its name to the Zaan after the Wilhelmina lock. This waterway runs north through Zaandam, Zaandijk and Koog aan de Zaan, known collectively as Zaanstad, and gives the best access to the attractions of this region. It links together two areas of open water and the width provides good sailing opportunities in between.

At its northern end the Zaan becomes the Tapsloot at Oost-Knollendam, which then connects with the Markervaart and the Nauernasche Vaart. The Knollendammervaart also branches off towards the northeast at this point to join the Noordhollandsch Kanaal at Spijkerboor. Several side canals join the waterway with lock access but these are restricted to air draught of less than 3.5m and so are not of interest here. Fuel is available from a bunker boat just inside the mouth of Zijkanaal G at its junction with the Noordzeekanaal.

Length 13km
Speed limit 12km/h except for bend north of Zaanbrug, 6km/h, and north of Prins Clausbrug, 9km/h
Locks Wilheminasluis and lifting bridge operates throughout the day, with a break for lunch at weekends only (1200–1300 Saturdays, 1200–1400 Sundays and holidays). VHF 20. Toll payable for lock and harbour passage (at office at north end of lock).
Bridges 8 opening: Dr J M den Uijl (7.1m when closed). Prinses Beatrix, Prins Bernhard, Prins Willem-Alexander and Coen (6.2m when closed) bridges operate the same hours as the Wilhelmina lock, VHF 20.
Zaan rail bridge operates throughout the day and opens at H+24 and H+58 although it normally stays open for 10–15

Lady Martina locking through the Wilhelminasluis with a pair of commercial barges

minutes if a train is not due. Tying up to wait for the rail bridge is difficult especially to the north, which is shallow on the east side.
Juliana, Zaan, Prins Claus (7.1m when closed) operate the same hours as the lock, VHF 18.

Make your own tour of the windmills at Zaanse Schans or take the *rondvaart* boat

ZAANSTAD

Where to stop

Immediately upon entering Zijkanaal G on the starboard side (opposite the bunker boat) is the Hierro boatcentre, providing rather austere moorings with adequate facilities and a boatyard next door. Good moorings are available south of Wilhelminasluis at WV De Remming in a large marina accessed by a self-service bridge. There are free 72-hours canalside moorings north of the lock on the west bank with coin-operated water and electricity. On the east bank south of Prins Bernard Bridge there are moorings for customers of the adjacent Dekamarkt supermarket. A further well-equipped yacht harbour is at WV De Onderlinge on the north bank of De Poel where there is a barge for visitors' reception and mooring or spaces in free boxes as available. Electricity is unmetered but water is from a single water berth so fill up on arrival or before leaving. This is a good place to stop for visiting the Zaanse Schans, but lies in an area of food manufacture and distribution and has an industrial outlook with developments going on around. In common with this entire area the air is pervaded with a smell of manufactured foods which can be quite sickly.

Around the corner and north of the Juliana bridge between the northernmost two windmills is a free 72-hour mooring for a single vessel with no facilities, right in the Zaanse Schans complex itself.

Further unserviced free moorings lie along the Zaan on the west bank near Z1 buoy (depth 1m), south and north of the Zaan bridge near to good local shops and the station, and north of Prins Claus bridge by the entrance to the Jisperveld De Poel. These are convenient for visits to the Zaandijk attractions which include a local museum and the Koog aan de Zaan windmill museum.

At the north end of the Zaan, where it widens out, there are several yacht harbours on the west bank offering good facilities for an overnight stop. Of these, JH 't Swaentje at the north end is distinguished by its attractive restaurant terrace.

Facilities Ashore

Fuel South of Den Uijl bridge
Repairs & Servicing Hierro boatcentre and others
Supermarket, Shops & ATMs Gedempte Gracht shopping street in Zaandam
Cycle hire At rail station in Zaandam

What to see

The Zaanstad area is a sprawling conurbation, combining some older settlements with extensive new development and is primarily a dormitory for people working in Amsterdam. It is however, an excellent shopping centre with many retail names familiar to English visitors. Zaandam no longer has a VVV office but retains an ANWB shop at the far end of the Gedempte Gracht shopping street which stocks digital and paper charts of the waterways. Of historical interest is the town's link with Czar Peter the Great, who lived here incognito in 1697 to pick up boat-building techniques from the local experts, soon dealt with by a visit to his statue and residence exhibition, which are linked together by pavement footsteps. North of here on the east bank the Zaanse Schans is a museum village consisting of traditional timber buildings which have been taken from the Zaan region and re-assembled to form a themed village. Within the complex is the Zaans Museum depicting the history of the Zaanstad region, working windmills, craft centre, clog-maker and museum of traditional dress.

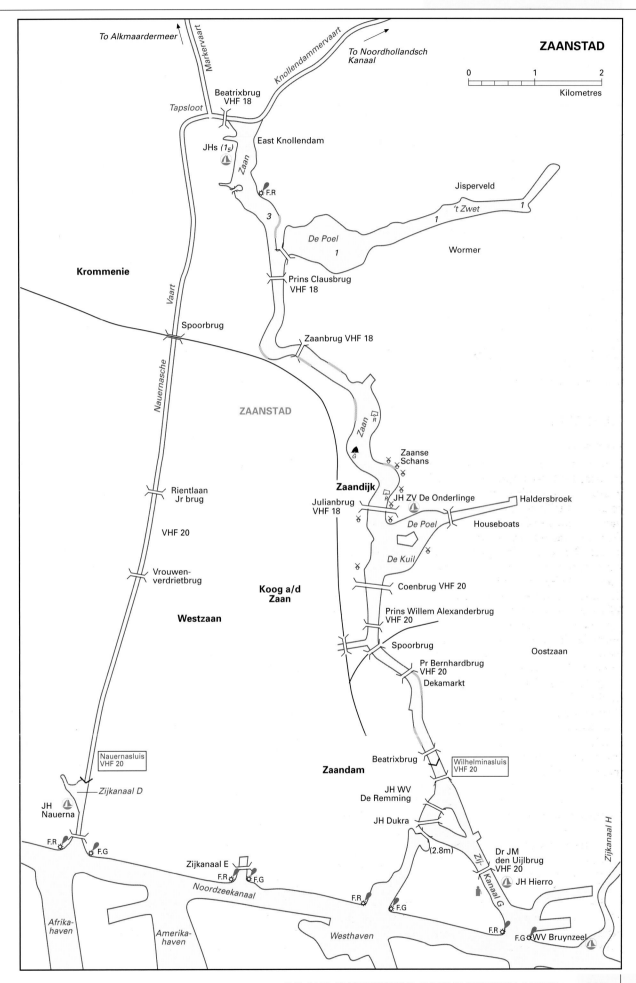

To Alkmaardermeer

Markervaart

Knollendammervaart

To Noordhollandsch Kanaal

ZAANSTAD

0   1   2
Kilometres

Beatrixbrug
VHF 18

Tapsloot

Zaan

East Knollendam

JHs (1.5)

F.R

Jisperveld

't Zwet

1   1

Wormer

De Poel

1

Krommenie

Vaart

Prins Clausbrug
VHF 18

Nauernasche

Spoorbrug

Zaanbrug VHF 18

ZAANSTAD

Zaan

R

G

Zaanse
Schans

Zaandijk

JH ZV De Onderlinge

Haldersbroek

Rientlaan
Jr brug

R

Julianbrug
VHF 18

De Poel

Houseboats

VHF 20

De Kuil

Vrouwen-
verdrietbrug

Koog a/d
Zaan

Coenbrug VHF 20

Westzaan

Prins Willem Alexanderbrug
VHF 20

Spoorbrug

Oostzaan

Pr Bernhardbrug
VHF 20

Dekamarkt

Nauernasluis
VHF 20

Beatrixbrug

Zijkanaal D

Zaandam

Wilhelminasluis
VHF 20

JH WV
De Remming

JH
Nauerna

JH Dukra

F.R

F.G

(2.8m)

Dr JM
den Uijlbrug
VHF 20

Zijkanaal E

Zij. Kanaal G

Zijkanaal H

JH Hierro

F.R

F.G

Noordzeekanaal

F.R

Afrika-
haven

Amerika-
haven

F.G

Westhaven

F.R

F.G   WV Bruynzeel

To see an example of the real thing, turn right out of WV De Onderlinge and cycle or walk past the factory buildings to the old village of Haldersbroek, situated on small dykes with limited car access. The 17th-century buildings are notable for their rustic construction, together with well-kept gardens, as a rural oasis surrounded by towering factories. Lining the canal on both sides east of the Haldersbroek bridge are hundreds of gaily painted traditional houseboats.

Restaurant tip

The Hoop op d'Swarte Walvis is very highly regarded restaurant with prices to match and lies within the Zaanse Schans complex with a single mooring place for customers. A more modest meal of traditional Dutch pancakes is available from Restaurant De Kraai near the Zaans Museum.

Connections

Train stations at Zaandam and Zaanstad are convenient for the moorings

Jisperveld

This area of lakes and channels connects the Zaan to the Noordhollandsch Kanaal, but a low bridge restricts air draught to 1.6m so for the purposes of this guide, only the lakes of De Poel and 't Zwet are navigable. Charted at only 1m depth and intended as a canoeing area, there are many shallow areas and the lake is only recommended for access to the two yacht harbours. A boatyard on the main navigation of the Zaan at this point offers servicing facilities including a 50-ton boat lift.

Lock Poelsluis and lifting bridge operate throughout the day with a break for lunch (1200–1300 Monday–Saturday, 1200–1400 Sundays and holidays)

Knollendam canals

The short Tapsloot channel connects the Nauernasche Vaart to the Knollendammervaart and the Zaan, and lies between West and Oost Knollendam. Halfway along, the Markervaart branches north, past Markenbinnen, to connect with the Alkmaardermeer via a turn to port into the Enge Stierop, and directly further north. As you turn into the Markervaart you leave the conurbations behind and head into typical Dutch countryside.

At the northeast end of the Knollendammervaart, the waterway joins the Noordhollandsch Kanaal at Spijkerboor This is also the junction with the Beemster ringvaart but this is not navigable to vessels with air draught of 2.5m or more. The Knollendammervaart is quiet and attractive, and lined with waterside properties. Its details are listed under Spijkerboor in the *ANWB Almanak 2*.

Speed limit Enge Stierop, 12km/h; Tapsloot and Markervaart, 9km/h; Knollerdammervaart, 6km/h
Bridges 2 opening. Beatrix bridge on the Tapsloot operates throughout the day with rush hour closures (0600–0800 and 1600–1800) and a break for lunch at weekends only (1200–1300 Saturdays, 1200–1400 Sundays and holidays). The bridge normally opens on the hour, at H+15, H+30 and H+45. The bridge will open for commercial vessels during rush hour closures and leisure boats may take advantage of these additional openings.
Spijkerboor lift bridge on the Knollerdammervaart operates throughout the day with a break for lunch (1300–1400)

No mooring is allowed along the Tapsloot or the Knollendammervaart.

The Knollendammervaart is lined with waterside properties at its junction with the Zaan

Alkmaardermeer

A large expanse of lake with several access points and a buoyed channel from north to south, the lake is reminiscent of a Norfolk Broad, but much bigger, and there is a large deep hole in the middle which drops to over 25 metres depth. Skippers are advised to follow the buoyage though, as areas outside the channels can be very shallow. A large area to the northeast is designated for water-skiing and small speed boats. In the northwest corner the buoyed channel leads to an opening that connects with the Noordhollandsch Kanaal. In the southwest corner at Uitgeest the Meldijk lock leads to the Assummervaart but this is restricted to air draught of 2m. Moorings also exist on islands in the meer; these are strictly speaking for members of a club, but other visitors are tolerated providing they don't cause problems.

Speed limit 12km/h

AKERSLOOT

Several lakeside harbours are clustered in the northwest corner of the meer at Akersloot. JH ARZV is the largest and has a fuel berth on the lakeside bank north of the harbour entrance. 't Hoorntje has less depth than some of the others and is mainly used by motor boats. Between WSVA and Jachtwerf Gebr. Verduin, substantial mooring stages with good depth at Laamens Jachthaven are serviced by the Café/Restaurant 't Kombuis, who do not advertise visitors' spaces but welcome them. Whichever harbour you choose in Akersloot, this a good place to eat especially if you choose their good value monthly set menu.

UITGEEST

Uitgeest is well-served with marinas on its southern bank as part of a modern waterside development, lacking the character of some of the other places. There is a popular lakeside swimming beach on the west bank north of the bridge and the village has good facilities, but the road noise from the nearby A9 can be a disturbance.

Sail away from it all on the open waters of the Alkmaardermeer

Noordhollandsch Kanaal

The Noordhollandsch Kanaal runs from Amsterdam to Den Helder and forms the main north-south route through this province. It is a major waterway of good depth and width, the northern section of which runs quite close to the coast, making it exposed in windy weather. The bridges include some unusual floating bridges to the north where the spans float sideways under the road. North of the Alkmaardermeer the canal runs through some lush pasture land and the avenue of poplar trees disperse noise from the road that runs alongside, but beware of cables belonging to the floating bridge at Akersloot, and a further one near the north end of the canal at Noorderhaven. Passage is not permitted whilst the flashing yellow light on the western ferry landing is lit. North of 't Zand the canal is a long straight drag with a busy road on one side and a row of wind turbines on the other, making its primary use the passage to Den Helder. Mooring along the canal is only permitted in the areas marked by boards, free for a maximum stay of 72 hours.

The canal is marked with kilometre posts, and at km 6 the Trekvaart van Het Schouw naar Monnickendam en Edam branches northeast. Passable by vessels with up to

3.6m air draught as far as Monnickendam, it provides alternative access or a through passage to the IJsselmeer (see details below). At Spijkerboor, there is a junction with the Knollendammervaart which runs southwest to East Knollendam (see details under Knollendam). At the northeast corner of the Alkmaardermeer there is a junction with the Markervaart, and at Akersloot there is open access to the Alkmaardermeer. Southeast of Alkmaar is the junction with the Kraspolderkanaal which continues northeast via Langedijk as the Kanaal Alkmaar (Omval)-Kolhorn; at Stolpen, the Kanaal Stolpen-Schagen is navigable as far as Schagen; and south of Den Helder at De Kooy, the Balgzandkanaal branches to the southeast to Van Ewijcksluis and the Amstelmeer.

Other connecting waterways are restricted to air draught of less than 3.5m and so are not detailed here. These include waterways north of Het Schouw leading to Het Twiske recreation area (1.9m); at Purmerend and at Spijkerboor, the Beemster ringvaart (2.4m); in Alkmaar, the Hoornse Vaart (2.8m); and at Groet, the Hargervaart (3.3m) and the Groote Sloot (1m). Also excluded, due to low air draught, is the Purmerringvaart which would otherwise link Edam with the Noordhollandsch Kanaal and forms the continuation of the Trekvaart Het-Schouw-Monnickendam-Edam, although the fixed bridge south of Edam is shown as opening on some maps.

Length 79km
Speed limit 9km/h
Maximum permitted draught 2.85m
Locks Willem I sluizen in Amsterdam operates throughout the day. Purmerend schutsluis and lifting bridge operates throughout the day with rush hour breaks on weekdays (0715–0815 and 1630–1730). VHF 20. Koopvaardersschutsluis in Den Helder operates 24 hours. VHF 22
Bridges 4 fixed (min 6.85m), 22 opening:
Gerben Wagenaar bridge (4.1m when closed) operates throughout the day with rush hour breaks on weekdays (0715–0900 and 1630–1815). Between 0700–0715 and 1615–1630 the bridge is only operated for southbound vessels. Operates from 0930 at weekends.
Meeuwenplein bridge (4.2m when closed) operates throughout the day with rush hour breaks on weekdays (0700–0900 and 1615–1815). Operates from 0930 at weekends.
Buiksloot bridge (4.15m when closed) operates throughout the day with rush hour breaks on weekdays (0700–0845 and 1615–1800). Operates from 0930 at weekends. Request via intercom or VHF 20.
IJsdoornlaan (4.75m when closed) operates throughout the day with rush hour breaks on weekdays (0715–0900 and 1630–1815). Between 0700–0715 and 1615–1630 the bridge is only operated for northbound vessels. Operates from 0930 at weekends.
Jan Blanken and the Purmerend rail (4.1m when closed) bridges operate throughout the day and open at H+10 and H+40.
Kogerpolder bridge (4.73m when closed) operates throughout the day with rush hour breaks on weekdays (0630–0910 and 1600–1830) when it opens twice on request for commercial vessels only (leisure vessels may take advantage of these additional openings if requested). Contact via intercom or VHF 20.
Leeghwater bridge (4.71m when closed) operates throughout the day with rush hour breaks on weekdays (0645–0900 and 1600–1800) when it opens only once VHF 20.
Friese bridge (3.8m when closed) operates throughout the day. During rush hour periods on weekdays (0700–0855 and 1600–1800) it opens at set 5 or 10 minutes intervals for any vessel. Ringers and Tesselse bridges operate throughout the day. For Friese to Koedijkervlot bridges call Post Tesselsebrug on VHF 20 or via intercom.
Alkmaar rail bridge operates throughout the day and opens at H+25 and H+55 (from 0925 at weekends). No VHF so ☎ 072 519 8557 if not seen.
Huiswaarder bridge (5.8m when closed) operates throughout the day with rush hour breaks (0720–0900 and 1630–1800) when it opens once only for any vessel.
Vlieland, Koedijkervlot, Schoorldammer, Burgervlot, St Maartens, Stolper and Vlot bridges operate throughout the day (from 0900 at weekends). For Schoorldam to De Kooy bridges request via push button or call Knooppunt De Kooy on VHF 20.
Koegras rail bridge opens throughout the day from 0752 at H+22 and H+52. Additional earlier opening times in *Almanak*. From 0852 at weekends. No VHF so ☎ 072 519 8557 if not seen.
Kooy bridge (8.2m when closed) operates throughout the day (from 0900 at weekends).

PURMEREND

There are free 72-hour canalside moorings on the Noordhollandsch Kanaal both sides of the Purmerend lock, or nearer to the town centre on the east side of the Beemster bridge. The town has an attractive old centre, and the weekly Tuesday market has its origins in the cattle market which had been held here for more than 500 years. Now the town has a good range of shops and facilities, with the small Purmerends Museum on the Kaasmarkt recording the history of the area. Next door, Museum Waterland presents exhibitions of contemporary art and design. From the moorings at Purmerend it is a pleasant cycle ride through the UNESCO listed Beemsterpolder to Middenbeemster, where two local history museums depict aspects of 18th and 19th-century life.

ALKMAAR

Where to stop

Municipal town centre visitors' moorings along the Bierkade with toilets, showers and launderette provided in the 17th-harbour office tower. Stop at the reception pontoon at the harbour office to be allocated a berth and take on water if necessary as

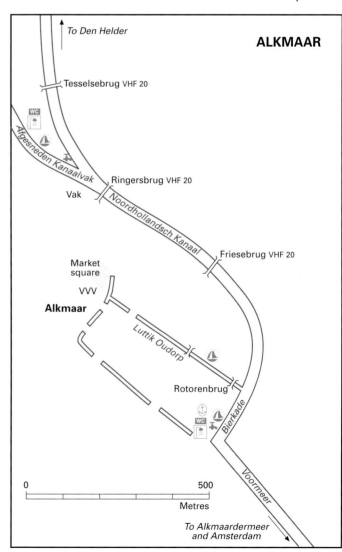

this is the only water point for the central moorings (€0.50/100ltrs). Turn to port under the Rotorenbrug (opened by arrangement with the HrMr) for more central berths along the Luttik Oudorp. The canal is quite narrow so is most suitable for boats under 13m in high season unless you can enter astern under close control, and a sill at the bridge restricts access here to 1.4m depth. For outgoing vessels the bridge opens Monday–Saturday only at 1000, 1200, 1400 and 1600 unless otherwise arranged.

Large and deep-draught boats moor south of the Bierkade in the Voormeer. Mooring boxes, for vessels under 10m, are situated in the Afgesneden Kanaalvak, north of Ringersbrug where a further water point is available. Electricity (16A) is available by coin meters in all moorings at €0.50/2kWh. The harbour staff speak good English, are very welcoming and have ample space for any number of summer visitors. Although cheese-market days in high season are obviously the busiest there is always space for everyone.

Facilities Ashore

Cheap Fuel By tanker at the moorings by arrangement (more than 150 ltr)

Extensive repairs, pump-out and small chandlers Jachtwerf Witsen at junction with Kraspolderkanaal has a large yard and slip facilities up to 300 tonnes.

Other Services Harbourmaster will give advice on a range of yacht services and spares suppliers who will visit.

Supermarket & Shops Aldi on Doelenveld, Albert Heijn across Ringersbrug or Super de Boer on Paardenmarkt

ATMs Nearest on Laat or Paternosterstraat and several others around town.

Cycle hire De Kraak on Verdronkenoord (also hires water-bikes) or at rail station

VVV office In De Waag at the end of Luttik Oudorp

What to see

Alkmaar (pronounced 'Alekmaar') has all of the things tourists look for in a Dutch town but its number one attraction is the famous cheese-market which is held every Friday from the start of April to the start of September, and is opened each week by a special guest. The festivities maintain a 600 year tradition although since 1945 the deals have been made only for show and the cheese returns to the factory after the market. The medieval town boasts some impressive architecture and a good way to tour the town is on the network of small canals, either by dinghy or on one of the frequent tripboats which depart from near the VVV on Waagplein. The tourist office also sells well-presented booklets describing (in English) walking and cycling tours in the town and surrounding area, and has a cheese museum upstairs. A highlight of the town tour is the network of narrow lanes near the Luttik Oudorp which are home to lots of individual and specialist shops. Take a break at one of the bars and restaurants which line the Waagplein or enjoy the extensive selection of shops along De Laat and Langestraat. A weekly market takes place on Saturdays until 1600 to complete the wide range of shopping facilities.

Also worth a visit are the National Beer museum and the contemporary regional museum. The former is situated in a 17th-century brewery near the Waagplein and includes samples of the exhibits and its own floating terrace. The Domestic Heating museum on Bierkade will probably have a less universal appeal. The town organises a full programme of outdoor events and concerts with annual highlights including the City Carnival (last week of August), Culinary Plaza (2nd weekend in September) and Jazz Festival (last weekend in September). Throughout the summer a series of outdoor music concerts are held on Canadaplein at weekends.

A pleasant day-trip can be made to the historic village of Bergen (5km), a popular residence for artists and writers and a long-standing resort area with substantial villas on tree-lined avenues. From here, a quiet and traditional beach lies just beyond the dunes. The Hoornse Vaart to the north of the old city is only navigable by craft of less than 2.6 m but is worth a cycle ride to see the chain of old windmills. You can take this route to make an outing to the fascinating floating vegetable market at Broek op Langedijk. See Kanaal Alkmaar (Omval)-Kolhorn for details.

Restaurant tip

The French style bistro De Koperen Pot will bring a menu to your boat if any of their seven tables are available that evening. If you are moored nearby and they are fully booked they have been known to bring plate service to your boat. There is a cheap day menu at De Bierbaron, next to the harbour office, or a very good pizza takeaway on the Bierkade called Pizza Sprint.

Connections

Train station to the northwest of the town offers a direct route to Amsterdam.

The cheeses are weighed in the age-old manner on the original scales

't ZAND

't Zand is a small stopping place along the canal just north of Stolpen where it runs close to the sea. This is just a short 3km walk or cycle ride from the popular Callantsoog beach resort, which is large enough to warrant a VVV office. A long visitors' moorings equipped just with rubbish bins is sited north of the Vlotbrug and pleasantly situated in a tree-lined setting. Mooring is free for a maximum stay of three days. Nearby is the Mandarin Wok Chinese restaurant and to the east of the canal, the large village itself, which is best visited during the second week of September for the Lily Show.

DEN HELDER

Where to stop

For vessels arriving from or leaving into the Waddenzee the Royal Marine Yacht Club (KMJC) in the Marinehaven Willemsoord is most convenient and has unmetered water and electricity. From the Noordhollandsch Kanaal this is accessed via the Koopvaardersschutsluis and the Vice-Adm. Moorman bridge. There is open access to the Waddenzee but vessels must clear movements with Traffic Control Den Helder on VHF 62 to avoid problems with the constant naval movements; from the west, when passing fairway buoys Molengat or Schulpengat; from the Waddenzee at about 4M from Den Helder (Texelstroom T8-T13, Malzwin M13-

Den Helder from the north; KMJC is in the left foreground with the Binnenhaven to the right of the photo

Patrick Roach

M14); when leaving the yacht harbour, prior to departure. Passage notes from Den Oever are mentioned in the introduction to this chapter. Remember that *Schengen* forms must be completed if this is your first port of entry.

For vessels arriving and returning via the Noordhollandschkanaal there are several yacht clubs in the Koopvaarders Binnenhaven that do not require passage through the lock. These are located on the starboard side (northeast bank) prior to the Van Kinsbergen bridge. Successively these are JH WSOV Breewijd, Marine WV, Panta Rhei ARZV and HWN. Recommended with three large hammerheads or boxes for visiting boats is Marine WV, where 6A electricity and water are unmetered. Access is by collective security gate and assistance out of hours can be sought from the duty bridge operator on the 3rd floor of the adjacent multi-storey harbour building. More spaces through the lifting Visser bridge are slightly nearer the town centre.

Lock Koopvaardersschutsluis and lifting bridge operates 24 hours.
Bridges Vice-Adm. Moorman and Visser bridges operate 24 hours with limited opening during morning, lunch and evening rush hours on weekdays. For exact times see *Almanak 2*, under Den Helder.

Facilities Ashore

Fuel At KMJC (cards accepted) and JH Den Helder
Chandlers Vaarshop van Kalsbeek on Zuidstraat
Repairs & Servicing Jachtwerf Den Helder
Supermarket & Shops None near the harbour but Albert Heijn on Julianaplein or Edah on Meeuwenstraat are both in the town centre
VVV office Bernhardplein

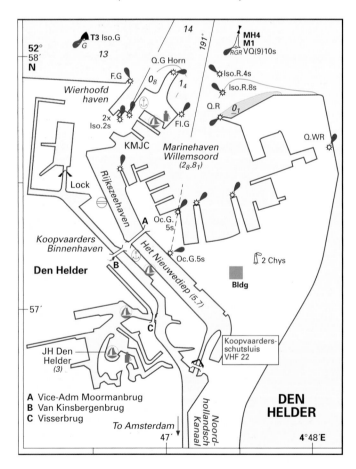

A Vice-Adm Moormanbrug
B Van Kinsbergenbrug
C Visserbrug

The Marine Museum includes a tour of a naval submarine

the small village of Huisduinen is now to be found and Napoleon built a fortress, Fort Kijkduin, here in 1811. After many years service as a lodging for soldiers it has found new life as a visitor attraction and, as well as a guided tour of the underground passageways, you can walk through the glass tunnel sea aquarium and see the North Sea from a very different angle.

Den Helder remains the main naval base of the Netherlands and most of the attractions follow a maritime theme. The Marine Museum offers the historical perspective, with a submarine and an ice-breaker amongst the vessels of interest to explore. Next door the Cape Holland attraction shares a site with the Dorus Rijkers rescue museum and offers well thought out entertainment for children as well as an informative overview of maritime rescue.

At the centre of the town some of the original star-shaped fortifications remain, although they are dominated by a modern and extensive shopping centre. Navy Days are held in July and amongst the town's attractions is a small beach.

What to see

Normally considered a refuge from the North Sea being sheltered from westerly winds, Den Helder also forms the northern terminus for those cruising the inland waterways in this region. The original settlement was sited on the North Sea coast where

Restaurant tip

Conveniently overlooking the yacht clubs and with an elevated terrace is the nautically-themed Neptunus bar/restaurant. Slightly expensive but provides a friendly welcome and a range of reading material of nautical interest. A good restaurant is also to be found at Fort Kijkduin.

Connections

Very popular, regular ferry service to Texel.

Trekvaart van Het Schouw naar Monnickendam en Edam

This waterway leaves the Noordhollandsch Kanaal at Het Schouw and runs via Broek in Waterland to Monnickendam. This forms the effective end of the navigation for the purposes of this guide as the onward section to Edam is restricted to an air draught of 3.2m, although in some guides this is shown as an opening bridge. It is a very attractive and pleasant cruise, and as you pass through the centre of Broek op Langedijk the waterway is lined with luxury houseboats. Remember that these are floating homes and mind your wash as the waterway is very narrow. The two bridges in the village are operated by one bridge-keeper so it is necessary to wait in the small space between them which can be difficult in windy weather. There is no mooring in Broek in Waterland except for some unsatisfactory places by the road between the two bridges, and there is no mooring allowed in the Havenrak. Arriving at Monnickendam via this route brings you into the inner berths of Marina Monnickendam. (See entry for under IJsselmeer for further details.)

Length 8km (Het Schouw–Monnickendam)
Speed limit 6km/h
Depth 1.3m
Locks Kloosterdijksluis operates throughout the day with a break for lunch (1300–1400). Grafelijkheidssluis and fixed bridge (3.6m) operates throughout the day. Both must be requested via pushbutton.
Bridges 1 fixed (min 3.9m), 3 opening. Broek in Waterland lift bridges (max 4.7m when open) operate 0900–1630. There are additional evening opening periods (1830–2000 on Fridays and 1830–1900 Monday–Thursday in high season) and they operate until 2000 at weekends. Monnickendam lift bridge (max 3.9m when open) operates 0900–1630 with additional evening opening periods (1630–1700 and 1800–2000 on Fridays; 1630–1700 and 1800–1900 Monday-Thursday in high season) and operates until 2000 at weekends.

Kanaal Alkmaar (Omval)-Kolhorn

North of Leeghwater bridge on the Noordhollandsch Kanaal, the Kanaal Alkmaar (Omval)-Kolhorn branches northeast. This is a combined name for three waterways which together form the route between Alkmaar and Kolhorn. These comprise the Kraspolderkanaal from Alkmaar to Huigendijk, the Langerdijkvaart, from Huigendijk to Oudkarspel, and the Niedorpervaart, from Oudkarspel to Kolhorn. The Hoornse Vaart/Huigenvaart which crosses the waterway after 2km has restricted air draught and is not covered by this guide. Red buoys mark the safe water along the southern stretch and these should be kept to the east as the direction of buoyage is from north to south. Free 72-hour canalside moorings are available in Noord-Scharwoude, 800m south of the Roskamsluis on west bank.

Speed limit 9km/h
Locks Roskamsluis operates throughout the day with a break for lunch (1300-1330 Monday to Friday, 1300-1400 weekends). Braaksluis operates throughout the day with a break for lunch (1300-1330).
Bridges 18 fixed (min 3.5m), opening. Kraspolder bridge operates throughout the day. Request on VHF 20. Heerhugowaard rail bridge (4.86m when open) is operated remotely throughout the day. 50m before the bridge in both directions there is an intercom on the right bank for communication.

BROEK OP LANGEDIJK

This small village on the edge of a larger development has its own municipal visitor harbour just north of the Horner bridge. There are recently renewed landing stages with toilets and showers

Broekerveiling auction clock installed as the height of modern technology in 1903

available, but no water or electricity. Alternatively, stop at Bijvoet Watersport on the west bank south of the bridge where the Volvo agent and small boat specialist also provides a number of moorings, serviced with water and electricity. (Toilets available but no showers.) Small shops are available near to the moorings and a supermarket is on Marktplein.

Whilst here you must visit the famous 'Broekerveiling' museum, a floating vegetable auction. Farms were situated on tiny islands in the adjacent lake and the auction building was designed so that boats could be brought straight in to save time-wasting loading and unloading. The adjacent Eetcafé Marktzicht has a popular waterside terrace with many customers also arriving by boat. Part of the museum visit is a whisper-boat trip through the 'thousand islands' but you can make your own visit by dinghy via the small lock next to the visitors' harbour during its limited opening hours. (Ask the harbourmaster at the lock or see Broek op Langedijk in *Almanak 2* for details).

NIEUWE NIEDORP AND WINKEL

Moorings are available at WV De Rijd in an old canal arm between Nieuwe and Oude Niedorp, and alongside the canal at Winkel. Niedorp is particularly known for Dahlia mosaic weekend when all the gardens are decorated with flower designs (3rd Sunday in September). A flower parade follows in Winkel the following weekend.

KOLHORN

At Kolhorn the municipal village yacht harbour is situated on the Kanaal Schagen-Kolhorn, just round the corner from the junction with this waterway. Its main feature is a very long visitors' pontoon that would amply provide the advertised 50 spaces for visitors. Easily accessible is the café/restaurant 't Anker, decorated with the internal décor of an English pub with an adjoining restaurant and covered terrace. Over the road the more upmarket Roode Leeuw provides another dining option. The small Museum De Turfschuur tells the history of the village from 1300 which began life as an anchovy-fishing port on the Zuiderzee before polderisation. The tiny village houses are notable for their separate gardens across the street and a popular Evening Market is held on the last Friday of June and two third Fridays after that.

Kanaal Stolpen-Schagen

This waterway runs east from its junction with the Noordhollandsch Kanaal at Stolpen and is navigable for the purposes of the guide as far as the town of Schagen. It passes through blooming bulb fields in the late Spring and is another bulb-growing region with visits and tours popular in April/May.

Length 4km
Speed limit 9km/h
Depth 2.5m
Bridges 2 opening. Stolperophaal and Zijper bridges operate throughout the day, VHF 20

SCHAGEN

WV Jan van Ketel has built a new marina in the Oude Industriehaven with modern pontoons and plenty of metered electricity and water points. Gated security covers most of the pontoons and it lies a short walk from the town in a commercial basin surrounded by small industrial units. New traffic controls are in place and efforts being made to improve its amenity. Opposite is the Automuseum Schagen, which specialises in VW Beetles and other historic vehicles.

The town boasts a good shopping centre and an attractive café-lined market square, with the nearby Slot Schagen housing the VVV. Best visited on a Thursday in the summer months for the special Westfriesche market when locals wear traditional dress, the church tower is open for panoramic views as are small museums in the castle towers, depicting the first world war Battle of the Somme and the impact of the second world war on the town. Under construction in 2006 was the Arc van Noah, which is a huge replica intended for launch and tours from

the area with its cargo of live animals on display. Museumboerderij Vreeburg is a restored farmhouse which has a permanent exhibition of 17th-century farm life open April-September on Wednesday to Sunday afternoons. On special market-days there are demonstrations of traditional crafts here.

The Battle of the Somme museum and the church tower are open for visits on Westfriesche market days

Wieringermeerpolder

The Wieringermeerpolder is crossed by a number of canals but for the purposes of this guide only two sections are navigable. These are the Westfriesche Vaart, from Kolhorn, via Middenmeer to Medemblik, and Den Oeversche Vaart and the Slootvaart, connecting Den Oever with the Amstelmeer. The others are restricted in air draught or navigable only by canoe.

Westfriesche Vaart

The Westfriesche Vaart completes a cross-country route from Alkmaar to the IJsselmeer and offers an alternative onward passage from Kolhorn, other than the Waardkanaal. Good moorings in Middenmeer with a range of facilities including pump-out.

Locks Westfriesesluis and lifting bridge near Kolhorn operates throughout the day with a break for lunch (1300–1330).
Overlekersluis with lifting and fixed bridges (5m) operates throughout the day Monday-Saturday with a break for lunch (1200–1300), but only morning and evenings on Sundays and holidays (0830–1030 and 1700–1900). Toll payable.
Westerhavensluis and lifting bridge in Medemblik operates throughout the day Monday-Saturday with a break for lunch (1200–1300), but only morning and evenings on Sundays and holidays (0900–1130 and 1600–1800). Toll payable.

Bridges 3 fixed (min 5m including Overlekersluis bridge), 2 opening. Alkmaarse bridge operates throughout the day Monday-Saturday with a break for lunch (1300–1330), but only mornings and evenings on Sundays and holidays (0900–1100 and 1600–1800). Kwikkels bridge in Medemblik harbour operates throughout the day with a break for lunch (1200–1300). VHF 9.

Slootvaart

The Slootvaart links Middenmeer with the Amstelmeer and connects to the onward route via the Balgzandkanaal to Den Helder. A former drainage dike, the waterway has high banks lined with reeds.

Length 9km
Locks Slootsluis and lifting bridge operates throughout the day Monday-Friday with a break for lunch (1300–1330) but only briefly at weekends (Saturday 0900–1100 and 1500–1700; Sunday 0900–1000 and 1600–1700).

Haukessluis and fixed bridge (5.6m) on Slootvaart operates briefly morning and afternoon only (1000–1100 and 1430–1530). Toll payable.
Bridges 1 fixed (Haukessluis bridge), 1 opening. Schager bridge operates throughout the day Monday–Saturday with a break for lunch (1300–1330) but only briefly on Sundays (0900–1100 and 1600–1800).

Den Oeverse Vaart

This waterway links Den Oever with the Slootvaart at Slootdorp. The northern section passes through the attractive Robbenoord woods.

Length 14km
Locks Stontelersluis and fixed bridge (3.8m) at Den Oever operates briefly morning and afternoon only (0830–0930 and 1600–1700). Toll payable.
Bridges 8 fixed (min 3.8 including Stontelersluis bridge)

Waardkanaal

The Waardkanaal forms an attractive waterway between Kolhorn and the Amstelmeer and, together with the Kanaal Alkmaar (Omval)-Kolhorn and the Balgzandkanaal, offers an alternative north-south route, instead of the Noordhollandsch Kanaal. The east bank is formed by the Wieringermeerpolder whilst the west bank is the old coast of the Zuiderzee. Green markers mark the safe water and should be kept to the west as the direction of buoyage is north to south.

Length 9km
Depth 3.6m
Speed limit 9km/h
Lock Ulkesluis flood lock normally stands open. For details of lifting bridge, see below.
Bridges 3 opening. Waard bridge at Kolhorn operates throughout the day Monday-Saturday with a break for lunch (1300-1330). Closed Sundays. Ring bell for service. Nieuwesluis and Ulkesluis bridges operate throughout the day Monday-Saturday with a break for lunch (1230-1300). Ring bell at Ulkesluis bridge for service.

One kilometre south of the Amstelmeer is the tiny rural settlement of Nieuwesluis where JH Nieuwesluis is situated on the south bank of the Pishoek, once an inlet on the coast of the Zuiderzee whose name originates from the drainage of water from the land. Lined with local boats and with just

two spaces for visitors this quiet location deep in the country has all the basic facilities but no amenities in the local village. A quiet retreat with fascinating rustic scenes, harvesting flowers in the season and tending goats, ponies and all manner of livestock at other times.

Tending the bulb fields at Nieuwesluis

Amstelmeer

A former coastal inlet and now a tideless lake, access from the northwest is via the Balgzand lifting bridge, from the east via the Haukessluis and from the south via the Ulkesluis, a flood lock which normally stands open. Channels of good depth connect the Balgzandkanaal, the Haukessluis and the Waardkanaal to the deep water in the middle of the lake and spar buoys mark the 1.5m depth

contour from May to November. Moorings at Van Ewijcksluis (see below), at WV Amstelmeer in the Haukeshaven and (very limited) at JH Amsteldiep.

Speed limit 12km/h

Balgzandkanaal

This completely straight section connects the Noordhollandsch kanaal at De Kooy with the Amstelmeer at Van Ewijcksluis. It is almost totally featureless and would be best avoided unless you wanted to take the alternative route south via the Waardkanaal. No moorings.

Length 6km
Speed limit 9km/h
Lock Kooysluis and lifting bridge operates throughout the day (except 0715–0800 and 1600–1645 Monday–Friday). VHF 20.
Bridge 1 opening. Balgzand bridge is operated remotely from the Kooysluis and works the same hours. Ring bell for service or call De Kooy, VHF 20.

Ewijcksluis, Van & the Van Ewijcksvaart

This winding waterway links the Amstelmeer with the Kanaal Stolpen-Schagen but is only navigable for the purposes of this guide as far as the Oude sluis south of Anna Paulowna, where a fixed bridge restricts headroom to 2.6m.

Length 4km
Speed limit 9km/h
Lock Van Ewijcksluis stands open
Bridges 2 opening: Van Ewijcksluis and Anna Paulowna bridges operate throughout the day with a break for lunch (1200-1300) and opens on the hour and at H+30.

VAN EWIJCKSLUIS

Van Ewijcksluis is a tiny village with moorings available at JH Anna Paulowna on the Van Ewijcksvaart, which has a long visitors' pontoon on the frontage. A single restaurant next to the lock, Vissers Tavern De Brug is the only amenity in the settlement, which forms a picturesque and sheltered refuge on an otherwise flat and featureless landscape.

ANNA PAULOWNA

The polder village of Anna Paulowna is named after the Russian princess who married Prins Willem in 1816. Moorings with basic facilities at WV Anna Paulowna which is south of the bridge on the east bank of the Hoge Oude Veer. A short walk back to the bridge finds the village the other side, where there is a popular local eetcafé, Café Ben. This is a small town populated mainly by bulb-field workers which comes to life during the first weekend in May when everything from bridges to streetlamps are bedecked with flowers.

Anna Paulowna polder is bulb country

IJsselmeer & Markermeer (West coast)

This section describes the harbours on the west coast of the IJsselmeer, including the section south of the Houtribdijk which is alternatively known as the Markermeer. These towns are part of the province of Noord-Holland and many have navigable links to the canals which cross this area.

The IJsselmeer is effectively an inland sea which was created in 1932 by the building of the 16-mile long Afsluitdijk (Barrier Dam) at the entrance to what was then known as the Zuiderzee. The outflow from the River IJssel led to its desalination and it now provides the area's water supply, as well as preventing flooding. The formation of a huge area for sheltered inland cruising is a happy coincidence and makes the whole area a popular watersports centre.

However, do not take the calmness of this inland water for granted. The fresh water outflow can create 1-1.5 knots of current, and when opposed to a northwesterly wind (especially Force 5 and above) it can develop into a short sharp sea. An onshore wind can create a significant swell, despite the relatively short fetch, creating an uncomfortable beam sea when cruising along one of the eastern coasts.

Buiten IJ

Access from Amsterdam is via the huge Oranjesluizen complex on the east side of the city, which provides a dedicated lock for leisure boats that operates throughout the day. Once through the lock, the Schellingwouderbrug presents little obstacle with 8m clearance under the fixed span, or three opening times per hour for yachts. The channel that runs east from the lock to the open water of the IJsselmeer is called the Buiten IJ (Outer IJ) and the regulations for busy commercial waterways apply here, i.e. keep to the starboard side of the channel, have a motor ready capable of making a minimum of 6 km/h and make use of radar in poor visibility if possible. Cheap fuel is available from the *Hollandia* bunker boat just east of the bridge by P27 green buoy. (Closed 1500–1600 and Sundays.)

Speed limit In the channels and near the shores, 20km/h; otherwise, no limit
Locks Oranjesluizen (to/from Amsterdam) operates 24 hours. Listen on VHF 18 but it is not necessary to call. Naviduct and Krabbersgatsluizen (at Enkhuizen) operates 24 hours Call Naviduct-Zuidzijde (from the south) or Naviduct-Noordzijde (from the north), VHF 22.
Stevinsluis and opening bridge (at Den Oever) operate 24 hours. Call Sluis Den Oever, VHF 20.
Bridges Schellingwouderbrug (8m when closed) operates 24 hours except for rush hour closures on weekdays (0700-0900 and 1600-1800) and opens on the hour, at H+20 and H+40.

Between the Oranjesluizen and the Schellingwouderbrug there are moorings at WSV Schellingwoude with water and electricity but no showers.

DURGERDAM

Further east at Durgerdam a reasonably sized linear harbour is accessed via a buoyed channel. The moorings of sailing club Het Y are the best equipped and these are the first you come to opposite the harbour entrance, with visitor berths hard to starboard and on the hammerhead. Services include unmetered electricity, water and wi-fi. The tiny village consists of different coloured houses with painted wooden gables and is the site of Fort Durgerdam, part of a 19th-century defence wall consisting of 42 fortresses around the capital city. A mobile shop visits on Tuesday, Thursday and Saturday and there is a single very acceptable bar-restaurant, De Oude Taverne. Snack-bar West Eind is open Wednesday to Sunday and serves breakast from 1000.

UITDAM

Continuing northeast along the coast, the next harbour is at Uitdam. The original fishing port lay in the southwest corner, but the large harbour is now given over to Camping-Jachthaven Uitdam and offers all facilities to the boating visitor although it is 6km from the village.

MARKEN

Where to stop

Approaching Marken you will notice it is connected to the mainland by a causeway to the south, and boats should pass well clear to the east of the Marken lighthouse to avoid the shallow water. Proceed northwest round the end of the mole into

BUITEN IJ

W.V.de Zuiderzee **Schellingwoude**
Oranjesluizen VHF 18
Schellingwouderbrug
Durgerdam
Buoyed channel
Tunnel
Buoyed
Buiten IJ
241° Buoyed Pampus Channel
Fl.R.5s
Work in progress
IJmeer
Nieuwe Diep
0   1000
Metres
Amsterdam-Rijnkanaal
Depths in Metres

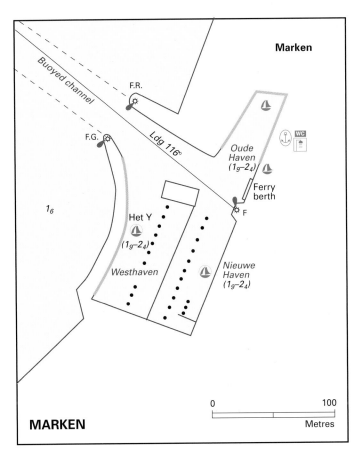

MARKEN

Traditional cottages huddle together on a *werf*

the Gouwzee where a buoyed channel avoids the thick weed marked on the chart as waterplanten. The channel forks in two with the left fork leading to Marken and the right fork to Monnickendam. Lit pierheads mark the narrow entrance, but look out for the regular ferryboat that plies between here and Volendam. Het Ÿ sailing club is based in the Westhaven, immediately opposite to starboard on entering. You can turn hard to starboard to moor alongside the harbour wall, close to the shell beach, or in an empty box and take advantage of unmetered water and electricity. Straight on the berths of WSV Marken are located in the Nieuwe and Oude Haven. The harbour office, toilets and showers are on the quay in the Oude Haven.

Facilities Ashore

Shops One small shop near the centre of the village
ATM Near the church

What to see

Formerly an island in the Zuiderzee, a causeway was built in 1957 to link Marken to the mainland. This has done little to alter the character of the place that is cherished for its olde-worlde charm. The situation would have been very different, however, if the planned Markerwaard polder had drained this entire area, incorporating the island into the new land mass. The causeway and northern mole were intended to form retaining dykes of the polder that would fill the area south of the Houtribdyke, with the Gouwzee remaining as an inland lake, but the

plan to drain the Maarkerwaardpolder was dropped after negative public reaction to the scheme.

Traditional cottages were built on artificial mounds, or *werfs*, to protect them from flooding, and on the limited higher ground seem to huddle together from the elements. Others around the harbour used stilts to avoid the ingress of the sea, although with the tides now tamed these under-houses have been walled in to provide additional accommodation. A cycle-path runs round the perimeter of the former island, providing fantastic views of the IJsselmeer and a close look at the *werfs*. At the eastern tip the lighthouse, Het Paard, is a famous landmark equally notable from land as from sea. The narrow promontory forms another narrow strip of shell beach, popular with bathers who all arrive by bike, enjoy the sun and eat ice-creams from the kiosk.

Marken from the southwest   *Patrick Roach*

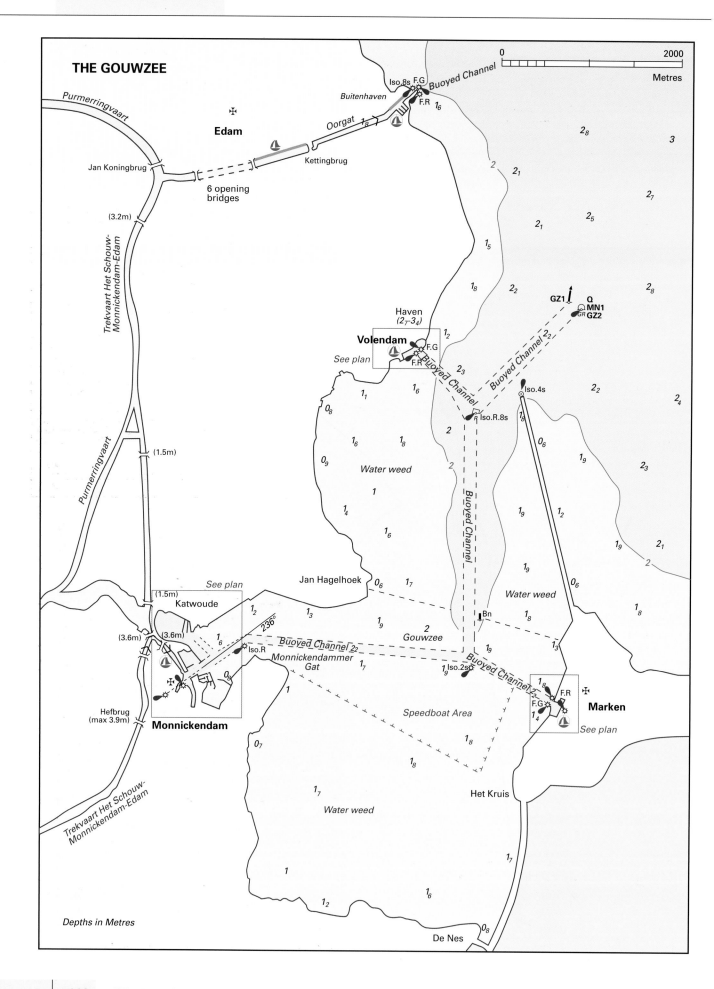

THE GOUWZEE

Purmerringvaart

Edam

Jan Koningbrug

(3.2m)

Trekvaart Het Schouw-Monnickendam-Edam

Oorgat 1₈

Buitenhaven

6 opening bridges

Kettingbrug

Iso.8s F.G

F.R 1₆

Buoyed Channel

2₈

3

2

2₁

2₇

2₁

2₅

1₅

1₈ 2₂

2₈

GZ1 Q MN1
GR GZ2

Haven
(2₇-3₄)

Volendam

See plan

F.G
F.R

Buoyed Channel

Buoyed Channel 2₂

1₂

1₆

2₃

2

R Iso.R.8s

Iso.4s

2₂

2₄

1₁

0₈

1₆

1₈

2

0₉

Water weed

1

0₆

1₉

2₃

Purmerringvaart

(1.5m)

1₄

1₆

2

1₉

1₂

1₉

Bn

2₁

(1.5m)

See plan

Katwoude

Jan Hagelhoek

0₆

1₇

1₉

2

Gouwzee

0₆

1₈

1₂

236°

1₃

Buoyed Channel 2₂

1₉ Iso.2s

Water weed

1₈

1₃

1₆

Iso.R

0₈

Monnickendammer
Gat

1₇

Buoyed Channel 2₂

F.R

F.G Marken

(3.6m)

(3.6m)

(3.6m)

1

Speedboat Area

1₄ See plan

Hefbrug
(max 3.9m)

Monnickendam

0₇

1₈

1₈

Trekvaart Het Schouw-
Monnickendam-Edam

1₇

Water weed

Het Kruis

1

1₇

1

1₂

1₆

Depths in Metres

0₈

De Nes

MONNICKENDAM

The harbour approach is clearly buoyed from the Gouwzee and there are several large harbours to choose from in addition to the municipal village centre moorings. De Zeilhoek is the first option to starboard and lies a little way from the town on the opposite side of a river inlet. Next, to port, comes the approach channel to Hemmeland, a yacht haven and camping site situated in an extensive parkland. Immediately beyond this is the entrance to JH Waterland, a large yacht charter base and harbour. Continuing towards the town, Marina Monnickendam lies to starboard with moorings both side of the harbour dyke. Fuel is available here. All four marinas have good facilities including wi-fi. If you continue straight on towards the Binnenhaven bridge there are municipal moorings by the harbour office; boats over 12m turn to port and there are alongside moorings to starboard in the Gemeentehaven. These are cheap moorings but with expensive metered electricity.

Access to the Trekvaart van Het Schouw naar Monnickendam en Edam (and on via the Noordhollands Kanaal to Amsterdam) is through the inner berths of Marina Monnickendam and the Grafelijkheidssluis and fixed bridge (3.6m). The lock operates throughout the day and there are push buttons both sides of the lock to request opening. See Trekvaart van Het Schouw naar Monnickendam en Edam for further details.

The route to Edam via the Purmerringvaart is restricted to 3.2m headroom.

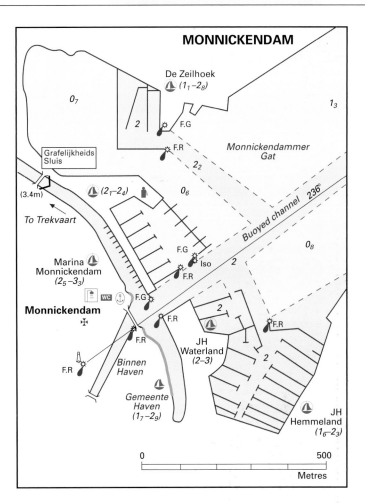

Facilities Ashore

Chandlers Hakvoort Watersport on Haringburgwal near Marina Monnickendam
Repairs & Servicing Good facilities at all marinas
Supermarket & Shops Selection of small shops on Zuidende
Cycle hire From JH Waterland or a shop on the Haven

Municipal harbour with small boat moorings and harbour office to starboard and moorings for larger boats to port

The old eel smoker on the quay at Monnickendam

What to see

Monnickendam is named after the Frisian monks who first built the dam and settled here in the 13th century. The main industry is eel-smoking, commemorated in statue form on the quay, with the produce available in several stalls around the town, including the excellent harbourside fishmongers. The Stadhuis is home to the local history museum and its clock tower is equipped with a 15th-century carillon from where every hour a procession of clockwork horsemen parade around the tower. Beyond the harbour office a selection of historic ships lie in the inner harbour.

Restaurant tip

De Waegh restaurant, housed in the 17th-century weigh building on Middendam (at the end of the Binnenhaven) is a popular choice.

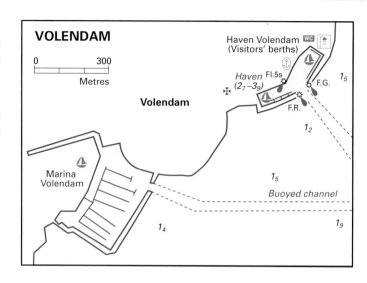

VOLENDAM

Where to stop

A buoyed channel leads into the harbour from just west of Marken's northern training wall. After dark line up the flashing white light on the fish auction building between the fixed red and green lights on the harbour moles. The small harbour is busy with fishing and trip-boats, but there is still room for visiting boats to raft up to the north of the entrance on the eastern and northern wall where water and electricity are available. Call the harbourmaster on VHF 71. Showers and toilets are provided on the quay and there are good facilities for servicing including a 50-ton boat hoist. A large new marina opened in April 2007 and offers all facilities including diesel, chandlers and servicing.

Facilities Ashore

Fuel and Chandlers At Marina Volendam
Repairs & Servicing Prins Scheepsreparaties on the haven
Supermarket & Shops Deen and other shops on Zeestraat

What to see

Volendam forms a joint municipality with Edam and is the most touristy of the Gouwzee ports, with many visitors arriving by coach from Amsterdam. The village is home to a form of traditional Dutch costume which is internationally recognisable, with the men in the loose trousers and short jackets once used by the fishermen and the women in the tight bodice and lace cap of the Dutch 'cheese girl'. For a permanent memento you can be photographed in costume at Fotoshop Volendam with or without their giant clog. Behind the dyke, something of the old atmosphere remains with traditional houses built on piles lining small waterways, which are crossed by hand-operated bridges. The original fish auction still sells fish on the quay and the Volendams Museum on Zeestraat displays traditional costumes, fishing equipment and more than a million cigarbands.

Volendam's busy quayside is lined with shops and cafés

The narrow entrance to Edam harbour, with short stay moorings to starboard

EDAM

Where to stop

The approach to Edam is narrow, but quite accessible, and once inside there is a lively holiday atmosphere, with Jachthaven Galgenveld on the port side and short-stay moorings to starboard next to a lakeside camp site. To reach the canal moorings close to the town centre in the Nieuwe Haven continue on through the small Zeesluis (L36m, W9.5m, D3.5m) which operates throughout the day with a break for lunch (1300–1400). Toll payable. Follow the Oorgat channel (depth 2m) and proceed under the Kettingbrug, a manually-operated bridge that opens

Edam harbour entrance from the west   *Patrick Roach*

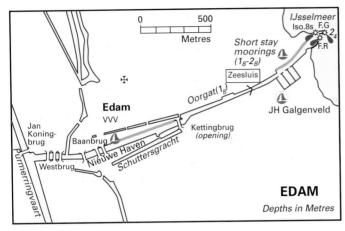

Edam

VVV

Jan Koning-brug

Baanbrug

Westbrug

Nieuwe Haven

Schuttersgracht

Kettingbrug (opening)

Purmerringvaart

Oorgat (1₈)

Zeesluis

Short stay moorings (1₈-2₈)

IJsselmeer Iso.8s F.G

F.R

JH Galgenveld

0   500

Metres

EDAM

Depths in Metres

on the half-hour in high season and on odd hours in April, May and September. There are moorings available all down the starboard side, with the only water and electricity from a single pod on the far end (16A, €0.50/2kWh). Unfortunately, this part is opposite a factory from where fork-lift trucks load lorries in the early morning and the area further back is quieter. Continuing on through the Baanbrug and five further opening bridges leads to the Purmerringvaart but this is restricted to 3m air draught.

Facilities Ashore

Repairs & Servicing Jachtscheepswerf Edam on the Oorgat

Supermarket & Shops Deen supermarket on William Pontstraat, south of the Nieuwe Haven, and selection of small shops around Damplein

ATMs Voorhaven & Jan Nieuwenhuizenplein

Cycle hire Ronald Schot on Grote Kerkstraat

VVV office Damplein

What to see

Edam is synonymous with cheese and the weekly market (every Wednesday in July and August) starts promptly at 1030. The traditional ceremony of the handclap bartering is used to agree a price between farmer and merchant and then the cheeses are taken to the scales in the weighing house. The festivities draw crowds of locals and tourists alike and a commentary is given in every necessary language for the benefit of the assembled throng. The need for the farmer's market died out in 1922 with the appearance of cheese factories, but its modern reincarnation seems to have an enduring appeal. On non-market days the Kaaswaag building houses an exhibition on cheese-making. The Damplein is the main square, overlooked by the Stadhuis and carillon tower, and here a 16th-century house contains the Edams Museum whose unique attraction is its floating cellar.

SCHARDAM

South of Hoorn in the bay area called the Hoornse Hop lies the small harbour of Schardam. It was formed as part of the outlet sluice for polder drainage and strong currents can run when sluicing is in operation. There is a short buoyed channel and fixed red and green lights marking the entrance. There are very limited facilities and no town nearby.

HOORN

Where to stop

The approach to the harbour is very straightforward with lit pierheads marking the main (west) entrance. Entry to the Buitenhaven is no longer permitted via the east entrance. To port and separated by Oostereiland, is Grashaven, home to the Stichting Jachthaven Hoorn — all conceivable facilities are available here including chandlers, supermarket and servicing. To starboard there is a sheltered anchorage in the Buitenhaven (harbour dues payable) and continuing on towards the Binnenhaven entrance there is a fuel berth to port. Leave the brown fleet mooring pontoon to port and you will see a second large marina to starboard in the Vluchthaven, home to WV Hoorn. Prices are slightly lower here, but they don't have the onsite shops like the Grashaven, although they do have a yacht club restaurant. Ahead the flood lock stands permanently open and leads inside to the town centre Binnenhaven (inner harbour), where there are visitors moorings on both sides. Those to starboard have the attractive wooded

Cheese bearers carry a batch to the weigh house

outlook, whilst those to port have the convenience of the sanitary facilities and the rest of the town closer at hand, as well as the free large water hose immediately opposite the binnenhaven entrance. Electricity is by chipknip or by arrangement with the harbourmaster.

Facilities Ashore

Fuel On Oosteiland, to port on entering the Buitenhaven

Chandlers, Repairs & Servicing Aqua Sport on Visserseiland in the Grashaven

Supermarket & Shops Supermarkts in the Grashaven, and on Kerkstaat with a large selection of shops in the town

ATMs On Veemarkt and others around town

Cycle hire Ruiters Rijwielshop, Stationsplein

VVV office Veemarkt

What to see

Hoorn started out in the 14th century as a settlement for merchants from Denmark and Germany and was granted town rights in 1356 by which time it already had a weigh house. The convenient natural harbour meant that Hoorn enjoyed a golden age in the seventeenth century when, as capital of West Friesland, it was home to one of the regional offices of the Dutch East Indies Company (VOC). To

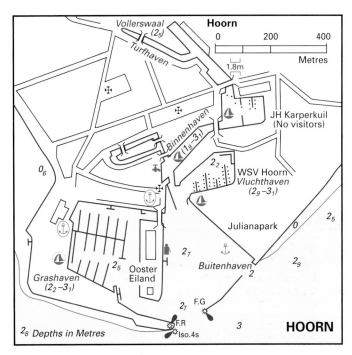

protect itself from potential invaders the town built four city gates as well as the pier tower (Hoofdtoren). This semicircular monument still stands watch over the harbour entrance although

Hoorn harbour from the north with the Binnenhaven in the foreground and the Grashaven to the right of the photo   *Patrick Roach*

Hoorn's Houten Hoofd tower stands watch over the Binnenhaven

now its occupants are customers of the popular fish restaurant of the same name. The similarity of the town's name with Cape Horn is no coincidence; it was local resident, Jan Pieterszoon Coen, who first rounded the southernmost tip of South America in 1616 and his statue stands in front of the weigh house. Now the home of the 'Brown Fleet' of sailing charter vessels, the three cabin boys of Bontekoe, heroes of a Dutch children's book, are immortalised in bronze on the quayside.

The town boasts a plethora of modern and historic attractions, with a comprehensive shopping centre and town centre supermarket supplemented by museums chronicling the history of the city. The Museum of the 20th century, housed in two former cheese warehouses on the old harbour, presents a nostalgic journey through time. As an adjunct to the rustic museum café, an audiovisual presentation and scale model tell the history of Hoorn and its significance through the ages. This includes the famous naval engagement in 1573, the Battle of the Zuiderzee, which took place just outside the harbour. The Westfries Museum on the Waagplein is an imposing building dating from 1632; the seven lions bear the coats of arms of local towns. Inside, as well as the structure of the building, archaeological

finds and the smell of cloves illustrate the town's history. A steam tram runs to Medemblik during the summer and from there you can continue by trip boat to Enkhuizen.

Restaurant tip

The Hoofdtoren restaurant is open every day for good quality Dutch specialities.

Connections

A train station to the north of the town centre connects with Enkhuizen, Medemblik and Amsterdam.

BROEKERHAVEN

The small harbour of Broekerhaven lies south of the Houtribdijk, but close to the town of Enkhuizen. A buoyed channel marks the approach from the Krabbersgat channel and after dark the white light on the bridge should be lined up between the red and green lights on the harbour piers. Only the buitenhaven (outer harbour) is accessible as a fixed bridge restricts access to the binnenhaven to 3.3m. Here, WSV De Broekerhaven offers spaces for visitors with a reasonable range of facilities.

ENKHUIZEN

Where to stop

From the south the approach to Enkhuizen is via the Krabbersgat naviduct, taking the starboard fork as you approach the lock complex. Follow the buoyed channel in a semi-circular arc to port, remembering that the direction of buoyage means that green buoys are to port. The lock operates 24 hours and can be called on Naviduct-Zuidzijde, VHF 22. (From the north, call Naviduct-Noordzijde.) On leaving the Naviduct lock continue to follow the channel with the green buoys to port and the red marks on the Krabbersgat wall to starboard.

Opposite the end is the lit entrance to the Buitenhaven, where you will find the municipal harbour – call on VHF 12 for a berth. To starboard in the Buitenhaven the Drommedaris lift bridge operates throughout the day and gives access to the most central canalside moorings in the Oude Haven, which are quieter than the large marinas and have water and electricity (€0.45/kw, 16A) available, both of which require an electronic V-shaped SEP-key, for which there is a deposit of €11.

Compagnieshaven, accessed further north along the Krabbersgat, is situated in a former harbour of the Dutch East Indies Company and was voted ANWB marina of the year in 2003. Every possible

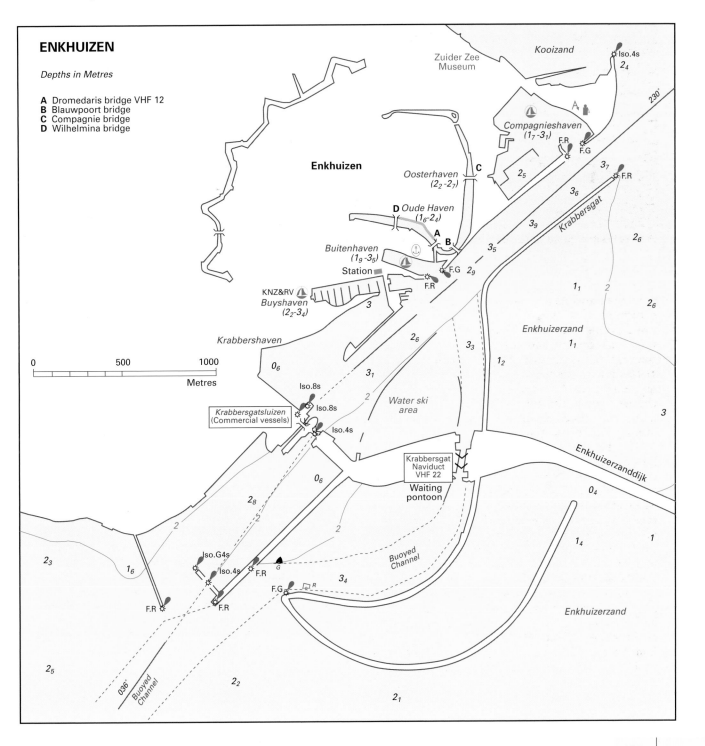

ENKHUIZEN

Depths in Metres

A Dromedaris bridge VHF 12
B Blaauwpoort bridge
C Compagnie bridge
D Wilhelmina bridge

The entrance to the Oude Haven is by the Drommedaris tower

facility is available here including wi-fi. This is the nearest marina to the Zuiderzee museum and still close to the town centre.

To the south, the Buyshaven is entered by going to port at the end of the initial buoyed Krabbersgat channel, crossing the approach to the commercial lock with care, and then going sharp to starboard into the Krabbershaven (reserved for charter vessels). This is home to the Enkhuizen base of the Royal Netherlands Sailing and Rowing Club (KNZ & RV, who have a second harbour at Muiden). Pontoons are on the south side, on the left as you enter; facilities are of a high standard, and include wi-fi. Both the Buyshaven and the Buitenhaven are very convenient for the station.

Facilities Ashore

Fuel, Chandlers, Repairs & Servicing Joosten
    Watersport in Compagnieshaven
Supermarket & Shops Supermarkets on Torenstraat
    and Clarrissenplaats. Good selection of shops in the
    town.
ATMs On Venedie Melkmarkt & Westerstraat
Cycle hire Dekkers Tweewielers, Nieuwstraat
VVV office Opposite rail station

What to see

Enkhuizen originally found prosperity through its successful herring fleet, but it was as a home base of the Dutch East Indies Company that it became better known. Many of the buildings from the golden age survive, when spices were unloaded on the quay and a fortress wall defended the city from intrusion. The town hall, jailhouse and cheese-weighing building

Ye olde herring smokery - one of the working exhibits at the open air museum

Enkhuizen from the south; Buyshaven to the left and
Compagnieshaven on the right   *Patrick Roach*

complete the picture of 17th-century life and the
VVV office provides a town guide in English. The
tour includes the Drommedaris tower, which stands
guard over the old harbour and displays an anchor
of the Gelderland fleet seized as a trophy of war. The
Houtribdijk, which links Enkhuizen to Lelystad was
intended to enclose the final polder in the southern
section of the IJsselmeer, but the Markerwaard
project was abandoned in 1986.

The main attraction of the town is the extensive
Zuiderzee Museum. An open air section presents
neighbourhoods of authentic villages, some
reconstructions and some actual buildings which
have been saved and relocated within the museum.
In the indoor museum a range of exhibits tell the
often turbulent history of the Zuiderzee but
interpretation in English is limited.

Restaurant tip
The Admiral on Havenweg offers an unlimited
mussel pot in season and a view of the Buitenhaven.

Connections
The train station lies very conveniently between the
Buitenhaven and the Buyshaven.

ANDIJK
Lying in a bay southeast of Medemblik, the well-
equipped harbour of JH Andijk lies nearer to the
village of Kerkbuurt. Good facilities are available
here including fuel, chandlers and cycle hire. The
nearby town of Andijk is home to 'Het Grootslag' on
Dijkweg, a museum charting the history of the
region and how it was polderised.

MEDEMBLIK

Where to stop
Regatta Centre Medemblik is a large marina outside
and south of the main harbour with very extensive
and modern facilities including a huge chandlers.
North of here the entrance to the old harbour is
clearly marked by two lit pierheads, but beware of
shallower water just south of entrance and approach
on a bearing of 232°. Immediately past Kasteel
Radboud the entrance to the Pekelharinghaven is to
port with plenty of visitors space and ample
facilities. Continuing straight on you pass through
the Oosterhaven and Middenhaven on route to the
Kwikkelsbrug and the Westerhaven. The bridge
operates throughout the day (except 1200–1300) but
likes to wait for three boats to gather before
opening. Here you will find the municipal yacht
harbour that is closest to the town centre. All three
harbours have wi-fi available.

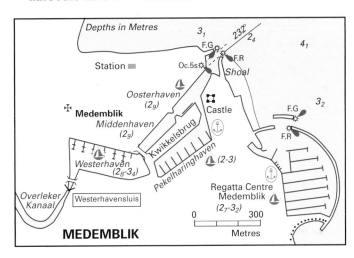

At the southwest corner of the Westerhaven you will find the Westerhavensluis leading to the Overleker kanaal and then the Westfriesche Vaart, which runs west across the region with a minimum air draught of 5m. See Wieringermeerpolder for details. The position of Medemblik makes it sheltered from southwesterly winds which is useful if you arrive from the sea in bad weather. In this case, the connections via the Westfriesche Vaart to other Noord Holland venues might offer a useful alternative cruise plan for vessels under 5m air draught.

Facilities Ashore

Fuel Fa. Kool & Co in Oosterhaven
Chandlers De Goede Watersport on Oosterhaven
Repairs & Servicing Medemblik Yacht Service
Supermarket & Shops Deen on Nieuwstraat

What to see

Standing guard over the entrance to the harbour is the Radboud castle, a 13th-century stronghold erected by Count Floris V as one of five that restrained the West-Frisians. Renovated in the late 19th century, the castle is now used primarily as a medieval-themed wedding venue, but there is also an exhibition in the tower on Medemblik in the middle ages and the history of the castle. A must-see visit at Medemblik is the steam tram that runs between Hoorn and Medemblik. The station is easily accessed at the end of Nieuwstraat and a round-trip is possible by catching the 1240 departure. Photos on

Medemblik steam train runs to Hoorn with a stop at the historic engine shed to see the old steam 'trams'

the train recall the heyday of the steam tram, although the carriages are now pulled by a more traditional locomotive. A short stop is made at the restored Twisk station, where uniformed staff preside over the authentically decorated waiting room, ticket and telephone booth and porter's store. At Hoorn there is time to visit the steam tram museum, housed in a former engine-shed, before the return trip to Medemblik. On the way back from the station you can stop off at Medemblik's

Kwikkeslbrug opens to give access to the Westerhaven

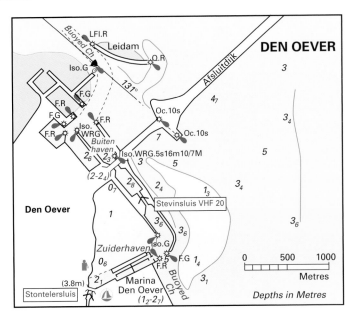

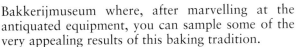

Den Oever lock complex from the north with the harbour
and canal entrance beyond   *Patrick Roach*

Bakkerijmuseum where, after marvelling at the
antiquated equipment, you can sample some of the
very appealing results of this baking tradition.

Restaurant tip
Chinese-Indian restaurant Danny Leung on
Nieuwstraat is a very good choice for a reasonable
price.

Connections
As well as the steam train there are convenient
connections from the station at the north end of the
high street.

DEN OEVER
Approaching Den Oever from the south you can
choose to take an inshore passage (min. depth 2m)
leaving the wind farm to starboard, avoiding the
shallow banks and the Breezand firing range.
Alternatively follow the marked channel though this
is more exposed in the southwesterly winds that are
common in this flat, featureless landscape. Marina
Den Oever is immediately to port as you enter the lit

lock approach channel and there is a reporting
pontoon on the north side of the central pontoon.
Electricity and water are by €0.50 meter. There are
good facilities including diesel, servicing, restaurant
and wi-fi. However, for visiting yachts the
attractions are minimal, being 3km from the small
town, isolated on the southern side of a large basin.
At the west end of the harbour the Stontelersluis
gives access to the Den Oeverse Vaart (see
Wieringermeerpolder for details).

The coast of Noord-Holland between Medemblik
and Den Oever is completely straight, being
reclaimed polder land, drained in 1930. The land
was reclaimed before the barrier dyke was built,
making it the only IJsselmeer polder to have been
reclaimed from sea water. The Den Oever harbour is
a popular place to keep a boat, having easy access
both to the IJsselmeer and the Waddenzee, just inside
the Stevinsluis at the west end of the Afsluitdijk.

Cruising in North Holland

From the descriptions and waterway plans in this
chapter, you can see that there is more to do than
cruise quickly along the mast-up route or visit the
IJsselmeer ports, and that alternatives do exist to
Sixhaven in Amsterdam. Alkmaar is already
appreciated by many visitors with time to stay and
investigate its attractions and charms, and some time
in the Zaanse Schans part of Zaanstad will reveal
lots more about the traditions and history of this
area, providing a nice counterpoint to the Zuiderzee
Museum at Enkhuizen.

Links to the canals of North Holland can be
found at the IJsselmeer ports of Monnickendam and
Medemblik, which together with circular routes
terminating at Den Helder, allow a good proportion
of North Holland to be seen without retracing your
path. By mooring and taking the ferry from Den
Helder to Texel, you can even sample the delights of
the Frisian Islands without offshore cruising.

5 Flevoland

including the Randmeren and the Kop van Overijssel

	Waterways	Principal venues	Other stopping places
	Markermeer	Lelystad	Almere
	Flevoland (Oost & Zuid)	(Lelystad)	Almere, Dronten
Randmeren	IJmeer	Muiden	Almeerderzand
	Gooimeer	Naarden	Almere-Haven, Huizen
	Eemmeer	Amersfoort, Spakenburg	Eemhof
	Nijkerkernauw		Nijkerk
	Nuldernauw		
	Wolderwijd	Harderwijk	Zeewolde
	Veluwemeer		Biddinghuizen
	Drontermeer	Elburg	
	Vossemeer		
	Ketelmeer		Ketelhaven, Schokland
	Ramsdiep and Zwarte Meer		
	Zwarte Water		Genemuiden, Zwartsluis
Kop van Overijssel	Meppelerdiep		
	Kanaal Beukers-Steenwijk	Giethoorn	Wanneperveen
	Kanaal Steenwijk-Ossenzijl		Steenwijk
	Ossenzijlersloot and Kalenbergergracht		Ossenzijl
	Linde and Mallegat		Oldemarkt
	Wetering and Noorderdiep	Blokzijl	
	Steenwijkerdiep		Scheerwolde
	Vollenhoverkanaal		Vollenhove
	Kadoelermeer		De Voorst
	Beulaker Wijde and Belter Wijde		
	Urk harbour	Urk	
	Noordoostpolder		Emmeloord, Marknesse

This chapter includes the waterways bordering and within the province of Flevoland, including the east coast of the Markermeer, and the group of lakes that make up the Randmeren. To the north, the waterways of the Noordoostpolder (also part of the province of Flevoland) are described starting at the IJsselmeer harbour of Urk and working inland. East of here, a small area known as the Kop (head) van Overijssel projects between the Noordoostpolder and Drenthe province, and is a little known but much loved cruising area. Easily accessible from the IJsselmeer, these waterways provide a mast-up route from the Randmeren to Friesland.

The province of Flevoland is divided into the Noordoostpolder on the one hand, and East and South Flevoland on the other, reflecting the various stages of polderisation. The draining of the Noordoostpolder was completed in 1942, making it the first to be reclaimed from fresh water. Draining of Flevoland followed in the 1950s and although East and South Flevoland are now one landmass, the southern section came into being some time after the eastern one.

The Randmeren (meaning 'peripheral lakes') is the collective name for the residual waters that lie between East and South Flevoland and the former coast of the Zuiderzee. In total they run for 79km with modern harbours and towns on the Flevoland side, and old sea ports along the Utrecht and Gelderland coast. Each section of these interconnected lakes has a separate name and is listed below and in the *ANWB Almanak* under that name, although details of all bridges and locks are grouped together in the *Almanak* under the title Randmeren van Flevoland.

The canals through East and Zuid Flevoland are also navigable although they are not recommended for sailing due to their heavily wooded nature. There is lock access into the network at Almere, Lelystad and the Ketelhaven and, with the opening of Sluis De Blauwe Dromer in 2001, a direct connection was made from the Veluwemeer. De Larsevaart is a short and attractive route from here to the Markermeer, but it is restricted to 3m air draught.

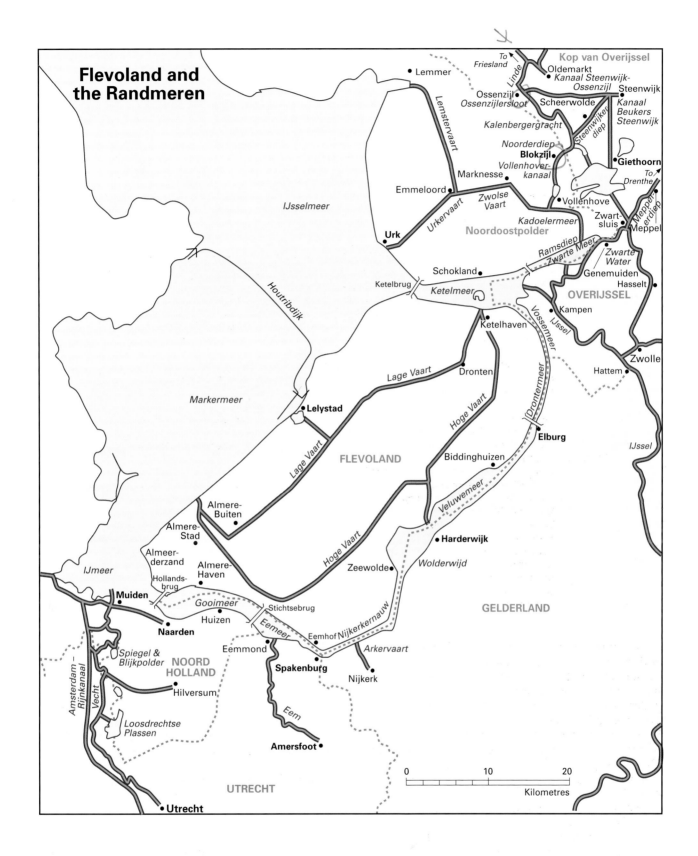

Flevoland and the Randmeren

A number of pumping engines were used to drain the polders and many of these areas are in the process of being converted to recreational use or are open to visitors as interpretation centres.

Map folio *1810* covers the IJsselmeer, Markermeer and Randmeren, whilst *ANWB Waterkaarts C* and *E* provide good coverage of the Noordoostpolder and

Flevoland. The *Schipper Vaaratlas* (Midden Nederland) published by Watersportverbond for the first time in 2006 provides combined coverage of these areas, along with details of navigational obstacles, yacht harbours and other facilities, although quoted bridge heights are often overly generous and can be misleading.

Markermeer

The Markermeer is the name given to the southern part of the IJsselmeer, between Amsterdam and the Houtribdijk. In good weather it is a calm, inland lake filled with watersports enthusiasts, but in strong winds its shallow fresh waters are converted into an uncomfortable and difficult short sea, which should not be taken lightly, particularly when taken on the beam away from shelter.

For those interested in a change of scenery, the Noordersluis lies at the northern end of Lelystad-Haven and gives access via the Lage Dwarsvaart to the Lage Vaart, which crosses the polder north to south. Further details of these waterways is given in this chapter and in the *Almanak* under Flevoland (Oost & Zuid).

Speed limit In the channels and near the shores, 20km/h; otherwise no limit.

Lock Sluis Houtrib and lifting bridge (7.2m when closed) operate 24 hours. VHF 20. A flashing white light indicates which of the two lock basins to use and leisure boats may be called in before commercial vessels depending on bridge openings. Listen out on VHF and for loudspeaker instructions.

ALMERE

A leisure marina, De Blocq van Kuffeler, has been established in the former vluchthaven (refuge port) and a number of visitors berths are now available. The harbour office is not manned full time but there are registration envelopes and information folders available for visitors out of hours. On site facilities are limited to showers and toilets, and the nearest amenities are 4km away in Almere-Buiten. The harbour borders a dune park and nature reserve and the information centre De Trekvogel is nearby.

The Zuidersluis gives access to the Hoge Vaart, the second of the main canals which run roughly north-south across Flevoland.

LELYSTAD

Where to stop

There are large marina complexes on both sides of the Houtribsluis. South of the lock, Lelystad-Haven is home to Jachthaven Lelystad Haven. Coin-operated electricity (€0.50/kWh) and water (€0.50/100 ltrs) are available. There is a bar-restaurant on the quay, and on-site facilities include chandlers, yacht servicing and wi-fi. The only downside is that the visitors' berths are on the outer pontoons, a long walk from the facilities.

DEKO Marine and WV Lelystad share the Houtribhaven north of the lock, with DEKO Marine to the north of the basin and WV Lelystad to the south. DEKO Marine offers a small supermarket and terrace bistro and has plenty of visitors spaces. WV Lelystad has the least expensive berths and fuel available, as well as launderette and chandlers. Visitors can make for the alongside berths near the

office or report by telecom or VHF 31 for a box. It is 10 minutes walk to Batavia Stad from here, the closest other than the municipal visitors' harbour.

Flevo Marina, to the north on the Houtribhoek, is pricey but has included unmetered 16A electricity and water, as well as a sauna, solarium and bathrooms that can be booked. An extensive chandlers, small supermarket and restaurant are available on-site as well as wi-fi and diesel.

A small municipal visitors' harbour at the Bataviahaven, immediately south of the lock, has coin-operated water and electricity as well as the usual basic facilities, and is most convenient for visits to local attractions.

Facilities ashore

Fuel WV Lelystad & Flevo Marina
Chandlers WV Lelystad, Flevo Marina & JH Lelystad-Haven
Repairs & Servicing All harbours
Supermarket & Shops On-site supermarket at Flevo Marina and Deko Marine. Local supermarket and shops close to Lelystad Haven
ATM Lelystad-Haven
Cycle hire Available at all harbours
VVV office In the town centre on Stadhuisplein

What to see

Named after Cornelius Lely, the engineer behind the Afsluitdijk and the polderisation schemes, Lelystad's (pronounced 'lay-le-stad') first residents arrived in the 1950s, living in temporary accommodation in Lelystad haven. The neatly planned development is the capital of the Flevoland province and the Agora community and cultural centre (which houses a cinema and library) marks the centre of the town. Most attractions are conveniently concentrated near the Markermeer harbours, although a bike is still useful to make your way between them.

Lelystad's little-used visitors' harbour is close to the lock and convenient for on-shore attractions

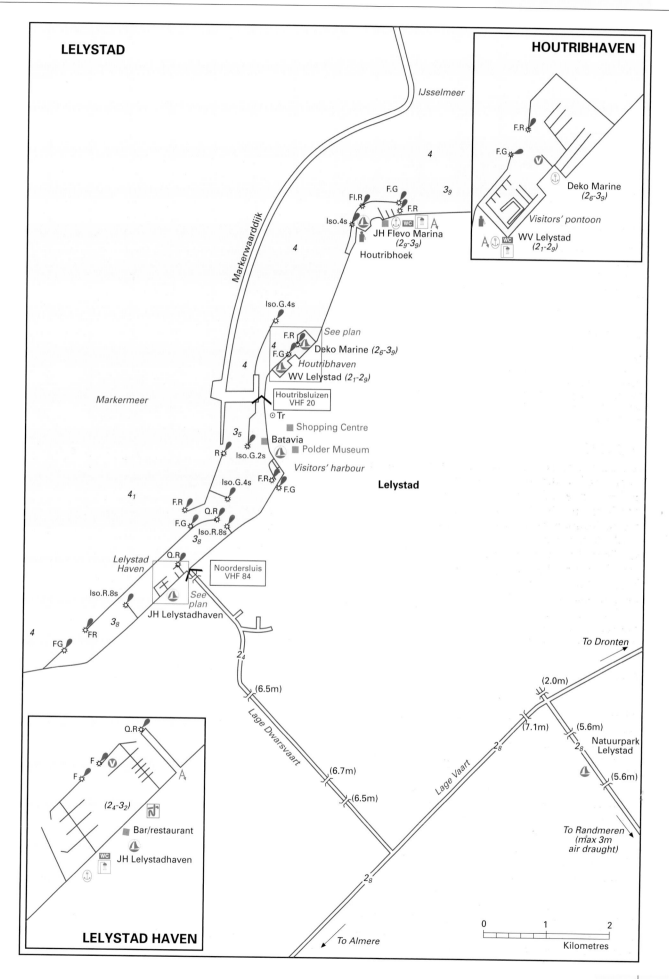

LELYSTAD

HOUTRIBHAVEN

IJsselmeer

4

3₉

F.R

F.G

Deko Marine
(2₆-3₉)

Visitors' pontoon

WV Lelystad
(2₁-2₉)

Fl.R

F.G

F.R

Iso.4s

JH Flevo Marina
(2₉-3₉)

Houtribhoek

4

Markerwaarddijk

Iso.G.4s

F.R

F.G

4

See plan

Deko Marine *(2₆-3₉)*

Houtribhaven

WV Lelystad *(2₁-2₉)*

4

Markermeer

Houtribsluizen
VHF 20

⊙Tr

■ Shopping Centre

Batavia

■ Polder Museum

Visitors' harbour

Lelystad

3₅

R

Iso.G.2s

F.R

F.G

Iso.G.4s

4₁

F.R

F.G

Q.R

Iso.R.8s

3₈

Q.R

*Lelystad
Haven*

Noordersluis
VHF 84

*See
plan*

Iso.R.8s

JH Lelystadhaven

3₈

4

FG

FR

2₄

(6.5m)

To Dronten

(2.0m)

(7.1m)

(5.6m)

Natuurpark
Lelystad

2₈

Lage Dwarsvaart

(6.7m)

(6.5m)

Lage Vaart

2₈

(5.6m)

*To Randmeren
(max 3m
air draught)*

2₈

LELYSTAD HAVEN

Q.R

F

F

(2₄-3₂)

Bar/restaurant

JH Lelystadhaven

To Almere

0   1   2
Kilometres

Visit the distinctive Nieuwe Land Erfgoed Centrum for a complete overview of the polderisation

The Nieuw Land polder museum was reopened in 2005 as the Nieuw Land Erfgoed (heritage) Centrum with a modernised presentation on the history of the province and the drainage of the polder. Next door, the national ships history and archaeology centre is housed in the Bataviawerf, and as well as finds from the many shipwrecks found during the drainage, a replica of the East Indiaman, the Batavia floats in the harbour. For shopaholics, Batavia Stad factory outlet shopping centre is also nearby offering discounts on a wide selection of designer wear.

The main maritime event in the harbour takes place at the end of June, when a Water Festival coincides with the National Sloop Show. As well as enjoying the maritime market and musical entertainment you can admire an impressive collection of sloops, traditional open boats which are ubiquitous in Holland's canal cities.

Connections

The train station in the centre of the city has regular services to Amsterdam.

Flevoland (Oost & Zuid)

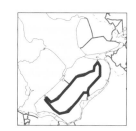

As well as sailing round the perimeter of Flevoland, either via the Markermeer, or via the Randmeren, vessels can also navigate the internal canals, which form surprisingly attractive and peaceful waterways. Heavily wooded for much of their length, these waterways are not suitable for sailing, but are ideal when the Markermeer is very busy or too windy for comfort.

The main waterways are the Lage (low) Vaart and the Hoge (high) Vaart and in each case there is a large drop down (around 5m) from the IJsselmeer level to reach them. Smaller waterways called the Lage Dwarsvaart and the Hoge Dwarsvaart connect these canals to coastal harbours. The Larservaart joins the two main canals near Lelystad but its bridges restrict air draught to 3m and so it is not covered by this guide. Furthermore, the Lange Wetering joining the Hoge Vaart to Almere-Haven has a minimum air draught of 2.5m. All locks have opening bridges except Sluis De Blauwe Dromer, which has a fixed bridge of 5.5m.

Free moorings are available along all canals for a maximum stay of three days (except for a fee payable at Biddinghuizen, for which use of the nearby yacht harbour's facilities is included).

Length: Ketelhaven – Lelystad-Haven, 31km; Ketelhaven – Blocq van Kuffeler Haven, 48km (via Lage Vaart) or 62km (via Hoge Vaart) ; Lelystad-Haven – Blocq van Kuffeler Haven, 28km; Ketelhaven – Harderhaven, 27km; Harderhaven – Blocq van Kuffeler Haven, 42km
Speed limit Not officially fixed but 9–12km/h is usual
Maximum permitted draught 2.4m
Locks: Ketelsluis and Kampersluis (at Ketelhaven), and their lifting bridges operate throughout the day with a break for lunch 1230–1330. VHF 18.
Noordersluis (at Lelystad-Haven), Zuidersluis and Vaartsluis (at Blocq van Kuffeler Haven) operate throughout the day with breaks at 1230–1300 and 1800–1830. (Only one break for lunch 1230–1330 at weekends.) Sluis De Blauwe Dromer (at Harderhaven) operates throughout the day with a lunch break at 1230–1300 (1230–1330 on Sundays).

Bridges: On Hoge Vaart: Fixed (min 5.4m); On Lage Vaart: Fixed (min 6.5m), 1 opening. Knip bridge is self-service and can be operated by push button throughout the day. On Hoge Dwarsvaart: Fixed (min 3.9m). At Sluis De Blauwe Dromer: Fixed (5.5m). On Lage Dwarsvaart: Fixed (min 6.5m)

ALMERE

Both the Lage and Hoge Vaart run through the built-up area of Almere-Stad and Almere-Buiten and there are stopping places provided along the canal at various points. The first residents arrived in the new town in 1976 and with that number now standing at more than 180,000 most of the area is taken up with extensive housing developments.

LELYSTAD

JH Liberty Maritime lies on the Lage Dwarsvaart, just inside the Noordersluis. Limited space for visitors up to 15m is available with the usual basic facilities. However, most boats on these waterways use the free canalside moorings, which are dotted along the canals.

What to see

Although many of Lelystad's principal attractions are located near the Markermeer harbours (described in this chapter under Markermeer), boats cruising the Lage Vaart should not miss a stop at the Natuurpark Lelystad, where a wide range of wild animals roam in a semi-natural environment. You can also see a shipwreck found during the polder

A moose lurks in the trees at the Natuurpark at Lelystad

drainage, which still lies where it was found, as well as a reconstruction of a pre-historic settlement.

The Natuurpark moorings are also the nearest stopping place from which to cycle to Aviodrome, an extensive indoor and outdoor exhibition of flight and flying.

DRONTEN

WV Dronten welcomes visitors up to 15m at its harbour in a large basin near the town centre. In addition to the usual basic facilities, fuel, pump-out and launderette are available. Alternatively, there are a limited number of semi-unofficial free moorings with no facilities at the northeast corner of the basin next to the 3m bridge.

Planning for the new town started in the 1950s with building begun in 1960 and the modern settlement has been blessed with a wide range of recreational amenities. The centre of the town is the architect-designed glass community centre, which acts as an extension of the market square. A weekly market is held here on Wednesday mornings and an annual market and music festival, the Meerpaaldagen, on the second weekend in August.

RANDMEREN

The Randmeren (meaning 'peripheral lakes') were the residual sea-space left as a boundary between the Flevoland polder and the original Zuider Zee coast and now make a very pleasant and easy cruising ground. Each section is given its own name and is described below starting at the southwest end and working northeast.

IJmeer

The IJmeer is the name given to the southern part of the Markermeer between the approach to Amsterdam and Almere in Flevoland. Although not strictly part of the Randmeren, it is described here as it forms the first stage of a cruise into this area. It extends as far as the Hollands Bridge in the southeast and in the centre lies the island of Pampus.

Speed limit 20km/h in the channels and near the shore
Bridges 2 fixed (12m). Hollandse bridge & rail bridge.

MUIDEN

Where to stop

A buoyed channel marks the entrance to the harbour, which has a maximum permitted draught of 1.8m. Prestige (and pricey) moorings are available on the edge of town at the KNZ & RV (Royal Netherlands Sailing and Rowing club) which lies on the west bank. This is the home harbour of the royal yacht De Groene Draeck, and facilities fit for a queen include a well-regarded restaurant and wi-fi, as well as chandlers and pump-out.

Further south on the east bank the cooperative harbour, JH Stichting Muiden, lies next to the castle and has fuel available, as well as unmetered water and electricity. Visitors' berths are on the outer pontoon and the harbourmaster is available by intercom if not on-site.

Although often visited as part of a Randmeren cruise, Muiden is also the mouth of the Vecht, and 500m south the Vecht sea lock gives access to this attractive river and popular cruising ground, as well as the Muidertrekvaart and the Naardertrekvaart. For further details of these waterways see Chapter 8: Central Netherlands.

Muiden from the northwest; KNZ & RV in the foreground with the Muiderslot behind *Patrick Roach*

Facilities ashore

Fuel JH Stichting Muiden
Chandlers KNZ & RV
Repairs & Servicing Jachtservice Muiden
Supermarket & Shops De Muidenier on
Weesperstraat and small shops around town
ATM Sluisstraat

What to see

The Muiderslot dominates the entrance to Muiden (pronounced 'mow-der' to rhyme with chowder) and was built as a defensive structure in 1280 by Floris V. Later occupied in the 17th century by a group of writers and poets known as the Muiderkring, today the castle and its extensive gardens are open to visitors. New sections were opened in 2006 and the guided tour tells of life at the castle from the Middle Ages to the Golden Age. From Muiden you can also take the ferry, or make a day trip in your own boat, to the island fort of Pampus, part of Amsterdam's defences completed in 1895.

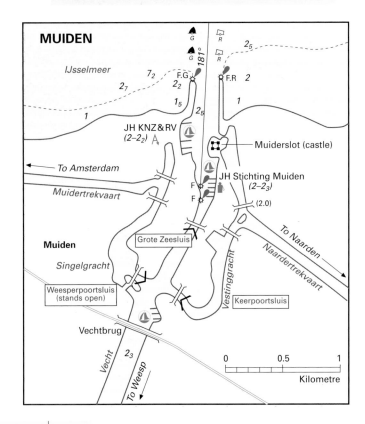

Stichting JH Muiden lies next to the Muiderslot, on the opposite bank to the KNZ & RV (visible in the background)

The double lock at Muiden provides endless entertainment for the customers at the quayside cafés

Back on dry land, the lockside cafés are a popular hangout for visitors and locals who enjoy watching the steady stream of pleasure boats making their way inland with the terrace of Omo Ko on Herengracht a particular favourite.

Restaurant tip

For the evening, move next door to Restaurant Graaf Floris V or the Brasserie Muiden.

ALMEERDERZAND

Almeerderzand (or Almere-Strand) is the name for the west coast of the Flevoland polder, which forms the eastern shore of the IJmeer. The edges of the waterway are shallow and vessels are advised to keep to the buoyed channel.

Marina Muiderzand is a huge yacht harbour with every facility including supermarket, restaurants and chandlers on site. The site also has water sports facilities and its own beach making it popular as a holiday destination, but not much good for visiting the surrounding area, or the nearest town of Almere which is 5km away.

Gooimeer

The Gooimeer is part of the peripheral lake south of Flevoland and stretches from the Hollandse bridge at Muiderberg to the Stichtse bridge, 5km east of Huizen. Spar buoys mark the 1.5m depth contour, and the southern part of the meer between Naarden and Huizen is designated as a nature reserve.

Speed limit 20km/h in the channels, otherwise, 9km/h

NAARDEN

Where to stop

The huge yacht harbour 2.5 km to the northwest of the historic fortress town is accessed from the Gooimeer. There is plenty of space and a reporting pontoon with intercom is provided near the entrance. There are extensive facilities including fuel, launderette and cycle hire, as well as chandlers and servicing.

A town centre visitors' harbour is planned and is due to open in 2007 with accommodation for around ten boats up to 12m long. For further details and a description of the Naardertrekvaart see Chapter 8: Central Netherlands.

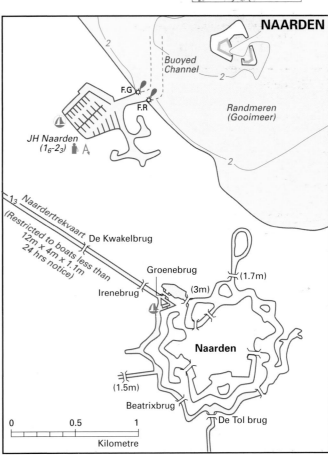

Tour the canal moat by trip-boat or dinghy

Facilities ashore

Fuel, Chandlers, Repairs & Servicing Jachthaven
    Naarden
Supermarket & Shops Small shop on site or Albert
    Heijn on Marktstraat in the centre
ATMs On Marktstraat
Cycle hire From the harbour
VVV office Adriaan Dortsman Plein

What to see

The original settlement of Naarden lay 3km
northeast of the present-day town but was rebuilt
after the civil war in 1350. The 17th-century
fortifications form a twelve-pointed star, surrounded
by a fortress wall and a double canal ring. The
Vestingmuseum is housed in one of the six bastions
and as well as an insight into the Dutch fortress
towns, you can see the 61m long passageway used
for listening for the enemy. To tour the fortifications
from the canal moat you can take the Vestingvaart
tour in a classic open boat, departing hourly from
the Nieuwe Haven. A detailed walking tour of the
fortress town is available (in English) from the VVV
and you can view the town from the top of the St
Vituskerk tower during guided climbs.

The centre of the small peaceful town is studded
with enticing boutiques, with the 17th-century Het
Arsenaal a particular highlight. Here, esteemed
Dutch furniture designer Jan van Bouvrie has created
an exclusive mall comprising shops, restaurant and a
modern art gallery.

Restaurant tip

De Kapschuur has a peaceful location behind the
church, whilst Eetcafé 't Hert is known for its diverse
menu, including game dishes in season. Poorters on
Marktstraat also comes highly recommended.

ALMERE HAVEN

WSV Almere-Haven lies to port on entering the
harbour and has space for boats up to 12.5m. Fuel is
available as well as the usual basic facilities and the
moorings lie in a quiet secluded part of the busy
harbour. Continuing to starboard, a large municipal
harbour provides fixed and visitors' berths in boxes
and alongside the town quay. Electricity is by SEP-
key by arrangement with the harbourmaster
(€0.50/kWh) and basic facilities are provided in the
blue harbour office building to the east of the
harbour by the lock, where you will also find the
VVV office.

Almere-Haven has been planned as the more
leisure-focussed area of the Almere conurbation and
is a popular outing for locals on summer weekends.
A host of restaurants of all persuasions relate well to
the harbour from the pirate-themed pancake ship to
the more sophisticated fish and seafood restaurant,
Krab aan de Haven. One street inland lies a modern
shopping precinct which is already starting to look
shabby and the topical exhibitions at the Corrosia
cultural centre look somewhat out of place.

HUIZEN

From the Gooimeer, a buoyed channel leads into the
harbour moles of Huizen harbour. The very large JH
Huizerhoofd is to port 100m after the entrance and
has all facilities including fuel, chandlers and cycle
hire. Beyond this and also on the port side, Huizer
Marina has limited visitors' spaces when members'
berths are free, but has good service facilities and
chandlers. The most convenient moorings for
visitors are at the head of the harbour at the
municipal harbour, which are the closest to the town
centre. A reporting pontoon is provided for arrivals
and visitors are normally put on the quay wall where
coin-operated electricity (€0.50/2kWh) and free
water are available.

Although Huizen (pronounced 'how-zer') is a
former fishing village its old fishing quarter is well
hidden behind extensive new industrial development
near the harbour. The Huizermuseum Het
Schoutenhuis has a fixed collection depicting the
traditional dress of the town and the interior of a
fisherman's cottage. Modern recreational amenities
are more in evidence and an indoor karting and laser
games centre is next to the municipal harbour, which
could be popular with youngsters (and which also
radiates free wi-fi.) A weekly market is held on
Saturdays on the Oude Raadhuisplein, which also
has a wide selection of shops and cafés.

Eemmeer

The Eemeer is a short wide part of the peripheral lakes between the Gooimeer and the Nijkerkernauw. Its western boundary is the Stichtse bridge and its eastern end is marked by the sharp bend east of Spakenburg. With the exception of the channels and the area around the Dode Hond island, the Eemeer is designated as a nature reserve. Anchoring is permitted around the island and moorings are provided on the south side, although those to the south-west can be uncomfortable or even dangerous in strong southwest winds.

Speed limit 20km/h in the channels, otherwise, 9km/h
Bridge 1 fixed – Stichtse bridge (12.9m)

AMERSFOORT AND THE RIVER EEM

A buoyed channel marks the entrance to the river Eem (depth 3m), which winds south from the Eemmeer through quiet rural countryside as far as Amersfoort. In the summer there is little or no flow and it is a pleasant detour to this lively and historic city. For navigation on the Eem use *ANWB Waterkaart E*. The cycle ferry collects and drops off cyclists along the river at the designated points shown.

Length 18km
Depth 3m
Speed limit 12km/h except 6km/h in central Amersfoort and by the Eembrugge houseboats,
Bridges 2 fixed (min 7.2m), 3 opening. Eembrugge operates throughout the day Monday–Friday with an evening rush hour break (1630–1730) and with an additional lunch break (1230–1330) at weekends, VHF 22. Koppel and Kwekers bridges operate throughout the day with an evening rush hour break (1600–1800) VHF 22.

Where to stop

There are free riverside moorings on the west bank around 800m from the entrance; in Eemdijk (short-stay only); by the Eemnesserbuitenvaart spur; by the Malesluis on the east bank; and downstream of the Eembrugge on the west bank. Visitors' places with reasonable facilities are available at yacht harbours at 't Raboes at Eemmond and at JH Eembrugge.

For moorings in the centre of Amersfoort a new visitors' harbour opened in 2007. This lies north of the fixed rail bridge, close to the historic centre and has good new facilities with SEP-key operated electricity (€0.50/2kWh) and water (€0.50/100 ltrs).

Alternatively, there are good facilities and a friendly welcome at WV De Eemkruisers just north of the Koppel bridge.

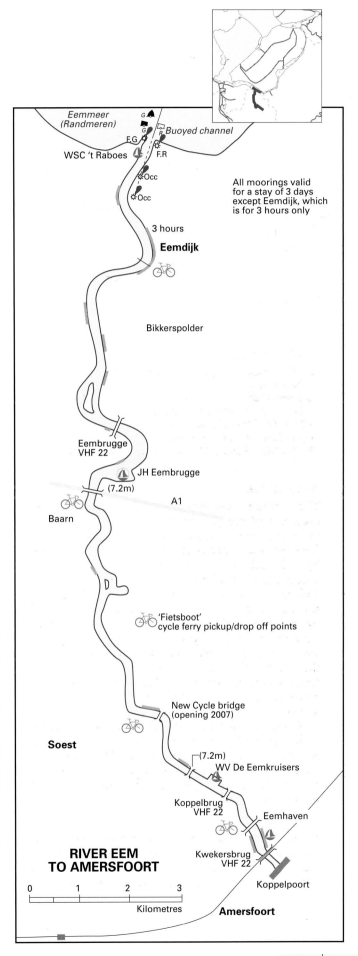

Amersfoorts's Koppelpoort defends both road and river

Facilities ashore

Chandlers, Repairs & Servicing Watersportbedrijf 't Vrouwezand
Supermarket & Shops Albert Heijn on Hellestraat
ATMs On Kortegracht and St Jorisplein
Cycle hire From the train station
VVV office Main office at the station, but information available at De Observant next to the Stadhuis, or from Museum Flehite.

What to see

Amersfoort originated at the confluence of several small waterways which still criss-cross the old town centre. After the granting of city rights in the 13th century the defensive walls and double canal ring were added with the Koppelpoort, built in 1400, acting as both a water and road gate. The muurhuizen (wall houses) were originally thought to have been built into the city walls but in fact were constructed from reclaimed bricks after its partial demolition in the 15th century. The Museum Flehite is located in three such wall houses and the well-interpreted exhibits give a good overview of the city's history, as does a detailed city walk available (in English) from the VVV. A special exhibition on the top floor recalls the German occupation of the town, especially in relation to the prison camp, Kamp Amersfoort, located on the south side of the city. The events here were a major influence for locally based artist Armando, whose work is displayed in the Armandomuseum on Langegracht.

For a more cheery view of the city, there are boat tours round the central canals, which depart daily from the Langegracht, or you can take the museum bus on Tuesdays and take your pick from the seven museum stops. The 98m high Onze Lieve Vrouwetoren is also open for visitors every day except Monday, with guided climbs on the hour.

Excellent shopping facilities and weekly markets on Friday morning and Saturday complete the range of amenities.

A 9-ton glacial boulder the Amersfoortse kei stands in the Zonnehof Rietveld pavilion on the south side of city, and the Keistad festival (2nd weekend in September) celebrates the day in 1661 when it was dragged from the outskirts of the city by 400 local residents.

Restaurant tip

There are plenty of eating options around the Hofplein square, or try Zandfoort aan de Eem, a lively bunker-style venue next to the harbour.

Connections

The train station is west of the harbour and has good services to Amsterdam, Utrecht and Zwolle.

SPAKENBURG

Where to stop

West of the main harbour entrance, a buoyed channel leads to the modern and well-equipped Jachthaven Nieuwboer. All facilities are provided including fuel, a large chandlers and wi-fi. The main harbour entrance is also buoyed and there are moorings along the harbour moles and all along the entrance which are administrated by the municipal harbour. These continue to starboard into the Oude Haven where traditional wooden botters are moored along the west quay and alongside berths for visitors are provided along the east quay. These have unmetered 16A electricity available but no water. The head of the harbour, beyond the traditional wooden boatbuilders yard, is called Museum Haven and is reserved for historic vessels. WSV De Eendracht lies to port opposite the harbour office in Nieuwe Haven but has space for boats only up to 10m. Fuel, pump-out and a launderette are available here.

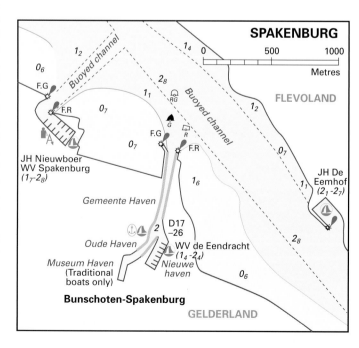

Local residents still turn out in traditional dress for the Spakenburg festival days

Many of the wooden fishing boats, known as botters, have been preserved and make an attractive backdrop to the old harbour. A wooden boatbuilder has been at work here for over 200 years and can still be seen maintaining the historic fleet.

Together with the adjoining farming village of Bunschoten, Spakenburg has retained a distinctive local culture and to this day around 300 of the older women still wear the traditional dress. These are joined on Spakenburgse Dagen (Spakenburg Days) by the rest of the community, for a day of special events including folk dancing, and arts and crafts markets. Spakenburg Days take place on Wednesdays from mid-July to mid-August and are followed by other mid-week events, and on the first Saturday in September by the Spakenburg harbour day.

A detailed guided walk in four languages is available from the VVV office to introduce you to the main sights in the village. Next door, in Museum 't Vurhuus or at the Klederdracht and Visserijmuseum you can learn more about the culture and history of these charming villages, or for the real thing drop into the weekly market on the Spuiplein on Saturdays.

Restaurant tip
Restaurant De Mandemaaker on Kerkstraat comes highly recommended, or for people-watching opt for Grand Café De Postkamer, which enjoys a central position on the market square.

Connections
There is no train station in Spakenburg, but from the bus stop by the supermarket you can take the regular service for a day trip to Amersfoot.

EEMHOF
Opposite Spakenburg on the Flevoland side Jachthaven Eemhof is a well-equipped and modern recreational harbour in an attractive wooded setting. Watersports lessons, on-site restaurant and wi-fi number amongst its many attractions.

Facilities ashore
Fuel JH Nieuwboer & WSV De Eendracht
Chandlers Van Halteren is a large chandlers based at JH Nieuwboer
Repairs & Servicing Available at JH Nieuwboer
Supermarket, Shops & ATMs Super de Boer on Broers Wetering (turn right at the carillon)
Cycle hire From JH Nieuwboer
VVV office Oude Schans (next to the wooden boatbuilders yard)

What to see
Spakenburg (pronounced 'spark-en-burek') was established as a fishing village in the 15th century and reached a peak of prosperity in 1900 when its fleet numbered over 200 ships. After the closing of the Zuider Zee this trade disappeared and now only a solitary eel catcher works out of the harbour.

Nijkerkernauw

The Nijkerkernauw is a narrow channel section of the Randmeren that spans both sides of the Nijkerkernauw lock complex, and connects the Eemmeer and the Nuldernauw. Outside the channel the shores are quite shallow and vessels are advised to follow the buoyage.

Speed limit 20km/h in the channels, otherwise, 9km/h
Lock Nijkerkersluis and lifting bridge (7.4m when closed) operates throughout the day (from 1000 on Sundays). VHF 18. On Arkervaart: Arkersluis and lifting bridge operate throughout the day Monday–Saturday with a break for lunch (1200–1300), and 0900–1015 only on Sundays. VHF 12.

Bridges On Arkervaart: 1 fixed (7.2m), 1 opening. Arkervaart bridge is opened by the Arkersluis operator and works the same hours. VHF 12 or ☎ 033 245 1207 to arrange a time. Two openings only on Sundays at 0900 outbound and 1015 inbound.

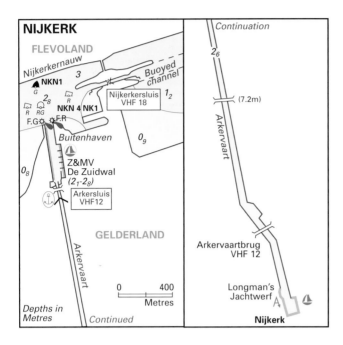

The Arkersluis and Z&MV De Zuidwal from the north
Patrick Roach

NIJKERK

Where to stop

Z & MV De Zuidwal lies at the harbour entrance, on the east side of the lock approach, with pontoon moorings and the usual facilities. Moorings along the harbour entrance are part of the municipal harbour and the lock-keeper comes round in late afternoon. Coin-operated water and electricity are provided here, and a bar-restaurant is available at the yacht club. Near to a small lakeside beach and some 3km from the town itself, these are popular moorings with boats looking for a quiet stop.

Passage through the Arkersluis gives access to the 3km long Arkervaart channel which leads to the municipal moorings in the town centre. The channel passes through extensive industrial areas, and the harbour itself lies next to the car park of the modern town hall. Facilities are housed in a locked portacabin and there is no water or electricity. On the opposite quay Langman Jachtwerf Watersport has an extensive chandlers and can undertake service and repair work.

What to see

The traditional town has been completely modernised and provides good facilities in an ordinary setting. Although Nijkerk (pronounced 'nigh-kerek') does not present its best face to the harbour some businesses, like De Havenaer home shopping centre, and the Herberg De Dolle Joncker, have done their best to make it appealing. A VVV office is situated in the old weigh-building and frequent events are held throughout the summer on the market square, as well as the weekly Friday market. West of the town on the Nijkerkernauw the Hertog Reijnout paddle-wheeled steam pumping station is the last of its kind still in use, and has a visitor centre for those wishing to learn more.

Nuldernauw

The Nuldernauw is another narrow channel section of the Randmeren between south Flevoland and the Veluwe coast. It connects the Nijkerkernauw with the Wolderwijd. JH Nulde has limited spaces for visitors up to 15m whilst Strand Horst is a large marina and watersports centre with all facilities.

Speed limit 20km/h in the channel; otherwise, 9km/h

Wolderwijd

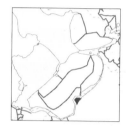

The Wolderwijd is, as the name suggests, a wider lake-like section of the Randmeren between Flevoland the Veluwe coast. It connects the Nuldernauw with the Veluwemeer at Harderwijk.

Speed limit 20km/h in the channels, otherwise, 9km/h
Bridge Harderbrug 7.2m is now replaced for leisure vessels by the adjacent aqueduct and is only to be used by commercial vessels. Maximum depth at the aquaduct is 2.3m.

ZEEWOLDE

Where to stop
The large JH Wolderwijd lies on the Flevoland side and predates the neighbouring new town by some six years. They offer a choice of the Bolhaven, to starboard, which is a 'nature' harbour open to the mere; the Bonshaven, a 'civilisation' harbour, which is bordered by waterside apartments; or the central 'drop in' harbour, the nearest to the town centre amenities. All moorings are administrated by the harbour office at the southern end of the Bonshaven, where you will also find the reporting and fuel pontoon. All facilities are available including servicing, repairs and chandlers.

Low cost moorings are also available on De Zegge island where camping is permitted.

What to see
The new town of Zeewolde has existed only since 1984 and has been designed with some notable modern architecture and a good range of recreational facilities, including a farmer's golf course at De Erkevelden as well as a traditional 36-hole course. It is best known for the large Hosterwold woods to the southwest of the town, which claims to be the largest deciduous wood in Europe.

The nearby De Wetering park includes the landscape art installation Sea Level, whose walls indicate where the sea level would be without the polder dykes. Also in the park is the visitor and interpretation centre De Verbeelding, which traces the interaction between landscape, art and nature.

HARDERWIJK

Where to stop
De Knar marina lies next to the aqueduct and is accessed via a short channel. There is ample space and facilities include launderette and cycle hire. Continuing into town there are good municipal moorings in the Vissershaven, both sides of the self-service lifting bridge. Coin-operated electricity (€0.50/2kWh, 10A) and water (€0.50/100 ltrs) is available and there is a well-equipped facilities block beyond the bridge on the north side. The most central, but more expensive moorings are those of JH Haven van Harderwijk, next to the Dolfinarium. A 14-year development project is underway which will open a new entrance to the west of the Haven van Harderwijk from the Wolderwijd, with significant changes to bridges and mooring arrangements. Work is expected to start on the new harbours in 2008.

Facilities ashore
Fuel & Chandlers Van Scherpenzeels in the Lelyhaven
Repairs & Servicing Polyarc Yachting and
   Scheepswerf Roelofsen are both in the Lelyhaven
Supermarket, Shops & ATMs Dirk van de Broek is
   near the post office and there is a large selection of
   shops in the centre
Cycle hire From the station or Fietsverhuur Boonen
   on Mecklenburglaan
VVV office With ANWB shop at Bleek 102

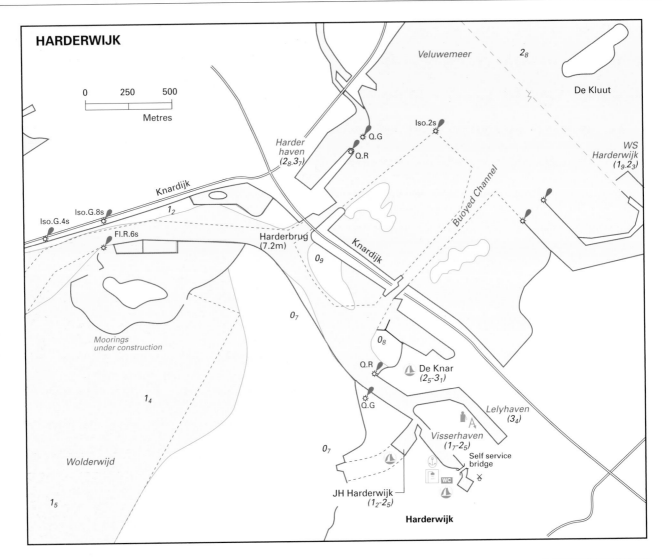

HARDERWIJK

0   250   500

Metres

Veluwemeer

2_8

De Kluut

Iso.2s

Harder haven $(2_8.3_7)$

Q.G

Q.R

WS Harderwijk $(1_9.2_3)$

Knardijk

1_2

Iso.G.4s

Iso.G.8s

Fl.R.6s

Harderbrug $(7.2m)$

Knardijk

Buoyed Channel

0_9

0_7

Moorings under construction

0_8

Q.R

De Knar (2_5-3_1)

1_4

Q.G

Lelyhaven (3_4)

0_7

Visserhaven (1_7-2_5)

Self service bridge

WC

Wolderwijd

JH Harderwijk (1_2-2_5)

1_5

Harderwijk

The harbours of Harderwijk are undergoing development which will see the car park (top right) turned into a waterside boulevard (Photo is looking towards the south)

Patrick Roach

What to see

Tickets for the fishy attractions of the Dolfinarium are available from the harbour office for boats staying at the Haven van Hardewijk which saves a few euros and a long queue – its nine daily shows feature not only dolphins but also sea lions, seals, walruses, rays and sharks. On a more traditional level the town's history museum is housed in an 18th-century mansion house, where special exhibits include reconstructions of an old-fashioned grocer's store and a first world war internment camp. An extensive shopping centre within the historic town walls and a Saturday morning market complement the range of attractions, and for wet days the indoor karting arena Harder's Plaza is not far away on the east side of town.

Restaurant tip

The popular on-site restaurant at Haven van Harderwijk offers regular dance nights as well as excellent food. Elsewhere you can enjoy good food at Restaurant Basiliek, or 't Nonnetje, both on the Vischmarkt.

Connections

The train station to the south of the town has services to Utrecht and Zwolle.

The giant walrus performs for the crowds at the Dolfinarium

Veluwemeer

The Veluwemeer is the section of the peripheral lakes between east Flevoland and the Veluwe coast. It connects the Wolderwijd with the Drontemeer at the Elburg bridge. Island moorings are available on Pierland island (halfway along) and De Snip, De Ral and De Kwak (at eastern end of wider section) and are accessible throughout the year. Access to De Kluut and De Krooneend (at the southern end) are restricted by bird-breeding seasons.

Speed limit 20km/h in the channels, otherwise, 9km/h
Lock On Hoge Dwarsvaart: Sluis De Blauwe Dromer and fixed bridge (5.5m) gives access to the Flevoland waterways (depth 2m) and operates throughout the day with a break for lunch (1230–1300). From 1000 on Sundays with longer break for lunch (1230–1330).
Bridge Harderbrug (7.2m) is now replaced for leisure vessels by the adjacent aquaduct and is only to be used by commercial vessels. Maximum depth at the aquaduct is 2.3m. Elburgerbrug (5.7m when closed) operates throughout the day with a break for lunch (1230–1300). From 1000 on Sundays with longer break for lunch (1230–1330).

BIDDINGHUIZEN

JH Aqua Centrum Bremergsehoek lies on the Flevoland side and has space for boats up to 15m with all facilities including chandlers, restaurant and cycle hire.

JH and campsite Riviera Beach is a large recreational complex opposite Elburg, which has plenty of space and all facilities. This is the closest harbour to visit Walibi World, formerly the Six Flags theme park, which is well worth a visit for families and those who enjoy white knuckles.

Drontermeer

The Drontermeer is a 10km stretch from the Elburgerbrug to the Roggebotsluis and lies between the Veluwemeer and the Vossemeer. Outside the channel the lake is shallow and vessels are advised to follow the buoyage. There are mooring places along the meer on the Flevoland side and also on Eekt island (depth 1.1m). Harbours both sides of the Roggebotsluis offer good facilities for a quiet stop.

Speed limit 20km/h in the channel; otherwise, 9km/h
Lock Roggebotsluis and lifting bridge (5.4m when closed) operate throughout the day (from 1000 on Sundays). VHF 22.
Bridge Elburgerbrug (5.7m when closed) operates throughout the day with a break for lunch (1230–1300). From 1000 on Sundays with longer break for lunch (1230–1330).

ELBURG

Where to stop

Immediately north of the Elburg bridge, the entrance to the harbour canal is on the east side (depth 2.8m, speed limit 5km/h). Municipal moorings lie alongside the canal and in the old fishing harbour at its head, which are closest to the town centre. Coin-operated electricity (€0.50/2kWh) is available at all berths, but water (€0.50/100 ltrs) is from a berth by the pump-out and harbour office. Alternatively, you can stop at Jachtcentre Elburg near the beginning of the canal, which is also served by a range of boatyards and chandlers.

Facilities ashore

Chandlers Touw & Watersport Deetman on Havenstraat and Loederman Watersportwinkel at the Jachtcenter.
Repairs & Servicing All services at the Jachtcenter
Supermarket & Shops Small grocers on main street.
ATMs At the Bruna bookshop on the main street
Cycle hire From Rijwiel Cash & Carry east of the harbour
VVV office Ledige Stede

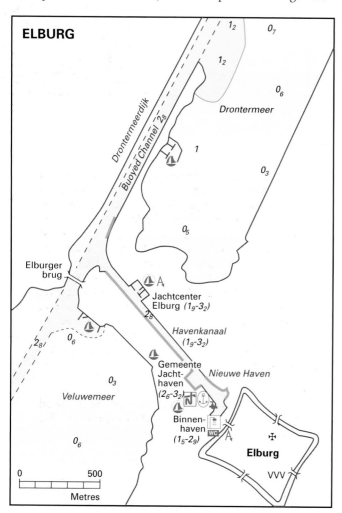

Elburg harbour canal from the northwest   *Patrick Roach*

Elburg's main street is watched over by the Vischpoort

What to see

Elburg was built as a fortress in a rectangular pattern with an encircling wall in the 14th century. The moat and ramparts were added soon after and not much has changed since. The VVV office provides a town walk (in English) which tells you about its history and development. Entry to the municipal museum on Jufferenstraat includes a visit to both the Vischpoort (originally a solid defence but converted to a gate in 1592) and to the Kazematten, an underground defensive structure which is entered near the gate. The town was an important fishing port for many centuries and on the harbour side of the Vischpoort a lantern served as the coast navigation light during the port's active years. Near the harbour you can still visit the old fish auction building, which is laid out ready for use.

Three kilometres southeast of the town a walk in the Alfred Vogel herb garden makes a welcome change to the usual diet of monuments and museums. Formerly in the nearby industrial estate, it has now been relocated to the Zwaluwenburg country park. A.Vogel is a major brand of homeopathic remedies in Holland, which are produced in Elburg from plants grown at Zwaluwenburg. Based on herbal recipes developed by Vogel from American Indian medicine, his products claim to address a vast range of symptoms.

A weekly market is held beyond the town wall on the southeast side on Tuesday mornings, when you can also enjoy free organ concerts in the St Nicolaaskerk. Midweek festivals are held on Wednesdays in July and August with music, market and special events.

Restaurant tip

Several nice restaurants in the town centre included Bistro Le Papillon and Café-Restaurant De Vischmarkt.

Vossemeer

The Vossemeer is a 7km stretch of the peripheral lakes from the junction with the Drontermeer at the Roggebotsluis to the Ketelmeer. Depth outside the channel is less than 1m and vessels are advised to follow the buoyage. There is no access to De Zwaan island.

Maximum permitted draught 2.5m
Speed limit 20km/h in the channel; otherwise, 9km/h
Lock Roggebotsluis and lifting bridge (5.4m when closed) operate throughout the day (from 1000 on Sundays). VHF 22

Ketelmeer

This lake is bordered by the northern dyke of east Flevoland, the southern dyke of the Noordoostpolder, and the Ketel bridge over the entrance to the IJsselmeer at its western end. At its eastern end it joins the Keteldiep channel which flows from the IJssel and the Ramsdiep channel which flows from the Zwarte Meer. Spar buoys mark the 1.3m contour at the eastern end

Speed limit East of the Ketelhaven and near the shores, 9km/h; otherwise, no limit.
Bridge Ketel bridge (12.9m) has an opening section which operates throughout the day with a rush hour break (1600–1830). VHF 18.

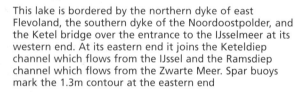

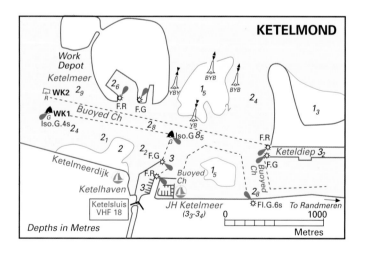

KETELHAVEN

On the south side of the Ketelmeer, the Ketelhaven forms the northern access into the Flevoland canals with a choice of two harbours outside the lock. Inter Harbour Marina lies immediately next to the Ketelsluis, whilst JH Ketelmeer has a separate entrance buoyed with small red can buoys from the Ketelmeer approach channel. The latter has the more extensive facilities, including cycle hire and pump-out, and an on-site restaurant serves both harbours.

SCHOKKERHAVEN

Marina Schokkerstrand on the north side of the Ketelmeer offers fuel and cycle hire, as well as launderette, restaurant, chandlers and wi-fi. Formerly an island before the Noordoostpolder drainage, the three villages on Schokland were abandoned in 1859 due to flooding. Now a world heritage site, Schokland symbolises the struggle between man and the sea, and the nearby Museum Schokland relates the island's past through archaeological finds. Walks between the three villages are illustrated by guidebook and the Gesteentetuin (stone garden) and visitors' centre concentrates on the early history of the area.

Nearby Nagele was architect designed in 1956 and is renowned for all the buildings having flat roofs. The Museum Nagele, itself housed in a flat-roofed building, describes the background to the village's architecture.

Ketelsluis from the south with the two harbours to starboard   *Patrick Roach*

Ramsdiep and Zwarte Meer

The Schokkerhaven also forms the entrance to the Ramsdiep channel, which runs east under the Ramspol bridge into the Zwarte Meer. The buoyed and lit channel is 3m deep, but beyond it the lake is immediately much shallower. The meer is designated as a nature reserve and so navigation is not permitted outside the marked channel. At the eastern end of the meer, the buoyed channel forks in two, running west of Vogeleiland to join either the Kadoelermeer to the north or the Zwarte Water to the southeast.

Depth 3m
Speed limit 20km/h
Length 17km
Bridge 1 opening (5.5m when closed). Ramspol bridge operates throughout the day as traffic flow allows (waiting pontoons provided on both sides). VHF 20.

Zwarte Water

The Zwarte Water continues east from the Zwarte Meer via Zwartsluis to Zwolle. The first (downstream) 5km link the Zwarte Meer to the Meppelerdiep at Zwartsluis and are included here to form the connection to the Kop van Overijssel route. Beyond Zwartsluis, the Zwarte Water continues south via Hasselt and is described in Chapter 8: Central Netherlands.

Free moorings are provided at Haven de Belt, close to the junction with the Zwolse Diep, and at the Vluchthaven (refuge harbour) De Ketting east of km20.

GENEMUIDEN

Visitors' moorings are in the inner harbour along the east quay, on the west quay by the Hotel, or on the marked hammerheads. Unmetered 16A electric is available here, but water (€0.50/100 ltrs) is only available from a berth next to the facilities and pump-out. The lock and bridge to the inner harbour normally stand open, but be aware that the footbridge is closed from Saturday evening to Monday morning.

Genemuiden (pronounced 'khener-mowder') was known for its mat-making industry, recalled in the Tapijt Museum on Klaas Benninkstraat, where there are demonstrations every Saturday. A little outside the town Stoomgemaal Mastenbroek was built in 1856 and used to drain the surrounding land. Steam days are held on occasional Saturdays in August.

ZWARTSLUIS

There are two large yacht harbours to choose from in Zwartsluis: the Stichting Recreatiecentrum lies on the Zwarte Water between the two locks and has an intercom on the reception pontoon for contacting the harbourmaster; De Kranerweerd lies on the Meppelerdiep beyond the opening bridge and has extensive facilities including 24 hour fuel, restaurant and service engineers. There are also alongside moorings by the Grote Sluis, which is not normally used for lock passage.

Zwartsluis lies at the junction of the Zwarte Water with the Meppelerdiep and forms the gateway to the nature reserves of De Wieden and De Weerribeen. The natural environment and traditional crafts of this region are showcased at the town's museum, the Schoonewelle Centre, and the town takes its name from the dark peaty or black water, which emanates from these fenland areas.

The historic inner harbour is home to a small fleet of brown boats and the whole area has a nautical feel. A large chandlers by the Grote Sluis bridge has a good selection and there are several boat engineers based locally. The last weekend in May in evenly-dated years are the National Sleepbootdagen (Tug boat days) which attracts hundreds of historic vessels to the town.

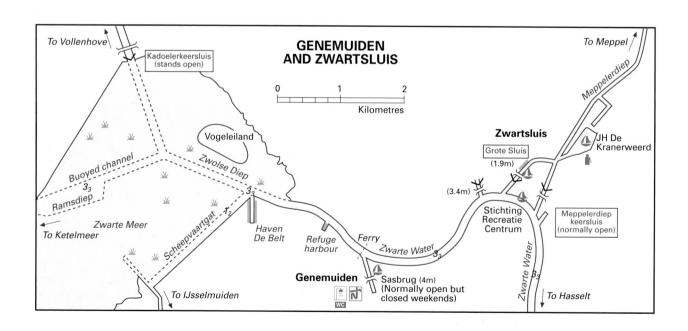

KOP VAN OVERIJSSEL

The Kop (meaning head) van Overijssel is the northern extremity of the Overijssel province which projects like a peninsular between the Noordoostpolder, Friesland and Drenthe. Towns on the west side were originally important trading and fishing ports on the Zuider Zee and then later on the IJsselmeer (after the closing of the Afsluitdijk) but the draining of the Noordoostpolder made them inland harbours and altered their character dramatically.

An area of extensive peat diggings, the fenland lakes so created have become important wetland nature reserves and the waterways dug in the 1920s to export the peat have been transformed into an idyllic leisure cruising ground. The circular route round the region can also be used as a through route to Friesland, which since the conversion of some bridges from fixed to opening, is also accessible to masted yachts.

The region is dotted with small villages and campsites and although it is only a short drive from major conurbations, it has a remote feel that makes it a popular camping and holiday destination. Only a day's cruise from the IJsselmeer, this underrated region is highly recommended in combination with cruises on the Randmeren or in Friesland.

Meppelerdiep

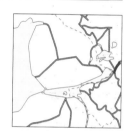

The Meppelerdiep leaves the Zwarte Water at Zwartsluis and runs northeast over the border into Drenthe and on to Meppel. The south-western stretch of this waterway connects Zwartsluis to the Kanaal Beukers-Steenwijk and the rest of the canal (including Meppel itself) is covered in Chapter 7: Groningen & Drenthe.

Length Zwartsluis to Beukerssluis, 4km
Depth 3.25
Speed limit 12km/h
Lock Meppelerdiepkeersluis & opening bridge (5.2m when closed at normal water level), VHF 22. The lock normally stands open and the bridge operates throughout the day (from 1000 on Sundays)

Kanaal Beukers-Steenwijk

The Kanaal Beukers-Steenwijk runs from the Beukerssluis northeast of Zwartsluis, north via Giethoorn to join the Kanaal Steenwijk-Ossenzijl, at a point west of Steenwijk. It is made up of the Kanaal Beulakerwijde, the Beukersgracht, the Belterwijde, and the Beulakerwijde. These waterways provide a mast-up route between the Randmeren and Friesland. Attractively lined with waterside properties, this area is very popular with leisure boats and is teeming with small boats on summer weekends.

Free 48-hour canalside moorings are available north of the Beukerssluis and dotted around the Belterwijde and the Beulakerwijde lakes.

Length 14km
Speed limit 9km/h
Maximum permitted draught 2.4m
Lock Beukerssluis and lifting bridge operates throughout the day with a break for lunch (1200–1300) except in July & August, VHF 20
Bridges 4 opening. Blauwe Hand, Giethoorn-Zuid, Giethoorn-Noord & Heerenbrug (6.9m when closed) operate throughout the day with a break for lunch (1200–1300)

WANNEPERVEEN

On the north side of the Belterwijde there are moorings at Waterpark Beulaeke Haven, west of the Blauwe Hand bridge on the north side. Extensive facilities are available including a restaurant, cycle hire and repairs.

The area around the bridge is called Blauwe Hand, supposedly in view of the condition of the residents after working in the ice-cold fens. To the east, the small village of Wanneperveen grew up around the peat digging industry that created the lakes, and on either side of the Veneweg (Peat Road) you can still see a variety of farms and labourer's cottages.

GIETHOORN

Where to stop

The large municipal visitors' harbour, De Zuiderkluft, provides ample space for visitors in its sheltered basin off the main canal. There is no reception arrangement so skippers should choose an alongside or box mooring and report to the harbour office after 1600. Coin operated electricity and water as well as a launderette and pump-out are available. The harbour also administrate the canalside moorings between Blauwe Hand and Giethoorn-Zuid bridges, but these are subject to heavy wash from passing hirecraft when the waterway is busy.

Alternatively, berths are available at JH Vos, just south of the Giethoorn-Zuid bridge where the facilities include pump-out and cycle hire.

Facilities ashore

Fuel & Chandlers Tankstation Prinsen
Repairs & Servicing Elzenaar Watersport
Supermarket, Shops & ATMs Ds T.O. Hylkemaweg
Cycle hire From Tankstation Prinsen or many cafés
  around the village
VVV office Eendrachtsplein

What to see

This internationally-known tourist attraction is also called Green Venice and the tiny canals which criss-cross the village are the best vantage point from

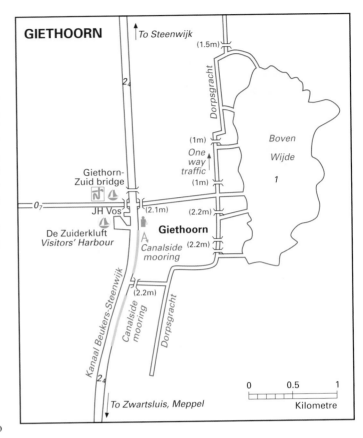

which to see the thatched farm houses which line the banks. The name originates from goat horns, victims of an earlier flood, which were found by the early inhabitants around 1200. There are covered boat tours of the canals with explanation from the guide which depart from several locations along the Binnenpad and the Zuiderpad, or you can take your dinghy into the small canals, taking care to follow the one way system south to north along the Dorpsgracht.

The museum farm 't Olde Maat Uus presents an image of the village around 1900 and the original rooms are furnished in the style of this period. Also on Binnenpad you can visit the Gloria Maris shell gallery or the Museum De Oude Aarde, a beautiful collection of precious stones and fossils from all over the world.

Restaurant tip

On the west bank of the main canal, Vistaria Hubanet specialises in fish dishes and transforms from a casual snack café and takeaway during the day, to a nautically themed restaurant by night. Another popular choice is De Witte Hoeve pancake restaurant with the unfeasibly wide range of varieties. You can also hire bikes and canoes here, or buy artisan candles. If you want to travel to dinner by dinghy a good location is Italian Restaurant and Pizzeria Fratelli, which has an attractive canalside terrace on the Binnenpad.

Take the dinghy or hire a whisper boat and explore Giethoorn's tiny canals

Kanaal Steenwijk-Ossenzijl

Kanaal Steenwijk-Ossenzijl runs from the centre of Steenwijk, close to the junction with the Kanaal Beukers-Steenwijk, to the Ossenzijlersloot at Ossenzijl. The bridges on this waterway are fully automated and an illuminated display board with the text *'brug wordt bediend'* indicates your presence has been detected and the bridge will open. Light signals indicate when passage is possible: a red light above a green flashing light indicates the bridge is about to close, and passage is not permitted.

Plenty of free canalside moorings are provided along the length of the waterway for a maximum stay of 2 days. Waiting pontoons at the bridges are only to be used until the next opening.

Length 12km
Speed limit 9km/h
Bridges 1 fixed (6.6m - only on the part into the centre of Steenwijk), 4 opening. Hogeweg, Meenthe, Hesselingen and Thijensdijk bridges and operate throughout the day with a break for lunch (1200-1300).

STEENWIJK

The visitors' harbour at Steenwijk is located in the end of the canal and lies close to the centre of the small town. There are berths on landing stages in a basin at the entrance to the harbour for boats less than 12m and thereafter quayside berths prior to a fixed bridge for boats over 3.3m air draught . Electricity is by token, which is available from the harbour office, halfway along on the north side. A free token is also needed to open the rubbish container. Water and pump-out are available near the entrance to the harbour.

Steenwijk (pronounced 'stain-vike') is the economic and cultural centre of this area and has a large shopping centre near the harbour. A large market is held on Saturdays and there are three supermarkets very close to the harbour, making it a good place for supplies. The 86m tower of St Clements church, dating from 1467, is open to visitors in July and August for a panoramic view of the town and you can also visit the local history museum, and the fun-fair and circus museum, both on the market square.

The town holds a series of mid-week festivals on Wednesdays from mid-July to August. Most amenities and attractions are closed on Monday morning except the supermarkets.

Popular canalside moorings on the Kanaal Steenwijk-Ossenzijl

Ossenzijlersloot and Kalenbergergracht

The Ossenzijlersloot forms the continuation of the Kanaal Steenwijk-Ossenzijl just south of the village and continues northwest to join the Linde. The Kalenbergergracht runs through the De Weerribben national park, to continue as the Heuvengracht and Wetering. There are free canalside moorings in the centre of Ossenzijl and along the Kalenbergergracht. The waterside houses and pretty villages make this a very pleasant cruise, with the waterway dotted with canoeists and reed punts as well as holiday cruisers and charter boats.

Length 6km
Speed limit Ossenzijlersloot 9km/h
Bridges 2 opening. Kalenberg and Ossenzijl bridges operate throughout the day with a break for lunch (1200–1300). Toll payable at Kalenberg.

OSSENZIJL

As well as the canalside moorings, the large JH De Kluft (depth 1.6m) just south of the canal junction is a popular camping and boating holiday destination. The extensive facilities include onsite bakers, café and restaurant, as well as cycle hire, launderette and pump-out.

The canal runs through the centre of the small village and the area's campsites and holiday chalets are popular with anglers and cyclists. De Weerribben visitors' centre is near the west end of the Kanaal Steenwijk-Ossenzijl, next door to JH De Kluft, and here you can find out all about the natural environment of this former peat-digging area which, together with the De Wieden nature reserve to the south, forms the largest marsh area in northwest Europe. Canoes and whisper boats are available to

hire from the centre or you can make use of one of their canoe route maps and take your own dinghy into the small, reed-lined channels.

The village has a single post-office/convenience store on the west bank of the Ossenzijlersloot, a fish shop and two restaurants.

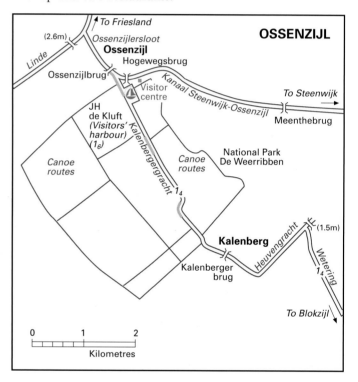

Linde and Mallegat

The Linde connects the Jonkers waterway (also known as the Helomavaart) to the town of Kuinre, and has a junction with the Ossenzijlersloot halfway along. Only the section north east of Ossenzijl is navigable for the purposes of this guide, as the southwest part is restricted to an air draught of 2.65m. At the east end of the Linde you come to an area called Driewegsluis (Three-way lock) where there are plenty of free canalside moorings and a pavilion restaurant and snack café. The old three-way lock was restored in 1995 but the normal navigation is through the Linthorst Homansluis. The Linde marks the boundary between Overijssel and Friesland and from here you can continue north, covered in Chapter 6: Friesland, or turn south on the Mallegat channel, which brings you to Oldemarkt.

Length 6km
Speed limit 6km/h
Maximum permitted draught 1.8m
Lock Mr HP Linthorst Homansluis and lifting bridge operate throughout the day with breaks for lunch and tea (1200–1300 and 1615–1715).
Bridges 1 opening. Wolvega bridge is self-operated and must be opened from ashore by releasing the safety catches and pulling the chain.

OLDEMARKT

The well-equipped harbour (depth 1.4m) lies at the end of the Mallegat channel and has plenty of space for visitors. Coin operated electricity and water are available together with the usual basic facilities. The harbour office is the most basic of all, residing in an old caravan round the back of the toilets. The harbourmaster works part-time sharing his time between here and Passantenhaven Steenwijk.

The small village dates back to the 15th century when an important butter and piglet market was held here. Its one main street has a handful of shops and a well-regarded restaurant, the Hof van Holland.

Wetering and Noorderdiep

The route from Ossenzijl to Blokzijl passes through the De Weerribben national park and (after the Kalenbergergracht) runs via channels called Heuvengracht, Wetering, De Riete, Valse Trog and Noorderdiep. South of the Scheere bridge the Steenwijkerdiep branches to the east, providing a mast-up route to Steenwijk. The De Riete buoyed channel passes down the west side of the Giethoornse Meer in order to continue on the Valse Trog, but an alternative channel to the east continues south to join the Beulaker and Belter Wijde. Navigational details for these lakes are given at the end of this chapter.

At Scheere is another of the automated bridges. A display board with the text *'brug wordt bediend'* indicates your presence has been detected and the bridge will open. Light signals indicate when passage is possible: a red light above a green flashing light indicates the bridge is about to close, and passage is not permitted. The lock at Blokzijl can be very busy during summer weekends and, with its slow operation, waiting times of up to two hours are not uncommon so allow plenty of time.

There are several canalside mooring places for a maximum stay of 2 days and moorings by the bridges which can be used until the next opening. South of the fixed bridge at Muggenbeet, the riverside café-restaurant, Geertein, is a pleasant stopping point with a few moorings.

Length 9km
Speed limit 6km/h
Maximum permitted draught 1.4m
Lock Sluis Blokzijl and lifting bridge operate throughout the day with a break for lunch (1200–1300) except in July and August.
Bridges 1 fixed (5.4m), 1 opening. Scheere bridge operates throughout the day with a break for lunch (1200–1300).

BLOKZIJL

Where to stop

The main visitors' harbour in Blokzijl lies in the old harbour pool, or kolk, just south of the town centre lock. The large basin has moorings on landing stages on the west side, or along the quay for boats over 12m. Coin operated electricity (€1/2kWh) and water (€0.50/100l) are available and a modern facilities block (including a launderette) is next door to the VVV office, who also provide washing machine tokens. The harbourmaster attends to these, as well as other moorings around the town, by calling by bike to collect your mooring fee when he can.

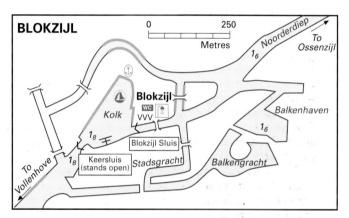

Facilities ashore

Chandlers, Repairs & Servicing Kielstra Watersport on Lage Wal
Supermarket & Shops Volume Markt on Boeffers Weidje
ATMs In the tea shop on Bierkade
Cycle hire From VVV office, or Zeinstra on Steenwijkerweg
VVV office Kerkstraat

What to see

The harbour basin in Blokzijl (pronounced 'block-sale') was the original harbour of the old town when it was an important port on the Zuider Zee. The high-water canon on the north side warned of impending flood conditions with a three-stage alarm, culminating in three shots for dykes broken. In the Gildenhuys museum on Kerkstraat, you can watch an informative film (in English) about the history and development of the town, which thrived as a result of its successful trading position, and later through peat-digging and reed-based products. The VVV also provide a town walk (in English), which gives the background story to the many historic buildings in the town. Many of these buildings now house specialist retailers who make a point of having unusual and interesting collections, such as the silversmith with her beautiful jewellery selection, or the tea house with its 80 varieties.

Today the town is a popular yachting centre and festivals are held in May and September to open and close the sailing season, which involve much music and merriment led by well-regarded shanty choirs from around the region. Other events during the summer include a ring-riding competition (a parade of horse-drawn carriages) and an annual tourist market, both held on weekends in August.

Restaurant tip

The Michelin-starred Kaatje bij de Sluis is named after a restaurateur from the 18th century who was notorious for her secret recipe dishes. Today you can buy some specialities which bear her name in the small grocer's behind the restaurant. For a more everyday dining experience, the Sluiszicht always has a busy terrace, whilst in the Prins Mauritshuis café-restaurant you can sample the traditional cake of the town, the Blokzijl Brok.

Connections

There is no station in the town, but there are regular bus services to Steenwijk and Emmeloord.

A cannon stands by the harbour ready to warn of impending danger

Steenwijkerdiep

The Steenwijkerdiep runs from Steenwijk to Muggenbeet and is a mast-up route across rural countryside. The waterway is very narrow and is most suitable for smaller boats, with the low speed limit designed to protect the banks from wash.

Length 8.5km
Speed limit 6km/h
Maximum permitted draught 1.6m
Bridges 2 opening. Halfweg and Kooiweg bridges operate throughout the day with a break for lunch (1200–1300). Toll payable at Kooiweg bridge.

SCHEERWOLDE

Scheerwolde was a new polder village inaugurated by Queen Juliana in 1952 and designed to provide convenient accommodation for those working nearby. The idea never took off and the village consists of only a few streets of houses from that time. There are free canalside moorings west of the Kooiweg bridge. The highlight of the visit is the eel-smoking house which is open to visitors every day with tours on Tuesday and Saturday afternoons.

Vollenhoverkanaal

The Vollenhoverkanaal runs from Blokzijl to Vollenhove along the border between north west Overijssel and the new Noordoostpolder. The bridge at Vollenhove can be requested by telephone, which is answered by an automated service. The answer machine registers your request and it is not necessary to say anything.

Free unserviced canalside moorings are available on the west bank to the south of Blokzijl.

Length 6km
Speed limit 20km/h
Depth 3m in the channel
Bridges 1 opening. Vollenhove bridge operates throughout the day with a break for lunch (Monday –Saturday 1230–1330, Sunday 1230–1330). Request by push button or ☎ 0527 241856 (automated answer service).

VOLLENHOVE

Where to stop

JH Vollenhove is a large harbour just south of the bridge which provides ample space for visitors. Most stop in the outer harbour where box and alongside moorings are available, with coin-operated water (€0.50/100l) and electricity (€1/2kWh). Limited space is available in the old inner harbour, accessed via a lifting bridge (3.7m when closed) which can be opened on request by the harbourmaster ☎ 06 20658979. The bridged entrance is narrow and moorings here are recommended for smaller boats up to a beam of 4.5m and draught of 1m. Rubbish disposal requires a token, available free from the harbour office, and bikes are also available to hire here.

Repair services and diesel are available from Jachtwerf Aquador, on the Vollenhove canal opposite the harbour entrance.

What to see

Once a Zuider Zee harbour and home of nobles, Vollenhove (pronounced 'follenhover') is also known as the town of palaces. Many of the great gardens remain and the Tuin van Marxveld, on Bisschopstraat is open to visitors and ablaze with colour in late summer. For more of a wilderness walk, the gardens of the Old Ruitenborgh manor house are also open to the public and include the ruins of a 16th-century castle. Today the Royal Huisman Shipyard is the main employer in the town, although its industrial buildings overlooking the harbour do not reflect the style and grace of the luxury yachts they produce. A statue on the quay remembers the three fishermen from Durgerdam who were stranded on a floating ice-flow in the Zuider Zee for 14 days before being rescued by a

Enjoy the stately gardens of Vollenhove's former nobles

boat from Vollenhove.

The town's Harbour Days take place over the Whit weekend (Pinksterdagen) and comprise a four-day celebration including visits from historic vessels and shanty choirs. On the last Saturday in August the town is ablaze with colour when the Bloemencorso (flower parade) rolls into town elaborately decorated with millions of dahlias.

Kadoelermeer

The Kadoelermeer forms the continuation of the Vollenhoverkanaal from Vollenhove to the Zwarte Water at Vogeleiland. There is good depth in the channel, but the waterway can be shallow outside this. The direction of buoyage is from south to north so green buoys lie on the east side of the channel. The flood lock at Kadoelen stands open and a moveable crane (which restricts air draught to 10m) is removed during the sailing season (1st May to 16th October).

At the De Voorst junction the Zwolse Vaart branches west into the Noordoostpolder, described below. At the three-way junction at Vogeleiland the waterway continues southeast as the Zwarte Water and to the southwest as the Zwarte Meer.

Length 3.2km
Speed limit 9–12km/h
Depth 3m
Bridges 1 opening. Kadoelerkeersluis bridge operates throughout the day with a break for lunch (Monday–Friday 1230–1300, weekends 1230–1330).

DE VOORST

Jacht Centrum De Voorst has space for boats up to 20m with the usual basic facilities although those on the outer pontoon do suffer from wash from passing vessels. The harbour stands on the edge of the extensive Voorster Bos woods and nearby is a former dyke-testing centre where much of the research for the Delta project was carried out. The dyke models have been installed in the neighbouring woodland with interpretative boards for the interest of those who walk there.

Beulaker Wijde and Belter Wijde

From the Giethoornse Meer, the Walengracht channel leads into the Beulaker Wijkde where buoyed channels cross to the Blauwe Hand bridge and the Arembergergracht. Outside the channels navigation is possible with a minimum depth of 1m, except for the area northeast of the Walengracht-Blauwe Hand channel. The Arembergegracht continues south to Zwartsluis but is restricted to an air draught of 3.4m at the southern end. There are good moorings on the islands to the west side of the lake and beyond these, in the the Kleine Beulaker, navigation is possible with depth of 0.8-0.9m.

The Belter Wijde is divided into two halves by a dam, with the east part forming part of the Kanaal Beukers-Steenwijk. Outside the channel navigation is possible with a depth of 0.8m, except for some areas near the banks. On the west side, an area is defined for waterskiing for which a local permit is required.

Speed limit 9km/h
Depth min 1.4m in the channels

Urk harbour

The entrance to Urk is clearly marked from the northwest or southwest, avoiding the shallow area known as the Vormt. The lighthouse makes a conspicuous landmark although it should be noted that the entrance is 0.9km to the southeast.

URK

Where to stop

There is plenty of space for visitors in the municipal harbour, either in boxes or alongside the quays. The harbour office is on the second pier to starboard and there are toilet and shower facilities on the third pier

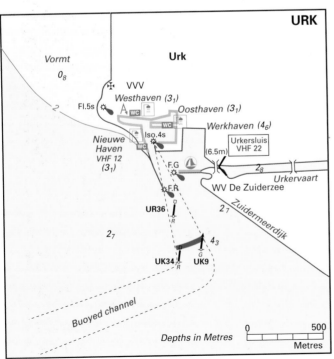

as well as on the north side of the harbour opposite, and by the beach on the west side. Water and electricity are unmetered and the token operated rubbish disposal system has been abandoned in favour of an unlocked container. There are also limited spaces at WV De Zuiderzee for boats up to 12m immediately to starboard on entering the harbour, near the Urkersluis.

A beach runs along the west side of the harbour and this is very popular in good weather with dozens of youngsters arriving on bikes. The south wall of the west harbour is their playground so be aware in this location that you are likely to be in receipt of a beach ball in the rigging and no peace.

Facilities ashore
Fuel Fuel by tanker from:
   K. de Boer ☎ 0527 681343 / 06 5126 0122
   BP Hoekman ☎ 06 5326 9456
   H. de Boer ☎ 0527 687080
Chandlers & Repairs Post Watersport (Yamaha Outboards agent & chandlers) Wijk 1-30a
Supermarket & ATMs Boni on Klifweg
Shops Small selection on Raadhuisstraat
VVV office Raadhuisstraat (By the Museum)

What to see

Formerly an island standing some 15km offshore, Urk was joined to the mainland by the Noordoostpolder in 1942, but a small fishing fleet remains and a fish auction takes place in the harbour most afternoons. The narrow, sloping alleyways of

Urk harbour and beach from the top of the lighthouse

Urk harbour from the west; the Urkervaart (top right) joins the IJsselmeer with the Kop van Overijssel   *Patrick Roach*

Urk's lighthouse gains stature from its position on the cliff

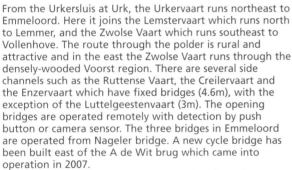

the old village still feature the occasional authentically dressed local, with more turning out for Urkerdag, the Saturday before Whit Monday. The Museum Het Oude Raadhuis presents the history of the island and the fishing industry, with a neighbouring fisherman's cottage added to the collection in 1998.

The 14m lighthouse was built on the high town cliff in 1844 and in summer months you can climb the 65 steps for a splendid view of Urk and the IJsselmeer. Nearby, the fisherman's monument depicts an anxiously waiting wife, and the 31 marble slabs which surround her list those seamen (right up to the present day) who never returned.

Restaurant tip

The inappropriately named Restaurant De Zeebodem is one of the few in this province which is not on the sea bottom, but its popular terrace is favoured for the view of the harbour and you will also find a T-mobile hotspot here. Round the corner on Klifweg the superb fish shop and café-restaurant run by G. Baarssen has every type of fish speciality.

Connections

There is no train station in Urk, but a regular ferry runs to Enkhuizen, from where the nearby train station provides connections to Amsterdam.

Noordoostpolder

From the Urkersluis at Urk, the Urkervaart runs northeast to Emmeloord. Here it joins the Lemstervaart which runs north to Lemmer, and the Zwolse Vaart which runs southeast to Vollenhove. The route through the polder is rural and attractive and in the east the Zwolse Vaart runs through the densely-wooded Voorst region. There are several side channels such as the Ruttense Vaart, the Creilervaart and the Enzervaart which have fixed bridges (4.6m), with the exception of the Luttelgeestenvaart (3m). The opening bridges are operated remotely with detection by push button or camera sensor. The three bridges in Emmeloord are operated from Nageler bridge. A new cycle bridge has been built east of the A de Wit brug which came into operation in 2007.

Free canalside moorings are provided on the Urkervaart both sides of the Tollebeek bridge, which are opposite a fuel station, café-restaurant and convenience store. Further canalside moorings are provided on the Zwolse Vaart halfway between Marknesse and Emmeloord, just west of the junction with the Luttelgeestenvaart, which are opposite a fuel station. These are both for a maximum stay of three days.

Speed limit Not officially fixed but 9–12km/h is usual
Maximum permitted draught 2.4m
Locks Urkersluis, Friese Sluis, Voorstersluis and Marknessersluis operate through the day with a break for lunch (1230–1300 Monday–Friday and 1230–1330 at weekends).
Bridges 4 fixed (6.5m), 7 opening. On Lemstervaart: Marknesser bridge; and on Zwolse Vaart: Kamper bridge. On Urkervaart (west to east): A de Wit, cycle, Tollebeek, Nageler (VHF 18) and Overstap bridges operate the same hours as the locks.

EMMELOORD

Where to stop

There are a large number of canalside moorings in Emmeloord between the Nageler bridge and the three way junction which have shower and toilet facilities and are close to the town centre. Those east of the Overstap footbridge have a more leafy outlook and are near to the sanitary facilities and a water hose, whilst those west of the bridge are near to two supermarkets and a car park. At the beginning of the Lemstervaart (between the viaduct and the hotel) Zuiderzee Yachting has limited space for boats up to 15m with the usual basic facilities including pump-out.

What to see

As the capital of the new Noordoostpolder, Emmeloord was laid out as a planned development. Its centrepiece is an unusual combination, a water tower with a 48 bell carillon, the design of which was the result of an architectural competition. Used for water storage until 2005, visitors can climb the 243 steps to the viewing platform and admire the carillon bells, which were donated and inscribed by each of the villages on the polder. For a taste of the tropics, take the bus or cycle to the Orchideeën Hoeve at Luttelgeest, a giant indoor orchid garden which would be ideal when the weather is less than tropical.

The functional town has the usual range of amenities with Eetcafe Chillers on the river the most popular dining venue, and a weekly market on Thursdays in the market square in front of the hotel, VVV and water tower. An annual tourist market is held on the third Saturday in July.

Expect deep drops at all the locks which connect the polders with the outside world

MARKNESSE

Canalside moorings are provided on the Zwolse Vaart just the west of the lock (toilets and showers are available) and halfway between Marknesse and Emmeloord, next door to a roadside fuel station. The small village has done its best to welcome visitors with an information point near the moorings and a signposted walk pointing out sites of interest.

The drainage of the polder was completed in 1942 and the first residents lived in temporary accommodation and houseboats until the end of the second world war, with fuel and food shortages hampering progress. Since then Marknesse has developed into a pleasant place to live and work with a single parade of shops in the main street providing for most day-to-day requirements.

Cruising in Flevoland, the Randmeren and Kop van Overijssel

With the polderisation of Flevoland, the character of the former IJsselmeers ports such as Naarden, Spakenburg, Hardewijk and Elburg has changed, but they still provide lots of interest, history and culture for the cruising yachtsman and crew to enjoy. The difference is now they can be visited in sheltered circumstances and without stress or worry.

Whilst these ports already attract some English-speaking yachtsmen that can pass under the twelve metre bridges near Naarden, and some of them complete the round trip back to the IJsselmeer via the Ketelmeer, almost none hitherto have sampled the peace and quiet of the Flevoland canals and emerged at Lelystad, Almere-Stad or opposite Hardewijk.

However the major oversight must be the under-exploitation by non-Dutch speakers of the Kop van Overijssel. Firstly, this area can be utilised as a mast-up route between the Randmeren and Friesland. Secondly, a circular route taking in Giethoorn, Ossenzijl and Blokzijl reveals much that is good about Dutch inland cruising and those visitors stowing a dinghy can enjoy a special insight into the Green Venice canal network at Giethoorn and the nature reserve adjacent to Ossenzijl. Combine this with emerging on the IJsselmeer at Urk and making excursions from the Randmeren to Amersfoort and Nijkerk and the crew can justly claim to have done the region a proper justice.

6 Friesland

Waterways	Principal venues	Other stopping places
IJsselmeer (east coast)	Hindeloopen/Hylper	
Lemmer canals	Lemmer	
Prinses Margrietkanaal	Grou/Grouw	Burgum/Bergum, Eastermar, Opeinde, Stroobos-Gerkesklooster
Harinxmakanaal, Van	Harlingen	Franeker
Leeuwarden canals	Leeuwarden/Ljouwert	
Dokkumer Ee/Dokkumer Ie and Dokkum canals	Dokkum	Burdaard/Birdaard
Dokkumer Grootdiep/Dokkumer Grutdjip		Dokkumer Nieuwe Zijlen
Lauwersmeer		Oostmahorn, Lauwersoog
Lange Sloot/Lange Sleat, Sloten and the Slotermeer/Sleattemer Mar	Sloten	Balk
Woudsend canals		Woudsend
Wijde Wijmerts/Wide Wimerts en Nauwe Wijmerts/Nauwe Wimerts		
Sneek canals	Sneek	
IJlst and the Geeuw/Geau		IJlst
Bolsward and the Bolswardervaart		Bolsward
Johan Frisokanaal	Stavoren	Heeg
Workum canal	Workum	Oudega, Gaastmeer
Trekvaart van Workum naar Bolsward (Workumertrekvaart)		
Makkum canals	Makkum	
Follegasloot/Follegasleat		
Tjeukemeer/Tsjûkemar		Echtenerbrug-Delfstrahuizen, St Nicolaasga
Tjonger/Tsjonger (or Kuinder/Kuunder)		
Jonkers (or Helomavaart/Helomavaort)		
Janesloot/Jaansleat		
Langweerderwielen/Langwarder Wielen	Joure	Langweer
Scharsterbrug canal (Scharsterrijn)		
Heerenveen and the Engelenvaart/Engelenfeart		Heerenveen
Buitenringvaart		
Sneekermeer/Snitser Mar and Terherne/Terhorne		Terherne/Terhorne
Akkrum canals		Akkrum
Nes canals		Aldeboarn/Oldeboorne
Opsterlandse Compagnonsvaart (Turfroute)/ Opsterlânske Kompanjonsfeart	Appelscha	Gorredijk, Donkerbroek, Oosterwolde,
Jirnsum/Irnsum canal		Jirnsum/Irnsum
Pikmeer/Pikmar and the Wijde Ee/Wide Ie to Drachten		Oudega, Drachten
Hooidammen-Veenhoop (Hooidamsloot)		Earnewâld/Eernewoude, Princenhof (Oude Venen)
Warten/Wartena canals		Warten/Wartena
Wergea/Warga canal		Wergea/Warga
Nauwe Greuns/Nauwe Greons		

The waterways of Friesland are formed by a series of large meers, being former peat or, as the Dutch say, 'turf' diggings, which are joined together by large and small waterways. The resulting network is a complex interconnected system, part of which forms a busy commercial route, and the rest of which are barely used rural waterways with very low headroom. In all, they therefore represent a range of places and landscape ideal for exploration by waterborne visitors. The waterways are described in a geographical sequence starting with the IJsselmeer in the west and with the major through routes, including the fixed-mast route via the Lauwersmeer. The remainder of the chapter is dealt with in two sections both working south to north, firstly addressing those waterways and meers to the west of the Prinses Margrietkanaal, and secondly those to the east.

Friesland has the most water of any of the Dutch provinces and has a wealth of boating facilities and places to stop. In order to give the visiting boater some guidance as to where to head for and to avoid swamping the reader with choices and keep this chapter to a manageable size, only the most popular venues have been featured in this guide. However, this does include some small village harbours as well as the larger cities and includes all of the significant, historic towns. A feature of boating in Holland, and particularly in Friesland is what might be called the resort yacht harbour, where Dutch boats might typically stop for several days. These are often combined with campsites and recreational facilities but are not always close to towns or amenities. Such harbours are very suitable for boats that are looking for this type of holiday and normally have excellent facilities, as detailed in the *Almanak*.

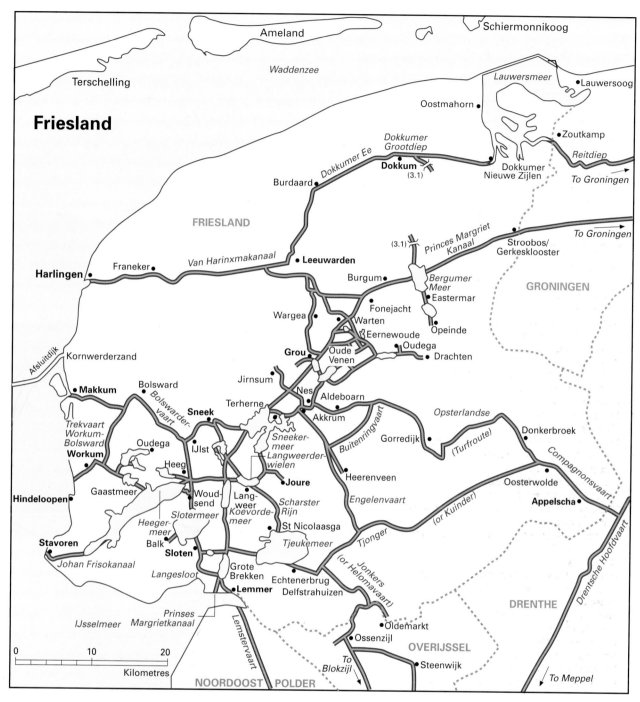

Friesland

The Frisian language is widely used in this bilingual province and causes particular problems for visiting boaters in the spelling and pronunciation of place names. In this guide, the most common version of the name is used, with the alternative name given second. This follows the authors' policy which is to both spell and pronounce the place names as they are done so locally. From 2007 the *ANWB Almanak* references many more towns and waterways under their Frisian spelling so you may need to use the alternative name in order to find it. This follows a decision taken by the local authorities in 2006 to make the Frisian names the official names which came into effect in March 2007.

English-speaking sailors find common cause and empathy with the Frisian people as they still encompass a maritime tradition, having retained the Waddenzee for much of their coast line rather than excluding the sea, and many of them have cruised the North Sea. They treasure their cultural and linguistic difference to the rest of the Netherlands and pronounce many of their words more closely to the English fashion (for example, the pronunciation of 'G' is more similar to the English than that difficult Dutch guttural sound) and they retain and have even revived the English habit of drinking tea in the afternoon rather than coffee morning, noon and night!

ANWB Waterkaart B covers the whole of Friesland including the area north of Leeuwarden, whilst a separate smaller chart 'Friese Meren' is produced at the same scale which covers only the lake area. The Opsterlandse Compagnonsvaart (Turfroute), whilst still part of Friesland province, is covered on *ANWB water atlas A 'Groningen & Drenthe'*.

IJsselmeer

The west coast of Friesland is bordered by the eastern shore of the IJsselmeer, an inland sea and so considered here as an inland waterway. For navigation on the IJsselmeer the *Dutch Hydrographic chart folio 1810* is recommended. At the northeast corner of the IJsselmeer the Kornwerderzand locks give access through the Afsluitdijk to the Waddenzee. A flashing white light indicates which of the two locks to use. Waiting pontoons are provided on both sides of the lock but these are not permitted for overnighting. No customs facilities are available here and boats arriving from outside the Netherlands should report instead at Harlingen.

Speed limit 20km/h in the buoyed channels; otherwise, no speed limit
Maximum permitted draught (at Kornwerderzand) 3.5m
Lock Lorentsluizen and opening bridge (at Kornwerderzand) operate 24 hours except in extreme high water conditions (NAP +2.15m) VHF 18

HINDELOOPEN

Where to stop

An important sailing centre and attractive village, Hindeloopen has a large and efficient yacht harbour which provides every conceivable facility including wi-fi. Not so much a marina village, but more a small town there is hotel, restaurant, shops, play area, pool, leisure centre and bowling alley all on-site, in addition to normal servicing, fuel, chandlery and laundry facilities.

Report to the harbourmaster at the *sluis-huis* for moorings in the Hylper Haven

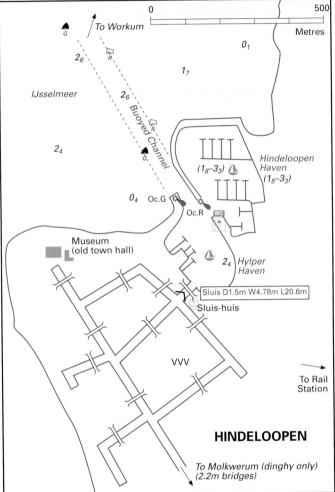

HINDELOOPEN

For a more traditional experience of Hindeloopen, berths in the old Hylper harbour are recommended in the centre of town, which have very low cost coin-operated electricity (€0.50/5kWh) and free water. The harbourmaster lives in the *sluis-huis*, the building with the distinctive tower next to the lock, and visitors can report here for guidance on where to moor. All the facilities of the adjacent marina are available to boats moored in the Hylper Haven and a new, separate toilet block is planned for 2007. Be prepared to be part of the scenery though, as this is a town much visited by tourists and looking at boats is what they do.

The lock at Hindeloopen gives access to a narrow waterway which is soon crossed by low fixed bridges (2.2m) and thus does not provide an access to the inland waterway network for the purposes of this guide, although you can take a dinghy and make an interesting round trip to Molkwerum.

Kornwerderzand lock complex looking from the northwest

Hindeloopen from the southwest. Hylper Haven is next to the town with JH Hindeloopen beyond

Facilities ashore

Fuel, Chandlers, Repairs & Servicing
  At JH Hindeloopen
Supermarket & Shops Small Coop and butcher/baker
  on Tuinen
Cycle hire From JH or the garage and fuel station on
  Suderseewei
VVV office On Nieuwstad

What to see

A former Hanseatic town, Hindeloopen (pronounced
'Hinder-lopen', and called Hylpen in Fries) prospered
through the sale of its hand-painted furniture, still
sold today in shops in the town and exported
worldwide. The tiny wooden bridges which cross the
narrow canals are reminiscent of that golden age
which saw trading for chintz with the Baltic and
other Northern European countries and is brought to
life in the local history museum, Hidde Nijland
Stichting, based in the old town hall. One of the
eleven towns of Friesland's Elfstedentocht (Eleven
Towns Race), the First Frisian Skating Museum on

Kleine Weide gives a detailed insight into this popular
winter sport. The Elfstedentocht is a skating race
which takes in the eleven towns of the Friesland
province and is held whenever the winter is cold
enough for the dykes and rivers to freeze to a
sufficient depth, the last time being in 1997. The
200km race attracts thousands of participants and
many more spectators. The current record, set in
1985, is just under seven hours.

Restaurant tip

De Gasterie on Kalverstraat is a good choice for a
special occasion and is known for its Frisian recipes
and home-smoked eel. Nearby Pizzeria Oost Acht is
where the locals go for something 'not-Dutch'. Away
from the main tourist area, the popular De
Brabander on Nieuwe Weide, is named after its
former owner, a native of the Brabant province.

Connections

A small railway station is 15 minutes walk from the
centre and is on the line from Stavoren to
Leeuwarden.

Lemmer canals

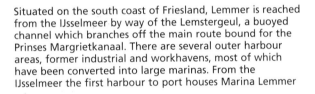

Situated on the south coast of Friesland, Lemmer is reached
from the IJsselmeer by way of the Lemstergeul, a buoyed
channel which branches off the main route bound for the
Prinses Margrietkanaal. There are several outer harbour
areas, former industrial and workhavens, most of which
have been converted into large marinas. From the
IJsselmeer the first harbour to port houses Marina Lemmer

and several boatyards. Continue past the red beacon on the
harbour mole to access either, straight ahead the Friesesluis
and the Lemstervaart, or hard to port, the Lemstersluis and
Lemmer's inner harbour. To the east of the Lemstersluis, the
Riensluis gives access to a defunct arm of the old
Lemsterrijn, now used as a dock.

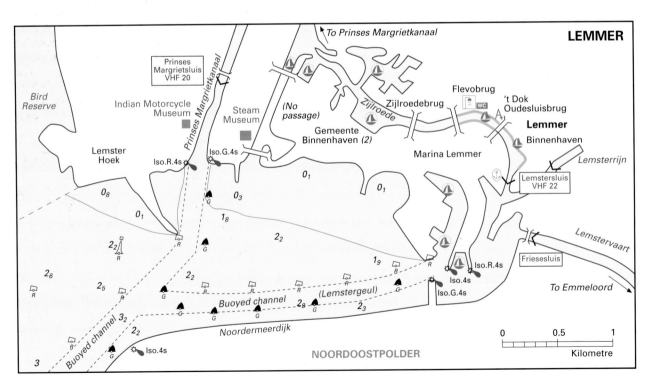

The channel which runs through the town is called the Zijlroede and this continues as the Stroomkanaal to connect the harbour with the Prinses Margrietkanaal. There are three lifting bridges which operate the same hours as the lock. A toll is payable for passage through the lock and bridges, which is collected either at the Lemstersluis for inbound vessels, or at the Flevobrug for outbound vessels.

Speed limit 9km/h
Maximum permitted draught 1.8m
Locks Lemstersluis VHF 22 operates throughout the day from 0800 with breaks for lunch and tea (1200–1300 and 1615–1715). Delays are predicted during summer weekends. Toll payable. The Riensluis opens on request only during office hours on ☎ (058) 292 58 88 and is not recommended for visitors. Opening times for the Friesesluis to the Lemstervaart are given under 'Noordoostpolder' (Chapter 5) and for Prinses Margrietsluis under 'Prinses Margrietkanaal'.
Bridges 3 lifting. Oudesluis, Flevo and Zijlroede bridges operate the same hours as the lock. Toll payable.

LEMMER

Where to stop
Municipal moorings are north of the Lemstersluis and between the Oudesluisbrug and the Flevobrug on both sides of the canal in 't Dok. These can be very busy in high season and although double mooring is permitted, the combination should not extend more than seven metres from the bank. Coin-operated electricity and water are available and a temporary facilities block, behind the Skipperland chandlers, is due to be replaced by new services as part of the apartment block under construction on the quay.

West of the Zijlroedebrug there are several marinas and mooring places, including the Gemeente Binnenhaven on the south side. Here 10A electricity and water are included in the mooring fee, and fuel is also available

Facilities ashore
Fuel Gemeente Binnenhaven
Chandlers Skipperland Watersport on Kortestreek
Repairs & Servicing Available at JHs and marinas or ask harbourmaster for contacts
Supermarket & Shops Super de Boer on Stationsweg. Spar shop on Lijnbaan and several small shops on Vissersburen.
ATMs On Schulpen by the Oudesluisbrug or others around the centre
Cycle hire De Boer on Kortestreek or Fietsplus Hoogma on Zeedijk
VVV office On Nieuwburen

What to see
A fishing port until the closure of the Afsluitdijk, Lemmer now relies on tourism and boating for its main industries. The town's strategic position between the IJsselmeer and the Friesland lakes makes it a popular base for boating and it boasts some ten yacht harbours as well as the numerous other marine businesses.

Just east of the Prinses Margrietsluis, Lemmer's steam pumping station, the ir. D.F. Woudagemaal can still be used for its original purpose and is called into service to protect Friesland from flooding in times of extreme rainfall. Guided tours of this 'steam

Stretching Lemmer's 7m beam restriction!

cathedral', built at the beginning of the last century, are given regularly during the summer months. Across the lock hidden within Lemmer's industrial estate is an Indian/Motorcycle museum, which claims to be the only one of its kind in Europe. An impressive collection of some 40 historic motorbikes with an American Indian theme are presented by their enthusiastic owner, who normally opens the museum on Saturday afternoons (race schedule permitting).

Annual events in Lemmer are organised around the sailing regattas, and include Lemsterweek at the beginning of August. A weekly market is held on Thursday afternoons on the Schans.

Restaurant tip
Dining on the quayside is the main activity in Lemmer and some of those on the main waterfront who cater mainly for tourists get a bit over-run in busy periods. A newly opened Tapas restaurant by the Oudesluisbrug has a reputation for good service, whilst next door the Restaurant Centrum serves a very acceptable range of traditional Dutch dishes. For something off the beaten track, try Pancho's Mexican restaurant on Nieuwe Dijk which the locals recommend.

Dining out on the quayside at Lemmer

Prinses Margrietkanaal

The Prinses Margrietkanaal leaves the IJsselmeer immediately to the west of Lemmer and runs approximately northeast to join the Van Starkenborghkanaal near Stroobos. It consists of a continuous series of waterways and meers, and forms, together with the Van Starkenborghkanaal, a throughway from the IJsselmeer, via Groningen, to Delfzijl. It crosses, or is connected with, most of the main meers of Friesland. The Prinses Margrietsluis, at the entrance from the IJsselmeer, operates throughout the day and has waiting pontoons with intercoms on both sides. This is a busy commercial route and there can be delays at the lock on weekdays.

Many stopping places can be found within easy reach of the canal, for instance at Koevordermeer (Recreatiepark Idskenhuizen) or Uitwellingerga south of the Sneekermeer. The Sneekermeer itself is dealt with in a later section, along with Terherne, which forms the main centre on the lake. In this section the principal stopping places which are likely to be of use to those making a passage for some distance along the canal have been featured.

Length 64.5km
Speed limit 12.5km/h
Maximum permitted draught 3.05m
Locks Prinses Margrietsluis, VHF 20, with liftbridge (7.25m when closed) operates 24 hours from Monday–Saturday and throughout the day on Sunday
Terhernesluis VHF22, normally stands open except in strong SW winds
Bridges 10 opening; 8 with minimum clearance of 7.15m when closed operate throughout the day with breaks for lunch and tea on Sundays only (1200–1300 and 1615–1715) and Schuilenburg and Stroobos swingbridges which operate the same hours as the lock.

GROU/GROUW

Where to stop

Grou stands to the west of the Prinses Margrietkanaal, where it crosses the west side of the Pikmeer. The main municipal harbour is on the west side of the Pikmeer, next to the Theehuis and a buoyed channel leads westwards to additional berths

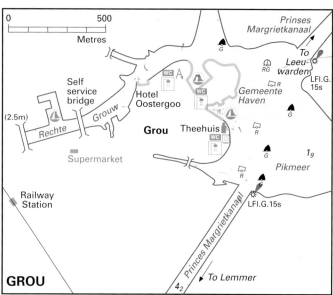

GROU

in the Hellinghaven near the centre of town and some boxes facing the canal. All berths have coin-operated electricity (€0.50/2kWh) and water (€0.50/100 ltrs) and there are facilities blocks by the Hellinghaven, near the church and by the Theehuis, the later also equipped with washing machine and dryer.

The buoyed channel continues on as the Rechte Grouw, but several fixed bridges soon prevent passage beyond the town. Yachting is the main industry here and moorings can be very crowded in high season, especially the last two weeks in July which are Skûtsje (traditional wooden boat) sailing weeks. Fuel is available from a pontoon in front of the Theehuis.

Facilities ashore

Fuel By Het Theehuis
Chandlers De Schiffart on Kerkstraat
Repairs & Servicing Numerous boatyards in town, ask harbourmaster for advice
Supermarket & Shops Super de Boer on Stationsweg or Poiesz on Gedempte Haven
ATMs Hoofdstraat
Cycle hire Zandberg cycle shop on Parkstraat
VVV office On Parkstraat

What to see

Formerly a fishing and ship-captains village, Grou (or Grouw in Dutch) was isolated by road but well-connected by water. The main church is the St Piterskerk, whose namesake St Piter was a Frisian saint named after apostle Peter, patron saint of

Quiet moorings in the centre of Grou at the Hellinghaven

Grou's church remembers the patron saint of fishermen, St Peter

fishermen. Grou is the only town in the Netherlands which instead of the St Nicholas festival in December, celebrates the St Piter festival in February.

The town's museum, De Trije Gritenijen, includes the history of two local brothers, who were significant in the development of the Frisian language. Small weekly markets are held on Tuesday and Friday afternoons and the local disco organises a foam-party every Wednesday in July and August, which may entertain younger crew members.

Restaurant tip

Het Theehuis is to be recommended for its lakeside terrace and wi-fi network, also detectable by boats moored nearby. In the main square, 't Wapen van Grou offers typical Dutch fayre, whilst Pizzeria Mio Amore is favoured by locals. Hotel Oostergo is a convenient lunch stop with its own free moorings for customers on the Rechte Grouw.

Connections

The train station is a 10-minute walk to the west side of town and is on the line from Stavoren to Leeuwarden.

BURGUM AND BERGUMER MEER

Burgum is one of the few stopping places at the east end of the Prinses Margrietkanaal and the efficient services of JH Burgumerdaam are convenient for refuelling and replenishing supplies. The aspect from the canal is somewhat uninviting, but once inside there is a friendly welcome from the harbourmaster and club members. There is a modest daily charge for the unmetered electricity, and diesel is available near the harbour entrance.

The harbour's welcome extends to a leaflet of special offers available in the town which range from a discounted white baguette to a half-metre sausage in luxury gift packaging! Restaurant 't Somerhuys offers a high standard of home-cooked dishes and offers free aperitifs for up to four diners. On a higher level, the regional museum on Menno van Coehoornweg incorporates a public observatory.

For a detour from the main canal route, the new yacht haven De Lits at Eastermar (Oostermeer) south of the Bergumer Meer offers excellent facilities or you can continue south across a further lake and stop at the free canalside moorings on the northern edge of Opeinde. This quiet village has a grocer and baker on the canal side south of the moorings as well as a Chinese restaurant advertising 'show-cooking' nearby.

STROOBOS/GERKESKLOOSTER

Passantenhaven De Landtong is a small yacht harbour on the north side of the Groningen–Leeuwarden route and is the most easterly stopping place en-route to/from Groningen. The moorings, sheltered from the industrial part of the large village by trees, have electricity and water, and diesel is also available. There is some (gentle) wash from the canal and the road opposite the berths is fairly noisy during the daytime. A small chandler and a mini-market are to be found at the other end of the village.

Harinxmakanaal, Van

From the Nieuwe Voorhaven at Harlingen, this waterway runs eastwards through Franeker, and then south of Leeuwarden. It changes its name to the Lang Deel southeast of Leeuwarden, before branching off eastwards, joining the Prinses Margrietkanaal at the Fonejacht junction, between Burgum and the Oude Venen (Old fens). Together with the Van Starkenborghkanaal it provides a throughway from Harlingen, via Groningen to Delfzijl.

Length 37.7km
Depth 2.6mm
Speed limit 12.5km/h
Locks Tsjerk Hiddessluizen VHF 22, with lift bridge (minimum 5.8m when closed) operate throughout the day with breaks for lunch and tea on Sundays only (1200–1300 and 1615–1715)
Bridges 11 opening; 10 with minimum clearance of 5.3m when closed, and Stationsophaalbrug in Franeker which operates throughout the day with breaks for lunch and tea on Sundays and holidays (1200–1300 and 1615–1715). Detailed opening times for the other bridges are given in table form in the *Almanak* under 'Harinxmakanaal, Van'

HARLINGEN

Locks Grote Sluis and Kleine Sluis (and fixed bridge 3.2m are operated by arrangement ☎ 06 5375 2587
Bridges Keersluis (4.5 m when closed) and Prins Hendrik bridges operate throughout the day and open at H+15 and H+45, VHF 11. Havenbrug operates throughout the day on request VHF 11. Bridges on the Franekervaart and Zuidoostersingel are operated in convoys: from the Industriebrug at 0900, 1030, 1400 and 1530 and from the Spoorbrug at 0945, 1115, 1445 and 1615 (includes Sundays June–August only). Franekereinds and Singel bridges are operated by arrangement ☎ 06 5375 2587

Where to stop

There are several mooring options for boats stopping in Harlingen, although by far the busiest spot is the Noorderhaven, accessed via two opening bridges when arriving from the IJsselmeer. Berths here and in the Zuiderhaven are administrated by Watersport De Leeuwenbrug and their rather expensive rates and coin-operated electricity (€0.50/kWh) do nothing to deter the crowds. Floating pontoons were added for most berths in 2006 which make managing the two-metre rise and fall much easier.

At the east end of the Noorderhaven the Grote Sluis was opened on a trial basis in 2006 and if successful, will provide an alternative access route to municipal moorings on the Franekervaart and Zuidoostersingel. These offer better value and a special weekly rate is available, although there are no toilets/showers until new facilities are provided in 2007.

Those in the know choose the secluded moorings of HWSV, considerably less expensive than the Noorderhaven, but close to the centre of town. They are reached through a nearly concealed entrance immediately to starboard east of the Tsjerk Hiddessluizen. After reporting to the harbourmaster at the clubhouse near the entrance, visitors are normally directed through the swing bridge (width 5m) into a broad canal with moorings alongside a

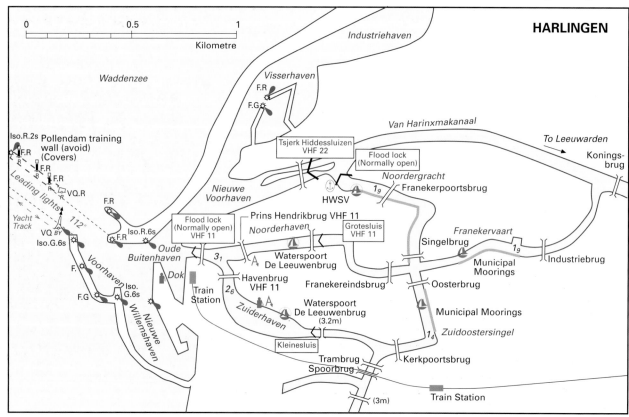

Harlingen's Waddenzee entrance and canals from the southeast

tree lined bank. Coin-operated electricity (€0.50/1.5kWh, 6 or 10A) and water (€0.50/100 ltrs) are available here, or unmetered electricity for those in boxes prior to the bridge. Very nice facilities in the clubhouse include washing machine and dryer, and the bar is opened by members on a Friday evening.

Facilities ashore

Fuel In the Buitenhaven (Dok) or at Dotinga Jachtservice in the Zuidhaven
Chandlers & Repairs Dotinga Jachtservice
Chandlers Van Meer Scheepswinkel and Ten Beaufort Watersport both on Noorderhaven
Supermarket & Shops Albert Heijn on Zuiderhaven or Super de Boer on Spoorstraat
ATMs On south side of Noorderhaven
Cycle hire BDS Fietsverhuur by the Willemshaven station
VVV office On south side of Noorderhaven

What to see

Harlingen is distinguished by having the most monuments (mainly historic buildings) of any Dutch city and a guided walk available (in English) from the VVV is a good way to see them. Many were the houses of sea captains and merchants, some being in charge of the whaling boats that sailed as far as Greenland until the 19th-century. Today the town is still a major port for shrimp and prawn fishing, with direct access to the rich fishing grounds of the Waddenzee.

The city centre is well provided with shops, with late night opening on Thursdays accompanied by evening markets in the summer. The regular weekly markets are held on Wednesday morning and Saturday on Voorstraat, and the last weekend in August is the annual Visserijdagen, a four-day festival of the sea.

Beware of the two metre tidal rise and fall in the Noorderhaven

The city museum Het Hannemahuis is also on Voorstraat, housed in an 18th-century residence and presenting the history of Harlingen and its maritime past. Around Harlingen are numerous statues to famous residents or characters with local connections, including the second statue of Hans Brinker to feature in this guide.

Restaurant tip

The Café-Restaurant 't Noorderke is convenient to the Noorderhaven and has a wi-fi hotspot. Nearby on Grote Bredeplaats the Nooitgedagt is a cosy spot for a casual dinner, or for a special event, the celebrated De Gastronoom is considered the best restaurant in Harlingen.

Connections

There are stations at the Buitenhaven and near the Zuiderhaven for the train to Leeuwarden, which connects with the regular ferries to Vlieland and Terschelling.

FRANEKER

This attractive town midway between Harlingen and Leeuwarden has limited mooring on the quay to south side of town where water and some electricity is available. These are adequate for a short stop or there is some space for boats up to 12m at JH WV Franeker to the west of the town centre.

The must-see attraction in Franeker is the Eise Eisinga planetarium, the world's oldest functioning example. Eisinga, a wool carder by trade, built the model of the solar system in the living room of his

Set your watch by the planetarium in Franeker

canalside house between 1774 and 1781. Still accurately depicting the movement of the planets in real time, it is driven by a gear mechanism using hoops and disks with 10,000 hand-forged nails as teeth. Other clocks depict the day, date, the rising and setting of the sun and moon and the position of the stars above the town, all driven by a pendulum and system of nine weights and culminating in the dining room ceiling and wall display!

There is good shopping close by in the centre of Franeker as well as markets on Wednesday afternoon and Saturday. For an insight into Frisian culture visit the Kaats museum, which explains the popular Frisian game of handball.

Harlingen's central canals make an attractive setting for the evening market

Leeuwarden canals

The canals through the centre of Leeuwarden link the Van Harinxmakanaal with the Dokkumer Ee and form part of the mast-up route from Harlingen (or Lemmer) to Delfzijl. The western section (which connects to the Van Harinxmakanaal east of Ritsumazijl bridge) is sometimes known as the Harlingervaart or the Harlingertrekvaart, the former name of the waterway to Harlingen. This leads via a series of lifting bridges to the Westerstadsgracht and Noorderstadsgracht where attractive and convenient bankside moorings are available. Continuing north takes you onto the Dokkumer Ee.

Speed Limit West of Verlaatsbrug, 12km/h, otherwise 9km/h
Maximum permitted draught 1.8m, length 40m, beam 6m
Bridges 6 opening. Slauerhoff, Hermes, Verlaats, Vrouwenports, Noorder and Ee bridges operate throughout the day with an evening rush hour break (1600–1800) Monday–Friday and breaks for lunch and tea at weekends (1200–1300 and 1615–1715). Spoorweg bridge is on a disused line and stands open. Toll payable in each direction (Verlaatsbrug and Eebrug).

LEEUWARDEN/LJOUWERT

Where to stop

The municipal moorings are on the Noorderstadsgracht on the northwest side of the city in the attractive woody surroundings of the gardens known as the Noorder plantage or Prinsentuin. The moorings were upgraded in 2006 and now include water, electricity and two new facilities blocks all operated using an access card, available from a machine outside the harbour office at the east end of the park. An initial payment of €10 (payable in notes as well as coins) includes a €5 deposit and the remaining funds can be used to pay for the required services. 16A electricity is charged at the modest rate of €0.50/7kWh and the card is also required to access the water hose, although no charge is made. The card can be topped up with more money, or returned for a refund of the deposit at the same machine. Pump-out facilities are available at both ends of the moorings and are operated by a key available from each of the neighbouring bridges.

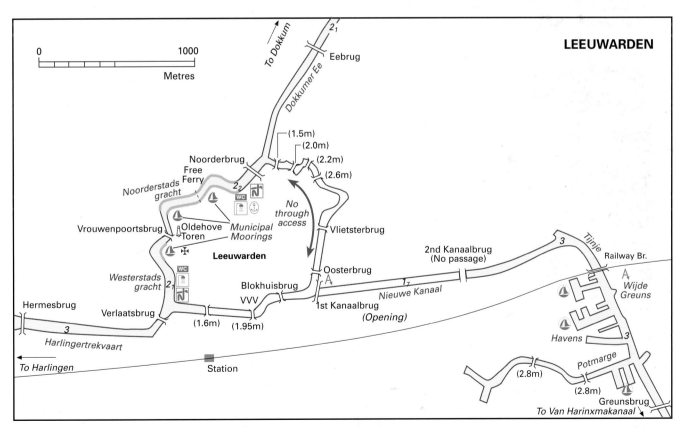

Facilities ashore

Chandlers Wagenaar Watersport, on Wijbrand de
Geeststraat, or Boatmax on the Wijde Greuns
Supermarket & Shops Albert Heijn on Zaailand or
Super de Boer on Hoekstereind. C1000 east of
Hermsbrug.
ATMs On Noordersingel or Spanjaardslaan
VVV office Willemskade Zuidzijde

What to see

As the provincial capital, Leeuwarden (pronounced
'Lay-oo-**ard**er', and called Ljouwert in Fries) has
plenty of things to do and see, including the Fries
Museum with its Mata Hari exhibition (devoted to
the first world war spy who grew up in the city).
Linked to this by an underground tunnel is the
Friesland Resistance Museum, whose central theme
is entitled 'Choices, then and now'. Resistance
sculptures around the Prinsentuin gardens give a
flavour of the museum.

Overlooking the moorings, the leaning Oldehove
tower was never completed due to subsidence and
the plan of the adjoining church (demolished in
1595) is marked out on the square. From the top
there is a view over the city and on a fine day the
Frisian islands are visible. The Prinsentuin garden
was the first public park in the Netherlands and in
the summer you can enjoy free music concerts on
Sunday afternoons.

Friesland's breed of cattle are world renowned
and the Friday cattle market and annual show are
still held regularly at the Expo centre. For more
routine supplies, the main weekly market is held on
Friday on Wilhelminaplein, with a smaller one on
Saturday morning. There is also an antiques market
on Thursdays in the summer. An annual culinary
festival takes place on Raadhuisplein in the middle
of September.

A free foot ferry links the moorings on the north side to
the facilities in the park

Restaurant tip

If you don't want to venture into the centre, De
Koperen Tuin in the Prinsentuin gardens reflects the
grandeur of the city and has a wi-fi hotspot.

Connections

The train station is about 15 minutes walk to the
south side of the city and is a main hub and has
services across the province and to the south to all
principal venues.

Leeuwarden resistance monument

Dokkumer Ee/Dokkumer Ie and Dokkum canals

The Dokkumer Ee continues north from Leeuwarden's Noordersingel, via Burdaard, to Dokkum and forms the only mast-up route to Groningen.

Length 22km
Speed limit 9km/h
Maximum permitted draught 1.95m length 40m, beam 6m
Bridges 6 opening. Van Steenhuizen, Birdaard and Klaarkampster bridges operate throughout the day with breaks for lunch and tea (1200–1300 and 1615–1715). In Dokkum: Ee, Altena and Woudpoort bridges are operated in convoy throughout the day with breaks for lunch and tea (1200–1300 and 1615–1715) expect a wait of up to 30 minutes for the next convoy. VHF 22.

BURDAARD/BIRDAARD

Burdaard (or Birdaard in Dutch) is a good stopping off village midway between Leeuwarden and Dokkum. There are canal-side moorings south of the Van Steenhuizen bridge but these are without electricity. Moorings also exist in the visitors' harbour for boats up to 12m (depth 1.3m) with places for one or two longer boats on the frontage (depth 2.1m) at the northeast end of village. Unmetered 6A electricity is available here as well as basic facilities, with a single water point by the showers.

Burdaard has a restored windmill 'De Zwaluw', dating from 1875, which claims to be the highest in Friesland and is regularly open to visitors. Also in the village is the Ruurd Wiersma house, a museum housing the simple paintings of a local artist. Eetcafé It Posthûs has a sheltered river terrace by the bridge from which to watch all the comings and goings on land and water.

DOKKUM

Where to stop

Moorings on the Zuidergracht and Woudpoortsgracht are managed by Rekreatie Dokkkum, who also have a campsite on the east side of town. Coin-operated electricity (€0.50/2kWh, 16A) and water are available and there also are facilities blocks on the south side of the canal near the windmill (De Zeldenrust), on Lutjebleek near the Woudpoortbrug, and at the campsite (where there is also a launderette).

Places on the north bank east of the Woudpoortbrug have particularly good depth and are reserved for deep-keeled yachts, but other boats can choose a space anywhere along the canal. The old rivers approaching the town from the east and west are both extremely attractive. As an important stop on the mast-up route Dokkum can get very crowded in high season but a place can usually be found.

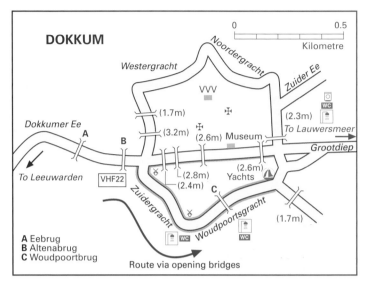

DOKKUM

Westergracht
Noordergracht
Zuider Ee
VVV
Dokkumer Ee
(1.7m)
(3.2m)
(2.6m) Museum
(2.3m)
To Lauwersmeer
To Leeuwarden
VHF22
Grootdiep
(2.8m)
(2.4m)
(2.6m) Yachts
Zuidergracht
C
Woudpoortsgracht
(1.7m)

A Eebrug
B Altenabrug
C Woudpoortbrug

Route via opening bridges

Facilities ashore

Fuel & Chandlers v.d. Zwaag on the Dokkumer Grootdiep (east of town)
Supermarket, Shops & ATMs C1000 on Strobossersteeg (north of Woudportbrug) and small shops on Grote Breedstraat & Nauwstraaat
Cycle hire Haisma Tweewielers, on Woudweg
VVV office Op de Fetze/Markt

Motorboaters should not forego Dokkum's understated attractions

What to see

Once a flourishing port, Dokkum is unusual in that it is built on a mound and has several steeply sloping streets. A ring of canals surround the centre, unchanged since 1650. Dokkum's history is dominated by the story of the evangelist Boniface who came here to convert the population in the 8th century. Some locals were offended by this idea and murdered him in 754. Museum Het Admiraliteitshuis tells the history of the town and has a permanent exhibition about Boniface.

As the most northerly town in the Netherlands and the largest in Lauwersland, Dokkum is a regional centre for north Friesland and is a lively spot during summer months. A weekly market is held on Wednesdays and there are fortnightly Friday evening tourist markets in the town centre.

Restaurant tip

De Posthoorn on Diepswal is popular for its riverside view whilst De Koffie Pot on Grote Breedstraat is on the main shopping street and, as well as the owner's coffee pot collection, you can see everything that goes on in the town.

Connections

There is no train station in the town but there are regular bus services to Leeuwarden.

Dokkumer Grootdiep/Grutdjip

The Dokkumer Grootdiep runs east from Dokkum to the Dokkumer Nieuwe Zijlen, the new locks built when the Lauwersmeer was closed off in 1969. Water levels can vary due to the flushing of excess water through the locks and although charted at two to three metres, the waterway is only recommended for boats with a draught up 1.95m.

Length 11km
Speed limit 9km/h (6km/h approaching the lock)
Maximum permitted draught 1.95m beam 6m, length 40m
Lock Willem Loréslûs at Nieuwe Zijlen with liftbridge (4.29m when closed), VHF 20. Operates throughout the day with breaks for lunch and tea on Sundays (1200–1300 and 1615–1715).

Bridges 3 opening. Schreiers and Stienfek bridges operate throughout the day with breaks for lunch and tea (1200–1300 and 1615–1715) VHF 22. Engwierum bridge is operated remotely from the lock and works the same hours (VHF 20).

DOKKUMER NIEUWE ZIJLEN

JH Lunegat lies on the north side of the locks and offers a comfortable berth and all facilities to boats on passage through the Lauwersmeer.

Lauwersmeer

Closed off from the Waddenzee in 1969, the Lauwersmeer (pronounced 'Low-ers-meer') is designated as a National Park and navigation is only permitted in the marked channels (see *ANWB Wateratlas A or Waterkaart B & Imray/CA Almanac*). The main channel (depth 3m) runs from Lauwersoog into the Vaarwater naar Oostmahorn, and via the Slenk channel into the Zoutkamperril to Zoutkamp. The Dokkumer Diep (depth 2–3m) runs from the Dokkumer Nieuwe Zijlen and joins the main Lauwersmeer channel in the SW corner of the meer. At Zoutkamp the waterway connects with the Rietdiep and continues to Groningen.

Speed limit Dokkumer Diep, Zoutkamperril and Raskes channel to Ezumazijl 9km/h; otherwise 12km/h

OOSTMAHORN

JH Oostmahorn is under new management and offers all facilities, including fuel and wi-fi, to boats looking for a quiet stop. Unmetered water and 4A electricity are provided and the latter will be increased to 10A in 2007. The bar-restaurant and children's play-area are shared by visitors to the on-site holiday chalets and the area has an out of the way feel.

The village consisted of a handful of farming and fishing cottages until the development of the new town of Esonstad nearby. A 'fortified' town built in the style of the Golden Age, Esonstad has an assortment of gabled houses as well as useful shops and amenities. There is a popular lakeside beach just to the southeast and in the nearby village of Anjum 2km to the west you can visit Museum Mill De Eendracht

LAUWERSOOG

Lauwersoog is a new settlement on the Lauwersmeer dyke which is a busy fishing port for Danish and

German as well as Dutch boats. The Vissershaven connects directly to the Waddenzee and the Robbengatsluis gives access from the sea to the Lauwersmeer. Two yacht harbours lie just inside this lock. Immediately to the south is JH Noordergat, a large harbour which operates on the red/green label principle for indicating free berths. Unmetered water and electricity are available together with extensive services and an on-site café-restaurant with views

over the meer. Further south, a new yacht harbour and camping site, Het Boze Wijf, has been established in the old state boat harbour.

Located in the fishing harbour are a chandlers, serving both the fishing and watersport trade, as well as numerous places where you can eat and buy fish and a cheap off-licence (much used by Danish fishermen).

Lange Sloot/Sleat, Sloten/Sleat and the Slotermeer/Sleattemer Mar

Beginning the description of Friesland west of the Prinses Margrietkanaal, the most southerly waterway is the Lange Sloot. From the southern end of the Groote Brekken, the Lange Sloot runs west (depth 1.7m) before becoming the Ee (or Boomsvaart) to Sloten. A second channel leaves the north end of the Groote Brekken, again running westwards (depth 1.7m) through the Brande Meer and joins the same waterway south of Sloten. North of the town the waterway continues as the Slotergat to the Slotermeer. On the Slotermeer there are 1.7m buoyed channels linking Sloten with Woudsend and back to Balk. An area for waterskiing and small speedboats is marked out on the northwest side.

Speed limit In the channels, 9km/h.
Maximum permitted draught 1.5m.
Bridges 2 lifting. Rengersbrug on Lange Sloot and Nieuwe Langebrug in Sloten operate throughout the day with breaks for lunch and tea (1200–1300 and 1615–1715). Tolls payable.

SLOTEN/SLEAT

Where to stop

At Sloten the JH Lemsterpoort is to the south of the town and has extensive on-site facilities including boat service yard and a large chandlers. Electricity is coin-operated and it is a short walk past the Lemsterpoort water gate to the centre of town. Canalside moorings both sides of the Nieuwe Langebrug (free until 1700) with a single water point near the facilities block to the north of the bridge (no electricity available). These places can be noisy due to the large milk factory which is just opposite.

What to see

The smallest of the eleven Frisian towns, Sloten (pronounced 'slote-en' and called 'Sleat' in Fries) is a fortified town on a miniature scale and the historic centre is preserved just as it was in the 18th century. The Museum Stêdhus Sleat, housed in the former town hall, is renowned for its collection of magic lanterns and has a film (in English) explaining the history of the town.

The flour mill, built in 1755, is open most afternoons. On Friday evenings a canon is fired from the grounds by Sloten's historic militia. A small canal

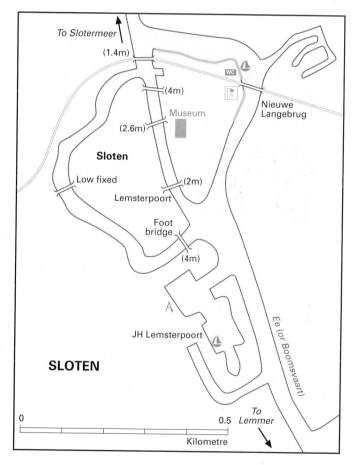

runs through the centre of the town and, although crossed by fixed bridges, is navigable by dinghy from the canal or the yacht harbour.

Many events in the town have the eleven-town theme, with cycle and vintage car rallies following the route of the famous ice-skating race. The annual fair, the Snipelsneon, takes place in June and there is a ring-tilting, or jousting competition, held in traditional costume during August.

Sloten's central canal can be explored by dinghy

Restaurant tip

Grand Café Restaurant De Zeven Wouden on Voorstreek has been an inn since the 17th century and is still a fine place to dine amongst the merchants' houses and ornamental lime trees.

BALK

Balk lies to the southwest of the Slotermeer and passage through the town is restricted to boats under 2.2m air draught. There are moorings on the canal side before the first (fixed) bridge without any facilities or yacht harbours further east of the town. Balk (pronounced 'balak') is a small town with an active charter industry and, although pleasant enough, is not particularly distinguished in an area rich with water-based recreational facilities. There is ample shopping and a choice of eating places and, for youngsters, there is more nightlife than some of the quieter towns. A Gondelvaart parade of illuminated boats takes place the last weekend of August.

Woudsend canals

The Ee runs from the north side of the Slotermeer to the town of Woudsend. North of the opening bridge the waterway branches into three arms. The Woudsender Rakken to port connects with the Heegermeer without obstacles, but beware of shallows on the north and west banks. The Noorder Ee continues north to connect with the Nauwe Wijmerts with a buoyed channel to guide vessels away from the shallow areas. The Wellesloot to starboard has 1.5m fixed bridges.

Speed limit 9km/h
Maximum permitted draught 1.5m, beam 5m, length 30m
Bridges 1 opening. Woudsend bridge operates throughout the day with breaks for lunch and tea (1200–1300 and 1615–1715).

WOUDSEND

Moorings on the quayside are limited and JH De Rakken on the west branch of the canal is the best bet (and no more expensive than the quay). Visitors' berths are on the outer quay and on the first pontoon near the harbour office, and there are toilet/shower blocks to the north and south of the basin. All facilities are available at this combined yacht harbour/campsite including a large children's play area and wi-fi internet. Alternatively there are free moorings on a grass bank to the northeast of the canal crossing, but then a dinghy would be needed to get to the town.

Woudsend's location at the junction of several waterways and between two lakes makes it a lively centre for water recreation. The village centre still has the charm of bygone days and includes monk's flourmill, De Lam, with its visitor centre and mill shop in the old miller's house next door. There is a selection of shops, a small supermarket and a good chandler, Multishop on De Dyk. The boating season gets off to a traditional start on even years in May with a three-day historic tug boat festival, the Friese Sleepbootdagen.

Restaurant t'Ponkje, has been housed in the converted chapel since 1969 and is run by a double husband and wife team, or you can enjoy a waterside view at Grandcafé-Restaurant De Watersport by the bridge.

Wijde Wijmerts/Wide Wimerts en Nauwe Wijmerts/Nauwe Wimerts

From the Noorder Ee north of Woudsend, the Nauwe Wijmert connects to the Johan Frisokanaal east of the Heegermeer. The best water is on the east side with a depth of 2.25m. Continuing north the channel changes its name to the Wijde Wijmerts and runs through Osingahuizen to IJlst, where it becomes the Bolswardervaart.

Speed limit 9km/h
Maximum permitted draught 1.95m, beam 6m, length 40m
Bridges 1 opening. Osingahuizen bridge operates throughout the day with breaks for lunch and tea (1200–1300 and 1615–1715). Toll payable.

Sneek canals

From the Prinses Margrietkanaal southwest of the Sneekermeer, the Houkesloot runs west towards Sneek. The waterways from the north, Sneeker Trekvaart and Franekervaart, have low fixed bridges so the only through routes of interest are to the south of the town; either continuing southwest along the Geeuw to IJlst, or turning southeast to return via the Woudvaart and Zwarte Brekken to the Prinses Margrietkanaal. Approaching Sneek via the Houkesloot, the navigation becomes the Zomerrak and at the end of this the route turns to port under the first of the three lifting town centre bridges, the Oppenhuizerbrug. Turning to port again after the next Van Harinxma bridge, through the Woudvaart bridge and then under a fixed bridge with 4.45m clearance brings you into the Zwarte Brekken. Continuing under the Lemmer bridge there are moorings in de Kolk in full view of the famous Waterpoort at the east end of the Geeuw.

Speed limit On the Houkesloot, east of the first Industriehaven, 12.5km/h; west of the Industriehaven, and on the Zomerrak, 9km/h
Maximum permitted draught 1.8m, beam 6m, length 40m
Bridges 4 opening, 1 fixed (4.45m) on the Woudvaart. Oppenhuizer, Van Harinxma and Lemmer bridges on the Sneek town ring, and the Woudvaart bridge on the Woudvaart operate throughout the day with breaks for lunch and tea (1200–1300 and 1615–1715). Toll payable.

SNEEK/SNITS

Where to stop

Quayside moorings are available throughout the town, on the Zomerrak approaching from the Sneekermeer, along the Koopmansgracht and in De Kolk in front of the famous Waterpoort. Those in the Zomerrak and Kolk have coin-operated electricity but the only water points are in front of Simon Watersport on Oosterkade and on the south side of De Kolk. There are toilet/shower blocks on both sides of the Zomerrak; at the west end of Koopmansgracht and on the north side of De Kolk.

Alternatively, there are berths at the many marinas on the east side of the town.

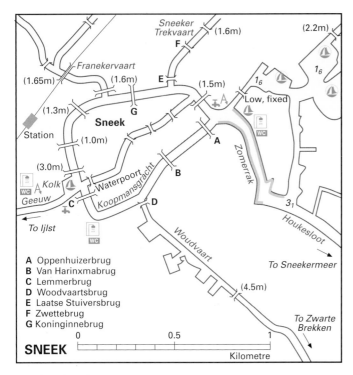

SNEEK

A Oppenhuizerbrug
B Van Harinxmabrug
C Lemmerbrug
D Woodvaartsbrug
E Laatse Stuiversbrug
F Zwettebrug
G Koninginnebrug

Sneek's famous water gate overlooks the Kolk moorings

Facilities ashore

Fuel & Repairs Brandsma Jachten on the Houkesloot south of the town
Chandlers Wels'Port on Geeuwkade by the Waterpoort; Simon Watersport on 1e Oosterkade; Dijkstra Watersport on Kleinzand
Supermarket & Shops Poiesz on Hoogeind Singel and many small shops in centre
ATMS On Martiniplein and Jousterkade
Cycle hire Twa Tsjillen on Wijde Noorderhorne
VVV office ANWB/VVV on Markstraat

What to see

Sneek (pronounced 'snake' and called Snits in Fries) stands at the centre of a vast network of waterways and has rightly earned itself the title of boating capital of Friesland. One of the eleven Frisian towns of the Elfstedentocht, Sneek's reputation comes from its Sneek week regatta, held on the nearby Sneekermeer.

The focal point of the town centre is the Waterpoort gate, claimed to be the only one of its kind in the Netherlands, and formerly the main defence of the town. The Fries Scheepvaart Museum on Kleinzand gives an insight into the town's past through historical paintings and reconstructions of ships interiors. The model rail museum in Sneek is the work of a single local collector and now boasts more than a thousand engines, carriages and goods wagons housed in a restored building near the current train station on Dr Boumaweg.

Throughout the summer, there are sailing events and regattas with the highlight being Sneek week, normally held at the beginning of August. Away from the water there are weekly markets on Tuesday morning on Grootzand and late night shopping on Thursdays. At the end of August, Swinging Sneek, is a major music festival in the market square.

Restaurant tip

On the Oosterkade, Cook & NY is a popular new lounge tapas bar, featured in the Quote Top 100 restaurants in the Netherlands (number 94). On Kleinzand, Eetcafé De Lachende Koe (The Laughing Cow) is also recommended.

Connections

The train station lies to the northwest of the centre and is on the Stavoren to Leeuwarden line.

IJlst and the Geeuw/Geau

The Geeuw runs from the Waterpoort at Sneek southwest to IJlst and connects with the Wijde Wijmerts at its junction with the Bolswardervaart.

Length 4km
Speed limit 9km/h; except in village centre, 5km/h
Maximum permitted draught 1.8m, beam 6m, length 40m
Bridges 2 lifting. Bridge over the Geeuw, and IJlst village bridge operate throughout the day with breaks for lunch and tea (1200–1300 and 1615–1715). Toll payable at IJlst village bridge.

IJLST

Limited canalside moorings are available both sides of the bridge, dotted amongst private riverside gardens, and served by a facilities block on the east side. There is a new visitors' harbour to the south of the town reached by the Jutrijpervaart or Het Schouw but the boxes are small and only recommended for boats up to 10m. Preferable for larger craft are the moorings at the Skipper Club charter base, to the east of the town next to the historic sawmill visitor attraction. They welcome visitors to their substantial landing stages when they have space free (normally during the week) and are (incidentally) a convenient place to hire boats when sampling the Netherlands before bringing over your own! Unmetered water and electricity are included in the mooring fee.

IJlst (pronounced 'eelst') is one of the oldest of the eleven Frisian towns and has a history of shipbuilding. Characteristic of the town are the ornamental lime trees which shade the canalside houses and border their private riverside gardens. The traditional wind-powered sawmill 'De Rat' was central to the town's industry and is still operational and open to visitors. There is a large supermarket near the centre as well as a handful of shops and café-restaurants.

Bolsward and the Bolswardervaart

The Bolswardervaart forms the continuation of the Wijde Wijmerts from IJlst and runs northwest to Bolsward, joining the Trekvaart van Workum naar Bolsward (or Workumertrekvaart) just south of the motorway bridge. It is an old and attractive waterway through very rural countryside.

Length 8.9km
Speed limit 9km/h
Maximum permitted draught 1.95m, beam 6m, length 40m
Bridges 5 opening. Nijezijl road and rail bridges, as well as Abbegasterketting and Wolsumerketting bridges operate throughout the day with breaks for lunch and tea (1200–1300 and 1615–1715). The Oosthem bridge is an automatic self-service foot and cycle bridge, although a bridge operator is normally available June–August. Tolls payable at road bridges.

BOLSWARD

Bridges Kruiswater bridge operates throughout the day with breaks for lunch and tea (1200–1300 and 1615–1715). 4 further opening bridges around the town canal operate the same hours.

Where to stop

The main town moorings are just north of the Kruiswater bridge in a large basin and more attractively, on pontoons under the lime trees. The mooring charges are higher than average but they include free water and electricity (6A) and interesting modern unisex toilets and showers in a bunker. Unusually the cost of the hot water in the showers is also included in the mooring fee. These are accessed by use of an entry card obtainable from the bridge-keeper at the Blauwpoort bridge, who also makes a round each afternoon.

Fuel is available from Tankstation De Kroon in the west branch of the canal, south of the Blauwpoort bridge, and helpfully this garage takes credit cards.

What to see

Bolsward is another of the eleven towns of the Elfstedentocht and a former Hanseatic town. The economic success of the town is reflected in its spectacular architecture spanning many periods. A famous Frisian writer and poet was born in the town in 1603 and the house where he was born is now a museum. Close to the moorings, a popular visit is the Sonnema Distillery tour where you can enjoy a Berenburg tasting – a liqueur that includes some 71 different herbs.

There are a good selection of supermarkets, shops, and café-restaurants in the centre, with the Pizzeria Ponte Vecchio (behind the town hall) recommended as being good value.

Johan Frisokanaal

From Stavoren at the southwest corner of Friesland, the Johan Frisokanaal connects the IJsselmeer with the Prinses Margrietkanaal just north of the Koevordermeer, via channels through the southwest lakes of the Morra, Fluessen and Heegermeer. The western section through Stavoren is also known as the Warnservaart and east of the Heegermeer, as the Jeltesloot.

This is one of the most straightforward entries into Friesland from the IJsselmeer and a much used route for leisure boats. Consequently lock delays are to be expected at weekends in summer. Buoyed channels cross the meers and boats are advised to stick to these in the Geeuw and the Morra as depths are minimal in other areas.

In addition to the principal stopping places, there are numerous yacht harbours and boat yards, particularly at Warns, a large watersports centre in a tiny village. In the Heegermeer and the Fluessen, there are four leisure islands where mooring is possible with a depth of 1.5m (except Leijepolle, 1m).

Length 25.6km
Speed limit 12.5km/h Outside buoyed channels on the meers a speed limit of 9km/h applies.
Maximum permitted draught 2.6m
Lock Johan Frisosluis and liftbridge, VHF 18, operates throughout the day with a break for lunch and tea on Sundays and holidays (1200–1300 and 1615–1715).
Bridges 3 lifting. Warns, Galamadammen, and Jeltesloot bridges all operate the same hours as the lock

STAVOREN

Where to stop

Marina moorings are available outside the lock at Marina Stavoren Buitenhaven and inside at Marina Stavoren Binnenhaven. Both share extensive facilities including wi-fi, restaurant, chandler and swimming pool. Alternatively, take the canal which runs north from the lock behind the small town and stop either at the municipal berths or in the small boxes of the local yacht club called 'VJS' (marked by the red and yellow flags) where costs are lower. These are individually labelled with size and tariff and share the (not very good) toilet/shower facilities to the west of the Koebrug, or those next to Restaurant Kruitmolen by the lock (which also has a launderette). Unmetered 16A electricity is provided at the yacht club and is to be added in 2007 for all of the municipal berths, in addition to the unmetered water.

For boats coasting on the IJsselmeer there are municipal berths in the old harbour on the north side of town, which has a historic atmosphere provided by the visiting charter boats, although there is no access through the old lock to the canal system. Coin-operated electricity (€0.50/2kWh) and water (€0.50/100 ltrs) is available here, and a facilities block is situated beneath the snack bar on the quay.

Facilities ashore

Fuel & Chandlers Jachttechniek van der Pol on Schans near the lock
Chandlers Also at the marina, or the near the old harbour
Supermarket & Shops Coop on Noord; fish shop on Smidstraat; butcher on Voorstraat
ATMs On Voorstraat
Cycle hire Annies Winkeltsje on Smidstraat
VVV office Stationsweg (near the old harbour)

What to see

Stavoren (pronounced 'sta-**voo**ren' or '**star**-vren' in Fries) was the oldest of the eleven Frisian towns, a former Hanseatic town with trading links to the Baltic and England. Trade flourished until the 14th century when the harbour silted up. The story goes that a rich merchant's widow demanded a precious cargo from her ship's captain and was so disgusted with the wheat he brought back that she had it thrown into the harbour, which locals believe began the silting process. Her statue, De Vrouwe van Stavoren, stands by the old harbour.

Today the town is an important link between the IJsselmeer and the Friesland lakes and numerous boat businesses operate from the area. For a taste of life in Stavoren and chance to meet a local character, take an open boat trip aboard Simmermoarn with the musical harbourmaster to the Gaasterland woods, departing from the back of the old lock near the VVV every Thursday at 1030. For an insight into the town's culture and history, visit the newly opened Ponthuus museum on the Hellingpad or browse at Het Hanzehuis, a ship's antiques and curiosity shop from the golden Hanseatic age.

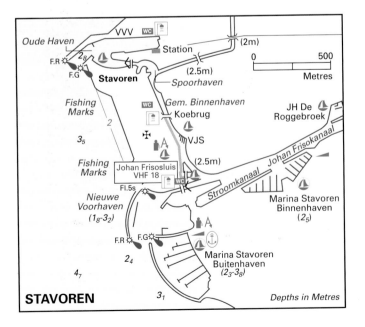

STAVOREN

The lady of Stavoren waits at the harbour for her 'precious cargo'

Restaurant tip

For a traditional Fries/Scots meal try the Stadsboerderij (town farm) De Koebrug with good quality home cooking and a choice of 350 single malts. For fish dishes, De Vrouwe van Stavoren stands by the old harbour or, near the lock, restaurant De Kruitmolen enjoys a breezy position and a busy view.

Connections

The train station is near the old harbour and has regular services to Leeuwarden. In the other direction you can take the ferry service to Enkhuizen.

HEEG

Where to stop

The visitors' harbour Heegerwal is convenient for the town centre and has a holiday camp atmosphere with many smaller boats arriving with tents as well as boats. 10A electricity (€0.50/kWh) and water (€0.50/100 ltrs) are coin-operated and facilities are busy in high season. In the centre there is a small town quay for daytime stops or you can find a berth at one of the harbours on the east side of town, the largest of which is JH Gouden Bodem. JH de Eendracht in the town centre has wi-fi as does Ottenhome on the Draei near the Graft. These have a longer walk to the town centre but there is a pedestrian tunnel under the Graft channel to the island.

For an out-of-town berth try a mooring on the large island (Rakkenpolle) on the south side of the Heegermeer channel and go across by dinghy. This island is well-equipped with quayside moorings, boxes, a beach and toilets. Uniquely for Friesland there is a small charge for an overnight stay but this is well worthwhile, especially over a fine weekend.

What to see

Heeg (pronounced 'haykh') has long been a fishing village, its eel trade with England going back to 1660. Visitors centre De Helling on the island gives an overview of this industry, as well as the traditional shipbuilding that accompanied it. Today the town is another of the major watersports centres in Friesland with popular waterside bars and restaurants and several good chandlers and marine businesses, including Stentec Software, specialists in PC navigation. Relax at De Watersport and watch the antics at the low swing bridge, or choose Restaurant Jonas in den Walvis for a more upmarket experience.

Stavoren from the north with the old harbour in the foreground and the Binnenhaven canal, and new marinas beyond

Workum canal

Further up the coast, the former sea port of Workum provides another access point to the Friesland waterways and connects with the Fluessen and Heegermeer via the Zandmeer and the Grote Gaastmeer. 'Het Zool' channel runs from the IJsselmeer 2km inland before reaching the Workum sealocks and bridges, which operate throughout the day with breaks for lunch and tea everyday. The Diepe Dolte channel continues in a northeasterly direction to the southeast of the old town and has three low lifting bridges. After a right angle bend the junction with the Trekvaart van Workum naar Bolsward is reached and the waterway changes its name to the Klifrak to continue on to the Zandmeer and the Grote Gaastmeer. From this, to the north, a channel leads to the Oudegaaster Brekken and at its eastern end, Oudega.

Length 10 km
Speed limit Through Workum 5km/h; otherwise 9km/h
Maximum permitted draught 1.5m, beam 5m, length 30m
Locks Workum zeesluis and liftbridge operate throughout the day with breaks for lunch and tea (1200–1300 and 1615–1715). Toll payable.
Bridges 5 lifting. 3 in Workum, then Sudergoa and rail bridge which open throughout the day with breaks for lunch and tea (1200–1300 and 1615–1715).

WORKUM

Where to stop

Workum is another of the main gateways between the IJsselmeer and the inland waterways.

There are few canalside moorings available but ample facilities exist in the many yacht harbours. Those on the east side of town are convenient for boats coming from the canals, and JH It Soal near the harbour entrance accommodates many of the boats stopping off from the IJsselmeer. For a cosy, central location choose Kuperus Watersport, with visitors' moorings along their quayside frontage, and spaces in boxes when permanent berth-holders are away. Unmetered 6A electricity and coin-operated water (€0.50/100 ltrs) are provided and there is an on-site chandlers and service yard as part of the family business. Tucked away behind a gate in a housing estate it is quiet and secluded whilst still being only a street away from the town centre; a popular stopping place, so arrive early to secure your berth.

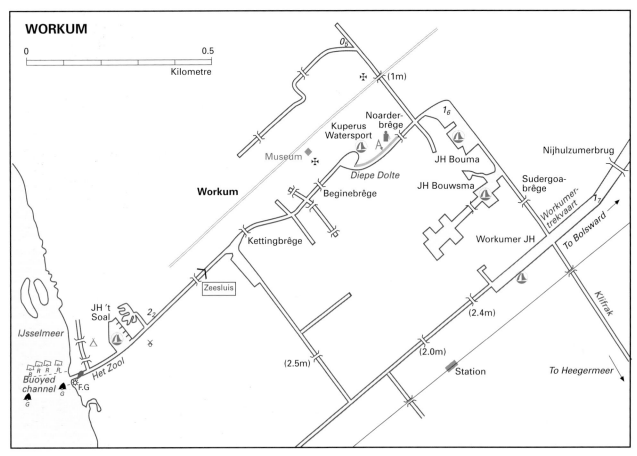

Facilities ashore

Fuel, Chandlers & Repairs Kuperus Watersport
Supermarket & Shops Poiesz on Noard; Super de
 Boer on Sud and small shops in between
ATMs Opposite the Markt
Cycle hire Fytsmakkerij Scheltema on Sud
VVV office Noard

What to see

The main street, originally the waterway through the
town, runs parallel to the canal, and boasts the usual
array of weigh house, VVV office, churches, and
town hall, as well as a selection of shops, cafés,
museums and supermarkets. Dominating the market
square, the great church and tower were originally
intended to be joined together. Unfinished, the plan
was abandoned in 1615 and they were left as
separate structures. The picturesque 17th-century
weigh house contains the Museum Warkums Erfskip
– delving into the history of the town and its
shipping and pottery industries. Workum also boasts
Friesland's most visited museum in the Jopie
Huisman Museum. Featuring the artworks of scrap
metal merchant Jopie Huisman, who died in 2000,
the collection depicts the daily grind and drudgery of
the ordinary tradesman and housewife.

Workum's IJsselmeer entrance and JH 't Soal from the
northeast

Workum's busy market square is the centre of the town

Restaurant tip

Hotel Restaurant De Gulden Leeuw on the market place offers a typically Dutch experience whilst across the road Bistro De Waag has a more rustic ambience.

Connections

The train station lies south of the canal and has services to Stavoren and Leeuwarden.

OUDEGA

Beyond the numerous free moorings in the Oudegaasterbrekken, there is a short canal in the village with some two dozen mooring places, two electricity pillars and water. Toilet/shower facilities are available at Camping de Bearshoeke, where you will also find a tourist information point. The moorings are pleasant but very noisy since, on the other side of the hedge, there is a road carrying a continual stream of farm vehicles at busy times. Oudega (pronounced 'owder-kha') has a minimarket and a single restaurant, and is favoured by cyclists and hikers looking for somewhere off the beaten path.

GAASTMEER

Gaastmeer is well located between several large lakes, although boats over 2m air draught cannot pass under the low foot bridge. The visitors' harbour to the north of the bridge has ample facilities for an overnight stop, or there are canalside moorings south of the bridge. The waterside terrace of D'Ald Herberch is the main place to watch the water-borne activities of small boats and canoes whose owners like to explore the area.

Trekvaart van Workum naar Bolsward

The waterway from Workum to Bolsward (labelled on the 2006/07 chart as the Workumertrekvaart) connects with the Workum canal to the east of the town and runs northeast to join the Bolswardervaart south of Bolsward. The canal has four toll bridges, which gobble up the loose change, and few mooring places. A short stretch southwest of the Workum junction has a fixed bridge of 2m and so is not navigable for the purposes of this guide.

Length 10km
Speed limit 9km/h
Maximum permitted draught 1.5m, beam 5m, length 30m
Bridges 4 lifting. Bridges at Nijhuizum, Parrega, Tjerkwerd and Eemswoude operate throughout the day with breaks for lunch and tea (1200–1300 and 1615–1715). Tolls payable.

Makkum canals

Half a kilometre south of the Tjerkwerd bridge on the Trekvaart van Workum naar Bolsward, the Van Panhuijskanaal connects with the waterway and runs west towards Makkum. West of the Hemmens bridge, the waterway changes its name to the Grote Zijlroede before running through the town centre and out of a sea lock into the IJsselmeer. There is little to see along the canal and the bridge midway along has no moorings to use if it is closed.

Length 7km
Speed limit 6km/h; except in Makkumer Diep, 9km/h
Maximum permitted draught 1.5m, beam 5m, length 30m
Lock Makkum zeesluis and liftbridge operates throughout the day with breaks for lunch and tea (1200–1300 and 1615–1715). Tolls payable.
Bridges Van Panhuijs, Allingawier and Hemmens bridges and the two bridges in Makkum all operate the same hours as the locks. Tolls payable.

MAKKUM

Where to stop

Arriving from the east there are canalside municipal moorings close to the town centre, with free water but no electricity. Basic facilities can be shared with the Gemeente Buitenhaven, which is immediately south of the lock and lies in the shadow of a large shipbuilding shed (it seems large enough to contain an ocean liner). There is space in boxes here for boats up to 11m and limited space on the hammerheads for larger vessels. Electricity and water are coin-operated and the toilet/shower facilities are due to be upgraded in 2008, when electricity will also be added to the Binnenhaven (canal) moorings.

For a full-service marina head for Marina Makkum or the WV Makkum, some 3km from the town centre on an artificial promontory south of the harbour entrance. All amenities including on-site restaurant and wi-fi are shared with the adjoining bungalow holiday park.

Makkum

Facilities ashore

Fuel, Chandlers & Repairs Denekamp Yachting and Kooi Yachting at Marina Makkum

Chandlers Silerswaar on Voorstraat or De Vries near Marina

Supermarket & Shops Small Coop (open late) on Workumerdijk or Jumbo supermarket further along

ATMs On Voorstraat

Cycle hire Fietsverhuur Venema on Voorstraat

VVV office Pruikmakershoek (close to Markt)

What to see

Makkum was an important fishing and commercial port in the 17th and 18th centuries and mainly owes its prosperity to the earthenware and tiles made in the town. During that period a host of ceramic building materials were produced locally, including roof tiles and building bricks but Koninklijke Tichelaar Makkum (pottery and tile supplier to the queen) is the only survivor of that time. You can visit the factory for a guided tour on workdays or watch a video presentation on Saturdays.

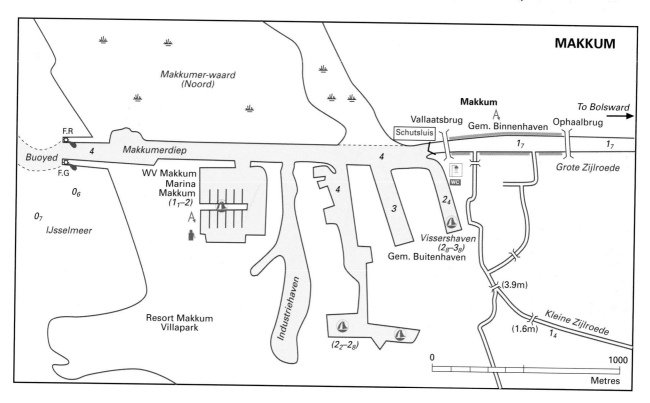

An interesting bicycle excursion from Makkum is to the Kazematten museum at Kornwerderzand. The seventeen bunkers are situated at the east end of the Afsluitdijk and were built in 1931 to supplement the defences of north Holland. Used during the second world war to defend against the 1940 attack, the bunkers remained in service for many years afterwards as a command post during the cold war.

As well as the modest shopping facilities in the town, there is a small weekly market on Wednesday mornings and tourist markets on Wednesday evenings in July and August.

Restaurant tip

Restaurant It Posthus is housed in the former Post and Telegraph office and the Irish chef commands a good reputation. Amongst several eating places on the Markt, Bistro De Waag is also popular.

Makkum's Buitenhaven is overlooked by a huge shipbuilding shed

Follegasloot/Follegasleat

Returning to the south of Friesland near Lemmer, the waterways east of the Prinses Margriet canal are now described. The first of these is the Follegasloot, which connects the north end of the Groote Brekken with the Tjeukemeer.

Speed limit 9km/h
Maximum permitted draught 1.8m, beam 6m, length 40m
Bridges 1 lifting. Follega bridge operates throughout the day with breaks for lunch and tea (1200–1300 and 1615–1715)

Tjeukemeer/Tsjûkemar

A large meer of over 2,000 hectares, there are buoyed channels east-west between the Follegasloot and the Pier Christiansloot, roughly north-south between the Follegasloot and the Scharster Rijn, and north from the Pier Christiaansloot, branching west to connect with the channel to the Scharster Rijn, and east to connect with the Broeresloot. An area for waterskiiing and small speedboats is designated to the north of the meer. The Broeresloot is crossed by a fixed bridge of 2.3m and is therefore impassable for the purposes of this guide.

A large motorway bridge cuts across the west side of the meer, with a fixed clearance of 12.4m. Immediately to port as you approach the Tjeukemeer from the Follegasloot, a buoyed channel (depth 1.5m) runs north, to the west of the bridge, to give access to St Nicolaasga. Air draught on this route is limited to 12m by the electricity cable, which crosses the St Nicolaasga channel.

The Tjeukemeer has had problems of insufficient depth in the past making it unpopular with sailors, but recent dredging has alleviated this problem. Its unfashionable

image makes it a quiet spot for those looking for peace and tranquillity and there are two man-made islands, each with a lagoon and about 80 mooring places, either on pontoons or alongside the grassy banks. There is no charge and no facilities on the islands, although a toilet is due to be added to Marchjepôlle in 2007.

Speed limit 9km/h in the channels
Bridges 1 fixed with a clearance of 12.4m

ST NICOLAASGA

The approach to St Nicholaasga is via a buoyed and shallow channel alongside the motorway. WSV St Nic is situated in a large rectangular basin with private moorings around the edges. The large village is 2km away along a country lane and is dominated by the neo-gothic St Nicolaaskerk. Unusually for this area, it is a catholic church behind which is a complete replica of the Lourdes grotto. The village especially celebrates its faith each year on the first Thursday in September with a carnival parade, the Allegorische Optocht.

ECHTENERBRUG-DELFSTRAHUIZEN

Where to stop

From the south side of the Tjeukemeer the Pier Christiaansloot runs southeast through the twin villages of Echtenerbrug and Delfstrahuizen which lie either side of the canal. There is a water point to the west of the bridge, on the north side.

Speed limit 9km/h
Maximum permitted draught 1.8m, beam 6m, length 40m
Bridge 1 lifting. Pier Christiaan bridge operates throughout the day with breaks for lunch and tea (1200–1300 and 1615–1715).

From the direction of the Tjeukemeer, the first moorings on the south side belong to JH De Meerkoet, where there are visitor places along the grassy bank, or in boxes when club boats are away. Unmetered 6 or 10A electricity (€1.50/day) and coin-operated water (€0.50/100 ltrs) are available and the resident harbourmaster normally greets visitors on arrival. Although a slightly longer walk to the village, this is a secluded and friendly place to stop, with an unspoilt view of the meer. Next door, JH De Merenpoort is a commercial harbour with servicing yard, small chandlers and fuel which also serve their charter fleet. On the north side, Oan's

Tjûkemar is a campsite and harbour with places for visitors along the canal bank, or there are further canal-side moorings beyond the bridge at the Turfskip charter base. Immediately south of the bridge, the fuel station doubles up as VVV information point, chandlers and post office but is not yet well prepared for English speaking visitors.

There are shops and cafés on both sides of the canal with the more upmarket Hotel Tjongervallei on the Delfstrahuizen side. Regular musical and sailing events are organised throughout the summer holidays, although dates vary from year to year.

Moorings at De Meerkoet have a view over the Tjeukemeer

Tjonger/Tsjonger (or Kuinder/Kuunder)

The Tjonger (or Kuinder) waterway connects with the Pier Christiansloot, south of Echtenerbrug and runs northeast as far as the junction with the Engelenvaart. On this section there is good depth of 2.4–2.5m and no restrictions on headroom. Northeast of the junction with the Engelenvaart the waterway continues as the Tjongerkanaal for 28km to join the Opsterlandse Compagnonsvaart but fixed bridges

of 3.25m restrict this section. South of the junction with the Pier Christiansloot there are fixed bridges of 2.75m.

Speed limit 9km/h
Maximum permitted draught 1.1m (applies north of Engelenvaart junction)

Jonkers (or Helomavaart/Helomavaort)

The Jonkers waterway (also known as the Helomavaart) connect the Tjonger with the Linde and forms part of the mast-up route between the Randmeren and Friesland. At the southern end a fork to the east leads via a self-operated bridge to the Mallegat channel and Oldemarkt described in Chapter 5: Flevoland and the Randmeren.

Length 7km

Janesloot/Jaansleat

A short but very narow channel which links the Prinses Margrietkanaal at the north end of the Koevordemeer with the Langweerderwielen, a meer to the east.

Length 1km
Speed limit 9km/h in buoyed channels; otherwise 6km/h
Maximum permitted draught 1.5m, beam 4m, length 25m
Bridges 1 lifting. Janeslootbrug operates throughout the day which breaks for lunch and tea (1200–1300 and 1615–1715).

Langweerderwielen/Langwarder Wielen

This attractive mere has several connections with other waterways but has shoal patches outside the buoyed channels, especially on the southeast shore of the Oudeweg, running to the northeast. There is depth of 1.75m in the main channels except in the entrance to the Janesloot, which has 1.4m.The channels connect the Janesloot with the Langeweerdervaart and from there on to the Scharster Rijn and Oudeweg at the eastern end. The two bridges lie over the Oudeweg section, which continues as the Noorder Oudeweg to join the Goingarijpster poelen, southeast of the Sneekermeer. The Langeweerdervaart joins the north-west corner of the meer to the Prinses Margrietkanaal at the junction of Het Nauw van de Brekken. The smaller waterways of the Stobberak and the Fammensrakken are restricted by low bridges of 2.6m. From the north end of the Oudeweg, a channel called the Zijlroede runs east to the town of Joure. A flood lock at the entrance to the canal normally stands open and there are moorings in the visitors' harbour, but there is no onward route as the Noordbroekstervaart (or Scheensloot) is restricted to 2.5m headroom.

Maximum permitted draught 1.5m, beam 5m, length 30m
Bridges 1 fixed with clearance of 11.5m. 1 lifting. Oude Weg bridge operates throughout the day with breaks for lunch and tea (1200–1300 and 1615–1715), but cannot open during bus service times which occur three times per hour for a period of 6–9 minutes each.

LANGWEER

Where to stop

The visitors' harbour at Langweer is regarded as one of the friendliest in Friesland and the husband and wife harbourmaster team greet boats on arrival from their Danish cutter by the entrance. Charter boats and young people are sent to the Oude Haven where they can stagger back from the pubs at night without disturbing boats in the Nieuwe Haven next door, where there is unmetered electricity and free water, with good facilities maintained personally by the duo.

Next door De Twirre Watersport has fuel and chandlers, and a wi-fi network which covers the visitors' harbour.

What to see

Langweer (pronounced 'longe-veer') is renowned throughout Friesland for the evening childrens' entertainment provided by harbourmaster Menno and his musical bike, at which regular adult devotees also enthusiastically join in the community singing and dancing. The happy couple, who met in Terschelling are planning ahead for their retirement in 2010 when the bike will be auctioned off, so do not leave your visit for too long! For those looking for more regular pastimes, the protected village street is lined with 200-year-old lime trees and chic nautical shops, one of which also offers cycle hire and angling equipment as well as tourist information when the VVV is closed.

Food shopping is limited to a good butchers/delicatessen and a modest grocers, but there are plenty of opportunities for dining out, with the Bistro De Oude Gevel, and Restaurant 't Jagertje recommended amongst the ample choice.

Menno and Marion demonstrate the actions to their favourite song

JOURE

Where to stop

The visitors' harbour at Joure is another of the popular holiday destinations with many boats returning each year for extended stays. Approached through an open lock and via an attractive canal, the harbour can be busy in high season but there is normally space along the banks or in boxes and the full-time harbourmaster does his best to make everyone feel welcome. Coin-operated electricity (€0.50/1.5kWh) and water (€0.50/100 ltrs), and good basic facilities are available including launderette.

As an alternative, there are free moorings on the island opposite the entrance lock or along the Noorder Oudeweg.

Facilities ashore

Pump-out, Fuel, Chandlers & Repairs Jachtwerf de Jong on Slachterdijk (at the end of the harbour)
Supermarket, Shops & ATMs Albert Heijn and all services on Midstraat, the main street through the town (turn right at the end of the harbour)
Cycle hire Profile Smit, on Tolhuswei
VVV office Midstraat

What to see

Joure (pronounced 'yow-rer') proudly describes itself as a vlecke, a settlement between a village and a town. Its industrious nature is still evidenced by the Douwe Egberts coffee factory on the outskirts and the traditional clock and barometer shop in the centre, where you are welcome to wander around. Both of these trades are imaginatively illustrated in Museum Joure, which (as well as having extensive exhibitions) includes the actual house where the founder of Douwe Egberts, Egbert Douwe, was born in 1723.

There are guided walks organised by the VVV every Monday at 1400 and a weekly market on Wednesday mornings. Annual highlights include a festival, renacting an old fashioned country wedding, and a four-day ballooning event, both held in July.

Passers-by admire Joure's church tower!

Restaurant tip

The restaurant opposite the church, De Jouster Toer, is run by a husband and wife team and whilst not speedy, provides a meal as good as you might find in countries that pride themselves on haute cuisine. At the harbour, De Oranjerie was originally part of the Heremastate country manor and you can dine amongst the tropical palms in the impressive glass conservatory.

Scharsterbrug canal

From the southeast corner of the Langweerderwielen, the Scharster (or New) Rijn runs southeast through the town of Scharsterbrug and then turns south to connect with the Tjeukemeer.

Speed limit 9km/h
Bridge 2 opening. Scharster and Rijksweg (3.5m when closed) bridges operate throughout the day with breaks for lunch and tea (1200–1300 and 1615–1715).

Heerenveen and the Engelenvaart/ Engelenfeart

The Engelenvaart runs roughly north from the Tjonger waterway to the town of Heerenveen, continues just to the west of the town as the Nieuwe Heerenveense Kanaal and then as Het Deel to Akkrum. The attractive waterways of the Heeresloot and the Monnikerak through the town are still passable but are restricted to 2.6m clearance at the southern end. For access to the Buitenringvaart (which gives onward passage to the Opsterlandse Compagnonsvaart) the Deelsbrug rail bridge at the north end of the Monnikerak opens twice per hour.

Length 14.5km
Speed limit 9km/h; except for north of Deelsbrug bridge, 12.5km/h
Maximum permitted draught 1.5m, beam 5m, length 30m
Bridges 1 fixed (5.7m), 3 opening. Nieuwe Schoot, Rottumer and Jouster bridges operate throughout the day with breaks for lunch and tea (1200–1300 and 1615–1715). All bridges operated from the Rottumer bridge. VHF 18.

HEERENVEEN

Bridges 1 fixed (7.4m), 4 opening. Terbandster, Stations and Tram bridges operate the same hours as above. Toll payable. Deelsbrug rail bridge normally opens at H+20 and H+40 but check the *Almanak* under 'Heerenveen' for latest timetable.

Where to stop

The visitors' harbour on the Nieuwe Heerenveense Kanaal is an unserviced, free basin with plenty of space on alongside landing stages. Situated in a modern housing estate, it is relatively quiet and a ten-minute cycle to the city centre. Alternatively take the hour-long detour down the old Heeresloot to free canal-side moorings in the centre of town. The best places are by a grassy bank south of the Tram bridge, but there is more space north of the Stations bridge and west of the Herenwalster bridge. Again there is no electricity available, but water (€0.50/100 ltrs) can be obtained by the 'super-loo' east of the Herenwalster bridge.

What to see

Heerenveen (pronounced 'hair-en-fain') means the 'Lord's Fen' and was named after the numerous Frisian nobles who established a fen colony here in the 16th century. Many of their manor houses still exist including Crackstate, built in 1648 and now in use as the city hall, and Oenemastate, which houses Restaurant De Herenkamer. Next door in the Museum Willem van Haren, is the permanent presentation on the culture and history of the town as well as temporary exhibitions.

There is extensive good shopping close to the town centre moorings including a supermarket on the main street and a weekly market on Saturdays.

A former mansion house, now in use as a restaurant

Buitenringvaart

From the Monnikerak north of Heerenveen, the Buitenringvaart (or Stroomkanaal), which includes the Nieuwe Pompsloot, runs northeast to join the Nieuwe Vaart (part of the Opsterlandse Compagnonsvaart). A fixed bridge just east of the Monnikerak junction has a clearance of 5.2m and the remaining bridges open.

Length 9km
Speed limit 9km/h
Maximum permitted draught 1.5m, beam 5m, length 30m

Bridges 1 fixed (5.2m), 3 lifting. Hooibrug is self-operated by a push button near the bridge, and along with the Pool and Warre bridges operates throughout the day with breaks for lunch and tea (1200–1300 and 1615–1715). Toll payable at Poolsbrug.

The waterway passes close to De Deelen, a fen-digging area where peat is still collected for horticultural use. From the canal-side mooring near km 5 you can walk along the dykes to a bird-watching hut to see the many species that congregate here.

Sneekermeer/Snitser Mar and Terherne/Terhorne

The Sneekermeer (pronounced 'Snake-er-meer') is one of the most popular sailing meers in Friesland and home to the famous Sneek week (akin to Cowes week) and held in the third week of August. There are many islands with good quality mooring pontoons and throughout the summer dinghy racing, and occasionally racing of larger old boats, dominates the area. It is also one of the few places in Friesland where anchoring is quite common. Terherne island, in the middle of the meer, is a camping and water sports centre and is accessible by lifting bridges on the north and south sides.

The Prinses Margrietkanaal runs across the northwest side of the meer, with the Teherne lock at the northerly end normally standing open. If in use, it can be difficult since there are no mooring places suitable for non-commercial craft. A flood lock at Heerenzijl also stands open in normal conditions but when it is closed with the Terherne lock, passage via this route is not possible.

There is an area designated for waterskiing and small speedboats to the north of the buoyed channel, where the speed limit does not apply.

Speed limit In the buoyed channel, 12.5km/h; elsewhere 9km/h, except on the small connecting waterways, 3km/h.
Locks Terhernesluis normally stands open. In strong SW winds the lock gates are closed but the lock operates for passage 24 hours from Monday–Saturday and throughout the day on Sunday.
Bridges 2 lifting. Heerenzijl bridge between Zoute Poel and Terkaple operates throughout the day with breaks for lunch and tea (1200–1300 and 1615–1715). Toll payable. Nije Sansleat bridge to the north of the island operates throughout the day with breaks for lunch and tea on Sundays only (1200–1300 and 1645–1745).

TERHERNE

Where to stop

There are several marinas and yacht harbours, but the nearest to the village is JH De Zandsloot where Joop de Schiffart Watersport has well-specified landing stages in a private harbour with unmetered electricity and coin-operated water (€0.50/100 ltrs). On-site chandlers, launderette and servicing yard are available.

What to see

Known to the Dutch as the setting of a popular series of children's books, Terherne (pronounced 'terherner' and called Terhorne in Dutch) is a small village which is dominated by watersports and tourism in season. Holiday markets are held every Saturday in July and August and all shops are open on Sundays from April, including the small Feijen supermarket, which also has an ATM and internet terminal. The island community was completely isolated until 1883 when the first bridge was built at Heerenzijl, and the residents made their living from shipbuilding, farming and fishing.

Regular summer entertainments include the Shanty festival in June, led by Terherne-based choir 'Ballast oer board', and the children's Klompkesilen competition, a race for model sailing boats made from real clogs. A popular stop for children is De Snoeperij (traditional sweet shop) that doubles up as the VVV office on the main street. Next door Eetcafé 't Far is known for its generous portions.

Every week seems to be regatta week on the busy Sneekermeer

Akkrum canals

From the east end of Nieuwe Zandsloot, north of Terherne island, the Meinsloot runs northeast to the town of Akkrum. After a lift bridge to the west of the town, the channel joins the Kromme Knillis which runs west to rejoin the Prinses Margrietkanaal at Oude Schouw, and east via two further lift bridges towards neighbouring Nes. The old waterway through the centre of the town is no longer accessible for through traffic and so the route takes the northern arm, known as the Leppedijk. Beyond the bridge, the waterway changes to the Boorne, part of the Opsterlandse Compagnonsvaart.

The Diepesloot and the Polsloot, which run from Het Deel to Akkrum, give access to two boatyards, Jachtwerf de Wit and De Kuypers, but the bridges which give access to the town itself are no longer operated.

Length 8km
Maximum permitted draught 1.5m, beam 5m, length 30m (Kromme Knillis and Zijlroede only)
Speed limit In the Pol and Diepesloot 12.5km/h; otherwise, 9km/h
Bridges 3 lifting. Meinsloot and Leppedijk bridge operate throughout the day from 0900 with breaks for lunch and tea (1200–1300 and 1615–1715). Toll payable at Meinsloot bridge. Boorne railbridge in Akkrum opens two or three times per hour at H+17 and H+55 (sometimes additionally at H+44) throughout the day (Check the *Almanak* under 'Opsterlânske Kompanjonsfeart' for latest timetable.)

AKKRUM

Where to stop
The visitors harbour in Akkrum has no facilities and is only suitable for small boats, and there are some central moorings on a concrete quay by the railway bridge. The most suitable mooring is at the large JH Tusken de Marren on the west side of town, which has ample facilities for visiting boats including launderette, pump-out and wi-fi. Fuel and a chandlers are available next door at Jachtwerf Oost.

What to see
Akkrum is half of the twin villages of Akkrum-Nes and is a favourite recreational village with plenty of shops and eating places. It is one of the start points of the turf route, described later under Opsterlandse Compagnonsvaart. In 1866, FH Kuipers emigrated from Akkrum to the United States where he became a successful businessman. During his yearly visits to see his father he saw much poverty amongst the older villagers and built Coopersburg in 1900 to accommodate and care for them.

Traditional local events, which are put on to entertain the visitors, include the Open Frisian mast climbing competition on the first Saturday in July, and in August 'Slingeraap', a competition which involves swinging across the river on a rope and trying not to get wet. The first Saturday in September is Shanty day in Akkrum, concluding with a combined choir of all participants.

Nes canals

Just across the railway from Akkrum is the neighbouring village of Nes. The waterway, which is known as the Boorne east of Akkrum, continues over the Leppe aquaduct and north of Nes to join the Zijlroede. To the north, the channel leads across the Bokkumermeer where buoys mark the safe water, and navigation continues without obstacles to the Wijde Ee and the Pikmeer. To the east, the Zijlroede skirts the village of Nes with two lifting bridges and then runs as far as Aldeboarn before a fixed bridge (3.4m) restricts onward passage.

Maximum permitted draught 1.1m, beam 5m, length 28m
Bridges 2 lifting. Nesserzijl bridge operates throughout the day with breaks for lunch and tea (1200–1300 and 1615–1715). Nes bridge is self-service, operated by a push button.

A boat makes its way through the hand-operated bridges in Aldeboarn

ALDEBOARN

Bridges
1 fixed (3.4m in the middle and 2.85m at the sides) 3 opening which operate the same hours as the Nes bridges.

There is a small yacht harbour on the east side of the village, but visitors normally stop on the canal where there is a new electricity pillar and water supply on the north bank. A modest toilet/shower block is on the north bank.

Aldeboarn (pronounced 'old-er-born' and called Oldeboorn in Fries) is one of the oldest villages in Friesland and its well-preserved centre has earned the status of village conservation area. Three antique cast-iron bridges span the narrow canal and are hand-operated by the bridge watcher who lives next to one of them. The parish church has an 18th-century tower and the three level open wooden lantern is visible for many miles around.

Normally a very quiet village, Aldeboarn comes to life on the last Friday in August for its Gondelvaart, a spectacular parade of illuminated boats accompanied by music and festivities.

Opsterlandse Compagnonsvaart (Turfroute)/Opsterlânske Kompanjonsfeart

Under this title are described the waterways of the Nieuwe Vaart from its junction with the Stroomkanaal to Gorredijk, the Opsterlandse Compagnonsvaart and the Witte Wijk as far as the Drentsche Hoofdvaart. At this point the route crosses the border into Drenthe, and continued coverage is given in Chapter 7: Groningen & Drenthe.

The Nieuwe Diep east of Aldeboarn to its junction with the Stroomkanaal is restricted by a fixed bridge of 3.4m clearance and so is outside the scope of this guide, but an alternative access can be made via the Buitenringvaart and the Stroomkanaal north of Heerenveen.

Also known as the Turfroute this is a peaceful series of waterways through a very different Friesland, as it was dug as transport for the extensive peat digging that was carried out here in the early 19th century.

A permit is required (valid for one circuit of the route) which costs € 15 and can be bought at the locks at Gorredijk, Damsluis or Sluis 1 on the Tjonger. Moorings on the canal-side and in the village harbours are free except at Olderberkoop, where more extensive facilities are available but showers and cycle hire are included in the overnight rate there. Toilets/showers, water and rubbish disposal are dotted along the waterways but there are no electricity points, except at Olderberkoop.

Some of the bridges are self-operated, using a handle stowed on the bridge itself, but these are sometimes manned by youngsters, who volunteer to perform the task for a € 0.50 tip per bridge. The route is specified as being safe for vessels up to 1.1m draught, although boats up to 1.2m regularly use the waterways at their own risk.

Length 45km
Speed limit West of Gorredijk, 9km/h; East of Gorredijk, 6km/h
Maximum permitted draught 1.1m, beam 5m, length 28m
Bridges & Locks
On the Nieuwe Vaart 1 fixed (5.85m), 3 lifting.
On the Compagnonsvaart from Gorredijk to the junction with the Tjongerkanaal, 1 fixed bridge (4.45m), 18 lifting bridges and 4 locks.
On the Compagnonsvaart and Witte Wijk, from the junction with the Tjongerkanaal to the Drentsche Hoofdvaart, 1 fixed bridge (3.7m), 9 lifting bridges and 5 locks (1 with an additional fixed bridge of 3.7m and 3 with additional lifting bridges).
All bridges and locks operate 0900–1700 with a break for lunch (1200–1300), including Sundays from July to mid-Aug.

GORREDIJK

A small visitors' harbour (toilets/showers, water and rubbish disposal) is provided on the west side of town and there are many moorings on the quayside on both sides of the lock. Possibly the most pleasant are those under the trees immediately east of the main bridge (water and rubbish/disposal). These require a short walk into town or the use of a dinghy.

Gorredijk (pronounced 'khorrer-dike') is a classic example of a peat-digging village, with the main street forming a crossroads with the central village canal. A booming market town in the 18th century, Gorredijk had many Jewish residents prior to the war. The regional museum gives a good insight into the history of peat digging and as well as models explaining the difference between high and low fens, there are numerous artefacts from that period.

Ample shops and café-restaurants, including De Vergulde Turf on Hoofdstraat, provide for daily needs, with a small market visiting on Wednesday afternoons.

Turf digging, as depicted at the Gorredijk museum

DONKERBROEK

Canalside moorings are available south of the bridge close to the small village with toilets/showers and water. There are a small selection of shops and cafés to the east of the canal, including a VVV information point in De Vosseheer on the canalside.

An old flour factory has been converted into a chic home shopping emporium 'Sil's Home', where you can also see an exhibition of photographs that depict the earlier use of the waterways. The family business was formerly involved in barge transport, now transferred to road haulage, and they keep one of the typical cargo vessels alongside for old times sake.

OOSTERWOLDE

The visitors' harbour at Oosterwolde has been rather poorly designed, with a fixed bridge over the entrance limiting access to 2.4m. Even for small boats it is well outside the village centre and so is seldom used and the alongside moorings further east are more popular. The toilet/shower block has been relocated here and lies on the north side of the canal, and water and rubbish disposal are also available.

Oosterwolde (pronounced 'oast-er-volder') lies in the middle of an agricultural region and is the centre of the Ooststellingwerf municipality. A good variety of shops and eating places serve the large village and a weekly market is held on Thursday afternoons.

APPELSCHA

There are plenty of canalside moorings available through the village with possibly the most popular lying east of the Remsdraai bridge, which are close to village amenities. The toilet/shower block is near number 66 Vaart Zuidzijde and water can be obtained here, as well as at Hotel 't Klaverblad and Pannekoekboerderij de Lindehoeve.

Appelscha (pronounced 'apple-scar') is a popular holiday resort on the edge of the Drents-Friese Wold national park and a cycle ride or walk in the woods is a must. Although there are good food shops and a delightful home-made ice-cream parlour close to the canal, the main village centre is a 5-minute walk to the south where you will find a dedicated VVV office and numerous café-restaurants. A nice visit is to the Tuin van Appelscha, a model village which concentrates on replicas of the northern provinces. For children, the Duinenzathe attraction park is also close by and has a host of rides and entertainments. Regular tourist markets are held on Wednesdays and Sundays and the Turfvaartdagen, a festival of the waterways, takes place every year on the last weekend in August.

The national park visitors' centre is a cycle ride away in Terwisscha but has excellent information (including in English) about the 6,000 hectare woodland. The dynamic Ervarium presentation uses images, sounds, light and wind to introduce you to the recreational possibilities. One of these is the Aekingerzand viewing tower from where you can enjoy a panoramic view of the park and watch out for the 'moor lark' or the wheatear.

Hand-operated bridges along the Turfroute at Appelscha

Jirnsum/Irnsum canal

Back again to north of the Sneekermeer and from the Prinses Margrietkanaal at Oude Schouw the Boorne channel runs northwest to the village of Jirnsum. There are several boatyards and charter outlets south of the town, but a fixed bridge (1.5m) prevents onward passage. On the southeast side of the Prinses Margriet canal there are moorings with electricity and water adjacent to Hotel and Restaurant De Oude Schouw.

JIRNSUM/IRNSUM

The only mooring appears to be an old wooden pontoon with a restricted stay of 3 hours but this is normally long enough. Jirnsum (pronounced 'yearn-sum' and called Irnsum in Fries) is distinguished by its tall FM transmitting tower, the highest in the Netherlands, and is a good example of ribbon development along the waterway. A small supermarket (closed on Wednesdays) and a single bar are the only amenities; but the town is en-fete on the third weekend in August.

Pikmeer/Pikmar and the Wijde Ee/Wide Ie to Drachten

The Pikmeer forms part of the Prinses Margrietkanaal at Grou and stretches southeast to join another meer called Wijde Ee (or the Peanster Ee) and the Sijtebuurster Ee. From the south-western end of this meer, a waterway runs south to Nes, taking on several names before becoming the Zijlroede. From the northeastern end, the Kromme Ee connects with another section of meer also called the Wijde Ee (listed separately in the *Almanak*) from where a buoyed channel leads east, becoming the Monniken Ee, the Monnikengreppel and then the Smalle Eesterzanding before arriving at Drachten. The shores of the Wijde and Monniken Ee are shallow and navigation is best restricted to the buoyed channel. The Ouddiep branches north from the Monnikengreppel to the village of Oudega (the second in this chapter with that name). The canal is marked as having a depth of 1.7m but is shallower in places.

There are numerous places to moor in the Pikmeer and Wijde Ee and along the small connecting channels. These are provided by the Marrekrite, a voluntary foundation that establishes and maintains countryside moorings in Friesland. You may be asked to buy one of their flags for a modest fee to support their endeavours when visiting the regions and it is customary to do so.

Speed limit In the channels, 12.5km/h (Hooidamsloot); 6.9km (Princehof); otherwise, 9km/h, except in the Nieuwe Drait, 6km/h.

OUDEGA

JH Oudega has space for a few visiting boats on the canal quay next to the harbour office. The small yacht harbour for local boats has well kept facilities including three unmetered electricity points on the office building, water and a good-value washing machine.

Oudega (pronounced 'owder-kha') is a large, quiet village with a single village store and a cosy pub, the Wellingbar, near the harbour. The medieval church is open for conducted tours on Wednesday afternoons in July and August.

DRACHTEN

There are several boatyards and yacht harbours on the western outskirts of Drachten, including JH De Drait where all facilities are available, including fuel, chandlers and boat servicing. These lie about 5km from the centre of the large town, although a plan to reopen the Drachstervaart to continue the waterway to the town centre is underway, and expected to be completed in 2008.

The commercial centre grew from a small village with the arrival of the Philips factory and today is a large modern town with considerable industry on the outskirts. Museum Smalleringerland is housed in a former monastery and has an exhibition of contemporary art from the 20th century.

Hooidammen-Veenhoop (Hooidamsloot)

From the western end of the Wijde Ee, the Hooidamsloot runs north to the Oude Venen, becoming the Fokkesloot as it passes Eernewoude to the east and continuing as the Lange Sloot to join the Prinses Margrietkanaal at its junction with the Warten canals.

Speed limit 12.5km/h (Hooidamsloot); 6–9km/h (Princenhof)
Bridges 1 lifting. Hooidamsloot bridge operates throughout the day with breaks for lunch and tea (1200–1300 and 1615–1715) on Sundays and holidays. VHF 20

EARNEWÂLD/EERNEWOUDE

There is a visitors' harbour on the north bank close to the village with coin-operated electricity (€0.50/kWh, 10A) and water (€0.50/100 ltrs). The harbourmaster lives in a house opposite and there is a nautical-theme children's play area at the southern end. Toilet/shower facilities are further south by the VVV office. Alternative berths are available at the large JH Westerdijk, which has places for boats up to 14m, or you can stop at Hotel Restaurant Princenhof, which has free moorings for restaurant guests.

Fuel is available from Watersportbedrijf G J Wester (and credit cards are accepted).

Earnewâld is also known as the Skûtsje village of Friesland on account of its long involvement with the Skûtsje sailing regatta and the Skûtsje museum is based here in the former De Stripe boatyard. It lies on the edge of the Âlde Feanen national park and the Reidplum visitor centre is a good place to find out more about the landscape and bird life that has made it their home.

Quiet moorings in the Âlde Feanen national park

A good selection of café-restaurants and a village store cater for the many camping and boating visitors and Museum It Kokelhûs, in the village centre, is still decorated as a fen-diggers cottage with tiled walls and rush mats.

PRINCENHOF

The Princenhof is the name given to the waterways which criss-cross the Âlde Feanen national park, which covers an area of about 2,000 hectares formed by old peat diggings. There are many narrow channels and the whole area is most attractive with bank-side mooring places and sheltered anchorages. Main channels have depth of 1.2m.

Warten canals

The Warten canals consist of the Rogsloot, the Wartenasterwijd and the Lang Deel. The Rogsloot connects with the Prinses Margrietkanaal north of the Oude Venen and runs north-west to the village of Warten, where it becomes the Wartenasterwijd through the village. West of the village the waterway changes its name to the the Lang Deel and runs north to a junction with the Wergea canal and the Lange Meer where it becomes part of the Van Harinxmakanaal as far as Leeuwarden.

Length 10km
Maximum permitted draught 1.8m
Speed limit 9km/h
Bridges 1 fixed (6.95m) and 2 lifting. Warten village bridge and the Rogsloot bridge (4.35m when closed) operate throughout the day with breaks for lunch and tea (1200–1300 and 1615–1715). Toll payable at Warten bridge.

WARTEN/WARTENA

A huge harbour lies on the east side of the bridge and has all facilities including fuel and chandlers. Some moorings are available in the centre of the village west of the bridge but these have no facilities.

Warten (pronounced 'vorten' and called Wartena in Dutch) is a small village on the narrow canal, which provides a short cut between the Prinses Margrietkanaal and Leeuwarden. The tiny Musea Súdwâl Warten is housed in a former almshouse and has limited afternoon opening in the season.

The bridge reopens to a queue after the lunch-time closure

A mini-market provides the only shopping but there is a good fish restaurant, De Brigantijn, with a terrace overlooking the canal.

Wergea/Warga canal

From the junction of the Lang Deel and the Lange Meer northwest of Warten, the Wargastervaart runs west and then south to the the village of Wergea. There is no passage through the Galle bridge, just north of Grou, but the De Meer channel connects the end of the Wargastervaart with the Prinses Margrietkanaal.

Length 9km
Speed limit 9km/h
Bridges 2 lifting. Wergea bridge operates throughout the day with breaks for lunch and tea (1200–1300 and 1615–1715). Toll payable. Tuutze bridge (3m when closed) opens Monday–Friday on request throughout the day with two hours notice by telephone ☎ (058) 292 58 88.

WERGEA/WARGA

A boatyard on the north side of bridge has space for visitors up to 13m and has fuel, chandlers and servicing on site. South of the village there are visitors' moorings with electricity and water (depth 1.4m).

Wergea (pronounced 'verkhea') has an attractive frontage to the waterside, and is a popular spot with smaller boats. It played an important role on a connecting waterway between north and south Friesland and tradespeople living there enjoyed a good life. Museum 't Ald Slot is furnished in the typical style of houses in the 17th to 19th centuries and open Wednesday to Sunday in the summer. The village has a mini-market, café and simple eetcafé.

Nauwe Greuns/Greons

Part of the former waterway which connected Grou with Leeuwarden, this short channel now runs only from the Lange Meer to Leeuwarden. The two lifting bridges are operated remotely from the Greunsbrug in Leeuwarden.

Length 3km
Speed limit 9km/h
Bridges 2 lifting. Hempens and Pyklwierster bridges can be requested via intercom or VHF 20 and operate throughout the day with a break for tea on weekdays (1600–1730). On weekends and holidays there are breaks for lunch and tea (1200–1300 and 1615–1715).

Cruising in Friesland

Friesland represents an almost endless proposition as far as cruising opportunities are concerned which is why so many Dutch boaters leave their home moorings and head to the area for holidays. It is also accessible for touring boats from the Frisian islands, the Waddenzee, the IJsselmeer and from the inland regions of Groningen, Drenthe and Overijssel, so there is plenty of scope for through routes and circular tours.

The traditional mast-up route starts along the Prinses Margrietkanaal taking in Lemmer, Grou and the Sneekermeer before passing east through Groningen and on to the Eems estuary, eventually to Germany and the Baltic.

Combining with Drenthe to the southeast, a circular route including the Turfroute reveals the historical origins of many of the meers and waterways, but taking a variety of channels through the large meers to the southwest makes for good sailing and exploration of open water. The upper transit close to the Waddenzee coast provides a very useful alternative to making the passage by sea, in times of poor weather, and can itself be combined into a circular route taking in Leeuwarden. Coastal access from Lemmer, Stavoren, Workum, Makkum and Harlingen also helps complete other routes and so the skipper is spoilt for choice.

Just leave plenty of time to explore this fantastic region and make the trip from Harlingen across the Waddenzee at least once to Terschelling to mimic what is often, for the Dutch inland motor boat, the nearest they get to sampling the North Sea!

~ <2.5m

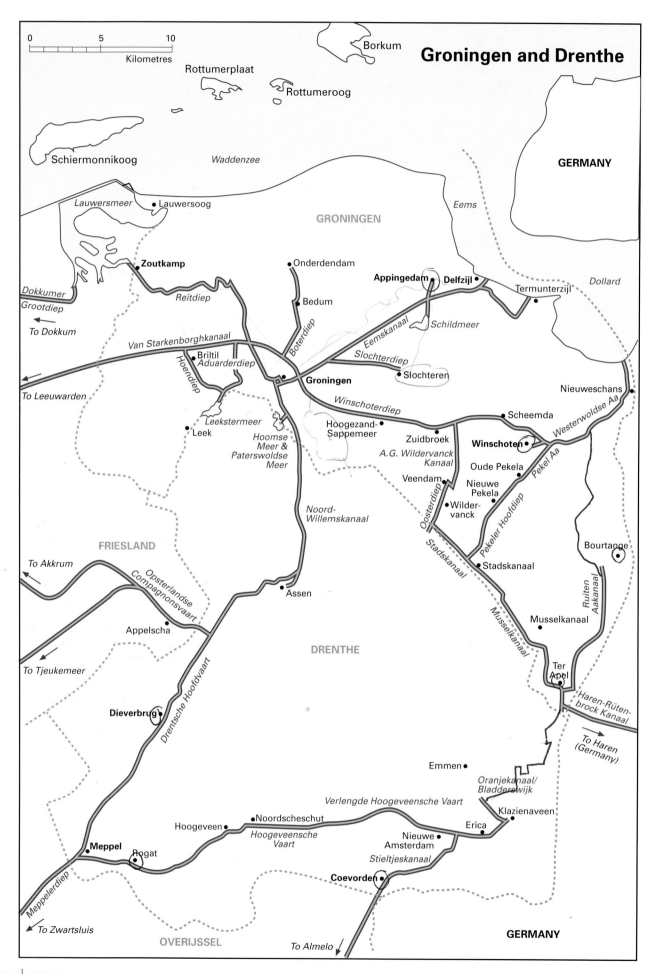

0   5   10
Kilometres

Borkum

Groningen and Drenthe

Rottumerplaat

Rottumeroog

Schiermonnikoog

Waddenzee

GERMANY

Lauwersmeer • Lauwersoog

GRONINGEN

Eems

Dollard

Zoutkamp • Onderdendam

Appingedam • **Delfzijl** • Termunterzijl

Dokkumer Grootdiep

Reitdiep

• Bedum

Boterdiep

Eemskanaal

Schildmeer

To Dokkum

Van Starkenborghkanaal

Briltil •
Aduarderdiep

Hoendiep

Slochterdiep

Slochteren •

Groningen

Nieuweschans

To Leeuwarden

Winschoterdiep

Scheemda •

Westerwoldse Aa

Leekstermeer

• Leek

Hoomse Meer & Paterswoldse Meer

Hoogezand-Sappemeer •

Zuidbroek •

A.G. Wildervanck Kanaal

Winschoten •

Oude Pekela •

Pekel Aa

Veendam •

Nieuwe Pekela •

Pekeler Hoofdiep

Noord-Willemskanaal

Wilder-vanck •

Bourtange

FRIESLAND

Oosterdiep

To Akkrum

Opsterlandse Compagnonsvaart

Ruiten Aakanaal

Musselkanaal •

Appelscha •

Assen •

Stadskanaal

• Stadskanaal

To Tjeukemeer

DRENTHE

Drentsche Hoofdvaart

Musselkanaal

Dieverbrug •

Ter Apel

Haren-Rüten-brock Kanaal

To Haren (Germany)

Emmen •

Oranjekanaal/ Bladderswijk

Verlengde Hoogeveensche Vaart

Klazienaveen •

Noordscheschut •

Erica •

Hoogeveen •

Hoogeveensche Vaart

Nieuwe Amsterdam •

Meppel •
Rogat •

Stieltjeskanaal

Coevorden •

Meppelerdiep

To Zwartsluis

OVERIJSSEL

To Almelo

GERMANY

7   Groningen and Drenthe

Waterways (north to south)	Principal venues	Other stopping places
Van Starkenborghkanaal		
Reitdiep	Zoutkamp	
Groningen canals	Groningen	
Hoendiep		Briltil
Leekstermeer		Leek
Aduarderdiep		
Boterdiep		Bedum
Eemskanaal	Appingedam, Delfzijl	Schildmeer
Termunterzijl canal		Termunterzijl
Slochterdiep		Slochteren
Winschoterdiep	Winschoten	Hoogezand, Zuidbroek,
Veendam canals		Veendam, Wildervanck
Westerwoldse Aa		Nieuweschans
Pekel Aa & Peker Hoofddiep		Oude Pekela/Nieuwe Pekela
Stadskanaal		Stadskanaal, Musselkanaal
Ter Apel canal		Ter Apel
Ruiten Aakanaal		Bourtange
Noord-Willemskanaal		Hoornse Meer/Paterswoldse Meer, Assen
Drentsche Hoofdvaart	Dieverbrug	
Meppelerdiep and Meppel	Meppel	
Hoogeveensche Vaart		Rogat
Verlengde Hoogeveensche Vaart		Noordscheschut, Nieuwe Amsterdam, Erica
Oranjekanaal/Bladderswijk		Klazienaveen
Stieltjeskanaal	Coevorden	

This chapter describes the waterways of Groningen and Drenthe from the border with Friesland in the west to Overijssel to the south. Although covering a larger geographical area than many other chapters there are currently not so many navigable waterways, and fewer attractive venues but initiatives are planned to add more waterspace.

The principal route of interest is that from Friesland to the Eems at Delfzijl, the gateway to Germany and beyond to the Baltic. This can be along the mast-up route via Zoutkamp to Groningen, or the more direct route along the Van Starkenborghkanaal as used by commercial traffic. A hidden gem along this route is Appingedam, between Groningen and Delfzijl, a historic town that has done much to encourage visitors. The development of a new harbour there will only enhance its desirability as a stop-over and although it lies on the lower air-draught Damsterdiep, it is only a short detour from the Eemskanaal.

The provinces of Groningen and Drenthe are doing their best to promote themselves as areas for water recreation and hope one day to rival their successful neighbour, Friesland. Most of the waterside towns and villages are still very underdeveloped from a boating point of view, but several projects are underway or in development to open up new waterways, provide new facilities and make more circular routes possible.

Many of the waterways are optimised for small motorboats with a minimum air draught of 2.5m, a common size in this area. Although this guide generally takes 3.5m as the cut-off point for minimum bridge height, brief mention has been made of some waterways and venues which can be reached by smaller boats.

Starkenborghkanaal, Van

This waterway forms the continuation of the Prinses Margrietkanaal from Stroobos on the Friesland/Groningen provincial border to the Oostersluis, just east of the city of Groningen. Fixed bridges and lifting bridges with a limited headroom (6.7m) make this route unsuitable for masted yachts, but it is a busy commercial waterway for barge traffic and forms part of the through route from Lemmer or Harlingen to Delfzijl. Leisure boats are advised to keep a good distance from commercial barges to avoid being drawn towards them by the displacement effect. There are no suitable places for overnight moorings on the canal itself, but there is a possibility to stop at Briltil on the Hoendiep, near Zuidhorn.

Length 27.2km
Speed limit 12.5km/h
Locks Gaarkeuken VHF 18, Oostersluis VHF 20. Operate 24 hours from 0600 Monday to 2000 Saturday and throughout the day from 0900 on Sunday.
Bridges 4 fixed (min 6.6m), 7 lifting. Eibersburen bridge (6.6m when closed) opens only on request with 24 hours notice ☎ 050 316 4692 / 316 4687. Zuidhorn, Aduard and Dorkwerd bridges (6.7m when open) are operated by the Gaarkeuken lock staff, VHF 86. Paddepoelster and Korreweg bridges are operated by the Oostersluis lock staff, VHF 68. All bridges operate 24 hours from 0600 Monday to 2000 Saturday and throughout the day from 0900 on Sunday.

Reitdiep

The Reitdiep (pronounced 'right-deep') forms the continuation of the route from the Lauwersmeer at Zoutkamp to Groningen's central canals. The downstream portion near Zoutkamp is buoyed and there are the remains of bank protection near the shores to watch out for. The waterway crosses the Van Starkenborghkanaal and continues south towards Groningen, joining the central canal ring at the Noorderhaven. All the bridges on this very attractive canal are self-operated; when the button on the mooring stage is pushed the time is shown on a screen and eventually the bridge opens.

At Zoutkamp there are three locks; the central lock, the Reitdiepbrug and Keersluis (normally open), is the only one of interest for boats of moderate air draft and connects the Lauwersmeer's Slenk channel to the Reitdiep.

The northern-most lock, the Hunsingosluis, leads to the Hunsingokanaal, restricted to 2.4m air draught, whilst the southerly lock, the Friesesluis (max length 10m), is the entrance to a small waterway that goes to Stroobos on the Prinses Margrietkanaal (air draught 2.6m).

Length 31km
Speed limit 9km/h downstream of Roode Haan bridge; 6km/h upstream
Locks Rietdiepsluis (VHF 85) and Lammersburensluis (VHF 84) normally stand open
Bridges 6 opening. Lammersburen (VHF 84), Roode Haan (VHF 85), Garnwerd (VHF 84), Wetsingersluis (VHF 84), Wierumerschouw (VHF 85) and Platvoet (VHF 85) bridges operate throughout the day. Details of bridges south of the Van Starkenborghkanaal to Groningen are given under 'Groningen canals'.

ZOUTKAMP

Where to stop

To the west of the Reitdiep bridge and lock is the large harbour of JH Hunzegat. A family run business, this friendly harbour does everything to make visitors welcome in this remote part of the world and as well as providing unmetered 4A electricity and water, and the usual basic facilities, it can offer an onsite chandlery and help with boat repairs. Additional services include cycle hire, wi-fi, fresh bread and grocery delivery.

East of the lock is the town harbour where there is coin-operated 16A electricity and water, and a part-time harbourmaster who calls in the evening. A new facilities block and harbour office has been built across the road on the dyke.

Facilities ashore

Fuel & Chandlers, Repairs & Servicing All at JH Hunzegat
Supermarket, Shops & ATMs On the Dorpsplein
Cycle hire From JH Hunzegat, Woddema on Schoolstraat or Zijlstra on Churchillweg
VVV office At the Fishing museum on Reitdiepskade

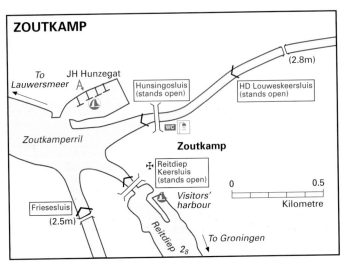

JH Hunzegat, looking west towards the Lauwersmeer

What to see

Zoutkamp (pronounced 'zowt-kamp') was established as a fortress by the Spaniards in the 16th century and later taken over and developed into a canon emplacement by the French. The defensive role was given up in the 19th century and the village then developed a successful fishing industry.

The boom years were at the beginning of the 20th century when a new harbour and fish auction hall were built. After the wartime occupation the fishing industry recovered until the closure of the Lauwersmeer from the Waddenzee in 1969 when the fishing boats, the state buoy service and the Schiermonnikoog ferry all moved to Lauwersoog. Relics of this industrious past can be seen in the old buoy shed, which now houses the fishing museum.

Today the village is the gateway to the Lauwersmeer national park, a 6,000 hectare wetland nature reserve which is the wintering site for thousands of migratory water birds. The village square offers a handful of shops and restaurants to meet most day-to-day needs, but the main attraction is the area's remoteness from everyday life.

The surrounding area provides plenty of opportunities for walking and cycling; a popular excursion is to the tea museum and tea shop in Houwerzijl where you can enjoy an English cream tea and browse the 300 varieties. Every year at Whitsun the village celebrates the start of the new shrimp fishing season with trips on historic cutters, markets, music and a carnival.

Restaurant tip

Restaurant ZK 86 recalls the heritage of the village and specialises in fish dishes from its harbour side location.

Visitors share Zoutkamp's Binnenhaven with a historic shipping vessel from the village's retired fleet

Groningen canals

Groningen's central canal ring provides a mast-up route for yachts on passage from Friesland to the Eemskanaal although the numerous lifting bridges can make it a lengthy journey. In the worst case, when all bridges must be opened and the trip coincides with rush hour delays the transit can take up to three hours. For boats with air draught lower than 6.8m the quickest route is via the Van Starkenborgh canal and the Oostersluis, approaching the Oosterhaven from the east for an overnight stop in the city. On the south side of the city a route leads from the Zuiderhaven to the Noord Willemskanaal, and continues south to Assen and the Drentsche Hoofdvaart. Bridges on the north and east sides of the ring (Schuitendiep) are only opened for trip-boats and the delivery of house boats. All bridges are closed and no passage is possible on 28 August, a public holiday known as Groningen's Relief (Gronings Ontzet). See below for details.

Locks Dorkwerdersluis and bridge operates throughout the day
Speed limit 6km/h

Reitdiep to the Oosterhaven

Bridges 15 opening. Zernike, Plataan, Pleiaden, Groningen rail, Herman Collenius, Plantsoen, Visser, A, Museum, Emma, Werkman, Here, Ooster, Tromp and Oosterhaven bridges operate throughout the day Monday-Saturday with breaks for lunch and evening rush hour (1200–1300 and 1600–1730. On Sundays there are convoys from Oosterhaven and Plataan bridges to the Zuiderhaven at 0900, 1300 and 1600; and in the opposite direction at 1030, 1430 and 1730, VHF 9.

Zuiderhaven to the Noord Willemskanaal

Bridges 8 opening (maximum 5.4m when open). Eelder, Van Hall, Rail, Park, Muntingh, Juliana, Van Iddekinge and van Ketwich-Verschuur bridges operate the same hours as the bridges above with Sunday convoys at the same times from van Ketwich-Verschuur bridge and Zuiderhaven.

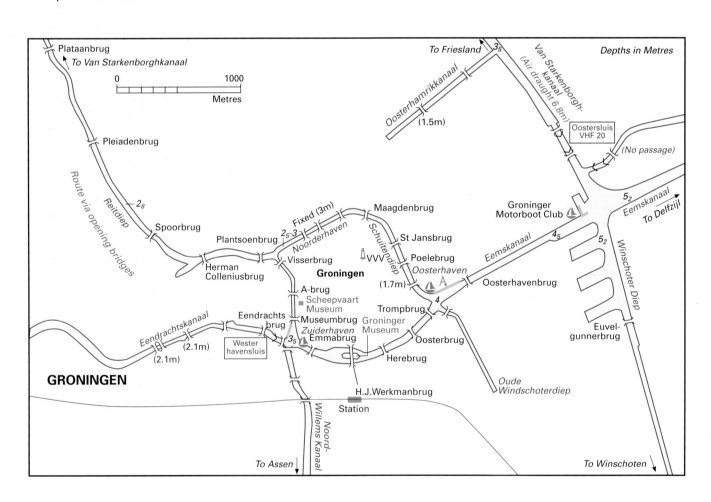

Groningen's Oosterhaven is close to the city centre

Where to stop

The main visitors' harbour is on the east side of town in the Oosterhaven where unmetered water and 10A electricity are included in the mooring fee. Chandlers and servicing are providing by Watersportcentrum Oosterhaven which is opposite the moorings on Oosterkade.

To the east there is space for visitors up to 15m at the Groninger Motorbootclub, which lies at the junction of the Van Starkenborghkanaal and the Eemskanaal. The usual basic facilities include a launderette and pump-out station.

Facilities ashore

Chandlers Watersportcentrum Oosterhaven
Supermarket, Shops & ATMs Albert Heijn on
  Gedempte Zuiderdiep and all facilities in the city
  centre
Cycle hire Rijwielhandel Kuis at the Centraal Station
VVV office Grote Markt, opposite Martini tower

Enjoy a panoramic view of the city from the Martini tower

What to see

Groningen's (pronounced 'khroan-inkher') perkily branded Tourist Office ('Er gaat niets boven Groningen' – 'There is nothing better than Groningen') is able to provide an ample range of maps, guides and walking tours in English and the option of a personally guided tour. It is a very major centre for all sorts of cultural and historical attractions with plenty to do and see. One of the city's main attractions is the modern Groninger Museum with its 'deconstructed' architecture and feature tiled staircase, or you can opt for the 251-step climb to the top of the Martini tower.

From here the panoramic view takes in the Stadhuis and Grote Markt, where an annual fair takes place mid May, as well as the Goudkantoor (gold office) in the background and the new Waagstraat complex, completed in 1996 and built in the style of the old city. On the south side of the square the historic facades remain, but the buildings to the north and east were destroyed in the struggle for liberation in 1945 and have been replaced by modern equivalents.

Groningen was once an important tidal port and the Noordelijk Scheepvaartmuseum in a medieval building on Brugstraat gives an insight into the lives of ship captains and their crews, from the Hanseatic traders to the peat barges from the last century. An important industry in the early years was the tobacco trade and the Royal Niemeyer Tabaksmuseum shares the same premises.

Large markets take place in the city centre on Tuesday, Friday and Saturday, and were recently voted second best in the Netherlands. Since the Groningen World Exhibition in 1903, it has remained a festival city with one-off and annual events occuring regularly throughout the year. Summer highlights include the annual flower market on Good Friday and 'Swingin' Groningen', a week-long music festival at the end of June. The Noorderzon festival is Groningen's answer to the Edinburgh Fringe, ten days of outdoor theatre, music and cabaret on the Noorderplantsoen. Every year, the 28th August is commemorated as the date in 1672 on which a major attack on the city by Bernard van Galen was resisted: 'Groningen's Relief'. This is celebrated with a major festival including music, fireworks and a carnival.

Restaurant tip

Of course there are plenty of places to dine out in Groningen and a good selection of modest options can be found on the Schuitendiep. Close to the Oosterhaven, the alley between Steentilstraat and Kattendiep has outdoor cafés with a Mediterranean theme.

Connections

The railway station is south of the canal, near the Groninger Museum and has services to Harlingen, Germany and the south. A growing regional airport, Groningen Airport Eelde, is 15km south of the city but the only direct UK services at time of writing are to Aberdeen.

Hoendiep

This waterway leaves the Van Starkenborghkanaal west of Zuidhorn in Friesland and then runs south and east to De Poffert. From here a narrow channel branches to the southwest to the Leekstermeer. The eastern section of the Hoendiep can be navigated as far as the Aduarderdiep, but the onward passage which connects with Groningen's central canals is restricted by fixed bridges to 2.1m headroom.

Length 10.6km to the junction with the Aduarderdiep
Maximum permitted draught 1.5m
Speed limit 6km/h
Bridges 7 lifting. Gabrug at the junction with the Van Starkenborghkanaal is self-operated by a push button. Passage through Briltil, Faner, Enumatil, Lage Meeden and Poffert bridges is by accompanied convoys which operate the following times: Southgoing – Depart Briltil bridge Monday to Friday 0830 and 1330, weekends and holidays 0915 and 1430, Northgoing – Depart De Poffert bridge Monday to Friday 1000 and 1500, weekends and holidays 1045 and 1600. Rail bridge in Hoogkerk operates throughout the day, opening once or twice per hour as train schedules permit with more limited opening on Sundays and holidays. Request via push button.

BRILTIL

JH Briltil is a friendly harbour and campsite south of the Van Starkenborgh canal and a potentially useful quiet stopping place to always bear in mind. Approached through a self-service bridge with moorings on the grassy bank and electricity outlets in the hedge. Water is available and there is a modest café-bar which provides simple food.

Leekstermeer

The Leekstermeer is approached by a small channel, which joins the Hoendiep at De Poffert. Crossed by a fixed bridge of 3.5m, the channel has a depth of 1.2m, with less outside the channel across the lake. The lake itself is quiet and peaceful and further exploration by dinghy is possible on the connecting waterways or to the moorings at Leek itself.

Depth 1.2m in the channel
Speed limit 6km/h
Bridges 1 fixed (3.5m)

LEEK

Access to the municipal visitors' moorings is restricted to an air draught of 2.5m by a fixed cycle bridge but there are possible mooring places at Paviljoen Meerzicht (depth 1.2m) on the northeast side of the lake or at WSC Cnossen (depth 0.9m) in the southwest corner. From here it is a short cycle ride to the moated manor of Kasteel Nienoord where you will find a host of entertainments including a family attraction park, a sub-tropical swimming pool and the National Carriage museum.

Aduarderdiep

Only the section of the Aduarderdiep from the Van Starkenborgh kanaal east of the Hoendiep, south to the Hoendiep at Hoogkerk is navigable by boats of 3.5m air draught or above. The northern section from the Van Starkenborgh kanaal to the Reitdiep at Aduarderzijl is restricted by low fixed bridges of 3.2m. Canalside moorings available at Hoogkerk and Nieuwklap for a maximum stay of three days.

Length 5.4km (Van Starkenborghkanaal to Hoogkerk)
Speed limit 11km/h
Bridges 1 fixed (minimum clearance 7m), 1 lifting (6.9m when open). Hoogkerk bridge operates throughout the day with breaks for lunch and tea on weekdays (1200–1300 and 1630–1730), and for brief periods in the morning and afternoon on weekends and holidays. VHF 22.

Boterdiep

From the Van Starkenborgh kanaal north of the Oostersluis, the Boterdiep runs north through Bedam to Onderdendam. The onward passage to Uithuizen is restricted by fixed low bridges of 2.9m.

Length 8km (to Onderdendam)
Maximum permitted draught 1.5m (to Onderdendam)
Speed limit 6km/h
Bridges 2 fixed (min 4.2m) 8 opening. Bridges operate to a fixed timetable with convoys starting from the Van Starkenborgh canal at 0915, 1215 and 1515 and from Onderdendam at 0840, 1220 and 1440. (Passage time is approximately 2.5 hours)

BEDUM

Canalside moorings are available on the north bank, east of Gele Klap bridge. Bedum is one of the oldest villages in the area with the first signs of a settlement from the year 600. The 12th-century church is named after St Walfridus, a devoted Christian murdered by the Normans, and is renowned for its leaning tower, which rivals that of Pisa. A weekly market is held on Thursday afternoon and late night shopping on Fridays.

Eemskanaal

The Eemskanaal forms the main commercial and leisure route from Groningen's Oosterhaven, northeast to Delfzijl, for onward passage to Germany.

Length 26.5km
Speed limit 13.5km/h
Bridges 6 lifting. Driebond, Borg, Bloemhof, Wold and Eelwerder bridges operate 24 hours from Monday morning to Saturday evening and throughout the day on Sundays, VHF 64.

Schildmeer

Maximum permitted draught 1.25m
Speed limit 12km/h (on Schildmeer); 6km/h (in the Groeve)
Lock Groevesluis-Zuid operates throughout the day, VHF 69
Bridge 1 opening. De Groeve bridge must be self-operated with a bridge key available from the lock office (deposit €20).

From the Eemskanaal at km19 the Groevesluis-Zuid gives access to the Groeve channel and the Schildmeer (depth 1m-1.5m) This 350 hectare lake is popular with dinghy sailors and windsurfers and offers smaller boats several choices of lakeside harbours or lakeside moorings to the west. Good facilities at 't Otter include unmetered electricity, pump-out and a log-cabin style restaurant.

APPINGEDAM

Lock Groevesluis-Noord operates throughout the day, VHF 64.
Bridge Eendrachts bridge operates throughout the day, VHF 64.

Where to stop

At km19.5 on the Eemskanaal, the Groeve branches north to join the Damsterdiep at Appingedam, where the municipal yacht harbour lies just east of the

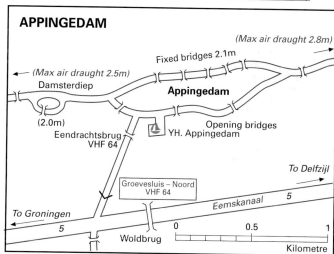

Groeve/Damsterdiep junction. At present there are ample facilities including unmetered electricity, but work on a new harbour was planned to start in 2006 and is due for completion in 2010. This will see all new facilities and an on-site restaurant added to the complex. Onward passage on the Damsterdiep is restricted to less than 3m airdraught in both directions.

Facilities ashore

Supermarket, Shops & ATMs Albert Heijn is next to the harbour
Cycle hire Lambeck Tweewielers on Farmsumerweg, or De Wapen van Leiden
VVV office Wijkstraat 38

The hanging kitchens of Appingedam

What to see

Appingedam (pronounced 'appingerdam') was the second city of Groningen province in the middle ages and originally a sea-port. The town centre has been thoughtfully restored and today provides an appealing combination of old-world charm and modern-day amenities. Guided tours of the town are organised by the VVV on Saturday afternoons, or you can choose a boat trip on the small canals, which depart near the harbour. During such a tour you will undoubtedly hear about Appingedam's distinctive hanging kitchens (which cantilever over the canal), devised to create more space when former warehouses were converted into houses. More about the town can be gleaned from the regional museum, housed in one of the town's oldest stone houses on Wijkstraat.

A popular excursion is to the Ekenstein country park, 5km to the west, where you can walk in the landscaped parks and dine in the stylish restaurant. A full programme of summer events take place on Fridays and Saturdays, starting with Appingedam Night, the fourth Friday in June, and closing on Damsterdag in mid-September with a parade of themed floats through the town.

As well as the good shopping facilities in the centre, there is a small market on Saturdays.

Restaurant tip

De Wapen van Leiden is one of a series of staging posts between Leiden and Rostock and, as well as free wi-fi, they also offer cycle hire.

Connections

The station is to the north of the town and has regular services to Groningen and Delfzijl.

DELFZIJL

Lock Kleine and Grote Sluis operate 24 hours, VHF 26 (Yachts normally use Kleine sluis but seek instruction.)
Bridges 1 opening. Brug 15 (over de Oude Eemskanaal) operates throughout the day with breaks for lunch and evening rush hour (1200–1400 and 1630–1830), VHF 22.

Where to stop

Delfizijl is the gateway to the river Eems for onward passage to Germany, the German Frisian Islands and the Baltic. The double lock complex south of the town connects the Eemskanaal with the sea harbour canal and there are yacht harbours both on the seaward and the canal side. For boats passing out to sea or on the way in, the yacht harbours in the sea harbour are probably most convenient, with ZV Neptunus offering unmetered electricity (4A) and water. Visitors' berths are at the southern end of the pontoon, behind some large commercial dry docks, and fuel is also available here.

For boats who wish to stay on the landward side of the locks, the Oude Eemskanaal branches northeast about three kilometres west of the locks and leads via an opening bridge to the large yacht club harbour of MV Abel Tasman in Marina 't Dok. Here you will find a friendly welcome from the volunteer harbourmasters although the clubhouse is closed during the summer when many local boats are away. Electricity and water are coin-operated and a launderette and pump-out facilities are also available.

Delfzijl's Oude Eemskanaal from the southwest, with ZV Neptunus in the background

Yachts make their way through the 'small' lock to Delfzijl's sea harbour

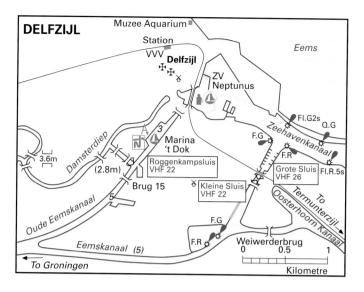

DELFZIJL

Facilities ashore

Fuel ZV Neptunus

Chandlers Jos Struyk on Eemskanaal Noordzijde (next to 't Dok); Datema (books and charts) on Landstraat

Supermarket, Shops & ATMs Super de Boer on De Vennen or C1000 on Jachtlaan

Cycle hire Rijwiel shop at the train station

VVV office In the station building

What to see

Delfzijl (pronounced 'delf-sail') is an important seaport, and the largest in the north of the Netherlands. It developed into an important industrial centre after the second world war, with its main industries being petrochemicals and the manufacture of soda, and boats cruising through the sea harbour to or from the Eems will have a good view of these industries.

Visitors to Delfzijl should not miss the MuzeeAquarium with its popular petting tank for close-up fishy encounters. It also displays one of the largest shell collections in Europe and includes exhibitions on Delfzijl's maritime history and one of the megalithic tombs found nearby. If you fancy a taste of the Waddenzee but are not sure about venturing out alone, you can always hop on one of the regular ferry boats to the German Frisian Island of Borkum, from where a narrow gauge railway takes you to the main town of the same name.

Ample shopping facilities in the city centre are supplemented by a weekly market on Wednesdays from 1000. Delfzijl celebrates its nautical heritage each year on the second weekend in September with a harbour festival, involving a parade of historic ships, to the accompaniment of shanty choirs and much merriment.

Restaurant tip

The best restaurants in Delfzijl try to look out to sea, although you might have seen enough of it if you arrived that way! Hotel Restaurant De Boegschroef (Bowthruster) overlooks the yacht harbour whilst the Eemshotel goes one further and stands on a pier with its legs in the sea, north of the harbour. Hotel du Bastion originally formed part of the town's defences and now offers free wi-fi to customers from its position opposite the train station.

Connections

As well as the train station offering regular services to Groningen, Delfzijl has ferry services to Borkum and Germany (Emden and Ditzum).

Termunterzijl canal

A new connection between the Eemskanaal and Termunterzijl was opened in 2001. The Oosterhornkanaal branches off the Eemskanaal 500m southwest of the sea locks and runs southeast behind the industrial area to Termunterzijl. The canal runs through a chemical processing harbour and is strictly regulated with camera monitoring and no mooring/anchoring except at the designated waiting places. Passage can be restricted if there has been a chemical spillage in the harbour.

The canal from Delfzijl joins the Termunterzijldiep 2km south of the village and for passage into Termunterzijl a self-service key for the remaining bridge is necessary. The Termunterzijldiep continues south to join the Winschoterdiep at Scheemda but is restricted to an air draught of 2.5m. Bridge keys are available for a deposit of €20 from the sea locks at Delfzijl, the VVV office in Appingedam or the yacht harbour in Termunterzijl.

This canal therefore offers an alternative outlet to the Eems with a slightly more inland and less exposed crossing to Germany.

Length 9km

Speed limit 6km/h

Locks Sluis Lalleweer VHF 11 operates throughout the day. Nieuwe Sluis (in Termunterzijl) operates throughout the day Monday–Friday with a break for lunch (1200–1300). At weekends operates 0900–1000 and 1700–1800 only.

Bridges 4 opening Weiwerder, Heemskes, and Borgsweer bridges are operated remotely throughout the day and can be requested by push button or VHF 11. Wartumerklap bridge is self-operated using a bridge.

TERMUNTERZIJL

Visitors' moorings are available alongside the canal inside the lock or at the tidal JH Termunterzijl (min. depth 1m). The harbour café the Golden Zieltje on Plankpad doubles up as the harbour office, and you can also collect a bridge key here.

Termunterzijl has had a lock since 1724 and was an important fishing harbour with a fish auction. Nowadays it is mainly used by sports fishers and several companies offer fishing trips on the Dollard. Nature lovers will enjoy a trip to the Dollard visitors' centre at Termunten where the permanent exhibition explains the importance of this brackish tidal marsh land.

Slochterdiep

Back inland and east of Groningen the Slochterdiep was formerly a part of the Damsterdiepcircuit but now runs only as far as Slochteren, once a commercial source of natural gas. A new watersports lane, 2,200 metres long, has been established south of the channel, which is home to a rowing and canoeing club. East of here, the Afwateringskanaal van Duurswold (which runs northwest to the southern end of the Schildmeer) is restricted by fixed bridges to 2.5m headroom.

Length 9km
Lock Slochtersluis operates throughout the day with a break for lunch (1200–1300)
Bridge 6 opening. Self-operated with a bridge key available from the lock (deposit €20).

SLOCHTEREN

At the end of the Slochterdiep a quiet and leafy visitors' harbour lies between the linear settlements of Slochteren and Schildwolde. There are no facilities but a VVV office is located on site. Nearby Fraeylemaborg is a large country estate where the house and gardens are open to visitors, the principal reason for visiting this location.

Fraeylemaborg gardens and park are open daily during daylight hours

Winschoterdiep

The Winschoterdiep runs from the Oostersluis at Groningen to connect with the Pekal Aa and Westerwoldse Aa east of Winschoten. Nearby, the Drentsche Diep (which branches southwest of Hoogezand and leads to the Zuidlaardermeer) is restricted to an air draught of 3m and access to the municipal harbour in Scheemda is restricted to 2.9m.

Length 35.4km
Speed limit 11km/h
Locks Zuidbroek and Scheemda locks normally stand open
Bridges 16 opening which operate throughout the day with a break for lunch on Monday–Saturday (1200–1300) and without a break on Sundays, VHF 22. Gideon bridge in Groningen (7.4m when closed) has restricted opening times and must be requested with 24 hours notice ☎ 050 318 8500. Rensel rail bridge operates throughout the day with a break for lunch Monday–Saturday (1200–1400) and for shorter periods morning and afternoon on Sundays.

HOOGEZAND-SAPPEMEER

The visitors' harbour at the end of an old arm of the Winschoterdiep consists of some untidy quay heading near the centre of this untidy town. There are no facilities at the harbour and a maximum stay of two days is permitted from March to September. Best accessed via the side channel east of the Rengers bridge, Hoogezand is home to several large shipyards which are known for their spectacular beam-on launching technique. Nearby amenities include a fish kiosk, supermarket and an attractive tea shop selling a selection of home-made tarts. A weekly market is held on Hoofdstraat between Hoogezand and Sappemeer on Saturdays.

ZUIDBROEK

The friendly visitors' harbour lies immediately west of the Zuidbroek bridge and there is a full-time harbourmaster on duty to assist with berthing. There are well-specified landing stages with good facilities, including unmetered 4A electricity and an industrial-sized water hose. The small village has a supermarket close by as well as a handful of shops and cafés. Boat services are available from the Pedro boatyard 1km to the west.

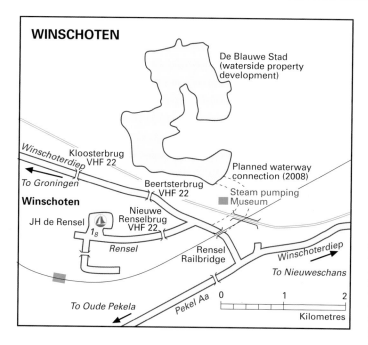

WINSCHOTEN

De Blauwe Stad (waterside property development)

Winschoterdiep

Kloosterbrug VHF 22

To Groningen

Winschoten

JH de Rensel

Nieuwe Renselbrug VHF 22

Beertsterbrug VHF 22

Planned waterway connection (2008)

Steam pumping Museum

Rensel

Rensel Railbridge

Winschoterdiep

To Nieuweschans

To Oude Pekela

Pekel Aa

0   1   2

Kilometres

you can also see the monument to the 389 Jewish residents of the town who never returned from German prison camps in the second world war.

On the edge of Winschoten (pronounced 'win-skoat-er') you can visit the historic bus museum or take a walk in the town's park, including the extensive rose gardens boasting over 320 varieties. Winschoten and the surrounding area is an international centre for the cultivation of roses and produces some 90% of the world's supply. Just north of the town the steam-pumping museum dates from 1895 and pumping days are held each Sunday in July and August.

A major new residential development, De Blauwe Stad, is underway north of the town with a large lake surrounded by a variety of different housing areas. A waterway link from here to the Winschoterdiep is planned to open opposite the river Rensel turning in 2008, and a yacht harbour will form part of the development on the north side. An information centre is already open on-site where you can inspect the 3D model and survey progress from the look-out tower.

WINSCHOTEN

Where to stop

The only mooring option in Winschoten is JH De Rensel, 2km along the old Rensel river. The approach passes under the Nieuwe Rensel bridge which is operated remotely from the Beertster bridge. There is a push button on the bridge or call on VHF 22 to request opening, which is worked for the same hours as the Winschoterdiep bridges. The harbour has clearly marked visitors' berths with coin-operated electricity and is located on the edge of a retail and industrial park – convenient if you want to visit the Konmar supermarket, home shopping stores or Macdonalds.

What to see

Beyond the retail park lies the centre of the town with an extensive pedestrianised shopping centre and Saturday afternoon market. In the market square

Winschoten's Jewish monument reminds shoppers of the fate of nearly 400 of their Jewish neighbours

Veendam canals

From the Winschoterdiep east of Zuidbroek the A.G.Wildervanckkanaal runs south to Veendam where it joins the Oosterdiep to connect with the Stadskanaal. The A.G. Wildervanckkanaal is a modern, wide waterway (depth 3m) built in the 1960s to replace a number of smaller channels. The Oosterdiep on the other hand is an old waterway (depth 2m) crossed by some 30 lifting bridges. The connecting channel at Veendam is crossed by a rail bridge that serves a museum line. The bridge normally stands open except for one passage of the museum train on Fridays and Saturdays.

AG Wildervanckkanaal

Length 6.7km
Speed limit 11km
Bridges 3 opening. Rail (4.5m when closed) operates on request throughout the day Monday–Saturday with a break for lunch (1200–1300). Closed Sunday. Meedenes and Geert Veenhuizer bridges are operated by a single bridgekeeper throughout the day with breaks for lunch (1200–1300) and tea (1630–1730) Monday–Friday, and a break for lunch only on Saturday. Closed Sunday. VHF 22

Oosterdiep

Length 6.7km
Speed 6km/h
Locks Wilhelmina, Participantenverlaat and Batjeverlaat operate throughout the day Monday–Saturday with a break for lunch (1200–1300). Closed Sunday.
Bridges 30 opening. Operated in succession by a team of mobile bridge keepers for the same hours as the locks
☎ 06 22 41 38 27

VEENDAM

The advertised yacht harbour at Veendam consists of some modern-looking landing stages along the north side of the connecting channel between the A.G. Wildervanckkanaal and the Oosterdiep. There are no facilities and the proximity of the road makes their security uncertain. The town centre is close by and there is a reasonable selection of shops and restaurants.

Veendam was a fen-digging village established in the 19th century, but the ribbon development of substantial dwellings along the canal has been overtaken by the modern town. The Veenkolonial Museum on Winkler Prinsstraat gives an overview of the town's history and development.

WILDERVANCK

A visitors' harbour lies north of a distinctive yellow bridge in a basin on the east side of the canal. The settlement is a continuation of Veendam and there is a small shopping centre nearby.

Westerwoldse Aa

The Westerwoldse Aa runs from the junction with the Pekel Aa at the Bulsterverlaat lock to Nieuwe Statenzijl on the Dollard. The upstream section from the Bulsterverlaat to Wedde is restricted to an air draught of 2.5m. A bridge key is required for the Klein Ulsda bridge which is available from the bridge-keepers at the Rensel rail bridge or in Nieuweschans, and in JH De Rensel in Winschoten for a deposit of €20.

Length 12km
Maximum permitted draught 2.6m
Speed limit 8km/h
Lock Nieuwe Statenzijl lock operates throughout the day with a break for lunch (1200–1300), depending on the tide.
Bridges 5 opening. Klein Ulsda bridge is self-operated and works throughout the day; the double A7 bridge (4m when closed) must be requested 24 hours in advance ☎ 050 533 4111 and operates throughout the day Monday–Friday with a break for lunch (1200–1400) but is closed weekends; the cycle, road and rail bridges in Nieuweschans operate throughout the day with a break for lunch (1200–1400) including Sundays.

NIEUWESCHANS

Limited canalside moorings are available on the west bank opposite a large industrial area. The train station is close by and there are a handful of shops and cafés in the small village, as well as a Vesting (fortress) museum on 1e Kannonierstraat. Nieuweschans has the destinction of being the most easterly village in the Netherlands and is popular for its spa resort, Fontana Nieuweschans, where day guests are welcome.

Pekel-Aa & Pekeler Hoofddiep

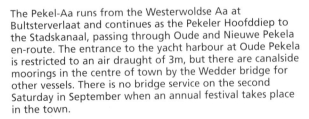

The Pekel-Aa runs from the Westerwoldse Aa at Bultsterverlaat and continues as the Pekeler Hoofddiep to the Stadskanaal, passing through Oude and Nieuwe Pekela en-route. The entrance to the yacht harbour at Oude Pekela is restricted to an air draught of 3m, but there are canalside moorings in the centre of town by the Wedder bridge for other vessels. There is no bridge service on the second Saturday in September when an annual festival takes place in the town.

Length 22km
Maximum permitted draught 1.2m
Speed limit 6km/h
Locks Bulsterverlaat is self-operated and can be worked throughout the day. Benedenverlaat, Middenverlaat, Bovenverlaat and Koppelsluis locks are operated as part of the convoy (see below).
Bridges 1 fixed (5m), 31 opening. Winschoterhoge bridge operates throughout the day Monday–Saturday with a break for lunch (1200–1300) and all day on Sunday, VHF 22. Remaining 30 opening bridges operated in convoy starting from Blijhamster bridge and the Koppelsluis at 0930 and 1330 (Monday–Saturday only).

OUDE PEKELA/NIEUWE PEKELA

Moorings are available on the canalside in Oude Pekela or at yacht harbour and campsite 't Dalheem south of Nieuwe Pekela. A linear town that developed during the fen-digging era, its only claim to fame is its annual boat procession, which takes place on the second Friday in September, followed by the annual market on the Saturday. A weekly market is held on Thursday afternoons.

Stadskanaal

The Stadskanaal runs from Bareveld at the junction with the Veendam canal (Oosterdiep) and this section includes details for the Musselkanaal and Ter Apelkanaal as far as Barnflair on the German border (junction with the Haren-Rütenbrock Kanal). The large number of opening bridges means this cruise takes about seven to ten hours. There is little commercial traffic and the canal is lined with residential development for much of its length.

Length 31km
Depth 1.4m
Speed limit 6km/h; or less by houseboats
Locks 7. Verlaat 1–7 operate throughout the day Monday–Saturday with a break for lunch (1200–1300). Closed Sundays.
Bridges 3 fixed (min 4m, or min 5m to Ter Apel), 26 opening. The rail bridge at Bareveld (3.7m when closed) must be requested 24 hours in advance ☎ 050 312 1710. The remaining bridges operate the same hours as the locks.

For the onward passage into Germany on the Haren-Rütenbrock Kanal there is automated opening of the bridges and locks, and it is necessary to start the passage at least two and a half hours before the published closing time in order to complete the transit. The yacht harbour at Ter Apel can advise further on transit arrangements.

Locks 4 locks (1 stands open). Lock on border operated from Verlaat 7 ☎ 06 5692 3547
Bridges 3 fixed (min 4.5m) 7 opening operate throughout the day with a break for lunch (1230–1300) Monday–Friday and mornings only (0800–1300) on Saturdays. Closed Sundays. ☎ 00 49 (0)5932 4376

STADSKANAAL

There are visitors' moorings dotted along the canal, normally only for one or two boats, with the most convenient being those by the Eurobrug where toilets/showers are available. (Key available from the bridge keeper for a small deposit.) Another of the

fen-digging communities, most of the residential development and shops are along the waterfront, whilst farms were built along a second, parallel canal. The Streekmuseum on Cerestraat gives a good overview of the distinctive history of the region and every Thursday in August you can climb the neighbouring water tower for an aerial view.

Stadskanaal is also home to the longest museum rail line in the Netherlands. The Star line runs 26km to Veendam every Friday and Saturday in the summer.

MUSSELKANAAL

Moorings for visitors are provided along the canal near the Stationsbrug and in front of Hotel Platen, as well as at the municipal JH Spoordok where toilet/shower facilities and water are available. Fuel is available from a bunker station between Musselkanaal and Stadskanaal, south of the 4e Verlaat lock.

TER APEL

JH Ter Apel has overnight places for visitors up to 20m (depth 1.5m) but a fixed bridge crosses the entrance which restricts air draught to 2.9m. Alternatively there are visitors' moorings in the village, including space near Hoofdstraat/Molenplein, where an overnight fee is collected.

The village owes its existence to the medieval monastery, which was in use until 1593. Now restored, Museum Klooster Ter Apel houses a collection of religious art and maintains an extensive herb garden. The surrounding woodland contains some rare species of plants and birds and is recommended for walking and cycling.

Ruiten Aakanaal

The Ruiten Aakanaal runs north from Ter Apel and, since 2001, connects via the BL Tijdenskanaal to the Westerwoldse Aa at Nieuweschans. However, for boats of 3.5m air draught or more this is a return trip from Ter Apel to visit Bourtange, as fixed bridges of 2.5m restrict the section north of Bourtange. The Bourtange Kanaal itself is crossed by bridges of 3m air draught before the visitors' harbour but there is a stopping place north of the Sellingersluis on the quay wall.

The bridge key for the self-operated bridges is available from the Potze fuel station and the bridge-keeper at Roswinkeler bridge in Ter Apel.

Length 14km (Ter Apel to Bourtange Kanaal)
Speed limit 6km/h
Locks 5 with opening bridges operate throughout the day
Bridges 4 opening are self-operated and require a bridge key (plus 2 fixed on Bourtange Kanaal, with a lowest air draught of 3m)

BOURTANGE

Situated in the Westerwoldse countryside, Bourtange was built in 1580 to defend the border with Germany, and isolate the Spanish in Groningen. After the end of the 80-years war the town became part of the northern Netherlands defence structure until 'modern' warfare rendered it obsolete in 1851. The community declined until a decision was taken some 100 years later to restore the town to its appearance in 1742, when the fortress had its heyday. A visit to the town today is a trip back in time, with fortification, museums and events of that age. The town comes to life at weekends, with re-enactments and parades from the historic militia.

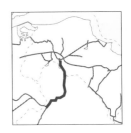

Noord-Willemskanaal

From Groningen's Zuiderhaven the Noord-Willemskanaal runs south to Assen to connect with the Drentsche Hoofdvaart. It was widened and modernised in 1972 and offers a pleasant view of the wooded landscape. Bridges as far as the van Ketwich-Verschuurbrug are managed by Groningen and details of opening times and Sunday convoys are given under 'Groningen canals'. A high-voltage electricity cable, which crosses the waterway west of Sluis Peelo, has an air draught of 7.8m

Various stopping places are provided along the waterway including a one kilometre long stretch of canalside moorings just south of the entrance to the Paterwoldse Meer . These are close to the lake and have a pleasant grassy bank on one side, but a motorway on the other side of the canal. At Jachtwerf Beuving De Punt (km17.5) there are moorings with electricity, water and toilets/showers available for a modest charge. Diesel, parts and boat repairs can be provided by the boatyard and chandlers. This is very close to Groningen's Eelde airport, if this proves to be useful in the future. Further moorings are available both sides of the De Punt and De Vries locks, and by most of the bridges between Oosterbroeksebrug and Taarlosebrug.

Length 28km
Speed limit In Groningen province, 6km/h; In Drenthe province, 9km/h, except from km post 1 to Brug Asserwijk, 6km/h
Maximum permitted draught 1.9m
Locks De Punt, De Vries and Peelo locks operate throughout the day with a break for lunch (1200–1300). Sunday service is only in July and August
Bridges 4 fixed (minimum clearance 5.4m), 17 lifting which operate the same hours as the locks.

HOORNSE MEER AND PATERSWOLDSE MEER

These are unusual meres below the level of the main canal which have to be entered through a small lock (max. beam 3.4m), which is hand-operated by the lockkeeper. Once beyond the lock, there are many mooring places on the islands offering a splendid and sheltered place to explore with a sailing dinghy. The small village of Paterswolde is in the southwest corner.

ASSEN

Where to stop

The diversion of the main waterway round the northern outskirts of Assen has meant that the only place to provide a visitors' harbour is on the extreme outskirts of the city, some 5km from the centre. This lies east of the Marker bridge in a large, leafy basin off the main canal, next to a quiet residential area. No facilities exist, except for rubbish bins and there are no shops or amenities nearby except for a bus service to the centre. Locals make the trip by bike, which takes about 20 minutes through housing and industrial areas. There is good ramp access from the mooring quays here, which is useful for those with bikes, pushchairs and wheelchairs etc.

Most visitors, however, prefer the canalside moorings both sides of the Asserwijk bridge which are slightly nearer the centre (about 3km away) and have a free, unmetered water hose available at the northern end. There is a single mooring stage on the Havenkanaal north of Marsdijk bridge, again in a residential suburb distant from any facilities. The closest moorings to the city centre are in the industrial harbour but are not to be recommended, being austere and occupied by displaced houseboats.

What to see

Assen (pronounced 'arson') is the capital of Drenthe province and is a modern, commercial city with a vaguely presentable centre hidden in the middle. The nicest parts are the woodlands that surround the city to the south and east, and these include an open clearing several metres below ground level which was used as the meeting place for the Provincial Assembly until 1602.

The Drents museum, housed in a series of historic buildings, has done a good job of presenting the local history and geology in an engaging style. Particularly impressive are the exhibits concerning the Neanderthal communities that lived nearby and artefacts from local *hunebedden*, the burial mounds for which the area is renowned. To the south is Westerbork, site of the notorious transit camp for Jewish prisoners, from where some 100,000 were deported to death camps such as Auschwitz. A remembrance centre and museum tells the story of the site, now used as a telecommunications centre.

Connections

A train service links the city to Groningen and Meppel.

Assen's generously-sized visitors harbour is remote from the town centre

Drentsche Hoofdvaart

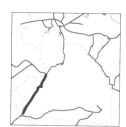

The Drentsche Hoofdvaart forms the continuation of the Noord-Willemskanaal and joins Assen with Meppel. The picturesque Opsterlandse Compagnonsvaart (Turfroute), described in Chapter 6: Friesland, joins the waterway south of Smilde. Much of the canal is dead straight with a road running alongside, although there is open countryside beyond and a border of poplar trees to absorb road noise.

Numerous canalside moorings are provided including those above each lock, which are next to grassy banks. In Bovensmilde there are moorings north of the bridge, and in Smilde on both sides of Koopbakkers bridge, next to a shopping centre, which includes two supermarkets and a Chinese restaurant. Those in Hoogesmilde have water and toilets/showers available on the east bank and there is a small shop and restaurant nearby.

Further good moorings are available near Uffelte and Havelte, where again toilet/shower facilities are available.

Length 41.8km
Maximum permitted draught 1.55m
Speed limit 6km/h
Locks Veene, Haar, Diever, Uffelter, Havelter and Paradijs locks operate throughout the day with a break for lunch (1200–1300) with Sunday service from July to mid-August only
Bridges 4 fixed (minimum clearance 5.4m), 25 opening which operate the same hours as the locks. The rail bridge operates the same hours but opens twice per hour depending on train services.

DIEVERBRUG

Where to stop

One of the nicest stopping places along the canal is the mooring by the lock at Dieverbrug, where there is a long stretch on both sides which are free for 14 days, equipped with a slightly eccentric toilet/shower block and pump-out facility. Fuel is available from a bunker station north of the bridge.

What to see

It is 2km to the nearby village of Diever (pronounced 'diva') and if you don't want to cycle or fancy the walk there is a bus stop right next to the moorings.

This is a popular holiday village on the southern edge of the Drents-Friese Wold National Park and, as well as basic shopping and a regular fish stall, there are plenty of options for eating out. The VVV office on the north side of the village doubles up as a visitors' centre for the national park, and they have good information about walks and cycle routes, which take in the megalithic *hunebedden*. A highlight is the delightful timber open-air theatre which has regular productions of Shakespeare plays throughout the summer. Unfortunately these are performed in Dutch but Shakespeare fans know the plots and words anyway! They used to give the characters Dutch names which would be really confusing but they have reverted to the traditional ones by public request.

There are summer markets on Monday afternoons in July and August and a *bos bus* – an old-fashioned 'woodland-bus', which runs a fixed schedule through the woods and serves all the different attractions.

Covered wagons are the old-world alternative to camper vans in the Drents-Friese Wold national park

Meppelerdiep and Meppel

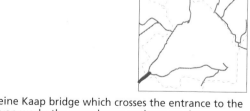

The Meppelerdiep runs from Zwartsluis northeast to the town of Meppel where it continues as the Drentsche Hoofdvaart. A connection through the town centre to the Hoogeveensche Vaart is no longer navigable and a new canal to the south of the town now connects the two waterways. Details of the downstream section of the Meppelerdiep are given in Chapter 5: Flevoland and the Randmeren as this gives access to the Kop van Overijssel waterways.

The Kleine Kaap bridge which crosses the entrance to the Buitenhaven works the same hours as those on the 'Meppelerdiep to the Drentsche Hoofdvaart' route. The Galgenkamp bridge opens only on the hour and at half past during the season. The Meppelersluis gives access to further moorings in the town centre and the following two bridges can be opened to provide more moorings along the canal if necessary.

Meppelerdiep to the Drentsche Hoofdvaart

Bridges 1 fixed (5.8m), 3 opening Eshuis (5.5m when closed), Kaap and Galgenkamp bridges operate throughout the day Monday–Saturday with a break for lunch (1200–1230). On Sundays the bridges open for brief periods morning and evening (0900–0930 and 1830–1930) in May, June and September, but throughout the day with breaks for lunch and tea (1200–1300 and 1700–1830) in July and August. VHF 22.

Meppel town centre

Lock Meppelersluis and lifting bridge operates throughout the day Monday–Saturday with a break for lunch (1200–1300) in June–August with shorter hours in low season. Closed Sundays.
Bridges Zuiderbrug and Emmabrug operate the same hours as the lock.

MEPPEL

Where to stop

The main municipal visitors' harbour is located close to the centre of the historic town, on the east side north of the Eshuis bridge (south of the Kaap bridge). There are further moorings beyond the Meppelersluis which are even nearer the centre but can be noisy until late at night on Meppel Thursdays (see below). Just south of the Kaap bridge, the Kleine Kaap bridge gives access to the Buitenhaven, where there are further municipal moorings as well as berths for commercial and trip-boats. Pricey electricity (coin-operated 10A, €0.50/kWh) is available at all berths or there is a double unmetered outlet close to the water point in the main harbour (6A, charged at €3.50/day). There is a half-price moorings offer for whole week stays. Coin-operated water points (€0.50/100 ltrs) are dotted around the moorings and there is a facilities block by the harbour office near the Kleine Kaap bridge.

Within cycling distance of the main town Jachthaven Meppel offers all facilities, including fuel and chandlers. Next door Holterman Yachting are mainly involved in producing swanky motor yachts, but do have a few spaces for visitors; as do Pro-Aqua yachting, north of the Galgenkamp bridge.

Facilities ashore

Fuel & Chandlers Leusink Marine Centre on the Meppelerdiep
Supermarket & Shops Aldi and Albert Heijn on Grote Oever (beyond the Pancake ship)
ATMs On Brouwersstraat
Cycle hire From the train station or Hoogwheem on Wheemplein
VVV office On Brouwerstraat

What to see

Meppel lies at the junction of several popular waterway routes, including the Tuin van Nederland, the Turfroute, and the Kop van Overijssel, which were dug for transporting peat in the 17th century. The town became an important transhipment point and continues the role to this day with a large container storage depot on the southern approach to the town.

Meppel is best known for its summer festivals, held each Thursday in July and August. Donderdag Meppeldag (Meppel Thursday) consists of a day-long programme of traditional entertainments and activities and is concluded with free multiple canal and town centre concerts until the early hours. The last Thursday of the season is accompanied by a parade of floats and a marching band. The church tower is open to visitors on Meppel Thursdays, and this also coincides with the weekly market, which is held on all Thursday mornings.

Meppel tower is open to visitors on Meppel Thursdays, when the market is also in town

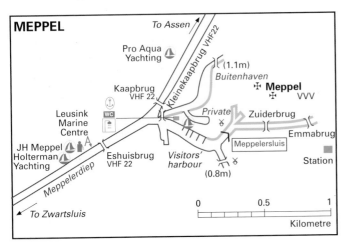

For a historical perspective on the town, you can join occasional guided walks organised by the VVV office on Saturday afternoons, which includes a trip up the Meppel tower, or visit the Drukkerij (printing) Museum, housed in an old grain warehouse which once stood directly on the canal. The restored Molen De Weert stands near the harbour and turns on most Saturdays and any other days the volunteer millers have to complete flour orders. As well as enjoying a free tour of the mill whenever you see the hand-reefed sails turning, you can buy hand-milled wholewheat and pancake flour, the latter coming with a recipe for genuine Dutch pancakes.

Restaurant tip

Meppel has a good choice of nice eating places, with the newly opened American Restaurant Het Pepermill a particular favourite.

Connections

The station is about 10 minutes walk on the east side of town and has good connections including a direct service to Schiphol airport and fast trains to the Hoek van Holland for home visits and crew changes.

Visitors' moorings beyond the Meppelersluis in the centre of Meppel

Hoogeveensche Vaart

The Hoogeveensche Vaart runs from the Meppelerdiep south of Meppel east to Hoogeveen. Beyond the town the waterway continues as the Verlengde Hoogeveensche Vaart east, towards Emmen.

There are several canalside moorings available, including near the Ossesluis, in Echten, by the Nieuwe Brugsluis. Moorings in Hoogeveen itself are very limited, with free places west of the Edison bridge on the south side of the industrial harbour your only option. More preferable are the moorings at Noordscheschut, which lie east of the town on the Verlengde Hoogeveensche Vaart.

Length 25km
Speed limit 9km/h
Locks Rogatsluis, Ossesluis and Nieuwe Brugsluis operate throughout the day Monday–Saturday with a break for lunch (1200–1230). Closed Sundays.
Bridges 13 fixed (minimum clearance 5.3m), 4 lifting. Staphorster Grote Stuwe operates the same hours as the locks. Vlinder, Tweelanden and Edison bridges are operated remotely from Nieuwe Brugsluis and open throughout the day Monday–Saturday with a break for lunch (1200–1300). Closed Sundays.

ROGAT

The quiet and attractive visitors' harbour lies in a backwater east of the lock and has a toilet/shower building and rubbish bins provided, but there is no water or electricity. The village consists of a handful of houses and a single riverside café but it is a nice starting point for walks or cycle rides; for instance to the nearby village of De Wijk. Here you will find more amenities, as well as an attractive windmill and a barrel-organ museum. Nearby on Schiphorsterweg you will find De Lokkerij, a stork station where you can learn more about these enigmatic feathered visitors. The Dutch share the legend of the English-speaking peoples about their baby-delivering role.

Verlengde Hoogeveensche Vaart

The Verlengde Hoogeveensche Vaart forms the continuation of the Hoogeveensche Vaart from Hoogeveen eastwards to the junction with the Oranjekanaal at Klazienaveen, south of Emmen. The frequent opening bridges are often hand-operated and it is not a waterway to be cruised in a hurry.

Length 32.5km
Speed limit 6km/h
Maximum permitted draught 1.1m
Locks Noordscheschut and Ericasluis operate throughout the day Monday–Saturday (until 1700) with a break for lunch (1200–1300). Closed Sundays.
Bridges 3 fixed (minimum 5.11m), 22 opening operate the same hours as the locks. The rail bridge in Veenoord is operated remotely and opens once or twice per hour and can be requested by push-button.

NOORDSCHESCHUT

Canalside moorings are provided both sides of the lock, with those on the east side equipped with coin-operated electricity and water, and a pump-out station. A modern facilities block is provided at the lock, for which a key is obtainable from the lock-keeper. The small village has a couple of cafés, including the friendly Café Troost, which also serves as the VVV information point. A supermarket and ATM are available on Zwarte Dijkje.

VEENOORD/NIEUWE AMSTERDAM

Free unserviced canalside moorings are provided through the centre of the small town with those west of the Kerkbrug close to several supermarkets and cafés. East of the Kerkbrug there are some quieter berths on the edge of the town. Nieuwe Amsterdam was named after the capital city when the first fen diggers arrived here in 1851, under the management of their head office in Amsterdam. Its claim to fame is the house where Vincent van Gogh stayed for two months in 1883, which stands east of the rail bridge on the south bank.

ERICA

Newly laid out canalside moorings are provided west of the Erica bridge, although no facilities have been provided as yet. Erica is another former fen settlement established at the end of the 19th century and south of the canal you can visit the narrow gauge railway, Smalspoormuseum, on Griendtsveenstraat.

Oranjekanaal/Bladderswijk

The Oranjekanaal was dug in 1853 and originally joined the Drentsche Hoofdvaart. Around ten years later it was continued from Emmen to the Verlengde Hoogeveensche Vaart, and it is this section which remains navigable today, from the junction with the Verlengde Hoogeveensche Vaart at Klazienaveen northwest to Emmen. It is still very much in use as a commercial waterway and the moorings in the centre of Emmen are in the main industrial harbour and not recommended for visitors.

A new waterway is currently in development that will link Oranjedorp with Ter Apel on the Stadskanaal making this a circular route for boats with air draught of under 3.75m. The details were still being finalised in 2006 and the project is likely to take 10 years to complete.

Length 7km
Speed limit 6km/h
Lock Oranjesluis operates throughout the day Monday–Saturday with a break for lunch (1200–1230). Closed Sundays.
Bridges 4 fixed (minimum clearance 4.25m), 1 opening. Brug 23 opens the same hours as the lock.

KLAZIENAVEEN

There are canalside moorings south of the Oranjesluis which are close to the village or near Brug 23 at Oranjedorp. A selection of shops and cafés are available in Klazienaveen and there is a bus service for excursions to Emmen or Coevorden.

Free moorings at the Oranjesluis close to Klazienaveen

Stieltjeskanaal

From Nieuwe Amsterdam on the Verlengde Hoogeveensche Vaart, the Stieltjeskanaal runs southwest via Zandpol to Coevorden, and then becomes the Coevorden-Vechtkanaal before crossing the provincial border into Overijssel. For the description of this onward passage south from the Bentheimerbrug, turn to Chapter 8: Central Netherlands, Kanaal Almelo-De Haandrik (& Coevorden-Vechtkanaal).

Dug at the end of the 19th century and named after engineer Thomas Stieltjes, the canal was later deepened to accommodate 600-ton ships, so for some of the cruise you are between high quay walls which restricts your view of the surroundings.

The Zijtak Stieltjeskanaal (which branches off the Verlengde Hoogeveensche Vaart to the west of the main channel and joins it at Zandpol) is restricted to 2.5m headroom. South of the lock, the rail bridge normally stands open, but can be operated remotely by rail staff when needed.

Length 12km
Maximum permitted draught 1.9m
Speed limit 9km/h
Lock Stieltjeskanaalsluis operates throughout the day Monday–Saturday with a break for lunch (1200–1230) Closed Sundays
Bridges 4 opening. Drieklaps, rail, Het Vonder and J Kuipers bridges operate the same hours as the lock

COEVORDEN

Where to stop

The municipal visitors' harbour lies in a spur off the main canal close to the centre of the fortified town. Unmetered electricity is available from quayside cabinets (which must be unlocked by the harbourmaster) and there is a free water point available in the toilet and shower building on the north side.

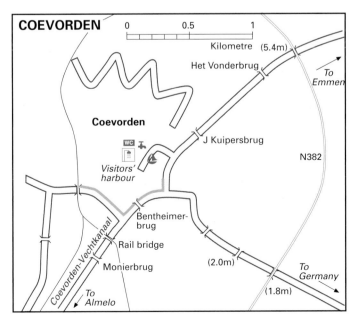

Quiet, alongside moorings close to the town centre in Coevorden's visitors' harbour

Alternatively, there are free unserviced canalside moorings on the Spoorsingel, between the Coevorden-Vechtkanaal and the rail bridge.

Facilities ashore
Supermarket, Shops & ATMs Albert Heijn in the Gansehof shopping centre, or Super de Boer on Spoorsingel
Cycle hire Scheerhoorn on Salladspassage
VVV office On Haven, next to the moorings

What to see
An important trading town in the Middle Ages, Coevorden (pronounced 'Coo-forder') remains one of Drenthe's most popular stops for boating visitors. Its historic centre is complemented by the attractive countryside that surrounds it and the town puts on a range of special events to entertain visitors throughout the summer. Behind the VVV office you will find the entrance to the local museum, Drenthe's Veste, which concentrates on the fortress towns of the province and gives an insight into the town's history.

The town has a selection of shops nearby including a covered shopping centre, De Gansehof, named after the annual goose market which is still held every second Monday in November. Also in the centre you will find Het Ambact, an artisan candle maker where you can visit the workshop and try your hand at crafting your own candle.

A harbour festival, the Historische Havendagen, is held over the third weekend in July, and the following weekend the annual market, the Piekiesmarkt, takes place on the last Saturday in July. The third weekend in August is also festival week, with the Horecadagen playing host to a range of musical entertainment.

Restaurant tip
Gasterie Het Kasteel is located in the cellar of the 12th-century castle and serves a special Drenthe menu, as well as Dutch and French specialities. The local recommendation is Eetcafe Miracle, a lower budget offering on Brentheimerstraat. On the same street is internet café De Bentheimer for those seeking connectivity.

Connections
The nearby train station has services to Emmen and Zwolle.

Coevorden's market square pays tribute to the success of its traditional goose market

Cruising in Groningen and Drenthe

Routes are already very much established for overseas visitors from the west of the region (and hence Friesland) via the mast-up route or Van Starkenborghkanaal on to the Eems estuary at Delfzijl. Also for the numerous Scandinavian and German visitors who arrive via that route or the network of canals that join the east side of Drenthe.

To these can be added connections to the picturesque Turfroute by using the Drentsche Hoofdvaart to complete circular routes. In the same way the Hoogeveensche vaart links Meppel with Coevorden to complete a circular route from the Central Netherlands. In the north of the region tours can be devised in their own right but many of the potential circuits are limited by bridge height restrictions.

In truth, many of the best aspects of Groningen and Drenthe province have yet to be fully exploited as, in addition to the improvements and extensions of waterspace mentioned in the text, ambitions include joining up the waterways in the southeast to complete a through route near the German border. The provinces seem very committed to follow the lead of neighbouring Friesland to encourage more watersports visitors and increase the waterspace accordingly, and we look forward to ever-improving facilities in the future.

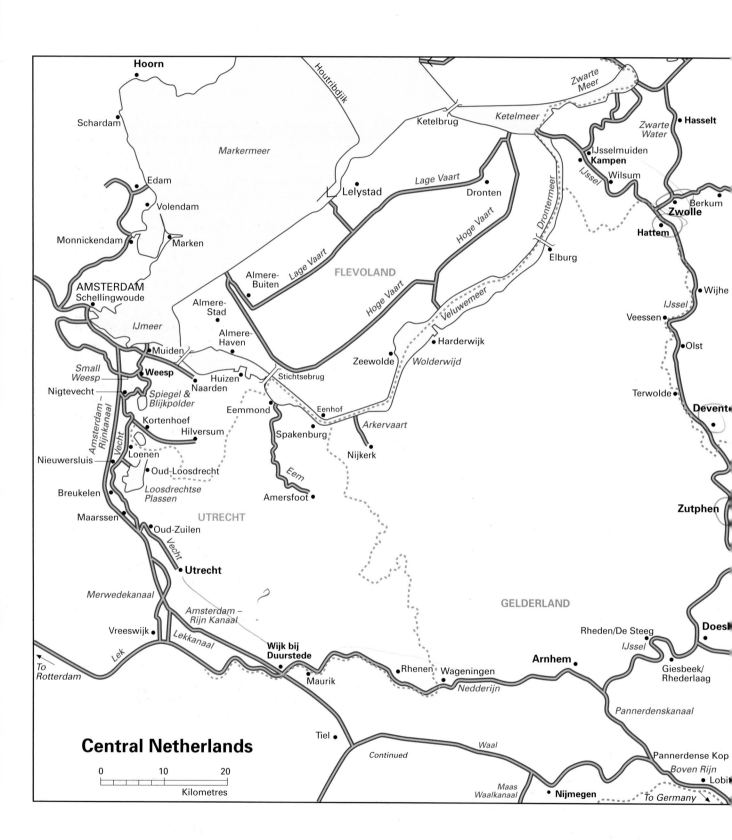

Central Netherlands

0   10   20
Kilometres

8 Central Netherlands

Utrecht, Gelderland and Overijssel

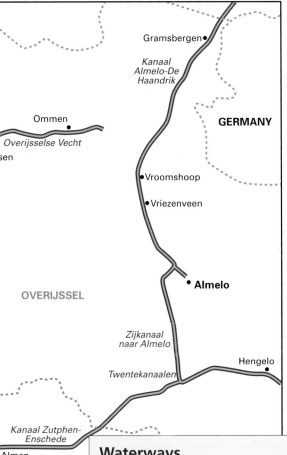

The Central Netherlands chapter comprises a large area of land, but one which has relatively fewer waterways than the rest of the country. The area is bordered to the west by the commercial artery of the Amsterdam-Rijnkanaal, although most leisure traffic tends to use the Vecht which winds its way north just to the east. South of Utrecht the region stretches as far as the Neder-rijn, where we turn east. A popular cruising route also follows this waterway, past Arnhem, to join the Gelderse IJssel. This flows north between the provinces of Gelderland and Overijssel, emerging into the Ketelmeer (and thence to the IJsselmeer) north of Kampen. To the east of the region, the Twentekanaalen are included which, together with the connecting waterways described in Chapter 7: Groningen and Drenthe, are often described as the 'Tuin van Nederland' (meaning 'Garden of Holland') route.

ANWB *Charts I (Vechtplassen), L (Grote Rivieren Oost)* and *D (Gelderse IJssel)* give good coverage of the main navigations, but there is only limited information available for the Twentekanalen.

Waterways	Principal venues	Other stopping places
Amsterdam-Rijnkanaal		
Muidertrekvaart		(Muiden)
Naardertrekvaart		(Naarden)
Vecht	Weesp, Utrecht	Loenen, Breukelen, Maarssen, Oud-Zuilen
Spiegel & Blijkpolder		
Hilversumskanaal		Kortenhoef, Hilversum
Loosdrechtse Plassen		Oud-Loosdrecht
Merwedekanaal benoorden de Lek		Vreeswijk
Lekkanaal		
Rijn	Wijk bij Duurstede, Arnhem	Maurik, Rhenen, Wageningen
Pannerdenskanaal		
Gelderse IJssel	Doesburg, Zutphen, Deventer, Hattem, Kampen	Rheden and De Steeg, Giesbeek and the Rhederlaag, Terwolde, Veessen, Wijhe, Wilsum, IJsselmuiden
Oude IJssel		Doetinchem
Twentekanalen (Kanaal Zutphen-Enschede & Zijkanaal naar Almelo)		Almen
Kanaal Almelo-De Haandrik (& Coevorden-Vechtkanaal)	Almelo	Vriezenveen, Vroomshoop, Gramsbergen
Zwolle-IJsselkanaal & Zwolle canals	Zwolle	
Zwarte Water	Hasselt	
Overijsselse Vecht		Berkum, Dalfsen

Amsterdam-Rijnkanaal

The Amsterdam-Rijnkanaal forms the main north-south through route between Amsterdam and the great rivers. It joins the junction of the Lek and the Nederrijn at Wijk bij Duurstede and then continues as far as the Waal, to the east of Tiel. There is very heavy commercial traffic and wash, except on Sundays when it is quieter. There are no mooring places along the waterway and leisure boats are advised to use the Vecht except for through traffic. Yachts must be able to make a minimum of 6km/h with a reliable motor, keep to the starboard side of the channel and use a radar reflector in poor visibility. VHF 66 is used along the canal for nautical information broadcasts at H+15. A listening watch should be kept as follows: Amsterdam to the Nieuwe Diep, VHF 60; in the vicinity of Maarssen, VHF 61; on approach to the junction with the Lek, call Wijk bij Duurstede on VHF 60 and stay on this channel until the junction is passed.

Connections between the Amsterdam-Rijnkanaal and the Vecht

There are connections via the Muider trekvaart and the Smal Weesp which are detailed separately below. Continuing south, there is a connection at Nigtevecht, where the lock normally stands open and the bridge opens throughout the day (VHF 21). There is a restricted view of oncoming vessels at this junction and passage is controlled by traffic lights. A yellow flashing light on the W-bank of the Vecht, south of the lock, indicates that vessels should wait for oncoming traffic from the Amsterdam-Rijnkanaal.

The only other usable connection is south of Maarssen, where the Vechtsluis connects the Vecht to the Amsterdam-Rijnkanaal and normally stands open. A fixed bridge crosses the flood lock with an air draught of 3.75m.

At Nieuwersluis, the Nieuwe Wetering waterway is crossed by a fixed bridge (3m) which puts it beyond the scope of this guide. (The western section of the Nieuwe Wetering, leading to the Vinkeveense Plassen, is described in Chapter 3, Holland South.) At Breukelen, the Kerkvaart-Danne connection is also restricted to 2.9m air draught and 2.8m beam, and in any case was out of service at the time of writing due to bridge reconstruction.

Length 72km
Speed limit 18km/h
Maximum permitted draught 4m
Locks Prinses Irenesluis in Wijk bij Durstede (VHF 22) and Prins Bernhardsluis in Tiel (VHF 18) operate 24 hours. Prinses Marijkesluis in Ravenswaaij is a flood lock which normally stands open.
Bridges 23 fixed (minimum air draught 9m)

AMSTERDAM

The only stopping places are at the north end of the Amsterdam-Rijnkanaal in Amsterdam's Nieuwe Diep. These include WV Het Nieuwe Diep and WV De Watergeuzen, but facilities at both are limited and visitors normally use the more central harbours described in Chapter 4: North Holland.

The lock stands open at Maarssen but you must negotiate the low bridge

Muidertrekvaart

This short stretch leaves the Amsterdam-Rijnkanaal south of the Diemen lakes and runs east to join the Vecht on the south side of Muiden. This waterway is restricted to modest sized vessels, and, as Muiden is more commonly approached via the Markermeer, full details of the stopping places and attractions are given in Chapter 5: Flevoland and the Randmeren.

Length 4km
Maximum permitted draught 1.1m, beam 4m, length 12m
Speed limit 6km/h
Locks Weesperpoortsluis often stands open, but the lifting bridge opens only for short periods morning and afternoon. See *Almanak* under Muidertrekvaart for exact times.
Bridges 2 opening. Pen bridge (requested by push button) and the Amsterdamse-Poortbrug also open restricted hours morning and afternoon.

Muiden forms the entrance to the Vecht from the IJsselmeer

Naardertrekvaart

The Naardertrekvaart forms the continuation of the Muidertrekvaart from Muiden to Naarden. It is again restricted to small vessels and has limited service times. Onward passage via the Karnemelksloot is restricted to 1m air draught and so vessels must return the same way. As most visitors use the large Jachthaven Naarden, accessed via the Randmeren, full details of Naarden and its attractions are given in Chapter 5: Flevoland and the Randmeren. However, a new visitors' harbour scheduled to open in 2007 is planned for Naarden, which will be accompanied by improved bridge opening times on the Naardertrekvaart. This will be sited at the end of the Naardertrekvaart, south of the 'Green bridge' (ANWB reference 768h).

Length 7.5km
Maximum permitted draught 1.1m, beam 4m, length 12m
Speed limit 6km/h
Locks Keetpoortsluis and lifting bridge open for a limited period in the afternoon on weekdays only and require 24 hours notice. See *Almanak* for details.
Bridges 4 fixed (minimum 5m) and 4 opening. Muiden, Hakkelaas and De Kwekel bridges open the same hours as the lock. Irene and Green bridges operate throughout the day Monday–Friday ☎ 035 694 1074. Closed weekends and holidays

Weesp canal

The Smal Weesp waterway forms the continuation of the Weesper trekvaart and connects the Amsterdam-Rijnkanaal to the Vecht at Weesp. There are municipal moorings all along the waterway, with those at the east end most convenient for the town centre. These have coin-operated water and electricity provided and a harbourmaster visits to collect the modest fee (€0.65/m in 2006). For full details of stopping places and attractions in Weesp, see the section on the Vecht, below.

Length 2km
Speed limit 6km/h
Maximum permitted draught 2.1m
Locks At either end of the waterway, normally stand open.
Bridges 4 opening. Sluis, Zwaantjes and Roskam bridges operate throughout the day with a break for lunch and tea (1230–1330 and 1630–1730). De Uitkomst bridge operates throughout the day. Early and late openings are only on request for commercial vessels, but leisure boats may make use of these openings if available. Toll payable at Zwaantjes bridge.

Vecht

The Vecht is an attractive, almost tideless river that connects Utrecht with Muiden and is linked to a series of large lakes. It is also connected at Weesp, Nigtevecht and Maarssen with the Amsterdam-Rijnkanaal (see details in that section) and forms a much quieter alternative to that waterway for leisure boats. The more northerly villages make convenient stops for those wishing to make faster passage on the Amsterdam-Rijnkanaal but beware of the restrictions to the crossing points as you get nearer to Utrecht.

Lined with parkland and impressive country houses, built in the 17th and 18th century by rich Amsterdammers, it is regarded as one of the most beautiful waterways in the Netherlands. Much of the downstream (northern) section is accessible to fixed-mast vessels, with opening bridges as far as Maarssen, although any boat with more than 3.75m air draught must return to Nigtevecht for access to the Amsterdam-Rijnkanaal.

Canalside moorings are provided along the length of the waterway including on the section between Muiden and Weesp and north of the Spiegelpolder and Blijkpolder lakes. (A small charge for these is administered by the neighbouring Thai restaurant.)

Vessels are locked and bridged as a convoy between the Roode bridge and the Weerdsluis in Utrecht. Last lock northbound 1815, southbound 1830.

Length 40km
Maximum permitted draught 2.1m to Loosdrechtse Plassen, 1.5m to Utrecht Weerdsluis; beam 5.5m
Speed limit Muiden to Nederhorst den Berg, 9km/h; Nederhorst den Berg to Utrecht, 6km/h
Minimum depth 1.5m between Utrecht and the Mijndense lock (Loosdrechtse Plassen)
Locks Muiden Zeesluis and lifting bridge operates throughout the day with two breaks on weekdays only (1145–1215 and 1245–1315). Toll payable. Utrecht Weerdsluis operates throughout the day with breaks for lunch and tea (1200–1300 and 1630–1730) on weekdays and for lunch only at weekends. Toll payable.
Bridges 5 fixed (minimum 4m), 16 opening as below:
A1 road (5.2m when closed) opens for restricted periods during the morning, lunchtime and evening (No lunchtime opening on Sundays).
Weesp rail (3.75m when closed) operates throughout the day at H+28. There is an intercom on the bridge to ask for the next opening; longer waits should be expected during rush hour periods.
Lange (or Vecht) bridge operates throughout the day with breaks for lunch and rush hour (1230–1330 and 1630–1730).
Uitermeer bridge operates throughout the day with a break for rush hour on weekdays (1630–1730). Normally opens at H and H+30.
Van Leer, Vreeland, Loenen (two) and Nieuwersluis bridges operate throughout the day with breaks for lunch and tea (1200–1300 and 1630–1730). Toll payable at Van Leer and Loenen bridges.
Breukelen, Vecht, Ter Meer and Plomp bridges operate throughout the day with breaks for lunch and tea (1230–1300 and 1630–1730 in high season).
Roode, David van Mollem and Stenen bridges operate throughout the day with breaks for lunch and tea (1200–1300 and 1630–1730). Break for lunch only at weekends.

WEESP

Where to stop

The most popular harbour in Weesp is the WSV De Vecht, south of the Lange bridge on the south side of town. Here there is a full time harbourmaster (good English spoken) who will greet you at the reporting pontoon. Smaller boats are normally allocated a box mooring whilst larger boats are rafted on the outside pontoons. Unmetered 4A electricity (€1.50/day) and coin-operated water (€0.50/100 ltrs) are available, as are a wide range of good facilities. Popular features are free tea and coffee in the clubhouse until 3pm when the bar opens for drinks and snacks and the adjacent large children's play area.

Municipal box moorings are provided north of the Lange bridge, where coin-operated water only is available, or beyond an opening bridge at the east end of the Smal Weesp, where coin-operated electricity is also available. These are both low cost and close to the town centre, but can get very busy.

Facilities ashore

Chandlers Weesper Watersportwinkel in the town on Buitenveer; or at De Bruyn or De Leeuw boatyards for larger items.
Repairs & Servicing De Bruyn Watersportservice and Jachtwerf De Leeuw
Supermarket & Shops Super de Boer at north end of Nieuwstad and lots of good small shops around the town
ATMs Several in the centre
Cycle hire Rijwielhandel Oldenburger on Stationsplein
VVV office On Hoogstraat (just north of Vecht bridge)

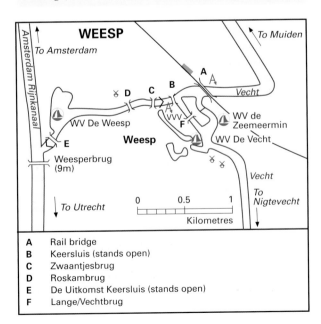

A	Rail bridge
B	Keersluis (stands open)
C	Zwaantjesbrug
D	Roskambrug
E	De Uitkomst Keersluis (stands open)
F	Lange/Vechtbrug

What to see

Weesp (pronounced 'waysp') celebrated its 650th anniversary in 2005 and the small town is a popular choice for boating and other visitors. The first Dutch porcelain was produced here in 1759, the coloured designs distinguishing it from the Chinese-inspired blue and white designs made famous by the Delft-based potters during the previous century. A varied collection of pieces made by Gronsveld's porcelain factory are displayed in the municipal museum, on the second floor of the 18th-century town hall. Here you can also see exhibits relating to the Van Houten chocolate factory which was based in the town until 1970, as well as prints and cards depicting the development of the town from the 14th century.

For more modern day entertainment you can enjoy Weesp's Juke box museum, open Sunday afternoons on Middenstraat, or the many tempting shops which line the small pedestrianised centre.

Restaurant tip

Greek restaurant Plaka on Hoogstraat has a special welcome for visitors from WV De Vecht, and although the outside is plain, the interior is gaily decorated. At Eetcafé 't Weesperplein on Slijkstraat you can enjoy a more traditional Dutch repast, in their secluded rear garden if the weather permits.

Connections

From the nearby train station you can make the short trip into Amsterdam for a day excursion, or to Schipol for crew changes.

LOENEN

The pretty village of Loenen has canalside moorings both sides of the bridge to the south, and if you are a keen walker this is a good starting point for a walk north on the east bank of the Vecht, then along the Alambertskade between the Wijde Blik and the Loenderveense Plas towards Oud Loosdrecht. From the road junction you can take the bus back to Loenen.

BREUKELEN

Free unserviced canalside moorings are provided north of the bridge, for a maximum stay of 24 hours. These are close to the centre of the small town, which gave its name to New York's Brooklyn, founded by Dutch settlers. The main square has a good selection of eating places with De Danne, by the junction with the Kerkvaart Danne, a popular choice. This is one of the areas popular for weekend retreats, and a VVV information point is located in the bookshop on the square. South of the town there are customer moorings at the riverside Restaurant Slangevecht and De Nieuwe Olifant.

MAARSSEN

There are plenty of canalside moorings north of the town, and just north of the Vecht bridge, as well as limited space south of the Ter Meer bridge on the west side. The town centre has many well-restored

Town moorings lie north of the Lange bridge and at the end of the Smal Weesp

old houses, as well as the villas and manor houses on the outskirts. One such villa is the 18th-century Goudestein, now in use as the town hall, which is open to visitors when it is not in use as a wedding venue.

OUD-ZUILEN

A small stretch of canalside moorings are provided just north of the Plomp bridge (maximum stay 3 days) from where you are very close to visit Slot Zuylen, a 15th-century castle now presented as a museum. Rooms decorated in the styles from the 17th–19th centuries depict the building's use over the years, with a special exhibition on the most famous occupant, Dutch authoress, Belle van Zuylen. Between the bridge and the castle, Restaurant Belle also remembers the 'rebel of the Vecht', who was known for her unconventional behaviour. For a longer excursion, head for Kasteel De Haar at Haarzuilens, the largest in the Netherlands, with fairy tale turrets and a wide moat.

UTRECHT

Where to stop

Coming from the north on the Vecht the nearest mooring place to the city centre is at the Nieuwe Kade, just south of the Weerdsluis. Here there are box moorings on the north side of the west spur for boats up to 10m, whilst longer boats can stop on the quay just north of the Zand bridge. Access to further places on the south side beyond the Monica bridge are restricted to 2.6m air draught. A water point, pump-out and rubbish disposal are available at the Weerdsluis, but there is no electricity. A toilet and shower block is located under the Monica bridge which is manned and open during high season only.

For vessels approaching from the south on the Vartse Rijn there are moorings on the Singelgracht, but a fixed bridge restricts access here to 3.3m. A major project to reconnect these two sections of waterway has been agreed. Due to start in 2007 it will take up to 20 years to complete.

Facilities ashore

Chandlers, Repairs & Servicing Jachtwerf De Klop between Oud-Zuilen & Utrecht

Supermarket & Shops Albert Heijn and all shops in the large Hoog Catharijne shopping centre near the station

ATMs Plenty in the city centre

Cycle hire Rijwielshop Tusveld on Van Sijpesteijnkade or from the Stadhuis and the station

VVV office 'RonDom' visitors information centre next to Dom tower on Domplein

What to see

Utrecht (pronounced 'oo-trekt') boasts a long and distinguished history with the first settlers making it their home in AD50. The Oudegracht which bisects the city centre was dug in the tenth century but flood risk meant that the street level had to be raised, giving the city its unique split-level design. The canal side wharves are used for cafés, restaurants and galleries, many connecting under the road to the buildings above. The trip-boats which ply along the waterway give a narrated tour and are a good way to see the city, or you can take your dinghy through the centre and make a round trip via the easterly Buitengracht.

For an aerial view of the city, the Dom tower at 112 metres really is the tallest church tower in the Netherlands, although the nave was destroyed, separating it from the remaining choir section, by a freak tornado in 1674. The fifty-bell Hemony carillon survived the disaster, and plays every fifteen minutes with a flamboyant rendition on the hour. The city is the site of the oldest water tower in the

Smaller boats can cruise through Utrecht's split-level canals

Netherlands, at a mere 40 metres high, which now houses an informative exhibition on water management, a subject in which the Dutch are well-versed.

Utrecht also boasts a host of other attractions which are well worth a visit including its Centraal Museum, the oldest municipal museum in the Netherlands; the Rietveld-Schröder house, a treat of Stijl design for fans of modern architecture; the University Museum with its extensive Botanic Gardens; and the newly opened Dick Bruna house, a tribute to the creator of cartoon rabbit Miffy, who still lives and works in the city.

As well as shops to suit all tastes and budgets, there are large markets on Wednesday and Saturday on the Vredenburg square.

Restaurant tip

The canal wharves that line the Oudegracht are a popular place for outdoor cafés and restaurants, with Tantes Bistro particularly recommended near to the Nieuwe Kade moorings, and further south, Café-restaurant Mevrouw Janssen.

Connections

The train station lies close west of the moorings and is a central hub for services throughout the country.

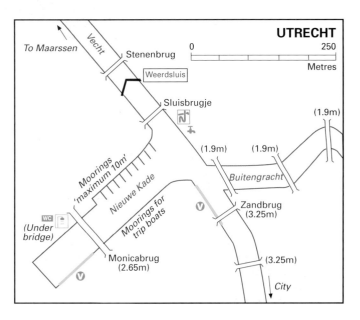

Spiegel & Blijkpolder

Gravel extraction formed these two lakes, now combined as one, to the east of Nederhorst den Berg. The limited opening hours of the lock deters some visitors, but if you are not in a hurry this is a quiet oasis with many free island moorings. If leisure traffic is very heavy during summer months, an extra lock opening is made during the afternoon.

Speed limit 6km/h
Maximum permitted draught 2.5m
Lock Zanderijsluis and lifting bridge opens for restricted periods mid-morning and evening.

The usual basic facilities are provided for boats up to 10m at WV De Spiegel, or free moorings at WV De Poldergeuzen, complete with toilets and showers.

Hilversumskanaal

This waterway runs from the lock at Het Hemeltje, north of the Loosdrechtse Plassen to the centre of Hilversum, and is restricted to vessels less than 12m long and less than 3.75m beam.

Length 8km
Speed limit 7.5km/h
Lock Het Hemeltje and lifting bridge operate throughout the day with breaks for lunch and dinner (1200–1300 and 1800–1900). From 1000 on Sundays.
Bridges 2 fixed (4.5m)

KORTENHOEF

There are canalside moorings at Kortenhoef for a maximum stay of two days or the well-equipped Maarten Fokke jachthaven on the north side of the canal, just west of the bridge. Although there is no water access to the Wijde Blik for vessels over 2.9m air draught, the marina makes a convenient stop from which to explore this quiet lake by bike or dinghy.

HILVERSUM

At the end of the canal, the Hilversumse WV De Sporthaven has space for visitors only when members are away, so it is best to telephone ahead before making the one hour detour from the Vecht. Larger boats normally use the hammerheads, and unmetered water and electricity are available here and at the box moorings. There is a friendly welcome for English visitors who are welcome to use the members clubhouse which is served by a selection of food delivery services, since the closure of the onsite restaurant. Two loan bikes are also available, and much needed as the nearest shops are 10 minutes away and the town centre a 30-minute walk.

Hilversum's modernistic city hall was the work of city architect Willem Dudok

Hilversum is known as the media centre of the Netherlands and those for whom 'Hilversum Radio' is a familiar call sign will be interested in the new broadcasting museum, opened in 2006 on the Media Park. The city is also famous for its modern architecture, much of which was the work of city architect, Willem Dudok. His signature piece is the 1931 city hall, where you will find an exhibition of his life and work. Tours of the building, including the 46m tower, are given on Sunday afternoon.

The well-planned city centre is home to the newly extended Museum Hilversum, as well as a good selection of shops and weekly markets on Wednesday and Saturday.

Loosdrechtse Plassen

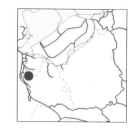

Access to this large expanse of lake is via the Mijndense lock south of Loenen. The Weersluis at the west end of the Weersloot has a sill depth of only 0.8m and an air draught of 1.8m. The Kraaienestersluis has an air draught of 2.3m and the Tienhovenskanaal to which it leads is lower still. A detailed chart of the lake is available in the *ANWB* series, and is highly recommended as there are many shallow patches which are not clearly marked on the overall *Vechtplassen Waterkaart I*.

Maximum permitted draught 1.2m
Speed limit Within 100m of shore and in channels, 6km/h; otherwise 12km/h
Lock Mijndense sluis and lifting bridge operate throughout the day with a rush hour break (1630–1730). Maximum draught in the lock is 1.9m and vessels are requested to switch off their engines whilst in the lock. Toll payable.

OUD-LOOSDRECHT
There are a host of yacht harbours all around the lake as well as many free island moorings which are ideal for getting away from it all. Most amenities are concentrated in Oud-Loosdrecht where you will find a good selection of eating places as well as watersport shops and sloops for sale.

In Nieuwe Loosdrecht, to the east of the lakes, you can visit castle-museum Sypestyn, rebuilt in the 1920s based on earlier illustrations.

Merwedekanaal benoorden de Lek

This waterway forms the continuation of the Merwedekanaal south of the Lek (bezuiden de Lek) which is dealt with in Chapter 2: Great Rivers. The northern part runs north from the Lek, joining the Hollandse IJssel to the west of the Amsterdam-Rijnkanaal. It then crosses the Amsterdam-Rijnkanaal, skirting the west side of Utrecht before rejoining the Amsterdam-Rijnkanaal further north. Near Utrecht it joins the Vaartse Rijn, which continues north through Utrecht to join the Vecht. This route through the city is restricted in air draught to 3.2m.

Fuel is available from a bunker boat at the northern end of the canal, at the junction with the Amsterdam-Rijnkanaal.

Speed limit 4.5km/h
Maximum permitted draught 2.8m

North of Vaartse Rijn
This section is not recommended for through traffic as the bridges and locks must be requested by telephone 24 hours in advance.

Vaartse Rijn to the Amsterdam-Rijnkanaal
Lock Noordersluis operates throughout the day
Bridges 1 fixed (6.4m), 1 opening. Liesbos bridge operates throughout the day with a lunch break on Sundays only (1200–1300).

South of Amsterdam-Rijnkanaal
Lock Zuidersluis, and Koninginnesluis and lifting bridge operate throughout the day (from 1000 on Sundays). The bridge to the south of the Koninginnesluis has a minimum air draught of 6.5m and is only operated for vessels which cannot pass under.
Bridges 1 fixed (6.7m), 3 opening. Blauwe, Nieuwe Rijnhuizer and Wierse bridges operate throughout the day with a break for morning and evening rush hour on weekdays (0745–0845 and 1645–1745). From 1000 on Sundays. Plattenburgse bridge (6.7m when closed) opens only for commercial vessels on request in advance, so is treated as a fixed bridge.

The eastern arm is no longer in use but the disused lock can be used for sluicing, creating strong currents.

VREESWIJK (NIEUWEGEIN)
JH WSV Plettenburg does not take visitors, which is just as well as it lies in the middle of an industrial estate and appears most unattractive. The adjacent Passantenhaven Vreeswijk is similarly uninspiring and, in 2006, was in the middle of an extensive building project of new riverside homes. Preferable moorings for a stop at Vreeswijk are at JH ZV De Lek, which lies on the Lek and is described in Chapter 2: Great Rivers.

Lekkanaal

This short stretch connects the Amsterdam-Rijnknaal at Jutphaas (south of Utrecht) to the Lek at Vianen and is very busy with commercial traffic, except on Sundays. Leisure traffic should only use this route if they have a reliable engine — otherwise the Merwedekanaal provides a quieter alternative. A board at the junction with the Amsterdam-Rijnkanaal gives the depth of water on the Lek.

Length 6km
Speed limit 9km/h
Maximum permitted draught 3.5m
Locks Prinses Beatrixsluis with lifting doors (air draught 9.3m) operates 24 hours. VHF 20
Bridges 1 fixed (9.1m) Overeindsebrug close to junction with Amsterdam-Rijnkanaal.

Rijn

The Rhine crosses the German/Dutch border near the town of Tolkamer where it changes its name to the Boven Rijn. Soon after crossing the border it splits into two, the northern arm being called the Pannerdens Kanal as far as km 873. Here it changes its name to Neder Rijn and then continues east as far as the Amsterdam-Rijnkanaal. From there it continues as the Lek, described in Chapter 2: Great Rivers. The southern arm is called the Waal, which is also described in Chapter 2: Great Rivers. This section deals with the Rijn navigation made up of the Boven Rijn and Neder Rijn. A description of the connecting Pannerdenskanaal follows below.

The Rijn is subject to special navigation rules, but for the leisure boater these still amount to keeping out of the way of all commercial traffic, and keeping to the starboard side of the channel except when instructed otherwise. It is also important to keep a sharp look out for the many ferries which cross the waterway, especially cable ferries which can only be passed when the cable is slack.

For eastbound traffic the Lek and Neder Rijn form a more pleasant route than the Waal, as there is less adverse current, less commercial traffic and more attractive scenery.

Two sluice complexes are found on the Neder Rijn section, at Amerongen and at Driel. These are closed in times of low water levels and passage is then by the adjacent locks. Both sluices have a minimum air draught in the raised (open) state of 12.1m, and unrestricted air draught through the locks, which operate 24 hours through the week and throughout the day at weekends. Lights and signs indicate which passage to take.

Speed limit 20km/h where applicable
Depth 3m
Length Boven Rijn, 10km; Pannerdenskanaal, 6km; Neder Rijn 54km
Locks Sluis Amerongen and Sluis Driel operate 24 hours from Monday–Saturday and throughout the day on Sundays VHF 20
Bridges 6 fixed (min 12.5m) all on Neder Rijn section

WIJK BIJ DUURSTEDE

Where to stop

One kilometre east of the junction with the Amsterdam-Rijnkanaal lies the entrance to the old municipal harbour at Wijk bij Duurstede. This is now used mainly by the boatyard which has one or two unserviced moorings. The best place for visitors is at the large yacht club in the defunct arm of the Rijn just to the east. WSV Rijn en Lek has a reporting pontoon in front of the large club barge and the harbourmaster is normally on hand to allocate you a berth. Coin-operated electricity (€0.50/4kWH, 6A) and unmetered water are available and the modern facilities are downstairs on the barge next to the club bar.

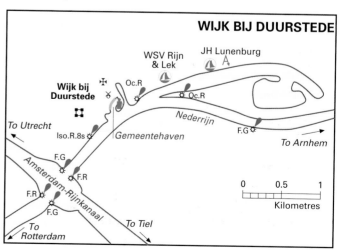

Take a walk in the grounds of Duurstede's 15th-century castle

Facilities ashore

Chandlers At JH Lunenburg
Repairs & Servicing Jachtwerf at Gemeentehaven or ask harbourmaster for contacts
Supermarket & Shops Albert Heijn on Steenstraat and others in the centre
ATMs Nearest on Steenstraat
Cycle hire 2 free loan bikes at WV Rijn en Lek or from Fietsdomain on Kloosterleuterstraat
VVV office On the Markt

What to see

Wijk bij Duurstede (pronounced 'vike-by-der-staider') was an important trading city of international importance from the 6th - 9th century because of its position at the confluence of the Lek and the Rijn. Abandoned after its destruction by the Vikings, the town enjoyed a resurgence in the 15th century when the Bishop of Utrecht chose it as his residence. Museum Dorestad on Muntstraat traces the history of the town and the excavations of the original settlement and includes a model of the original harbour. On the west side of town, the remains of the moated Kasteel Duurstede has an impressive 15th-century round tower and the extensive parks are a listed monument. The 17th-century windmill the 'Rijn en Lek' was built over one of the original town gates and, if you walk along the

adjoining city wall, you can enjoy a view over the river and the town. For longer excursions, the bus takes you to the centre of Utrecht in 30 minutes which is a worthwhile visit if you are not going there by boat.

The town centre has all the necessary shopping amenities and a small market is held on Wednesday morning. Jazz by Duurstede is a music festival held every first Saturday in June; and on every first Sunday of the month the galleries and artists around the town hold an open house.

Restaurant tip

The pretty market square is full of restaurants, but special mention goes to Café-Restaurant De Engel and Restaurant Pippijn.

MAURIK

Just east of Wijk bij Duurstede, a defunct river arm has been expanded by gravel extraction and now houses Watersports Centre De Loswal (which has wi-fi) and the larger JH Eiland van Maurik which has good facilities including fuel, chandlers and cycle hire.

RHENEN

On the west side of town the visitors' harbour consists of a few pontoons directly on the river which have a water tap and rubbish disposal facility. All usual amenities can be found close by in the large town. The Cunerakerk clock tower was originally finished in 1531 but has suffered several accidents since then. The most recent was in April 1945 when allied bombers targetted the church, believing it to be in use by the Germans as an observation tower. The restoration lasted until 1974 but one brick was left missing to discourage further misfortune. Rhenen (pronounced 'rain-en') is best known for its large zoo that has over 1,600 animals including an aviary of exotic birds, a primate house, a dolphinarium and

The annual fair takes place by the moorings during the first week of July

aquarium. On the wild side are brown bears, wolves and tigers which can be observed from the safety of a pedestrian walkway. A Dutch military cemetery is one kilometre east of the town at Grebbeberg with the National War Monument which commemorates the battle that took place here in 1940.

A station is on the east side of town for services to Utrecht.

WAGENINGEN

The comfortable harbour of WSV VADA (depth 2.5m) lies at the southern end of the harbour canal. The reporting pontoon is in front of the harbour office to port after entering and there is normally plenty of space. Coin-operated electricity (€0.50/2kWh, 16A) and fuel is available, as are good facilities in the modern clubhouse. The centre of the town is around 2km away and you will need your own bike as there are none available. Local shops are a 15-minutes walk away.

Wageningen (pronounced 'varkhen-inger') is internationally renowned as the site of the German capitulation which was signed at the Hotel De Wereld, on 5 May 1945. You can still visit the hotel, which holds a photographic exhibition to coincide with the Liberation Day celebrations. Although the town dates back to the 13th century it is known today as the location of an Agricultural University and the related activities make it one of the largest centres of agrarian research in Europe. Two university botanical gardens are open to visitors on Generaal Foulkesweg.

The old town centre has a good selection of shops, cafés and restaurants and a weekly market is held on Wednesday mornings.

ARNHEM

Where to stop

East of the John Frost bridge two marinas are located near the entrance to the Haven van Malburgen. First to port is R&ZV Jason (pronounced 'yarson') which has space for boats up to 15m. There is no reporting pontoon, so it is best to phone on arrival or in advance to arrange a berth. Coin-operated electricity and free water are available with other basic facilities in the riverside clubhouse. Beyond here is the smaller commercial marina of JH Valkenburg where a small restaurant is available.

Facilities ashore

Fuel & Chandlers Bunkerstation Fiwado downstream of John Frost bridge
Repairs & Servicing Jachtwerf van Workum or ask harbourmaster for contacts
Supermarket, Shops & ATMs Lidl and other shops 700m east of the harbour
Cycle hire Rijwielshop, Stationsplein
VVV office Next to the Musis Sacrum building on Velperbinnensingel

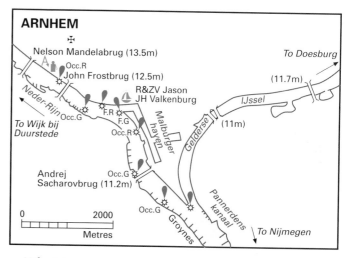

What to see

As capital of Gelderland province and a prosperous trading town, Arnhem has long been considered a coveted prize and has seen many territorial battles over the years. During its history it has been occupied by the Spanish, the French and the Austrians, as well as most recently by the Germans, prompting the infamous 1944 battle. A pillar of the old Law Courts, destroyed in the fighting, now stands as a monument in Airborne Plein and offers a 'bridge to the future'. The history of the town's wartime experiences is thoughtfully displayed at the town's Oorlogs (War) Museum 1940–45, located in a former school which was used as a German command post, to the north of the town on Kemperbergerweg. For a detailed exhibition on Operation Market Garden and the Battle of Arnhem head to Oosterbeek where General Urqhart's former headquarters at Hotel Hartenstein house the Airborne Museum.

Another victim of those years was the 93-metre high Eusebius church tower which has been carefully reconstructed and again stands watch over the market square. Its modern manifestation includes a glass lift which take visitors effortlessly to the lookout platform. The views of the notorious bridge and the other vistas are explained with the aid of plans.

The Eusebius church remembers the Airborne landings of 1944

On the outskirts of town are two attractions that are well worth an excursion. The Open Air Museum is a collection of authentic buildings assembled to illustrate rural life in bygone days with the very high-tech HollandRama, a simulator capsule, getting your visit off to a stimulating start. Next door the Burger's (People's) Zoo is laid out in a series of themed eco-zones which allow the animals to live in something close to their natural environment.

Connections

The train station is on the far side of town, but there is a convenient bus service from the yacht harbour (timetable and map in the clubhouse).

Pannerdenskanaal

The Pannerdenskanaal splits from the Boven Rijn at Pannerdense Kop (km867) and flows northwest towards Arnhem. Just south of the city the Gelderse IJssel branches off to the north and the main navigation continues west as the Neder Rijn (listed under Rijn in the *ANWB Almanak*). There is a small downstream (north-going) current and no locks or bridges. The small yacht club of WV Loowaard is located in a gravel pit at Gat van Moorlag but has limited space and facilities.

Gelderse IJssel

The Gelderse IJssel runs north from the its junction with the Neder Rijn, south of Arnhem, to its mouth in the Ketelmeer. There is normally an appreciable (2–3 kn) downstream (north-going) current and many of the frequent barges will display the blue board to indicate their wish to pass starboard-to-starboard. This is another important area for gravel and sand extraction and there are a growing number of lakes in various stages of the process; some where work has been completed and the area given over to recreation, and others where extraction continues making it less pleasant to visit.

When turning into the IJssel from upstream on the Rijn it is important to leave a wide berth around the tight corner, as the oncoming current flows strongly towards the rocky mole.

Length 118km
Depth At average river levels, 3m in the main channel
Bridges 12 fixed (minimum 9m at average river levels), 4 opening (minimum 5.3 when closed, maximum 10.4m when open). Zutphen rail bridge (maximum 5.75m when closed) opens at H+10 and H+ 41 (VHF 20); Zwolle rail bridge (5.3m when closed) opens at H+26 throughout the day (VHF 18); Kampen Stads bridge operates 24 hours Monday to Friday and throughout the day at weekends (VHF 18); and Eiland bridge (15m when closed) operates throughout the day (VHF 84)

RHEDEN AND DE STEEG

Limited spaces are available for boats up to 12m at WV De Engel, which lies in a pleasantly sheltered defunct arm of the river. A fixed bridge crosses the entrance which has an air draught of about 9m at normal river levels. Free boxes are indicated by a green board and visitors should find a space and report to the harbour office towards the southern end of the moorings. The usual basic facilities are available.

The moorings lie on the edge of the Veluwe National Park, 4,600 hectares of pine and birch forest which is popular for walking and cycling. The visitors' centre occupies an old farmhouse on Heuvenseweg in Rheden, whilst to the north in the village of De Steeg, Kasteel Middachten, preserved with its original furnishings and double moat is open to visitors.

GIESBEEK AND THE RHEDERLAAG

The Rhederlaag is a large lake area created by gravel extraction opposite Rheden, which is now popular for recreation and water sports. There are several yacht harbours and places where you can more bow-to the sandy shores, but WV Giesbeek is a good choice for a well-equipped harbour near to a small village. A board by the reporting pontoon directs visitors to an appropriate pontoon and there are good facilities including fuel, launderette and on-site restaurant. A nice play area and the many beaches make this is a popular stop for boats with children on board.

The nearby village of Giesbeek has a small selection of shops and amenities, and a weekly market is held on Tuesday mornings. Moorings to the west of the lake are the nearest to the Veluwe and the famous 100-metre high Posbank (a hill – a rarity in the Netherlands) from where a good view of the valley can be enjoyed.

DOESBURG

Where to stop

A spacious visitors' harbour is situated close to the town in the Industriehaven, and unmetered electricity and coin-operated water (€0.50/150ltr) are available. The helpful harbourmaster, who was voted Harbourmaster of the Year in 2003 by a Dutch motor boat association, is on duty for published periods during the day. The electricity points are mainly near to the harbour office, but amongst his services the harbourmaster can provide a long extension cable if necessary. Good basic facilities are due to be expanded in 2008 to coincide with an increase in the number of moorings when the industrial activity ceases. There is already space for boats up to 18m, but it is advisable to reserve these in advance.

WV De Oude IJssel has limited space for visitors in their small harbour beyond the Oude IJssel lock and north of the town in the Zwarte Schaar, a defunct arm of the river, there are three campsite/yacht harbours with all facilities.

Facilities ashore

Repairs & Servicing Jachtwerf Doesburg is nearby
Supermarket & Shops Albert Heijn and Coop on Ooipoortstraat
ATMs On Kerkstraat and elsewhere around town
Cycle hire Sonneveld Rijwielen on Gasthuisstraat
VVV office On Kerkstraat

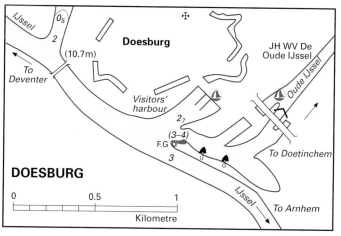

Visit the old mustard factory and shop on Boekholtstraat

What to see

Doesburg (pronounced 'doos-burekh') was one of seven Hanseatic towns along the river IJssel, one of the protected trade routes between European cities. The height of its prosperity was in the 15th century and the church, the town hall and the weigh house all date from this period. A town walk is available (in English) from the VVV to point out the highlights or you can join the guided walk on Tuesdays and Thursdays at 1500. The church tower was blown up by the retreating Germans a couple of weeks before their surrender to prevent its use by the Allies, but its contemporary replacement can be climbed under the leadership of a volunteer guide on Wednesdays and Fridays at 1500. Gerardus Mercator (1512–1594), of projection fame, is buried in the church.

Doesburg is best known for its mustard and you can visit the old factory, founded in 1457 where they still use the original methods and equipment. A mustard shop, café and avenue of traditional shops complete the visit. Also of interest are De Roode Toren regional museum which includes reconstructions of an old grocer's shop and a tobacco workshop; and the Fotografica museum, which traces the history of photography from 1900.

The small town centre has ample shopping facilities and you must stop at Peters the bakers for some Doesburgse Moppen, the traditional local biscuits. Weekly markets are held on Wednesday and Saturday mornings, and a four-day festival is held mid-July which includes music, theatre and dance.

Restaurant tip

Café-restaurant De Waag claims to be the oldest restaurant in the Netherlands, having been the town's inn since 1478. Inside you can see the original weigh-house scales as well as enjoying one of their traditional Hanseatic dishes. For an indulgent lunch or afternoon tea try Croissanterie La Fleur which has a garden terrace accessed via a reconstruction of an old sweet shop.

The Vispoorthaven is overlooked by the imposing St Walburgis church

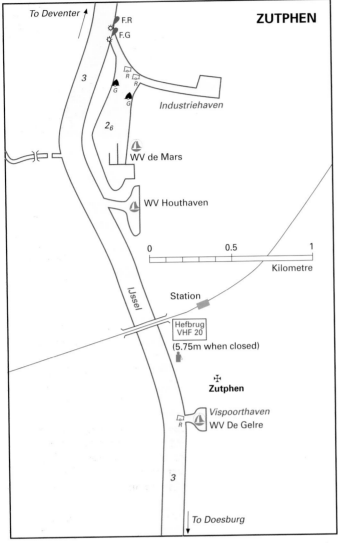

To Deventer

F.R
F.G

Industriehaven

WV de Mars

WV Houthaven

0   0.5   1

Kilometre

IJssel

Station

Hefbrug
VHF 20

(5.75m when closed)

Zutphen

Vispoorthaven
WV De Gelre

To Doesburg

ZUTPHEN

ZUTPHEN

Where to stop

The best place to stop for a visit to Zutphen are the central moorings of WV De Gelre in the Vispoorthaven. The harbour is quite small and skippers should beware of a strong eddy on entering which pushes you towards the starboard side. Inside (on the starboard side) is the reporting pontoon and just round the corner is the water pontoon.

North of the town WV De Mars is a larger harbour in the Marshaven, which offers a quieter lakeside outlook, but they are not so accustomed to receiving visitors. A harbourmaster will greet you from the reporting pontoon and allocate you a berth, but a gate deposit of €20 is required if you want to leave the site. Coin-operated water and electricity (10A) and an on-site bar-café are available.

Facilities ashore

Fuel & Chandlers Slurink-Zwaans Bunkerstation on Ijsselkade

Repairs & Servicing Jachtwerf de Marshaven is next door to WV De Mars or ask harbourmaster for contacts

Supermarket & Shops 15-mins walk to C1000 on Stationsplein or Albert Heijn on Polsbroek

ATMs In the centre

Cycle hire Rijwielshop Kranendijk on Stationsplein

VVV office On Stationsplein

What to see

Another former Hanseatic town, Zutphen (pronounced 'zut-fer') is capital of the Achterhoek region, and its name comes from Zuid Veen, or southern fen. It was an easily defendable site in the surrounding marshland and it became a prosperous trading town between the 14th and 16th centuries.

A rare treat in Zutphen is a visit to the St Walburgis church library which was constructed in an elaborate vaulted style in 1564. The extensive collection includes many unusual works and illuminated texts handwritten by monks. A selection are displayed on wooden stands and it is one of the few remaining in Europe in its original state.

For an introduction to the history of the town and its attractive medieval buildings take one of the guided tours from the VVV office or a whisper boat trip on the small river Berkel, once used as a trading route to Germany.

Restaurant tip

Bij D'n Open Haard on the Houtmarkt has a whole menu of medieval dishes to take you back to the golden age of the Hanseatic league. For ambience choose the Wijnhuistoren, where you can dine Italian-style either in the trattoria Coretto, or in the more upmarket Ristorante Prima Piano.

Connections

Trains from the central station run to Apeldoorn, Arnhem and Deventer.

Whisper boat tours depart from the 14th-century Berkel gate

DEVENTER

Where to stop

There are free unserviced riverside moorings close to the town which are convenient for a daytime visit but not suitable for overnight stops. A strong current runs past the moorings so it is advisable to approach from downstream and beware of commercial barges who share the quay.

A more peaceful berth can be had just north of the city at JH ZMV Deventer where there is normally plenty of space for visitors in summer. Boats over 15m are advised to phone ahead as spaces for these sizes are limited. Coin-operated electricity (4A) is available at all berths, but water (€0.50/100 ltrs) is only from a pontoon near the entrance. Good basic facilities are available and a popular on-site bar-restaurant is run by the harbourmaster from May to September. Further limited moorings are available at the southern end of the same lake at RV & ZV Daventria which boast 16A electricity.

Facilities ashore

Fuel None nearby but the harbourmaster will lend you his trolley and jerry cans if you want to wheel them to the nearby garage.
Repairs & Servicing Diesel Service Deventer and Wolf Rozenburg can help with engine problems
Supermarket, Shops & ATMs 10-min walk to local shops and amenities or 10-min cycle to the centre
Cycle hire 5 bikes available from the harbour
VVV office On Keizerstraat

What to see

Another of the seven Hanseatic towns along the IJssel, Deventer (pronounced 'day-fenter') was the site of an 8th-century wooden church built by an

The extravagant finale to the Deventer Op Stelten festival

Irish missionary, and the Lebuinis church, rebuilt in the 15th-century was named after him. The 62-metre church tower can be climbed every afternoon except Sunday. The town is most famous for its gingerbread cake, which is available in the traditional style cake shop, Bussinks Koekwinkel, on the main square, De Brink.

In the 16th and 17th centuries printing was an important part of the town's industry and several printers and publishers are still based here today. Every first Sunday in August an international book market, billed the 'largest in Europe' is held in the town.

Guided tours of the historic town centre are available by foot, cycle or horse-drawn tram and take in the local history museum in the 16th-century Waag (weigh-house) as well as the Speelgoed en Blikmuseum, the largest collection of toys in the country. A programme of summer concerts and events take place throughout the summer, with a highlight being the international stilt festival, Deventer Op Stelten, which takes place over the first weekend in July.

Restaurant tip

De Brink square is packed with pavement cafés and restaurants; if you want wi-fi opt for Hans en Grietje, which has a T-mobile hotspot. The neighbouring Greek restaurant offers good service and a late-opening kitchen. On Roggestraat, Chez Antoinette is a well-regarded Portuguese-style bodega in a restored property from the 14th-century.

Connections

The train station is close northeast of the centre of the town and, as well as connections to Arnhem, Utrecht and Leeuwarden, this would be a good place from which to make an excursion to Apeldoorn to visit Het Loo, the former palace of William of Oranje which was used by the present royal family until 1975.

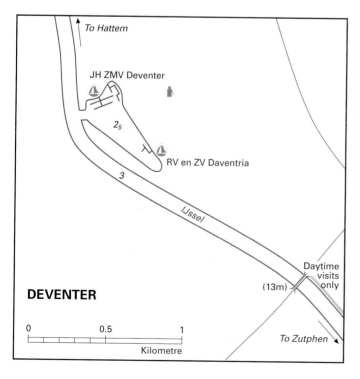

DEVENTER

To Hattem

JH ZMV Deventer

2₅

RV en ZV Daventria

3

IJssel

Daytime visits only
(13m)

To Zutphen

0   0.5   1
Kilometre

TERWOLDE

JH Terwolde is part of the Schepenhof campsite and recreation complex. Although places are advertised for boats up to 15m it is mainly used by much smaller boats. Good facilities are available on site including cycle hire and supermarket.

VEESSEN

JH IJsselzicht at Veessen is another village camping location with good on-site facilities for a quiet stop. A beach café and play area make it suitable for families.

WIJHE

Halfway between Deventer and Zwolle, Wijhe is a traditional resting point and the visitors' harbour has space for boats up to 12m with limited basic facilities (no electricity). In the nearby village you can visit Veerman's Hof, a large garden specialising in wild flowers particular to the local area. If you are cycling look out for Het Tuinpad, a network of farm shops from whom you can buy regional speciality products. For children, the covered play centre Ballorig is nearby.

HATTEM

Where to stop

JH Hattem lies on the Apeldoorns Kanaal, just 300m from its junction with the IJssel. There is a reporting pontoon just inside the entrance and one of the two harbour staff is normally on hand to allocate a berth and take your lines. The harbour do not take reservations but can normally find space for overnight visitors, and are planning an expansion

Bread baked at the bakery museum uses flour from the town's corn mill

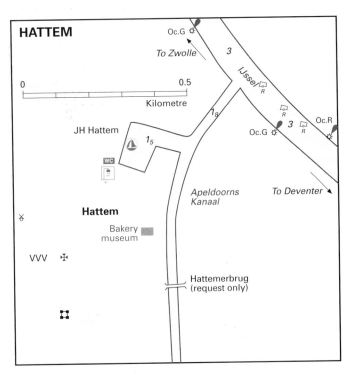

which will triple the number of berths. Coin-operated electricity and water, and good basic facilities are available.

Facilities ashore

Supermarket & Shops Boni on Kleine Gracht
ATMs In the nearby town centre
Cycle hire Veltkamp on Kruisstraat
VVV office In the Primera bookshop on Kerkstraat

What to see

Hattem (pronounced 'hart-em') was a less influential member of the Hanseatic league than some of the other towns along the IJssel, but still claims an allegiance during its latter years in the 16th and 17th centuries. The town certainly prospered at this time, as is evident by the Dijkpoort gate, the St Andreas church and the tower mill, De Fortuin. The windmill still grinds corn on Saturday afternoons and, as well as buying flour on site, you can also visit the National Bakery Museum on the opposite side of town, where they use it for bread-baking demonstrations. The best way to learn about the history of the town is to pick up the English language walking tour from the VVV office, or opt for one of their guided walks on Tuesday afternoons in July and August.

The Voerman Museum, and next door the Anton Pieck Museum, are dedicated to well-known artists who lived and worked in the town. The Voerman museum also holds the remains of the town's medieval castle, whose outline is picked out on Tinneplein. On Kerkstraat, De Franse Hof is a public herb garden, where anyone is invited to pick samples, provided they do so neatly. Amongst the good shopping facilities in the town, Bonbon Atelier, near the Dijkpoort, is certainly worth a visit, where you will find a chocolate emporium to satisfy all cravings. A market is held on Wednesday afternoons.

The town lies at the northern extremity of the Veluwe National Park where cycle and walking excursions are popular. Also nearby is the Molecaten, a country estate that has large parks open to the public. If you want to see more of the water you might like to try klompvaren (clog sailing), or one of the other novelty boats for hire from Vadesto.

Restaurant tip

Across town on Adelaarshoek, 't Spookhuys is located in the only remaining part of the old castle. For a gastronomic treat with a twist, book a place on the 8km Culinary Walk on selected Sunday afternoons, which takes in the old town centre and the Molecaten park as well as four of the best restaurants in town.

ZWOLLE

Two kilometres north of Hattem you will see the entrance to one of Zwolle's two visitors' harbours, but the best moorings for a visit to the city are accessed via the Zwolle-IJsselkanaal and details are given in that section below.

WILSUM

The visitors' harbour at Wilsum offers free moorings for a maximum of two days stay (but recent signs show there is less than 1m depth). Shops and restaurants are available in the nearby village and the harbour itself is situated in a quiet and attractive location.

IJSSELMUIDEN

A district of Kampen rather than a town in its own right, IJsselmuiden's visitors' harbour lies immediately south of the Kampen Stadsbrug. Facilities are limited to coin-operated electricity and rubbish disposal, but the low-cost moorings are still close to the town centre just across the bridge.

KAMPEN

Where to stop

The most central moorings are those of WV Buitenhaven, which lies downstream (north) of the Stadsbrug and are convenient for visitors approaching from the Randmeren, as well as those cruising down the IJssel. There are places in both the Oude Buitenhaven and the adjacent Nieuwe Buitenhaven, and both are managed by the full time harbourmaster based in the new clubhouse and office building between the two. Visitors with special requirements can phone ahead to reserve a space, but you are normally greeted on arrival and directed to a berth. Coin-operated electricity and water are available, and there is a fuel and pump-out berth near the entrance to the new harbour (downstream entrance). The all new facilities are of an exceptional standard and upstairs there is a small bar for drinks and light snacks.

Further moorings are available upstream at WV De Bovenhaven (depth 2.6m) or on the opposite side of the river, but these are not so convenient for the town.

Facilities ashore

Fuel Nieuwe Buitenhaven and Bunkerstation Verweij (km 997)
Chandlers Aquashop on Oudestraat
Repairs & Servicing Ask harbourmaster for contacts
Supermarket & Shops Albert Heijn on Meeuwenweg
ATMs Opposite Oude Buitenhaven on Bolwerk
Cycle hire From harbour, Tweewielercentrum Kok next door, or from the station
VVV office On Oudestraat

What to see

The most northerly of the former Hanseatic cities along the river IJssel, Kampen is famous for the ship, the *Kamper Kogge*, invented here. More seaworthy than its predecessor, it facilitated international trade and prompted Kampen's economic boom in the 14th century. A replica lies in the Oude Buitenhaven and occasional tours are given. The manufacture of cigars took over as the major industry in the 19th and 20th centuries and the last of the hundred or so businesses to survive now houses the Tobacco Museum on the Botermarkt.

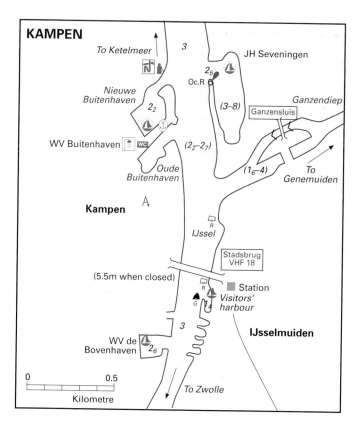

For an introduction to the history and culture of the town, you can follow one of seven themed walking routes or join the guided walks which depart from the VVV office on Saturdays in July and August. Characteristic of the town is the so-called 'New Tower', completed in 1664, which features a cow hanging from the top every summer. The tradition is based on an old story that grazing was available there; this and other unlikely tales are called the 'Kamper Uien' – available in booklet form from the VVV. For a closer inspection and an aerial view of the town you can climb the tower on Wednesday, Friday or Saturday afternoons.

Good shopping facilities in the town include a large fish shop near the harbour on Hagenkade and weekly markets on Monday and Saturday mornings.

Restaurant tip

De Bastaard is known for its good value and generous portions whilst De Vier Jaargetijden (Four Seasons) emulates its namesake and provides fine dining for special occasions.

Connections

The station is across the river on the IJsselmuiden side and has services to Zwolle only.

Look out for the cow grazing at the top of the new tower

Oude IJssel

The Oude (old) IJssel runs from the junction with the Gelderse IJssel at Doesburg to the weir in Ulft, near the German border. For the purposes of this guide it is navigable only as far as Doetinchem, above which a fixed bridge at Sluis De Pol restricts headroom to 3m. It is an attractive, quiet waterway and the trip from Doesburg takes between one and two hours.

Length 25km (12km to Doetinchem)
Maximum permitted draught 2.5m, air draught 6m
Speed limit 9km/h
Locks Doesburg and lifting bridge (4.2m drop) operate throughout the day with a lunch break (1200–1245). VHF 20.
Bridges 1 fixed (8.1m), 4 opening. Hoog Keppel, Laag Keppel (VHF 20) and the bridges in Doetinchem (VHF 18) operate the same hours as the lock.

DOETINCHEM

Where to stop

WV De Ank in Doetinchem lies 50 metres before the Europa bridge on the starboard side and offers a quiet berth close to the town. There are visitors' reception pontoons on the river just by the entrance, or just inside to port where unmetered water and electricity are available. Good basic facilities include a 20-ton boat lift and small club bar.

Alternatively, continue through a further two bridges and you will find a free, unserviced visitors' pontoon on the starboard side, also close to the town.

What to see

Although Doetinchem (pronounced 'doo-ti-kem') dates back to the 13th century it was badly damaged by bombing in 1945 and today is a modern industrial and commercial town. It is a popular shopping centre at the centre of the Achterhoek region and the pedestrianised centre is nicely laid out. A large market takes place on Tuesday mornings and on Saturdays, and the town boasts three windmills, which are open to visitors on selected days. Look out for the sails turning which signifies the miller is present.

The town's museum, which includes a model as it looked in 1940, and the Staring Institute, recount the town's history, and guided walks are available on Saturdays. The town's annual festival, the Stadsfeest, takes place over the first weekend in September.

Restaurant tip

There are lots of good eating places around Simonsplein, and the town seems to have a particular South American connection, with Gringo's Mexican, and Gonzales barbecue restaurants gaining strong recommendations.

Twentekanalen

The small waterways which cross the Twente region are known collectively as the Twentekanalen. The primary navigations are the Kanaal Zutphen-Enschede and the Zijkanaal naar Almelo. This second waterway continues north as the Kanaal Almelo-De Haandrik, which is described separately in the *ANWB Almanak*, and below. The Kanaal Zutphen-Enschede connects with the Gelderse IJssel just north of Zutphen and runs east to Enschede. The waterway is a combination of industry and countryside as far as Hengelo, becoming increasingly industrial as you approach Enschede.

The most useful section is that as far as the junction with the Zijkanaal naar Almelo which branches to the north, just west of Hengelo and Delden lock. The onward passage to Hengelo and Enschede is not a through route, and boats must return the same way. Mooring facilities on this final stretch are limited to out-of-town yacht clubs and the towns themselves are mainly industrial, with less touristic appeal than other possible destinations.

Unserviced municipal moorings are available in Lochem, Goor, and Delden but nearby amenities and attractions are limited. Those at Lochem are in the process of being redeveloped and may offer a more desirable visitors' harbour in the future.

Length IJssel-Zijkanaal naar Almelo, 34km; Zijkanaal naar Almelo, 16km
Speed limit 12km/h
Maximum permitted draught 2.5m, air draught 6m
Locks Sluis Eefde operates 24 hours Monday–Saturday and throughout the day on Sundays. Sluis Delden operates throughout the day. Sluis Hengelo operates throughout the day during the week, for limited periods on Saturday, and is closed on Sunday.
Bridges On Kanaal Zutphen-Enschede: 25 fixed (minimum 6.5m); On Zijkanaal naar Almelo: 11 fixed (minimum 6.5m).

ALMEN

De Nieuwe Aanleg visitors' harbour and café-restaurant is a nice stop a short way from the junction of the Twentekanalen with the IJssel. The small harbour has space for boats up to 15m (depth 2.5m) and 6A electricity is included in the modest fixed fee. Skippers are advised to secure their boats well with long lines in view of surges created by passing barges. Good basic facilities are available including an on-site restaurant with skittles and bowling alleys. The harbour is also a good starting point for several cycle and walking routes through the surrounding wooded countryside and, as well as hiring bikes, the helpful harbour/restaurant proprietors keep illustrated maps of the various themed routes.

South of the canal in the village of Almen you can visit the Museum Oude Boekdrukkunst where you can see an old printing press used for clandestine newspapers during the war, as well as printing your own postcard. Boat trips in a traditional wooden boat, called a Berkelzomp, on the old Berkel river are offered during the summer and depart from the swimming pool centre. For supplies, a market comes to the village on Tuesday mornings with one each of fish, meat, cheese and vegetable stalls.

Hotel De Hoofdige Boer has a popular garden where you can sample traditional specialities of the Achterhoek region and, across the street, visit the mustard, spice and sweet shop run, for 35 years, by the Boesveld family, for a variety of old-fashioned delicacies.

Kanaal Almelo-De Haandrik (and Coevorden-Vechtkanaal)

From its junction with the Zijkanaal naar Almelo, the Kanaal Almelo-De Haandrik continues southeast for a further 2km into the centre of the town.

Heading north it forms the continuation of the Zijkanaal naar Almelo to its junction with the Overijsselse Vecht at Gramsbergen. The Overijsselse Vecht is not navigable at this point but it marks the point at which the waterway changes to the Coevorden-Vechtkanaal, and continues north across the border into Drenthe to Coevorden. North of Coevorden the waterway continues as the Stieltjeskanaal, described in Chapter 7: Groningen & Drenthe.

Bridges are divided into five groups of 3-4 bridges and vessels transit in convoys. Skippers should advise the bridge operator if they are not intending to continue to the next bridge. Times of the next convoy are available from Sluis Aadorp ☎ 0546 575541 / 06 2043 8229

Length Almelo-Gramsbergen, 32km; Gramsbergen-Coevorden, 5km
Speed limit 8km/h
Maximum permitted draught 1.9m
Locks Sluis Aadorp, operates throughout the day with a break for lunch (1200–1230) Monday–Saturday in high season. Closed Saturday afternoons in low season, and on Sundays. VHF 22.
Bridges 5 fixed (6.5m), 16 opening, which work in convoys the same hours as the lock

Take tea and visit the bakery museum in the Bolletje winkel

ALMELO

Bridges 2 opening. Dollegoor and Eiland bridges operate throughout the day with a rush hour break Monday-Friday (1600–1730) and for shorter periods at weekends; Saturday 1030–1530 and 1730–1830, Sundays only on request in advance ☎ 06 5337 6887, VHF 20

Where to stop

There are three possible mooring options in Almelo. The most central is the municipal Jachthaven Almelo-Centrum which has plenty of space in the newly-equipped harbour, as well as convenient access to the town centre amenities. Facilities include launderette, pump-out and high-tech biometric security for the gate access. The two lifting bridges listed above are opened by the harbourmaster, who is available by VHF or telephone.

WV De Brug is convenient if you don't want to go out of your way and is just south of the Almelo lock, opposite the start of the Zijkanaal naar Almelo. The third option, Almelosche WV is to the west of the town on the Zijkanaal naar Almelo. There is fuel available here as well as the usual showers and launderette. The nearest shops and restaurants are in the neighbouring village of Wierden, where you can also climb the church tower and visit the local museum, which has an impressive collection of irons.

What to see

As you approach the harbour you will notice the sweet smell of biscuits baking, which emanates from the Bolletje biscuit factory, the products of which often grace traditional Dutch breakfast tables. The company started life on a site in the town centre, which is now given over to a bakery museum and traditional tea shop. The speciality is a 'dolled up' pot of tea, served by the attractive ladies, who will provide the necessary instruction!

The town was an important textile centre and monuments are dotted around the centre to recall this heritage. In the town museum this history is recounted in a restored rectory, but the town walk, which starts at the Bolletje shop, is available only in Dutch. One of the oldest farms in the town still stands near the centre and you can visit this quiet corner for a look at life in the past as well as visiting their contemporary exhibition and coffee garden.

VRIEZENVEEN

There are free unserviced canalside moorings in the 6km long village. Hotel-Café Zandwijk is nearby, whilst the Historisch Museum Oud Vriezenveen, with its unusual Russian collection (from the time when active trading links existed with St Petersburg) is in the centre.

VROOMSHOOP

A well laid out visitors' harbour offers a free stay for up to two days complete with electricity and water (ask harbourmaster for access). A small market visits Vroomshoop and Vriezenveen on alternate Wednesday mornings.

GRAMSBERGEN

The yacht harbour 't Hooge Holt is opposite the bungalow park/campsite of the same name, and the facilities and covered swimming pool are available free to visitors. The on-site facilities include launderette and pump-out, whilst bikes are available to hire from the camp site.

Being close to the German border Gramsbergen was once an active smuggling area, and the guided tour of the town highlights notorious spots with tales of contraband and customs battles. It also lies at the confluence of the Kanaal Almelo-De Haandrik with the Overijsselse Vecht. No longer accessible to large boats, this attractive river is still popular for canoeing and angling and several long distance walking paths pass through the town. A pleasant outing is to the Ada Hofman pond garden, which boasts over 30 themed gardens and 50 water features and ponds. In poorer weather you could try the Historisch Cultureel Infocentrum Vechtdal for a contemporary exhibition about the surrounding area.

The last weekend in August is the Gramsbergen Lichtstad festival, when all the houses are decorated and the streets elaborately illuminated.

Zwolle-IJsselkanaal and Zwolle canals

The Zwolle-IJsselkanaal runs north of the city from the IJssel to join the Zwarte Water on the northwest side of the city. Turn south for Zwolle central moorings or north to continue on the Zwarte Water.

Length 3km
Speed limit 13.2km/h
Maximum permitted draught 3.25m
Lock Spooldersluis with lifting bridge operates throughout the day (from 1000 on Sundays), VHF 22
Bridges 3 fixed (9m)

ZWOLLE

Speed limit Up to 1.25m draught, 9km/h; Up to 1.5m draught, 7.5km/h; Over 1.5m draught, 6km/h
Bridges 1 fixed (8m), 2 opening. Holtenbroek and Hofvliet bridges operate throughout the day with three rush hour breaks Monday–Saturday (0730–0845, 1200–1330 and 1630–1730). Operate Sundays throughout the day. VHF 20. No service for central city bridges

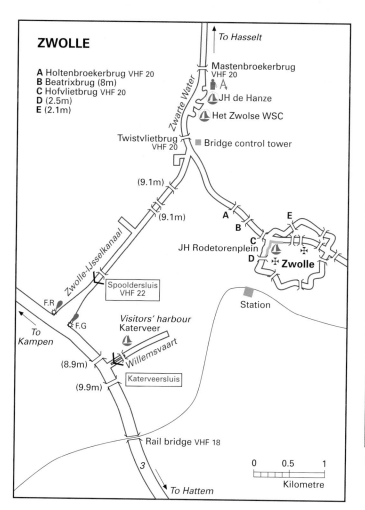

ZWOLLE

A Holtenbroekerbrug VHF 20
B Beatrixbrug (8m)
C Hofvlietbrug VHF 20
D (2.5m)
E (2.1m)

To Hasselt
Mastenbroekerbrug VHF 20
JH de Hanze
Het Zwolse WSC
Twistvlietbrug VHF 20
Bridge control tower
(9.1m)
(9.1m)
Zwarte Water
A B C D E
JH Rodetorenplein
Zwolle
Zwolle-IJsselkanaal
Spooldersluis VHF 22
F.R
To Kampen
F.G
Station
Visitors' harbour Katerveer
Willemsvaart
(8.9m)
Katerveersluis
(9.9m)
Rail bridge VHF 18
3
To Hattem
0 0.5 1
Kilometre

Where to stop

There are three options for visitors' moorings in Zwolle. The municipal visitors' harbour has two locations: one in the old Willemsvaart, accessed via the restored Katerveersluis (operates 0900–1200 and 1400–2000), just north of the IJssel road bridge. These are quiet and peaceful but not convenient for the city. The second, Jachthaven Rodetorenplein, is accessed via the Zwolle-IJsselkanaal and is much more central and convenient for shops and restaurants, although noisier and more public. Adequate basic facilities are provided at both locations.

The large Jachthaven De Hanze is north of the city on the Zwarte Water and has all facilities including fuel and a large chandlers.

Facilities ashore

Fuel & Chandlers JH De Hanze
Repairs & Servicing Jachtwerf Dijkzicht near De Hanze
Supermarket, Shops & ATMs Albert Heijn on Klein Grachtje is near the centre; C1000 on Beethovenlaan is near De Hanze
Cycle hire Rijwielshop at the train station
VVV office Grote Kerkplein

Step back in time at Zwolle's Drostenhuis museum

What to see

Zwolle is the capital of the province of Overijssel, and along with other towns along the IJssel, was an important member of the Hanseatic League. Only a few metres of its city walls remain but the town's canals still form a star-shaped moat and are bordered on the southwest side by the attractive Park Eekhout. A much larger country park, the Engelse (English) Werk is close to the Katerveer yacht harbour. Laid out as typical of English landscape it offers extensive opportunities for walking and cycling.

The municipal museum on the Melkmarkt is an effective combination of old and new with a permanent collection depicting the culture and history of the region and the city in the restored Drostenhuis, and temporary exhibitions in the modern wing next door. Zwolle is also home to Ecodrome Park, on Willemsvaart close to the centre, where the natural environment of the past, present and future is brought vividly to life.

Amongst Zwolle's traditional specialities are Zwolse *balletjes*, cushion-shaped sweets with different flavours; and *blauwvingers*, shortbread biscuits dipped in chocolate.

Restaurant tip

Zwolle is home to one of the best restaurants in the Netherlands, De Librije, on Broerkerkplein which has not one but three Michelin stars and so deep pockets are advisable.

Zwarte Water

The Zwarte Water runs from the central Zwolle canals and winds north through Hasselt and Zwartsluis to the Zwarte Meer. Free lakeside moorings are available at the southern end of the Noorderkolk and in the lakes north of the junction with the Overijsselse Vecht. The upstream section as far as Zwartsluis is described here, and the remainder in Chapter 5: Flevoland and the Randmeren.

Length 18km
Speed limit 20km/h
Maximum permitted draught 3.25m
Bridges 3 opening (fixed spans 5.5m). Twistvliet and Mastenbroek bridges operate throughout the day, VHF 20; the Zwarte Water bridge at Hasselt operates throughout the day Monday–Saturday but only for limited periods on Sundays (0900–1100 and 1700–1900), VHF 22

HASSELT

Where to stop

Jachthaven De Molenwaard is a large modern yacht harbour to the north of the town with coin-operated 10A electricity and unmetered water. Good facilities include launderette, fuel, a small chandlers and yacht servicing. Next door WV Nadorst is a private yacht club where visitors are welcome when space permits. There are also low cost municipal moorings (coin-operated water only) along the river quay and the small canals that run through the town centre, but those on the main river can be affected by wash from passing barges on weekdays. A half-finished visitors' pontoon in the Haven de Beer has been delayed over a planning dispute and may or may not be available in future years.

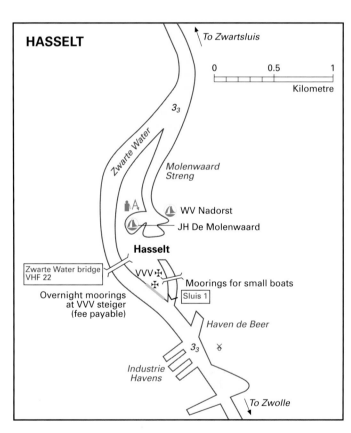

Visit Hasselt's historic limekilns for an insight into the town's industrial heritage

Facilities ashore

Fuel & Chandlers, Repairs & Servicing JH De
   Molenwaard
Supermarket & Shops Golff, Buiten de Venepoort;
   C1000 Van Viandenplein
ATMs On Nieuwstraat
Cycle hire Van Dalfsen, on the quay
VVV office In the Stadhuis, on the Markt

What to see

Hasselt (pronounced 'har-sell') is a small Hanseatic town which played an important role in the textile industry in previous centuries. Its inner centre retains some 70 buildings listed as historic monuments and many are carefully labelled and their history explained (in Dutch). The old Gothic town hall houses a permanent exhibition about life in Hasselt in the Middle Ages, as well as a notable collection of antique firearms. Limekilns to the east of the centre were used from the 16th century to make lime from shells, although those standing there today date only from the 19th century. After production ceased, the kilns were restored and since the 1990s have been open to the public for tours including a video presentation.

The first corn mill was built on the Stenendijk in the 16th century and the current De Zwaluw (the Swallow) was in use until 1955. It is open to visitors when the blue flag is flying, normally on Saturday mornings. Alternatively, you can climb the tower of the St Stephanus church on Tuesday mornings or Thursday afternoons. In the last week of August the town is brought to life by the hay festival, when the town earns its nickname 'Northern city of lights'.

Restaurant tip

Onder de Luifel is a lively spot popular with locals and serves an unchallenging menu on their quayside terrace.

Dine alfresco on the quayside at Onder de Luifel

Overijsselse Vecht

The Overijsselse Vecht leaves the Zwarte Water near Hasselt and runs east as far as Junne and is lined with castles, windmills and woodland. For the purposes of this guide the waterway is effectively only navigable as far as Dalfsen. Beyond this, the lock at Vilsteren is restricted by a fixed bridge with an air draught of 3.4m. (Junne is a further 3km on from Ommen after which navigation is only possible by canoes or rowing boats which have to be carried over the weir.) Although an attractive river, boats must return the same route making it less practical for visitors. The rain-fed river supports a rich variety of fish life and anglers from all over Europe come here to fish.

Length 15km (to Dalfsen)
Speed limit 9km/h
Depth 1.7m above Sluis Vechterweerd. Below this the normal summer level is NAP-0.2m although it can vary significantly.
Locks Sluis Vechterweerd. Operates throughout the day Monday–Saturday with a break for lunch (1200–1300). Last locking is 20 minutes prior to closing time. Sundays have one locking in each direction: downstream 1700, upstream, 1730.
Bridges 3 fixed (min 4.9m), 1 opening. Dalfsen bridge opens at H+30 throughout the day Monday–Saturday with a break for lunch (1200–1300). Sundays 1615 and 1815 only.

BERKUM

JH/Campsite Terra Nautic provides all necessary facilities in a basin off the main river. The distant village of Berkum is a commuter village of Zwolle and not of great historic interest. However, a walk along the river brings you to the hand-operated Haerst ferry, by which you can reach De Agnietenberg, a campsite and recreation area where you can lunch in style in the tea house or the winter garden.

DALFSEN

The municipal visitors' harbour (depth 1.2m) is just before the bridge on the port side where basic facilities are available. Mooring boxes up to 5m beam are available with a single coin-operated electricity point and water berth opposite the entrance. Tucked away behind the town hall, the moorings are private and peaceful. Further quayside moorings without facilities are available both sides of the bridge, except for the space reserved for a trip boat.

Dalfsen's main shopping street, Prinsenstraat, is nearby and includes the VVV information point (which is housed in a travel agency). Outdoor activities are well-provided with Hiawatha-Actief hiring canoes and riverbikes from the harbour, or 'step-scooters' and bikes from its nearby Activity Centre, where you can also enjoy a round of farmer's golf. The Westermolen mill is open to visitors when the blue flag is flying, which is normally on Saturday mornings.

The surrounding area is dotted with country estates and residential castles, many of which have large country parks open to the public. These include Den Aalshorst, which has an English style landscaped garden noted for its water features. For a day-trip you could take the 10-minute train journey to the Hanseatic town of Ommen, where the National Tin Figure Museum on the Markt includes a 10,000 figure re-enactment of the Battle of Waterloo.

Kampereiland

Under this heading are the waterways between Kampen and the Zwarte Meer. The most used route follows the Ganzendiep from Kampen, then takes the more easterly Goot channel. At the junction with the Zwarte Meer the Scheepvaartgat runs east to join the Zwarte Water south of Vogeleiland. The northern end of the Ganzendiep joins the Zwarte Meer at an unbuoyed shallow area and is therefore not safe for normal navigation. Variations in the level of the IJsselmeer can cause the depth to vary significantly, so great care is needed for this navigation.

There are no suitable stopping points or attractions on these waterways but they are included as through routes for shallow-draft boats.

Length 14km
Speed limit 9km/h
Depth 1m (at IJsselmeer winter level)
Locks Ganzensluis (at Kampen) (max air draught 5m) operates throughout the day with a break for lunch (1200–1300)
Bridges 1 opening. Mandjeswaard bridge operates the same hours as the lock.

Cruising in the Central Netherlands

For those often in the vicinity of Amsterdam and the IJsselmeer, there is much interest and variety to be found by cruising up the Vecht and sampling the lakes near Weesp and Loosdrecht. Cruising further to Utrecht presents all of the attractions of a historic regional centre, but committing further time will bring all of the rewards of undertaking a circular route up the Rijn and down the IJssel to discover what the Dutch describe as the true heart of the Netherlands.

Motoring upstream on the Rijn (and thus downstream on the IJssel) is by far the most preferable direction to go as almost all of the adverse flow is diverted in the summer, unlike that of the Waal. There are few people speaking English as a first, second or even third language for whom the historic significance of Arnhem is not important as a pilgrimage and then the pleasant downstream passage along the IJssel takes in seven of the old Hanseatic ports that were so formative in moulding Dutch cultural and economic history.

For those with explorative tendencies, the cruise along the Twentekanalen east from near Zutphen leads close to the German border and then turns north near Hengelo. Eventually crossing the border into Drenthe, the waterways complete a circular route which returns via Meppel.

9 Southeast Netherlands

Noord Brabant and Limburg

Completing our clockwise circular tour of the Netherlands, this chapter comprises those waterways in the provinces of Noord-Brabant and Limburg, bordered to the north by the river Maas and to the south and east by the borders with Belgium and Germany. The Maas flows from Belgium, arriving in the Netherlands at Eijsden and flowing north through Maastricht, changing its name to the Andelse Maas when it finally arrives at Woudrichem. This chapter includes the lesser-known canals across North Brabant which are not included in the series of *ANWB* charts. A free overview map is available locally, although it does contain some errors and is due for reprinting in 2007.

The Southeast Netherlands, characterised by the combination of long busy commercial waterways with the extended leisure areas of the Maasplassen, has seen its fortunes fought over in many ways at different times. Projecting as it does as a peninsula deep into the neighbouring countries of Germany and Belgium it has been something of a historical through route with the past conflicts having shaped its boundaries and towns. Many of the settlements have retained their historic fortifications enclosing compact and attractive town centres whilst others are very modern having been totally rebuilt and redeveloped. Although certain of

Waterways	Principal venues	Other stopping places
Andelse (or Afgedamde) Maas & Heusdenskanaal	Woudrichem	Aalst, Wijk en Aalburg, Nederhemert-Zuid
Bergse Maas	Heusden	Waalwijk
Oude Maasje		Raamsdonksveer, Waspik, Sprang-Capelle
Amertak (& Kanaal naar de Amer)		
Donge (& Noordergat)		Geertruidenberg, Raamsdonksveer
Mark & Dintel, and Markkanaal (including Mark-Vlietkanaal and Leursche Vaart)	Oudenbosch	Dintelsas/Dinteloord, Roosendaal, Zevenbergen, Etten-Leur, Terheijden, Breda
Wilhelminakanaal	Tilburg	Oosterhout, Beekse Bergen, Biest-Houtakker/Hilvarenbeek
Beatrixkanaal	Eindhoven	
Dieze	's-Hertogenbosch	
Zuid-Willemsvaart		Veghel, Aarle-Rixtel/Helmond,
	Nederweert, Weert	
Kanaal Wessem-Nederweert		
Noordervaart		
Maas (& Julianakanaal)	Maastricht, Maasbracht, Stevensweert and the Maasplassen, Roermond	Eijsden, Venlo, Arcen, Wanssum, Well, Boxmeer, Gennep, Cuijk, Mook and the Mookerplas, Heumen, Grave, Ravenstein, Maasbommel, Lith, Heerewaarden, Alem, Kerkdriel, Hedel, Ammerzoden

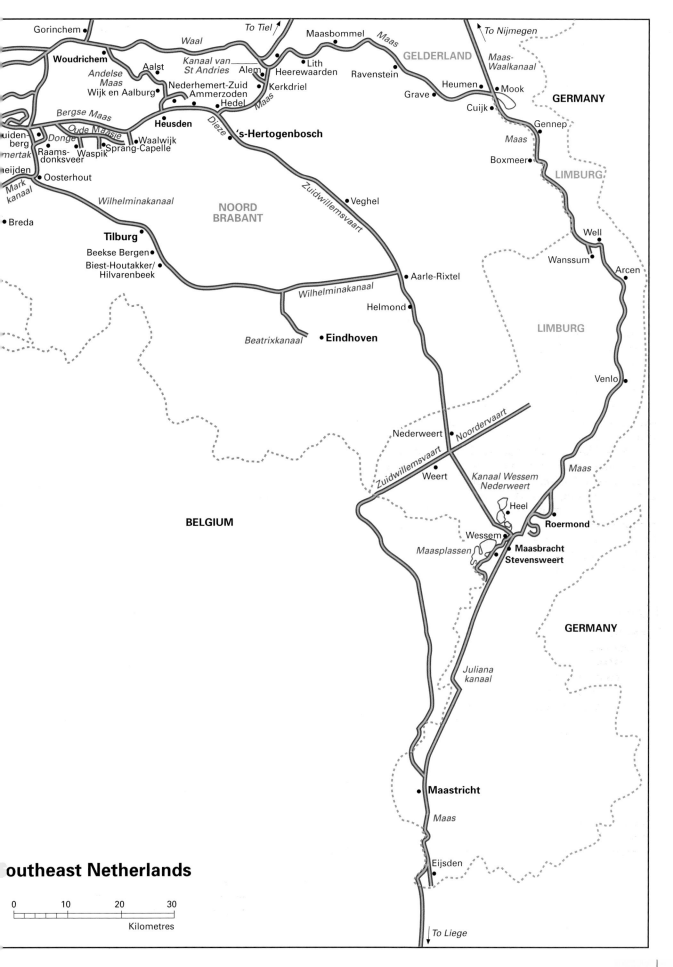

Gorinchem

Woudrichem

Aalst

Andelse Maas

Wijk en Aalburg

Bergse Maas

Oude Maasje

Heusden

Donge

uiden-berg

mertak

Raams-donksveer

Waspik

Sprang-Capelle

Waalwijk

eijden

Oosterhout

Mark kanaal

Breda

Wilhelminakanaal

Tilburg

Beekse Bergen

Biest-Houtakker/ Hilvarenbeek

Nederhemert-Zuid

Ammerzoden

Hedel

Kerkdriel

Dieze

Waal

Kanaal van St Andries

Alem

Heerewaarden

To Tiel

Maasbommel

Lith

Maas

Ravenstein

GELDERLAND

To Nijmegen

Maas-Waalkanaal

Heumen

Grave

Cuijk

Mook

GERMANY

Gennep

Maas

Boxmeer

LIMBURG

's-Hertogenbosch

Zuidwillemsvaart

Veghel

NOORD BRABANT

Wilhelminakanaal

Aarle-Rixtel

Helmond

Beatrixkanaal

Eindhoven

Well

Wanssum

Arcen

LIMBURG

Venlo

Nederweert

Noordervaart

Zuidwillemsvaart

Weert

Kanaal Wessem Nederweert

Heel

Maas

Roermond

BELGIUM

Wessem

Maasplassen

Maasbracht

Stevensweert

GERMANY

Juliana kanaal

Maastricht

Maas

Eijsden

To Liege

Southeast Netherlands

0   10   20   30

Kilometres

the rivers and canals are fairly long and featureless they nevertheless provide pleasant cruising, bordered as they are by trees and vegetation.

Some of the most interesting landscape for boaters is man-made and has been created in the Maas valley. Former sand and gravel extraction and subsequent flooding has created a network of lakes or *plassen* and although in Belgium this work is continuing and water areas increasing, it has by and large run its course in the southeast Netherlands to give wide open waters for recreational use. Whilst the earlier conflicts of the area led to the battlements of the fortress towns, 20th-century conflict has led to a number of first and second world war cemeteries, monuments and museums, which are also of interest to English-speaking visitors. Scene of preliminary action in Operation Market Garden, the countryside is dotted with sites and small monuments with the National War and Resistance Museum at Overloon bringing it all together.

The area is often blessed in the summer months by being included within the continental high pressure areas which enable the use of the many inland lake and river sandy beach venues. This is in direct contrast with the winter conditions on the Maas especially, where, because of the regular flooding, many of the harbours are emptied of boats during the winter. Since the last bad floods in 1995 increased protection work has taken place in many of the towns and villages, with extra dykes built and flood gates being installed.

Hitherto, the principal foreign boating visitors have been Germans, many of whom base their boats in the Maasplassen and spend very enjoyable holidays there. With the increase of information and interpretation in the English language, the area has great potential for further visits by motor boats from England who will enjoy the relatively lock-free environment and high bridges for canopy clearance. Already a through route for boats coming from Belgium to the Netherlands, its proximity to the

Fortified towns line the waterways in Southeast Netherlands

Belgian border has been used in the past to provide a useful opportunity to fill up with low cost diesel before continuing to explore the rest of the Netherlands. The whole area has been something of a well-kept secret for local boaters with little information available in the English language. Parts of it are not included in the series of *ANWB* charts, and such information as is available has proved out of date or unreliable. We have made special efforts with these waterways to provide authoritative information in this chapter, even where that has meant adding more detail than normally provided. Much of this has been the result of first hand investigation by boat, together with considerable help from local experts for which we have been very grateful.

For those people who are thinking of basing a boat in the Netherlands there are extensive facilities and plenty of space. Good transport links to Ejndhoven or the airport at Niederrhein across the border in Germany have persuaded many British boaters to do that already, with Roermond a favourite choice.

Andelse Maas & Heusdenskanaal

The official name for the Andelse Maas is Afgedamde Maas, but locally and in the *ANWB Almanak*, the name Andelse Maas is used. Together with the southern section called the Heusdenskanaal, the waterway runs from Heusden to Woudrichem. Despite being a locked waterway, its attractive course winds through quiet countryside. At only 17km the whole waterway can be cruised in around two hours.

Riverside cafés and restaurants which are situated along the waterway with their own moorings make pleasant stops, although there can still be variation in water level and wash from passing vessels. In view of the shallow banks, deep-draught vessels should stay within the buoyed channel. There is a flood protection barrier near the southern end of

the Heusdenskanaal which is normally kept open with an air draught of 11.4m.

The Dode Maasarm runs east from Aalburg past Nederhemert-Zuid and you can anchor off the beach at the end (1.8m depth at LW).

Length 17km
Speed limit 20km/h except in Dode Maasarm, 9km/h
Locks Wilhelminasluis and lifting bridge operate throughout the day. VHF 22.
Bridges 1 fixed (11.4m) Kromme Nolkering flood barrier is closed only in very high water conditions. The bridge can be opened for masted yachts but there are no published service times.

WOUDRICHEM

Where to stop

WSV Woudrichem is entered just south of the foot-ferry to Loevestein at km 247. The usual facilities are available including unmetered electricity and water. JH 't Gatje to the south does not take visitors. The historic harbour, accessed from the Merwede, has been restored to its original appearance in 1650, even down to its naturally overgrown banks. The first section is intended for historic yachts, but beyond these and the outdoor fishing museum is a visitors pontoon for stays of up to two nights. Coin-operated electricity and water (€0.50/100 ltrs) and the usual basic facilities are available. Both harbours are situated within the town's fortress canals and have a peaceful ambience surrounded by grassy banks.

The municipal visitors pontoon outside the harbour near the ferry terminal is only to be used with the permission of the harbourmaster.

Facilities ashore

Supermarket, Shops & ATMs On 't Rond in the new town

Cycle hire Step-scooter hire for groups from the Pannekoekenbakker next to WSV Woudrichem

VVV office On the corner of Kerkstraat & Hoogstraat

What to see

The tiny fortified town of Woudrichem (pronounced 'vowdrikem') has been supplemented by new development to the south and so the old centre presents a step back in time. The bastioned ramparts were part of the Hollandse Waterlinie (Dutch Water Line of defences), and you can walk around the intact fortifications although the Gevangenpoort is the only one of the five town gates remaining. Salmon fishing was an important industry in the

A visiting boat arrives at Woudrichem's historic *stadshaven*

town following the granting of fishing rights to the population and although there is no salmon left, there is still fishing for eels and the Visserij museum (Fishing museum) depicts the history of this important trade.

A popular excursion from Woudrichem is to the solidly-built castle Slot Loevestein on the opposite side of the Maas. Dating from around 1360, the encircling moat made it effective as a prison when it was converted in the 15th century. The tale of a legendary escape inside a book chest is displayed inside the castle, along with the famous chest. Catch the small ferry by the yacht club or the larger one from nearer the Stadshaven. Also accessible by ferry is Fort Vuren, another in the Hollandse Waterlinie.

Shopping in the old town is restricted to items of touristic interest but you can buy bread in the cornmill at weekends. All facilities on 't Rond in the new town including a weekly market on Thursdays. On Sunday afternoons you can visit the brewery on Hoogstraat for a taste of the local ale.

A fishing festival complete with salmon cooking competition is held on Hemelvaart weekend in May and the fortress town festival is held every three years on the last weekend in August.

Restaurant tip

Even if you don't want to hire a step-scooter, the Pannekoekenbakker next to the yacht harbour has 230 delicious varieties and a scenic riverside terrace. Kruiden & Jasmijn on Kerkstraat is well-suited for a special occasion and have a range of set menus which can be served in their garden adorned with statues, or enjoy the air-conditioned comfort of Restaurant De Gevangenpoort.

In the Stadshaven, De Stroming has a nautical atmosphere and a harbour-side terrace, or if your boat has the best table in town call Gourmet to Go who will deliver a feast to your pontoon ☎ 0183 661406.

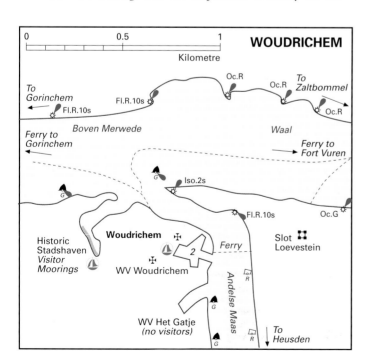

Restaurant De Gevangenpoort is housed in the only remaining city gate

Connections

The easiest way to get anywhere from Woudrichem is by ferry to Gorinchem and by onward train.

AALST

WSV Esmeer has a small number of visitors' spaces in a gravel pit off the east bank of the Maas. Just north of km 236 the Rietschoof campsite and yacht harbour offers extensive on site facilities including a beach, swimming pool and bar/café. Further to the south are free municipal visitors' pontoons for short-term daytime mooring.

WIJK EN AALBURG

On the west bank near km 234, WV Trident offers a small number of visitors' moorings for boats up to 12m on the edge of the village. The largest of seven villages that form the municipality of Aalburg, Wijk en Aalburg holds a weekly market on Tuesday afternoons and has a handful of shops for basic needs. Good times to visit include the during music festival in June or the harbour festival in September.

NEDERHEMERT-ZUID

On the south side of the Dode Maasarm the tiny harbour of Nederhemert only takes visitors by prior arrangement. Nederhemert castle has been completely restored after standing in ruins since 1945. Officially reopened by Queen Beatrix in 2005, the building is partly used as office space and for weddings, but the gardens and café can be visited daily and there are limited open days during the summer.

Bergse Maas

The Bergse Maas is the name given to the section of the River Maas from the mouth of the Donge to a point at km 226.5 (between Heusden and Ammerzoden). Continuing on from the Amer (See Chapter 2: Great Rivers) it is a wide and attractive waterway although, with no speed limit for much of its length, it is heavily used by speedboats and jetskiers which can be a nuisance. This is a pleasant river to cruise with plenty of space and only the occasional barge on weekdays.

There are several small, free harbours along the waterway but these are not recommended for visitors. A harbour marked on the 2005/06 Waterkaart as being under construction just inside the Oude Maasje east of the Keisersveer bridge was taking shape in 2006. In future years this will be very convenient for a visit to the National Automobile museum just across the A27. The café and moorings marked at Bokhoven are convenient for a short stop but are exposed to passing traffic and are therefore not suitable for overnighting.

Speed limit 20km/h where applicable
Bridges 2 fixed (minimum 8.9m). At Keizersveer (9.6m under central span at HW) eastbound traffic should take the southern span, and westbound traffic the central span.

WAALWIJK

WSV Waalwijk have a reception pontoon for visitors to port just before the lock. The large pontoon prior to the entrance is for boats longer than 12m, but there are boxes for smaller boats inside. Free 3A electricity and water are available and the small clubhouse is opened by members at the weekend. Beyond the lock the harbour canal is entirely industrial and not navigable for leisure boats, but you can hire a bike from the harbour or take a bus from across the lock for the 3km trip to the town centre.

There are plenty of shops including a small chandlers and a weekly market on Wednesday morning. Waalwijk (pronounced 'varl-vike') is the centre of the Netherlands leather and shoe industry and a museum includes a reconstruction of a 1930s shoe factory and a tannery from 1870. The fantasy theme park De Efteling is 8km away and you can ask at the harbour office for details of the 30-minute cycle route or take the special bus from the town centre. The highly-landscaped park has a good range of white knuckle rides as well as more leisurely attractions and is well worth an excursion for children of all ages.

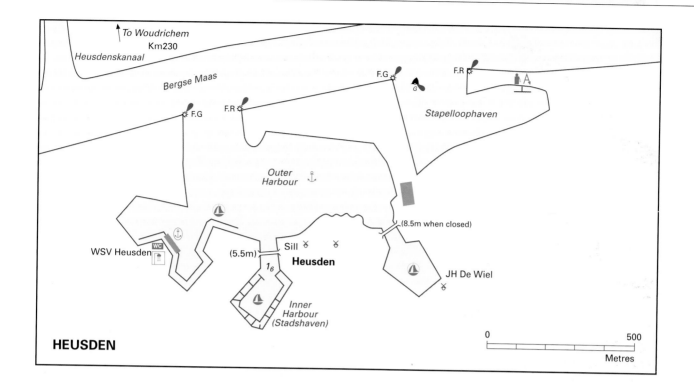

HEUSDEN

HEUSDEN

Where to stop

Heusden has two yacht clubs which are both accessed via the western outer harbour (opposite km 230). WSV Heusden is to starboard upon entry and the visitors' pontoon is next to the old bridge into the Stadshaven. Further moorings are available in this inner harbour but the fixed bridge has an air draught of 5.5m and there is a sill at a depth of 1.6m at normal water level. An old stone gauge under the bridge showing the depth of the sill is only visible from inside the harbour but the harbourmistress will advise on request. Facilities and the harbour office are located on a barge at the west end of the harbour, which was originally used during the Normandy landings. JH De Wiel is to port and through a second bridge into another small basin, but moorings are double the price of WSV Heusden and not normally preferred by visitors. Unmetered water and 4A electricity are available on the outer moorings but not in the Stadshaven. The harbour gets busy in the summer months and reservations are taken but not essential. There is also a free sheltered anchorage in the outer harbour and crews are normally permitted to use the shore-based facilities.

Facilities ashore

Fuel, Chandlers, Repairs and Servicing
  Legerstee Watersport in the Stapelloophaven
Supermarket & Shops Hoogstraat & Vismarkt
ATMs Near the Wijkse Poort and on Hoogstraat
Cycle hire From the harbour office or the cycle shop
  on Burchtplein
VVV office Junction of Hoogstraat and Pelsestraat

What to see

After 600 years of service, Heusden's (pronounced 'whose-den') fortifications were dismantled in 1821 and the ground used as allotments. The old harbour was drained and filled in 1908 and the new square named Wilheminaplein, after the Queen who came to open it. The town hall and church tower were destroyed by the retreating Germans in 1944 but escaped a process of 'urban renewal' after the war in favour of authentic reconstruction. This process was continued when in 1965 the town council decided to rebuild the fortifications and excavate the inner harbour and restore them to their original condition. Although the inhabitants did not want the town to become an 'open-air museum' they receive 350,000 visitors a year who come primarily for this attraction.

The tourist office sells a detailed booklet (in English) describing the history of the town and a walk around its main sights, or you can take a guided tour on Sunday afternoons. The VVV office is part of Heusden's visitor centre, which features a detailed scale model of the town with computerised explanations of the principal features (in Dutch only).

A good selection of individual and specialist shops are to be found mainly on Hoogstraat, including one which sells nautical books and charts. Jansen the butchers on Vismarkt is described as the 'best in the Netherlands'. A market is held on Thursday afternoons but unusually for the Netherlands other shops close on Tuesday afternoon. If shopping is your priority the wine merchant De Heeren van Heusden will deliver to your boat and you can sample the wares in the town's remaining brewery at the weekends.

Lie on the visitors' moorings by the bridge or inside the historic harbour

A walk around the city ramparts takes about an hour, and includes the three post mills as well as the island defence posts. You can make a nice excursion by bike to the Loonse & Drunense Dunes National Park and a cycle route is available from the VVV.

Restaurant tip

It is a short walk via the Stadshaven bridge to the Vismarkt square where many of the bars and restaurants are to be found. Eetcafé Havenzicht is ideal for a simple meal and the adjacent Pancake House is renowned for its extensive range of fillings. On the opposite side of the square Restaurant Brasserie Centraal is a very nice choice but for something extra special head for Hotel/Restaurant De Verdwaalde Koogel (The Lost Cannonball – which you can still see embedded in the wall).

Connections

There is no train station in Heusden but there is a bus every half-hour to 's-Hertogenbosh.

Visit the highly regarded Jansen butcher's shop on Heusden's market square

Oude Maasje

This old arm of the Maas remains tidal and joins the Bergse Maas just upstream of the bridge at Keizersveer. After 300m a flood lock crosses the waterway and normally stands open but can be closed in periods of high water levels. The lock forms a constriction in the waterway creating faster flow through the opening. Whilst this is normally less than 2km/h, it can reach 8km/h and in strong flow conditions the direction and strength of the flow are given on a board by the lock. There is a waiting pontoon for leisure boats on the west side of the lock but as there is not one on the east side, westbound vessels should ensure they can complete their passage through the lock before departing. Beyond the Capelle bridge the waterway continues as the Zuiderkanaal towards Waalwijk, but the navigation is discontinued just west of the Waalwijk harbour entrance.

Length 11.2km
Speed limit 9km/h in blue areas on ANWB chart; otherwise, 20km/h.
Maximum permitted draught 2.5m
Bridges 2 fixed (min. 5.6m)

RAAMSDONKSVEER

The well-equipped JH Hermenzeil lies close to the mouth of the Oude Maasje. There are a large number of good-sized boats, but visitors' spaces are only in free boxes. It is 2km to the nearest village, but on site facilities include a bar, restaurant, chandlers and play area. A foot and cycle ferry crosses from here to a popular recreation area between the Oude Maasje and the Bergse Maas. It is also a convenient stop for a visit to the National Motor museum in Raamsdonksveer.

WASPIK

The moorings of WV 't Oude Maasje lie on the main river, just before the bridge and the harbour canal. This is home to an active motor boating club but being 2.5km from the village it is not ideal for visitors. Entering the canal to port, the moorings of JH Scharloo line the end of the Kerkvaart and are ten-minutes walk from the village centre. The facilities include on-site chandlers.

SPRANG-CAPELLE

At the head of the 2km long harbour canal, a further fixed bridge (5m) crosses the channel, before the moorings of JH Aquapelle and the municipal quays. Moorings are available at both, but the JH charge half that of the municipal moorings. These are near to the small village, with its one main street.

Amertak (& Kanaal naar de Amer)

The Amertak is a new waterway that joins the Amer and the Wilhelminakanaal to the west of Geertruidenberg. For boats above 5m air draught this avoids the new fixed Noordergat bridge on the Donge.

Length 3km
Depth 4.3m
Bridge 1 opening. Steelhoven bridge (7.3m when closed) opens only on request with 24 hours notice to Sluis 1 at Oosterhout ☎ 0162 45 42 41.

Donge (& Noordergat)

The Donge forms the original eastern mouth of the Wilhelminakanaal to the Bergse Maas. It is heavily industrial although most of the traffic has been diverted onto the more direct Amertak route to the west. Fuel and a large chandlers are available at Bunkercentrum Dongemond on Rivierkade 4 on the west bank north of the marinas.

Speed limit 11km/h
Maximum permitted draught 3m
Bridges 2 fixed (minimum 5m) including Noordergat bridge (new in 2006).

GEERTRUIDENBERG

Limited moorings are available at the two yacht club harbours of WV De Donge (up to 10m boats inside the harbour and up to 15m in the riverside boxes), and WSV Geertruidenberg (up to 12m boats). Just north of the bridge the visitors' harbour advertises space for nine boats not bigger than 12m by 3.5m (depth 1.2m), but if it is quiet there is ample space to manoeuvre a slightly larger vessel. No facilities are available but it is quite close to the town centre.

Geertruidenberg (pronounced 'kheer-trowder-bereg') claims to be the oldest town in the province of Holland, whose name originates from the mountain or *berg* of St Gertrudis. The former fortress town has been comprehensively modernised but some of the fortifications to the north and west of the town are intact and feature in the historic town walk. Museum 'De Roos' on the Markt depicts the history of the town and the triangular 'square' comes to life on Friday mornings for the weekly market. The 15th-century tower of the St Gertruidskerk is open to visitors on selected dates during the summer. A fortress festival is held every odd year in June.

RAAMSDONKSVEER

WV Zuidergat just south of the bridge does not take visitors but there are spaces at JH De Meerpaal along the Zuidergat channel for boats up to 16m.

The former bargeman's town is now a modern conurbation with lots of shops, cafés and bars. As well as the National Automobile museum with its 200 vehicles on display, you can take a tour of the old corn mill, d'Onvermoide, and buy their home-milled flour. An international Cajun cultural festival is held every year in June.

Mark & Dintel

The Mark and the Dintel are treated as one waterway that runs from Dintelsas lock on the Volkerak east to Breda. Upstream of Breda the waterway is navigable only by canoe. It runs mainly through polder countryside, which is dotted with the occasional sugar beet factory, but is not an unpleasant cruise. Fuel is available from Bunkerstation Dintel at Dintelsas which lies between the piers.

Existing published charts of this area have errors and omissions and our best efforts have been made to provide accurate details here.

Length 35km
Maximum permitted draught 2.6m
Speed limit Dinteloord-Stampersgat 12km/h; upstream of Stampersgat 9km/h
Locks Mandersluis (at Dintelsas) normally stands open, except in warm summers when the waters are susceptible to algae bloom. In this case the lock is operated throughout the day. Passage through the lock is controlled by lights.
Bridges 2 opening, 10 fixed (min 7m). Prinsenlandse bridge operates throughout the day on the hour and half-hour (from 0930 on Sundays) with a break for lunch (1230–1400) weekends and holidays only. VHF 20.
Zevenbergen rail bridge opens throughout the day at H+58. The bridge is operated remotely from Roosendaal and there is an intercom by the bridge.

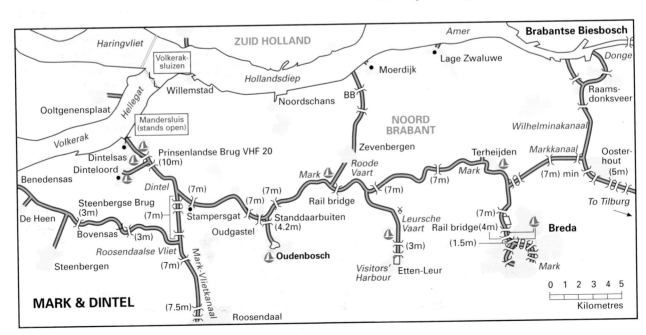

DINTELSAS/DINTELOORD

Just inside the lock at Dintelsas there are three harbours at the mouth of the Dintel river which is a convenient stopping place if want to make your way inland. WV De Dintel is the first to starboard and although they do not have designated visitors' spaces it is a large yacht club and if any of their members are away you can have a good cheap mooring. All the facilities were built by the members and the toilet/shower block is a credit to their workmanship. Electricity is by €0.50 coin-meter (4A) or ask to have the unmetered tariff (€1.50/night, 16A). You can use their mast crane if you are planning an inland cruise and they can store masts temporarily during the summer.

Alternatively, choose one of the two marinas: Jachtcentrum Dintelmond to port charges the most but has the best facilities including fuel, chandlers and wi-fi; to starboard JH Waterkant always has space on their dedicated visitors' pontoon but toilet and shower facilities are not so good.

If you continue under the Prinsenlandse bridge and turn to starboard you can follow the short harbour canal to a visitors' quay close to the town. Here there are free moorings (no facilities, depth 1.25m) for a maximum of 2 nights.

The village is some 3km away from the marinas but you can take a dinghy and stop at the town quay or hire a bike from JH Waterkant (from 2007). Although mostly dominated by the sugar beet factory, Dinteloord still has an old centre with a selection of shops and cafés, as well as a market on Tuesday mornings. If you can't make it to the centre you can get a good value meal in the pub, De Kajuit, on the corner by JH Waterkant.

MARK-VLIETKANAAL TO ROOSENDAAL

Just west of Stampersgat the Mark-Vlietkanaal (10km) branches to the south to give access to the large town of Roosendaal. There are five fixed bridges with a minimum of 7m to the harbour at WV De Vliet, which has limited space for boats up to 12.5m (depth 1.5m). A link with the Roosendaalse and Steenbergse Vliet (See Chapter 1: Zeeland) is restricted to an air draught of 3m.

The modern town has a popular factory outlet shopping village, the Rosada, for discount designer shopping and a music festival in the harbour in June.

OUDENBOSCH

Where to stop

Opposite Standdaarbuiten a harbour canal turns south off the main river to the old town of Oudenbosch. A bridge crosses the waterway near the boatyard at the entrance which is not marked on many of the charts but has an air draught of 4.2m. At the head of the canal is the friendly harbour of Jachthaven Oudenbosch. A reporting and water pontoon (€0.50) is provided by the harbourmaster's house, who will allocate you a space in the basin or in the boxes up to the head of the navigation. All

The striking dome of the basilica in Oudenbosch is visible from the harbour

moorings have unmetered electricity (10A) charged at €1/night. Good basic facilities and an informal bar are provided at the harbour office.

Facilities ashore

Workman-like chandlers and repair facilities
  Bootservice Van der Krogt at junction with Mark
Supermarket, Shops & ATMs Several between the
  harbour and the Markt
Cycle hire From Boere Tweewielers at Markt 1

What to see

Also known as Little Rome, Oudenbosch (pronounced 'Owdenbosh') is famous for its replica of St Peter's Basilica built in 1892. Complete with 68m dome, the interior is really worth a visit and is open every day. As well as seeing the museum you can climb the 70 steps to see the decorative artwork of the dome at close quarters. Continuing on a papal theme, the Museum of Pontifical Zouaves recalls the 19th-century defenders of the Papal States. Also on Markt is the entrance to the highly regarded Arboretum which has 4.9 acres of carefully selected specimens and several themed gardens. Tours are run on Sunday afternoons.

The nearby shopping centre is convenient for supplies and there is a market on Tuesday afternoons.

Restaurant tip

Hotel/Restaurant De Kroon on Markt does not look much from the outside but offers a good value three-course menu from Tuesday to Friday. The food is very good at the Brasserie Het Vrolijke Schaap on Fenkelstraat, which can be enjoyed either inside or in their shaded private courtyard.

Connections

A train station is 10 minutes away and the single line runs to Vlissingen and Dordrecht.

ZEVENBERGEN

Limited spaces are available at the small harbour at the river end of the harbour canal 2.5km from town, and daytime moorings only on the Roode Vaart near the centre of Zevenbergen.

LEURSCHE VAART TO ETTEN-LEUR

There are no bridges on this stretch as far as the large harbour of Jachthaven De Turfvaart. It is quite a distance from the large town but is popular with families because of its small beach and on site facilities, which include a chandlers and terrace restaurant. A fixed 3m bridge restricts access to the municipal moorings at the head of the canal.

A harbour festival is held on the last weekend in May and an Annual market on the second Sunday in September. You can cycle along the canal and visit the only polder mill in West Brabant, the Zwartenbergse mill, or enjoy the ample shopping facilities in the restored centre.

TERHEIJDEN

Jachthaven Terheijden is a municipal harbour near to the village centre and as well as boxes there are alongside moorings at the head of the inlet. Coin-operated electricity and free water are available as well as basic facilities.

This former fortress town was occupied by the Spanish and one of the unusual moated 'Schans' forts lies next to the quiet harbour. A cycle ferry crosses the river at this point and connects with the 5km route to Breda. A supermarket and small selection of shops are available on Hoogstraat.

BREDA

The last section of the Mark runs through some industrial harbour areas and does not present the best face of Breda to waterborne visitors. On arrival, the visitors' harbour is alongside a busy road and trains cross the nearby rail bridge until 0200. A major project was underway in 2006 to restore some of the town's central canals around the old fish market but it is not intended to create any new moorings as part of the scheme. It is a shame the moorings are so uninviting as the town could be nice to visit with its Spanjaardsgat water gate and castle occupied by the Royal Military Academy. In light of this visitors might prefer to stop at Terheijden and make an excursion using the cycle ferry described above.

Breda (pronounced 'braid-ar') owes its name to a contraction of the Brede (wide) Aa and the city is located at the confluence of the two rivers, the Mark and Aa. The Breda Museum depicts the culture and history of the city and you can get a bird's eye view from the tower of the Onze Lieve Vrouwe Church. The small War & Freedom museum on Ginnekenweg opens only by arrangement.

A four-day Jazz festival is held over the Ascension Day holiday weekend and a balloon festival is held in August.

Markkanaal

This short straight stretch links the Mark near Terheijden to the Wilhelminakanaal at Oosterhout.

Length 6km
Speed limit 10.8km/h for vessels of 1.5m draught or less

Maximum permitted draught 2.5m, air draught 7m
Locks Marksluis and opening bridge at Oosterhout operate throughout the day (until 1600 on Saturdays, 0900–1700 Sundays). VHF 18.
Bridges 3 fixed (min 7m)

Wilhelminakanaal

The Wilhelminakanaal connects with the Amertak and forms the route from Geertruidenberg, via Oosterhout and Tilburg, to the Zuidwillemsvaart. Commercial traffic on the waterway is moderately heavy and although passage through the electrically-operated locks is normally prompt, vessels should beware of frequent container barges between Oosterhout and Tilburg. The section from Geertruidenberg to Oosterhout is very industrial with little to see but beyond here the landscape is more attractive, especially around Oirschot, with wooded sections dotted along the banks. Overhead cables cross the waterway but the lowest of these has a height of 27m.

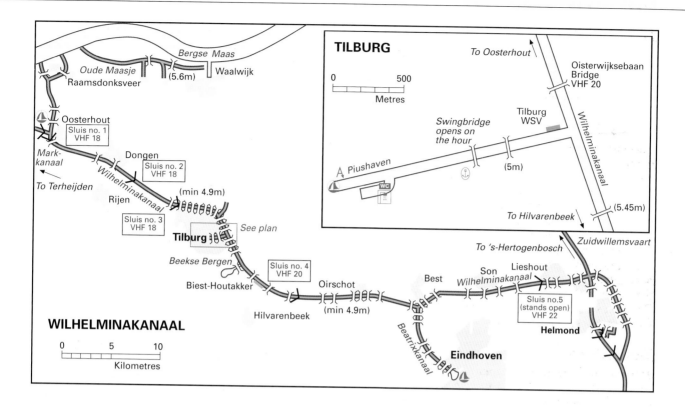

Length 73km
Speed limit 10.8km/h
Maximum permitted draught 1.9m
Locks 5 (of which that at Lieshout normally stands open) operate 24 hours throughout the week (until 1600 on Saturday, 0900–1700 on Sundays)
Sluis 1 Oosterhout and lifting bridge, Sluis 2 and Sluis 3 Tilburg. VHF 18
Sluis 4 Haghorst and lifting bridge. VHF 20. Sluis 5 Lieshout and lifting bridge. VHF 22.
Bridges 29 fixed (min 4.9m), 18 opening which operate the same hours as the locks. Deelenlaan, Waalstraat, Lijnsheike, Heikantsebaan, Enschotsestraat, Bosscheweg, Oisterwijksebaan, Trappisten, Holenakker, Biesthoutakker, Kattenberg, Groenewoud and Heuvel bridges. VHF 20. Houtens, Son, Hooydonk, Stad van Gerwen and Oranjelaan bridges. VHF 22.

OOSTERHOUT

Jachthaven Oosterhout, just north of Sluis 1, has space only for boats up to 12m length and 3.5m beam. A reporting pontoon is provided by the outer boxes and the usual basic facilities are provided. The centre of the large town is about 2km away. There is a large modern shopping centre and the town is known for the extensive collection of toys from the 18th century to 1950 in its museum, 'Op Stelten' on St Vincentiusstraat.

TILBURG

Where to stop

Visitors should make for the Piushaven which lies at the head of the harbour canal just south of the city centre, after a fixed bridge of 5m and a swing bridge which opens on the hour throughout the day. The harbourmaster is based in the office by the bridge and normally spots arriving boats, who can wait on the pontoon on the starboard side. The bridge

operates throughout the day Monday to Saturday, but must be requested by telephone for Sunday openings (at 0900, 1300 and 1700, with extra July and August openings at 1100 and 1500) ☎ 013 542 9440. You are welcomed with an electronic SEP-key, for which a deposit of €25 is required, which gives access to the water and electricity as well as the toilets, showers, washing machine and the key to the rubbish skip. These are located at the east end of the moorings, with the entrance hidden behind the fire escape of the adjacent block of flats. The friendly and helpful reception makes up for the unprepossessing surroundings and the highlight of the harbourmaster's services is a specially adapted bike for watering the hanging baskets.

The present Tilburg WSV has very basic facilities and is not to be recommended. It is due to move to a new location in the near future.

The harbourmaster demonstrates his specially adapted watering bike outside the harbour office on the Piushaven

Lakeside moorings at the Beekse Bergen Safari park

Facilities ashore

Chandlers & service Wetsports Divecenters opposite the harbour has certain useful supplies and are handy for underwater problems.

Supermarket & Shops Jumbo supermarket is between the two harbour bridges and a market is held every Saturday on Koningsplein

ATMs Nearest is on Jan Aartestraat

Cycle hire Fietspoint Derks, Spoorlaan

VVV office Kiosk on the harbour (accessed by SEP key) and main office on Spoorlaan

What to see

This large, modern industrial town was dominated by the textile industry until the 1960s; the Textile museum is located in one of the last surviving factories and includes a working steam engine from 1906. The De Pont foundation for modern art is housed in a former woollen mill and the naturally lit space is perfect for displaying the varied and internationally renowned collection. Near the station, the North Brabant Natural History Museum deals with the flora and fauna of the region and, next door, Scryption is a museum of written communication. Amongst the facilities in the harbour in future years will be a modern floating hair salon which was under construction in 2006.

The Festival Mundial celebrates world music and culture and takes place in the middle of June, whilst the annual town fair is held at the end of July and is one of the largest in Europe.

Restaurant tip

Head for the Korte Heuvel and the Oude Markt around the pedestrianised Heuvel for a choice of good eating places.

Connections

The train station is close to the town centre for services to all destinations and a convenient bus from the central station also serves the De Efteling theme park.

BEEKSE BERGEN

East of Tilburg is the large recreation and camp site of Beekse Bergen. The yacht harbour is accessed via a lifting bridge where the Beekse Bergen lake joins the Wilhelminakanaal. The bridge opens every two hours (1000–1800) and there is a waiting pontoon outside the bridge on the starboard side. The moorings are grouped around a wooded peninsula in about 1.5–2m depth, although those against the quay wall are a little deeper. Unmetered 4A electricity and water are available, as are good basic facilities. No reservations can be taken and the moorings are very busy in high season. The harbour is administrated from the campsite reception where you should report on arrival.

The overnight mooring fee not only includes admission to the extensive adjacent children's playground, but also to the large Safari park that is home to over 1,000 animals. You can take the safari bus or a water tour, as well as the mini-train around the complex, which also features a restaurant, supermarket and small indoor splash pool. For anglers, day permits are available from the reception for fishing on the lake.

BIEST-HOUTAKKER/HILVARENBEEK

Southeast of the Beekse Bergen lake and the Biest-Houtakker bridge there are free unserviced pontoon moorings on the west bank at the small village of Biest-Houtakker. These are advertised as being for daytime stays only and although hitherto it has been customary for boats to stay overnight, new 24-hour lock opening could lead to this rule being more strictly enforced. Opposite the moorings a family run café-restaurant has a popular children's playground, and you can cycle to the village of Hilvarenbeek for further amenities and attractions, including the National Likeurmuseum on Goirlesedijk. It is also 4km to cycle to the Beekse Bergen Safari Park from here.

Beatrixkanaal

This short section runs from the Wilhelminakanaal at Best to Eindhoven. Opened in 1933, it serves the industrial areas south of Eindhoven but the banks are thickly wooded so it is not an unattractive waterway.

Length 8.4km
Speed limit 10.8km/h
Maximum permitted draught 1.9m; height, 4.95m
Bridges 10 fixed (5.2m)

EINDHOVEN

Where to stop

EJV Beatrix does not seem accustomed to visitors, being at the end of a dead-end canal some 6km distant from the city centre. For those determined to visit, the location is not unpleasant, lying in a wooded area which almost shields the sound of the nearby motorway. Facilities are quite adequate with unmetered water and electricity, diesel and pump-out. The advertised chandlers comprises only a small trailer but the café-bar has a sunny terrace with a pleasant aspect.

What to see

You will need some persistence to visit Eindhoven (pronounced 'I-ndhover') but bus and cycle routes do run near the harbour. The centrally located VVV at the bus/train station has a range of information in English including a walking tour of the city which points out where the historic sites used to be. Most of the city's significant buildings were destroyed during the second world war because of heavy bombing due to its industrial significance, and it is now distinguished by its wealth of modern architecture.

Already the fifth largest city in the Netherlands, Eindhoven continues to grow. Its expansion was helped by the success of the Philips factories, which as well as lighting made all manner of electrical appliances. Most of the manufacturing has now moved out-of-town, but the Incandescent Lamp Museum on Emmasingel remains to recount its history. Van Doorne's Aanhangwagen Fabrieken, known throughout the world as DAF, is also based here and their story is told at the DAF Museum along with an exhibition of their lorries, buses, trailers and cars.

The Eindhoven Open Air Museum is a representation of life through the ages based on local archaeological finds, with sections on the ice-ages, middle ages and Vikings. The museum is located in the Genneper Parken recreational area, on Boutenslaan to the south of the city.

Connections

Close to the yacht harbour is Eindhoven Airport from where Ryanair flies to Stansted twice daily.

Dieze

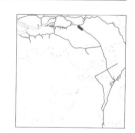

The Dieze and the Gekanaliseerde Dieze, form the connection between the Maas at km 221.4, and the Zuid-Willemsvaart at 's-Hertogenbosch, and is detailed in the *ANWB Almanak* by the town, Engelen, that it passes near. There can be a long wait at the Engelen lock which has a 1.5m change in water level and heavy barge traffic. The waterway is planned to be supplemented in the future by a new canal which will leave the Maas between Empel and Gewande and run south between 's-Hertogenbosch and Rosmalen. Joining the Zuid-Willemsvaart south of 's-Hertogenbosch near Berlicum, the new waterway will provide an easier connecting route for through traffic.

The Dieze runs into the Ertveld lake north of 's-Hertogenbosch and continues into the city emerging on the other side as the Zuid-Willemsvaart. There are moorings south of the Engelen lock alongside a rough quay but they would be affected by wash from the heavy traffic.

Length 5km
Speed limit 11km/h
Locks Sluis Engelen and lifting bridge operates throughout the day (from 0930 on Sundays). VHF 18.
Bridges 4 fixed (min 5.8m)

'S-HERTOGENBOSCH

Where to stop

WV De Waterpoort is located at the mouth of the river Dommel which branches southwest just south of the Dieze bridge. Box moorings at the yacht club are available only when members are away with unmetered water and electricity (6A). The visitors' moorings lie beyond the opening Havenbrug (3.2m when closed, opens at 1000 and 1900 only) and in the second inlet to the south under the fixed Boom bridge (4.2m). Alongside space with coin-operated water and electricity (€0.50/1.5kWH, 10A) is always available on the visitors' berths and you can telephone for reservations at the yacht club. The harbourmistress lives on a boat at the head of the Dommel moorings and looks after both these and

'S-HERTOGENBOSCH

the yacht club berths. Report on VHF 31 if available, or stop at the reporting pontoon between the Havenbrug and the Diezerbrug and telephone for a berth. Showers and toilets for all moorings are available free in the harbour office by the Boom bridge.

Two further yacht clubs are available off Plas Ertveld. WV Viking on the east side of the lake and WV Neptunus in the old Industriehaven via the opening Gordelweg bridge, which operates throughout the day on request to the harbourmaster during the week, but only 0900–1000 Saturdays, and 1830–1930 Sundays. South of Sluis 0 on the Zuid-Willemsvaart there are further unserviced canalside moorings.

Facilities ashore
Fuel & Chandlers At WV Viking on Plas Ertveld and south of Sluis O
Repairs and Servicing Bogamat supply a range of technical consumables or ask harbourmaster for contact for engine problems.
Supermarket & Shops Albert Heijn in the Arena Centre and all supplies available in nearby town centre
ATMs Nearest on Visstraat
Cycle hire From the harbour, the VVV or the train station
VVV office In the Markt

What to see
Capital of the Noord Brabant province, 's-Hertogenbosh (pronounced 'Certo-gabosh' and meaning the Dukes Wood) is also commonly referred to as Den Bosch.

The focal point of the town is the St Jan's Cathedral, the most elaborate gothic church in the Netherlands and complete with its own explanatory museum. Tours of the cathedral and the tower are available Tuesday–Sunday in the summer. For a more leisurely activity, take a horse-drawn tram tour of the city from near the cathedral (Saturday afternoons only) or one of the regular canal trip-boats which not only cruise through the city but also under it. These run Tuesday–Saturday and depart from Molenstraat and on Saturday evenings in the summer you can cruise to a special music concert by visiting artists. There are also guided walking tours of the city departing from Diezehuis on Molenstraat or an explanatory booklet available (in English) from the VVV. The highly regarded Noord Brabant museum presents temporary exhibitions as well as the work of Jeroen Bosch, a characterful religious artist who may or may not have lived in the city in the 15th century. Funpark Autotron, an automobile theme park in nearby Rosmalen, is due to reopen after refurbishment in 2007.

Weekly markets are held on Wednesdays (until 1400) and Saturdays (until 1600) in the central square and the nearby De Moriaan, the oldest brick-built building in the city, houses the VVV. Shopping is a popular recreation in the city and, as well as the markets, you can find a wide choice of boutiques and stores as well as a guide to an exclusive selection from the VVV. The Arena shopping centre provides a covered mall for all-weather shopping enjoyment.

Music and culinary festivals take place throughout the summer with the bi-annual Maritiem festival (3rd weekend in September in odd years) a highlight for boating visitors.

Restaurant tip
There are dining possibilities to suit all tastes and the harbour provides a summary leaflet with some local suggestions including Brasserie De Eeterij on Brede Haven with their good value three course choice menu, or Wok City on Havensingel, which offers a wide choice of dishes for a fixed price. For a typically Den Bosch experience head for the narrow streets off Visstraat where Spoon, on Lepelstraat, is highly recommended amongst a host of individual terrace restaurants and bistros. For a longer walk, Korte Putstraat is another area where you will find a good choice of dining options a little off the beaten track.

Free wi-fi is available at Bagels and Beans on Hooge Steenweg.

Connections
The train station is nearby to the west of Visbrug and is a hub for regular services to all destinations.

The canal tour heads underground along the Binnendieze

Zuid-Willemsvaart

The Zuid-Willemsvaart runs from 's-Hertogenbosch southeast via Helmond to Nederweert, then turns sharply to the southwest and crosses the Belgian border. At its confluence with the Kanaal van Bocholt naar Herenthals it continues southeast as the Zuid-Willemsvaart towards Maastricht. Just west of Maastricht the waterway splits into two, with the easternmost fork continuing as the Zuid-Willemsvaart back across the Belgian/Dutch border to join the Maas at Maastricht. This section is mainly of interest to boats wishing to access the marina at Maastricht and is dealt with in that section. The original course of the waterway passed west of Helmond, but this arm is now closed except for a short section at the southern end, and all navigation must take the eastern arm. This closed off arm gives access, under special permit, to the Eindhovenskanaal, but this is restricted to 2.7m headroom, so is not considered here.

For the most part the Zuid-Willemsvaart is a quiet canal with some wooded landscape, which is mainly used by small commercial barges. Built as a short cut between Liege and 's-Hertogenbosh when Belgium was still under Dutch rule, it has been largely surpassed by the Maas, which can accommodate bigger vessels. It is still popular with leisure boats and the Belgian section is described in *Inland Waterways of Belgium* (Imray).

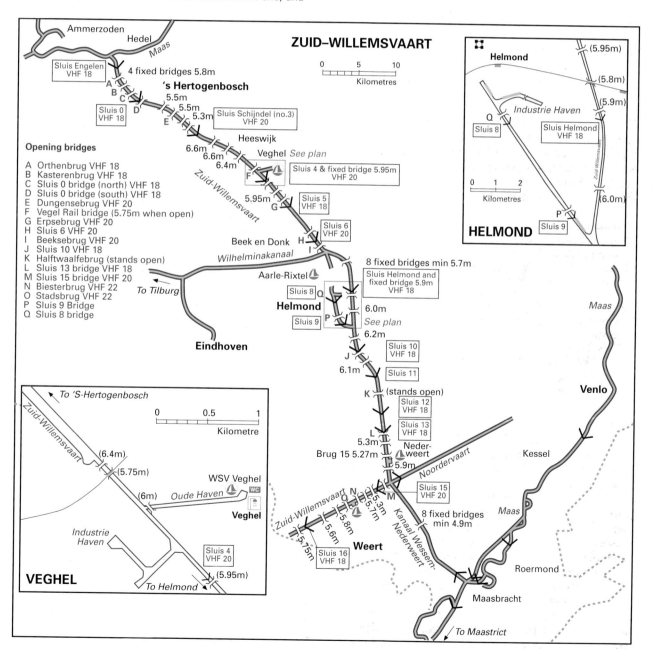

In 2006 some of the locks were being modernised whilst others were already computerised and worked efficiently when they weren't suffering from software failures. The level changes in the locks are significant (~2 metres at each one) and it is advisable to use the vertical poles to tie to.

's-Hertogenbosch to Nederweert

Length 61km
Maximum permitted draught 1.9m
Locks Sluis 0 (VHF 18), Sluis Schijndel, 4, 5, 6 (VHF 20), and Sluis Helmond, 10, 11, 12 & 13 (VHF 18) operate throughout the day (but only until 1600 on Saturdays and 1700 on Sundays).
Bridges 20 fixed (min 5.3m – maximum permitted air draught 5m), 5 opening. Orthen & Kasteren (VHF 18), and Dungense, Erpse and Beekse (VHF 20) bridges operate the same hours as the locks.

Nederweert to the Belgian border

Length 18.5km
Maximum permitted draught 2.1m
Locks Sluis 15 in Nederweert (VHF 20) and Sluis 16 in Weert (VHF 18) operate throughout the day (but only until 1600 on Saturdays and 1700 on Sundays).
Bridges 6 fixed (min 5.1m), 2 opening. Biester and Stadsbrug Weert operate throughout the day with rush hour breaks on weekdays (0800–0900 and 1600–1700) and until 1600 on Saturdays and 1700 on Sundays.

VEGHEL

At Veghel (pronounced 'fay-khel') a 6m bridge gives access to the visitors' harbour where WSV Veghel have good moorings on fixed landing stages. Water and pump-out are available at the reporting pontoon by the entrance and coin-operated electricity (€0.50/2kWh) is at all berths. The harbourmaster is based on site during the season and will allocate you a berth. In summer the harbour does get busy, but telephone reservations are not taken and there is normally space for everyone. Good basic facilities including two free loan bikes, which were a gift from the local cycle shop.

The harbour is close to the town centre, which was on the route taken by the land-based troops from Eindhoven to Nijmegen during Operation Market Garden. There is a large pedestrianised shopping centre close by and a market is held on Thursdays. Opposite the harbour, Eetcafe Havenzicht is recommended as being good value.

AARLE-RIXTEL/HELMOND

Free unserviced canalside moorings are available north of the Aarle-Rixtel bridge on the east bank in the closed (western) arm of the Zuid-Willemsvaart. There is room for about 20 boats of up to 12m length (depth 1.8m) and a maximum stay of 3 days is permitted. To the west of the canal, the small village has a handful of local shops and cafés.

The main navigation follows the eastern arm of the Zuid-Willemsvaart and there are free canalside moorings on the east bank of the closed (western) arm just south of Sluis 9. A rubbish bin and free water hose are available at the lock. For access to the town, Sluis 9 and 8 do operate throughout the day Monday–Friday and until 1400 on Saturday (closed Sundays) and there are moorings against a disused commercial quay on the east bank south of the Houtse Parallel bridge (north of Sluis 8). These are next to a large residential development site and a new bridge planned for 2007 may prohibit access here in the future. Immediately south of this quay an inlet to the east has moorings used mainly by barges with free water and electricity which are also a possibility for leisure boats. If you don't mind a cycle ride the moorings at Aarle-Rixtel or south of the lock are slightly more pleasant and are linked to Helmond by a canal-side cycle path.

The large town centre is north of the railway bridge and as well as the street organ museum you can also visit Kasteel Helmond which houses the municipal museum, and has open-air concerts in July and August. The old arm of the navigation has been converted into a town centre water feature and now bars and restaurants overlook the spot where the moorings used to be. The central train station is convenient and for an excursion this would be a suitable place from which to take a train to visit Eindhoven.

NEDERWEERT

A free visitors' harbour (depth 1.5m) has been provided south of bridge 15 which despite its narrow entrance experiences surges from passing barges. It is important to tie up well and although it is advised not to moor on the outside of the harbour in fact this spot is less susceptible to the surges, albeit more at risk of collision. Water and rubbish disposal is provided and boats may stay for a maximum stay of 2 days, but with the waterway destined to operate 24 hours this is not an ideal mooring and it is unlikely you would want to.

From here you could visit the Limburg Open Air Museum at Nederweert Eind which as well as turf huts, forge and farmer's ice-cream, has demonstrations of traditional crafts on Sundays, with the second Sunday in August being a special festival day. A weekly market is held in the village on Wednesdays and you can also cycle to the ice-cream farm and the artisan butcher which are near the museum.

For a longer excursion, the National Park De Grote Peel is about 4km to the northeast and cycle routes are marked from the harbour. A peat bog of some 1,400 hectares, the area is renowned for its diversity of bird life, and is also an important habitat for dragonflies and butterflies. There are boardwalk trails crossing the area and a new visitor centre and birdwatching hut.

WEERT

Just east of the Stadsbrug on the south bank is the modern visitors' harbour that has box moorings and unmetered electricity. The water berth is to port on entering next to the single automatic toilet. The harbourmaster is based in the bridge control office and you should report here if you intend staying longer than two hours.

One of the largest towns in Limburg, Weert (pronounced 'veert') has plenty of pedestrianised shopping streets and a covered mall, De Munt, on the site of the town's former mint, which lies to the south of the canal. St Martiniskerk dominates the market square with its 72-metre tower that, despite a 10-year maintenance programme scheduled until 2012 is open to visitors a number of times per year.

The regional museum, De Tiendschuur, depicts the history of life and work in Weert and the surrounding area and has changing exhibitions of temporary art.

To the west of the town is the IJzeren Man recreation park which has a sub-tropical wave pool as well as a Nature and Environment centre with permanent and changing exhibitions.

Kanaal Wessem-Nederweert

The Kanaal Wessem-Nederweert was excavated in the 1920s to connect the Zuid-Willemsvaart with the Maas without leaving Dutch territory. As straight as a die, it is bordered by trees on both sides and although the only features are the coots and anglers it is not an unpleasant cruise. Downstream of Panheel is the entrance to three large gravel pit lakes with a fixed bridge over the entrance (7m). The northern part of the first lake is very shallow and it is advisable to follow the buoys as far as the bridge over the connecting channel but elsewhere there is plenty of depth.

Length 16km
Speed limit 20km/h
Locks Sluis Panheel and fixed bridge (9.5m) operates throughout the day (until 1600 on Saturdays, 1700 on Sundays) VHF 84 (8m drop)
Bridges 9 fixed (minimum 5.0m)

Unserviced canalside moorings are available in Ell and north of the Trambrug. Further places are on the east bank north of the lock which are close to one of the wood-fringed Maas lakes and a small café. Beyond the lock the lakes provide further stopping opportunities or yacht harbour facilities are available after continuing into the Maas and stopping at Wessum. (See section on the river Maas, below.)

Noordervaart

This short stretch of waterway runs northeast from the junction of the Zuid-Willemsvaart and the Kanaal Wessem-Nederweert as far as Beringe but it does not connect with any other waterways and is little used.

Length 15km
Maximum permitted draught 1.65m
Lock Sluis Hulson is operated only on request with 24 hours notice to Sluis 16 in Weert ☎ 0495 532018.
Bridges 1 fixed (5.0m), 2 opening which operate in conjunction with the lock.

Maas (& Julianakanaal)

The river Maas is one of the four major rivers which flow through the Netherlands, starting in France and flowing through Belgium as the canalised Meuse. It reaches the Belgian/Dutch border downstream of the lock at Visé and forms the border between the two countries for the next 63km to Stevensweert. Much of this border section, north of Maastricht, has been bypassed by the Julianakanaal,

completed in 1934, which forms the normal route for water-borne traffic. The Julianakanaal rejoins the Maas at Maasbracht and just north of here the Lateralkanaal Linne-Buggenum forms another short cut, bypassing the Roermond loop. At Buggenum the Maas then continues as a canalised river for a further 129 km (to St Andries) to its confluence with the Bergse Maas west of Ammerzoden.

Although the official end of the Maas is at km 226.5, the actual distance is about 8km less due to the shortening of bends by cuttings.

To cross between Belgium and the Netherlands boats must join the Albertkanaal to pass through Sluis Lanaye; northbound, via the locked channel at Vise or at Luik/Liege; and southbound at km9 (north of Eijsden).

It is advisable for leisure boats to report to the locks on arrival, especially when there is heavy traffic, although they will normally be called in after the commercial vessels. Be prepared for light signals or loudspeaker instructions, and delays at busy times. Some locks have intercoms installed and all are contactable via VHF as given below. Leisure boat waiting pontoons are sometimes available, and at Born and Maasbracht overnighting is permitted. Locks on the Julianakanaal have large drops, especially those at Maasbracht (11.85m) and Born (11.35m) but these are equipped with floating bollards to aid mooring, with those to the rear of the locks spaced for leisure boats.

The Maas is bordered by a series of gravel pits or *plassen* which have been connected to the river for recreational use. These are home to a variety of yacht harbours and moorings, although some parts can be shallow. Bridges on these side channels are not less than 7m air draught.

The river is fed primarily by rainfall and there can be large variations in the depth and current. There is normally at least 2.8m depth in summer, and more in winter when floods and ice can occasionally close the waterway. Persistent heavy rain in Belgium can increase the normally negligible current to between 3–7km/hr. Boats navigating the Maas must have an engine capable of a minimum of 6km/hr and must keep to the starboard side of the channel except when directed otherwise, such as by barges showing the blue board signal (see CEVNI for details).

Red diesel was available from JH De Spaanjerd at the southern end of the Spanjaardplas (which is in Belgian territory) near Maasbracht but this was formally terminated in 2007.

Length 218km
Maximum permitted draught 2.8m
Speed limit 9km/h near moorings and on lakes, otherwise 20km/h
Locks 7 on main route. Operate 24 hours from Monday morning to Saturday evening and throughout the day on Sundays. These are from south to north:
Sluis Limmel (Julianakanaal) VHF 20 (normally stands open) Maximum permitted air draught under raised gate 6.75m
Sluis Born (Julianakanaal) VHF 22 (11.35m drop)
Sluis Maasbracht (Julianakanaal) VHF 20 (11.85m drop)
Sluis Heel (Lateralkanaal Linne-Buggenum) VHF18 (6.7m drop)
Sluis Linne (southern end of Roermond arm) VHF 22 (4m drop)
Sluis Roermond (northern end of Roermond arm) VHF 20 (2.7m drop)
Sluis Belfeld VHF 18 (3.25m drop)
Sluis Sambeek VHF 22 (3.25m drop)
Sluis Grave VHF 20 (2.6m drop)
Sluis Lith (also known as Prinses Maximasluis) VHF 22 (4m drop) South lock gate has an air draught of 7.1m when raised; North lock, no restriction
Bridges 37 fixed (min 6.75m), 1 opening – St Servaas bridge (5.85m when closed, 8.1m open) Operates throughout the day on request. VHF 20

EIJSDEN

Where to stop

WV Eijsden and the even smaller WSV Aqua Viva are located in a side arm of the river opposite km 5.5 on the east bank. WV Eijsden has limited space for boats up to 11m with basic facilities and a pleasant terrace café, whilst WSV Aqua can accommodate boats up to 14m but has only water and electricity.

Both are close to the village along a riverside footpath. Further north in the large leisure lake complex, Jachting Sondagh has a pleasant lakeside location and the usual basic facilities. It is also close to a popular lakeside beach park where you can hire pedalos and canoes.

What to see

The most southerly town in the Netherlands, Eijsden (pronounced 'Eyes-den') is a sleepy spot with a handful of small shops and some nice restaurants which cater mainly for parties of walkers and cyclists. Just south of the main street the gardens of the 17th-century Kasteel Eysden are open to the public during daylight hours. The riverbank walk continues along Voerbeek where there are three watermills.

If you take the cycle ferry across the Maas and then continue via Lanaye over the Albert canal, you can visit Fort Eben-Emael, an impressive complex of second world war bunkers with a permanent exhibition of Germany's secret weapons. Public tours restricted to one weekend per month.

MAASTRICHT

Where to stop

There are three options for mooring close to the city, the simplest of which are the free visitors' moorings between the St Servaas and the Wilhelmina bridges. This has no access or headroom restrictions, but facilities are limited to a rubbish disposal service.

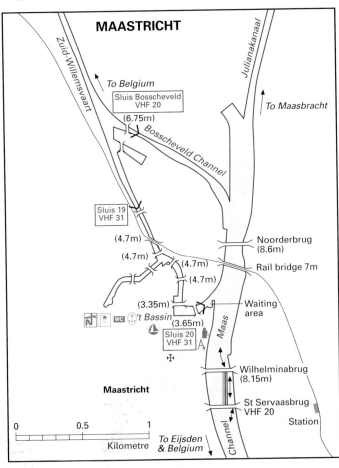

The Stadshaven 't Bassin is surrounded by chic harbourside bars and restaurants

There is no limit on length of stay and it can be very busy in the high season, with the usual reluctance from some boats to double moor. Although the barge traffic takes a separate channel, there can be some wash from the regular trip-boats that pass in something of a hurry.

To the north, the Bassin is situated in the historic inner harbour a few hundred metres from the Markt. Access from the Maas is via Sluis 20 which operates throughout the day but is restricted to 3.65m air draught by a fixed bridge. There are waiting berths just before Sluis 20 in the Voorhaven inside the piers, but these are not recommended for overnight stays. An alternative route to the Bassin is from the Zuid-Willemsvaart via Sluis 19. This route is restricted to 3.35m air draught, but there are moorings just outside the Bassin with access to the same facilities

which are accessible by boats up to 4.7m air draught (and not as shown on the *ANWB* chart). Sluis 19 can be accessed via the Bosscherveld channel on the left bank just south of the junction of the Maas and the Julianakanaal. You will need to call the harbourmaster on ☎ 06 5396 0349 (or VHF 31 if you have it) to request lock service which is available from 1100–1200 and 1530–1700 (summer only). Sluis Bosscherveld is crossed by a fixed bridge (6.75m) and operates throughout the day.

Also known as the Historische Stadshaven, the Bassin (or 't Bassin as it is known in Dutch) has unmetered 16A electricity and water as well as all usual facilities including launderette and pump-out in a facility beneath the bridge. It is often very busy but you can normally find space in the large basin and wi-fi is available. Surrounded by popular harbourside cafés and restaurants it is a lively spot, especially at weekends.

To the south of the city WV Treech '42 is a popular boat club with an active social programme. Founded in 1942 as a rowing club, 'Treech' is the name of the city in the local dialect. It lies to the south of the JFK bridge, in an inlet on the left bank. Here there are good facilities including unmetered water and 4A electricity, onsite swimming pool and restaurant. The quiet leafy location is still only 2km from the centre and there are local shopping facilities close by.

Immediately south and still on the left bank, a further inlet is home to WV MCC and diagonally opposite this JH Pietersplas is situated in a small gravel pit and has wi-fi. Petrol is available opposite the ENCI cement factory. Fuel and a well-stocked chandlers are available at the Shell bunker boat on the left bank of the main river, 200m north of the Wilhelmina bridge.

Take a boat trip to the Zonneberg caves from opposite the St Servaas visitors' quay

Facilities ashore

Fuel & Chandlers Nautica Jansen (Shell) bunker boat 200m north Wilhelmina bridge (cards accepted)

Repairs and Servicing Ask the harbourmaster at WV Treech for advice on local contractors

Supermarket & Shops All facilities at Centre Ceramique to east of JFK bridge. City centre markets on Wednesday and Friday.

ATMs West end of JFK bridge or all around the city

Cycle hire Courtens Bike Sport on Calvariestraat, or Aon de Stasie, Parallelweg (Train station)

VVV office Het Dinghuis on Kleine Staat

What to see

Located at the site of a Roman ford across the River Meuse, Maastricht (pronounced 'mars-trikt') has for centuries been a strategic location which has had to withstand many sieges. As a result the city was heavily defended and parts of the medieval fortifications still remain. To the south of the centre an area of parkland has been laid out around the city walls, which include the Helpoort gate, claimed to be the oldest in the Netherlands. An exhibition in the tower explains the history of the fortress of Maastricht, and a fortifications walk available in English from the VVV describes the whole route.

Just outside the city, Berg St Pieter is notable as the only hill in the area, but its significance lies below the surface where a labyrinth of underground tunnels are the result of centuries of marl excavation for building stone. Tours of the 20,000 passages take place in English at the Zonneberg (southern) caves every day in July and August. The caves have been used as a place of refuge for local citizens for centuries and most recently, during the second world war, as a storage vault for a large part of Holland's national art treasures. Fort St Pieter, constructed in 1701, lies at the northernmost point of the complex and from the terraces you can enjoy a view across the entire city.

Maastricht is rich in ecclesiastical treasures, and many of these are on display at the Treasury Basilica St Servaas and the Basilica of Our Lady. The Romanesque churches date from the 10th and 11th centuries and the Basilica of St Servaas is the only church in the Netherlands built above the grave of a saint. Next door, the St Janskerk has a 70-metre tower open to visitors daily during the summer. For a novelty tour of the city, there is the Maastricht City Tram, an English Double Decker, or an American School Bus, which all depart from the Vrijtof in front of the Basilica St Servaas. From Onze Lieve Vrouwenplein you can take the horse-drawn coach tour every afternoon except Monday. Or on water, the Pallieter boat tour departs from the Stadshaven Bassin and there are more trips departing from the Maas Promenade, opposite the St Servaas bridge moorings. The VVV provides good information in English on local attractions including a walking tour of the city and the central square has general markets on Wednesday and Friday mornings. On other days there are speciality markets on Boschstraat and Stationstraat.

The harbour day band gets into the swing at Maasbracht

Every weekend is festival weekend in the summer and annual highlights include the main town festival of St Servaas in May and the Burgundian food festival in August.

Restaurant tip

There is a good choice around the Bassin harbour and the Vrijtof square, or the VVV office provides a free gastronomic guide to the city.

Connections

The train station is on the east bank nearest to St Servaas bridge for services to Roermond and all points north, as well as international services.

MAASBRACHT

Where to stop

There are no stopping places on the Julianakanaal, except for waiting places both sides of the Maasbracht locks, at which overnighting is permitted. The best place to stop for a visit to Maasbracht is north of the locks, in the dead-end arm on the east side. At the southern end of this arm, near Restaurant De Kolentip is the municipal visitors' harbour (depth 1.8m) where unmetered electricity and water are provided. Moorings are supposed to be restricted to boats up to 10m length but longer vessels can be accommodated if space allows. A maximum stay of three days is permitted and an overnight charge is payable after 1800.

Alternative mooring places can be found in a spur off the Maas river, west of the Maasbracht lock at Maasbrachter WSV or Van der Laan Yachting – which is recommended as a good place to keep a boat for the winter.

Fuel is available from the bunker boat to the north of the lock on the west bank.

What to see

As one of the largest inland ports in the Netherlands, the quayside at Maasbracht is always lined with barges, and nautical facilities in the town run to three chandlers, of which the biggest is Wim Houben on Kloosterstraat. If you like Linssen boats you will also be interested to visit their showroom in the

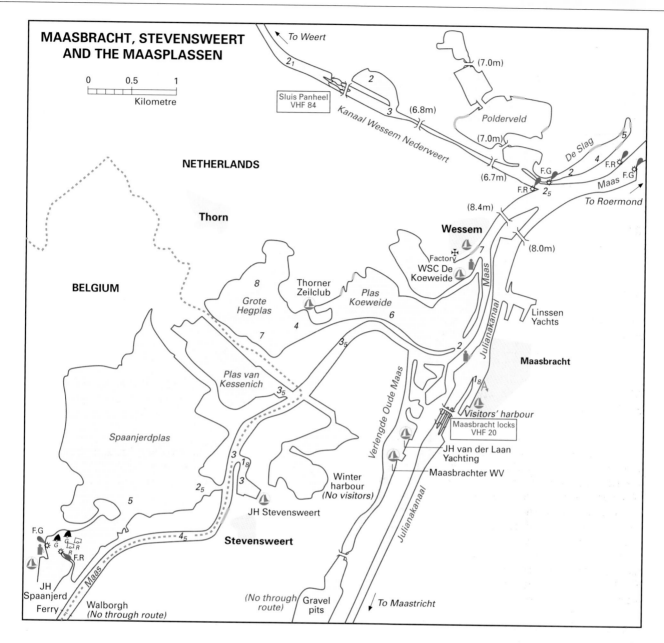

MAASBRACHT, STEVENSWEERT AND THE MAASPLASSEN

Industriehaven, but they no longer offer moorings to visiting boats. The history of the port and shipping on the Maas is depicted in the small Maas & Scheepvaart Museum on Havenstraat, which also serves as the VVV information point. One of the most popular sights in town is a visit to the lock complex, where a gallery is provided for onlookers to observe the 12m drop, the largest in the Netherlands.

A good time to visit is the last weekend in June when more than 80 marine businesses set out their stalls on Havenstraat and the town is *en fête* with music and merriment. Once every five years on the last Sunday in September (next in 2009), a huge waterborne procession takes place through the harbour.

Restaurant tip

Groups of four can book a tour of the harbour guided by a former barge skipper finishing with lunch or dinner at Restaurant De Kolentip.

STEVENSWEERT AND THE MAASPLASSEN

North of Maasbracht the Julianakanaal rejoins the Maas and the west fork of the river that continues south gives access to a complex of lakes, known as the Maasplassen, which have been formed through gravel extraction which continues apace. There is no through route south on this arm but it is well worth a detour to visit the attractive and historic small towns nearby.

Where to stop

The first stopping place you come to is at Wessem, where there is a visitors' pontoon on the west side near the town. These are suitable for a short visit but are exposed to wash from passing traffic. On the east side, beyond the yacht service and fuel barge is Watersport Centrum De Koeweide which enjoys all facilities including wi-fi, but has an unfortunate view of the neighbouring gravel plant. The town has an attractive cobbled market square where the last vestige of the weekly market is a solitary cheese stall on Thursday afternoons.

Continuing south on the Maas you will come to the entrance to Spanjaardplas on the west side of the river at km 62, where JH De Spanjaard, because of its unique position in Belgian territory, was once a popular refuelling point. The best place to stop is JH Stevensweert, which lies to the east of the Maas, opposite Spanjaardplas. Here you will find a friendly welcome from the on-site harbour managers and good facilities including wi-fi.

What to see

The small village was originally a Spanish fortification and the web-shaped street plan reflects the encircling canal that once protected it. The cycle shop on the square not only hires bikes, but is also the post office and VVV and can provide details of the historic town walk and regional museum.

A nice excursion by bike from Stevensweert crosses the Maas on the Walborgh ferry just south of the village and then continues north to Thorn. Known as the 'white village', Thorn was founded as a home for noble ladies and the gothic church was the focal point of the secular convent foundation to which they all belonged. The baroque interior is typical of the feminine touch throughout the village, and a visit to the church includes a slide show explaining the history of the town (with English commentary). For the Dutch the highlight of the visit is a stop at the Pannekoekenbakker, but you can find many other nice hostelries around the village.

Restaurant tip

Restaurant Chambor in Stevensweert does not have a fixed menu but offers a daily four-course selection based on seasonal specialities. On the Markt, 't Oad Kloaster offers traditional Dutch fare, except for Thursdays which is 'Schnitzel day'.

ROERMOND

Where to stop

Continuing north from Maasbracht you have a choice of taking the Lateralkanaal Linne-Buggenum, or the original winding course of the Maas which it bypasses. This longer route threads its way amongst a number of large lakes, again formed through sand and gravel extraction and now used for recreational boating. The lack of commercial traffic makes it a tranquil oasis and there are excellent facilities for watersports, making it an attractive place to keep a boat, especially for Germans from across the nearby border. To the south of Roermond, the suburb village of Herten has good facilities at JH De Rosslag (owned by the same company as JH Stevensweert), including unmetered electricity and water, on-site café-restaurant and wi-fi. There are local facilities in the village, where a harbour festival is held mid-July, or it is 10 minutes by bike along the riverside path to Roermond.

Close to the city centre in Haven La Bonne Aventure, WV Nautilus has prime position with a large harbour in a sheltered inlet off the main river. Their visitors' berths are very popular in summer and it is a good idea to phone in the morning to

The magnificent high alter in Thorn's abbey church

reserve a berth. Water and 6A electricity are unmetered but you won't find any hoses as they worry about Legionnaires disease. Gated access ensures security close to the city and there are good on-site facilities. No launderette here, but a local firm will collect and deliver if required.

For a more peaceful berth there are harbours in most of the lakes with all usual facilities, or free unserviced lakeside moorings in the Zuidplas. Between WV Nautilus and the bridge there are free town centre moorings which are for daytime stays only.

Facilities ashore

Fuel & Chandlers JH Snellens in Herten
Chandlers Driessen Watersport or Helenwerf, both at Haven La Bonne Aventure
Service facilities Ask the harbourmaster for advice on local contractors
Supermarket & Shops Jan Linders in Herten, or Jumbo in Roermond. City centre markets on Wednesday and Saturday.
ATMs In the Markt
Cycle hire At the train station
VVV office Kraanport, near the Markt

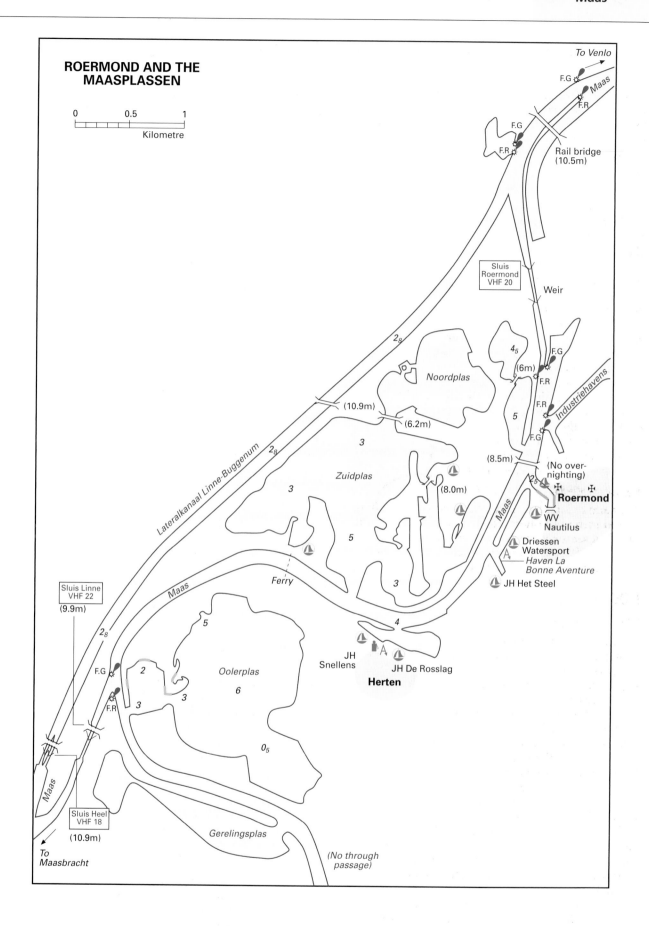

ROERMOND AND THE MAASPLASSEN

0   0.5   1
Kilometre

To Venlo

F.G
F.R

Maas

F.G
F.R

Rail bridge
(10.5m)

Sluis
Roermond
VHF 20

Weir

4_5

(6m)

F.G

F.R

2_8

Noordplas

F.R

5

Industriehavens

(10.9m)

(6.2m)

F.G

3

(8.5m)

Zuidplas

5

(No over-
nighting)

2_8

(8.0m)

2_5

Roermond

3

WV
Nautilus

5

Lateralkanaal Linne-Buggenum

Driessen
Watersport
Haven La
Bonne Aventure

3

JH Het Steel

Maas

Ferry

Sluis Linne
VHF 22
(9.9m)

4

2_8

5

JH
Snellens

JH De Rosslag

F.G

2

Herten

3

Oolerplas

3

6

F.R

0_5

Maas

Sluis Heel
VHF 18

(10.9m)

Gerelingsplas

(No through
passage)

To
Maasbracht

Take a carriage tour from the Munsterkerk on Sundays

What to see

A bishopric was founded in Roermond (pronounced 'ruur-mont') in 1559 and to this day it remains the religious capital of this very Catholic province. It is dominated by its churches of which the oldest is the 13th-century Onze Lieve Vrouwe Munsterkerk. On the edge of town, the 14th-century Rattentoren is the only remnant of the city wall. Today Roermond is a busy commercial and industrial centre and its extensive central shopping streets are supplemented by a popular designer outlet village nearby.

The town was the home of the renowned Dutch architect P. Cuypers and his house on Andersonweg is now the municipal museum. Weekly markets are held on Wednesdays and Saturdays and the market square is also used for special events on Sundays in the summer. Tours of the town can be made by horse-drawn carriage on Sundays from the Munsterkerk or by trip boat from the town quay.

Restaurant tip

The Markt square is packed with café-restaurants and on Sundays you can enjoy the free concerts and speciality markets.

Connections

The central train station is nearby for services to Maastricht and Eindhoven.

ROERMOND TO VENLO

Several small villages have yacht clubs or visitors' moorings, starting with WV Ascola on the Asseltse Plassen, to the east of the river. At Neer, WSV Hanssum has the usual basic facilities and the nearby nature reserve is a popular area for walking and cycling. Home to over 100 species of birds, there is a visitor centre in an 18th-century grain mill which is still in working order. At Kessel you can stop in the small visitors' harbour at the north end of the trip boat and ferry quay. A weekly market is held on Tuesday mornings and you can visit the remains of the Roman castle, blown up by the Germans at the end of the second world war. For a more sheltered berth opt for WV Poseiden to the north of the town. Just south of Venlo, Blerick has a visitors' harbour near the centre of the old agricultural village which is now part of the municipality of Venlo. Facilities limited to rubbish disposal and a quayside café.

VENLO

North of the road and rail bridges a visitors' harbour has been established on the east bank, close to the city centre. Moorings are on pontoons with 16A coin-operated electricity and rubbish disposal provided. These are convenient for a visit to the city but are not the most attractive or comfortable berths being surrounded by a half-finished quayside development project and open to wash from passing traffic. Alternatively, WV De Maas is a further 2km downstream, next to the industrial harbour. Usual basic facilities are available and the nearby Noorderbrug makes it just a 10 minute cycle ride to the town.

A settlement has existed on this site since Roman times, although many of the historic buildings were destroyed in the second world war. The VVV office on Koninginneplein provides details of a walk around the significant sites, which include the Limburgs Museum. This striking building recalls the ramparts that stood on this site and was opened in 2000. Twelve themed presentations tell the history of the region from prehistoric hunter to modern man, starting with the multi-media presentation, 'Historoscoop', narrated by Mother Maas.

Venlo (pronounced 'fen-lo') is the centre of the market gardening region and just to the north is the asparagus capital of the Netherlands at Grubbenvorst. North of the town you can visit the National Asparagus and Mushroom Museum, De Locht. Good shopping facilities and train station are close to the city centre.

ARCEN

The small town of Arcen (pronounced 'arson') has become quite a resort and boasts a thermal baths as well as a sauna park. A small municipal visitors' harbour is provided for short visits but is not permitted for overnight stays. The town is most famous for its 18th-century castle which has 80 acres of themed gardens, including a Rosarium, oriental garden and sub-tropical glasshouse. Hertog Jan

Visitors' harbours are provided at most towns and villages on the Maas; but many, like this one at Arcen, are not permitted for overnight stops

Brewery is 1.5km north of the town and at their onsite brewery tap De Proeverij you can sample their range of brews, as you can at every terrace in town. The watermill is used for milling grain to make *jenever* (Dutch gin) and asparagus liqueurs.

WANSSUM

Beyond the container depot and the numerous silos the slightly run-down moorings at JH Wansum offer adequate basic facilities in a sheltered harbour. A supermarket and chinese restaurant are close at hand, and for a longer excursion it is a 30-minute bike ride to the National War and Resistance Museum at Overloon. Sited at the location of a major tank battle of Operation Market Garden, the extensive collection includes a permanent exhibition on the plight of those held in POW camps and is next door to the Overloon War Graves Cemetery.

WELL

North of the village a lakeside recreation area lies east of the river in the Leukermeer. There are free places for bow-to mooring against a grassy bank in the Voorhaven, whilst the fully serviced JH 't Leuken is situated beyond the 8m bridge. The visitors' pontoon is outside the main harbour overlooking the lake, and water, electricity and pump-out are available here. Opposite at Recreatiecentrum Leukermeer there are a few alongside moorings by the restaurant, pool and beach, where pedalos and canoes can also be hired. The small village is some 3km away and the 14th-century Kasteel Well is used as a school by Emerson College (Boston, Massachusetts) but the gardens are open to the public.

BOXMEER

The small harbour of WSV Boxmeer lies in a quiet leafy spot in a closed arm of the river but is too isolated from the village to be of significant interest to most visiting boats.

GENNEP

Where to stop

WSC De Paesplas is located in the northern most of a series of early gravel pits, and enjoys a pleasant rural aspect, although visitors should take care at the shallow entrance. The reporting pontoon and outer berths are due for renewal by club members but those nearer the shore are suitable for larger boats and there is a harbourmaster on hand to direct you to a berth. The mooring fee includes unmetered water and 6A electricity (16A on the quay wall) and there are the usual basic facilities provided. The clubhouse is limited to liquid refreshments, but there is a special barbeque area away from the moorings equipped with fixed grills, tables and chairs.

What to see

The town is about 1.5km away but the harbour has free loan bikes for shopping excursions. Gennep (pronounced 'khennep') lies on the site of a former Roman settlement and archaeological finds have provided evidence of centuries-old pottery works. The town remains an important centre for pottery to this day and the North Limburg Pottery Collective is based locally. Examples can be seen in the mosaic on Ellen Hoffmanplein and in the Museum Het Petershuis on Niersstraat. An international ceramics fair is held every third weekend in September. South of the town lies the 4,200 hectare Maasduinen National Park and you can view the variety of amphibians, reptiles and birds from the Observation Hut on the shores of Westmeerven.

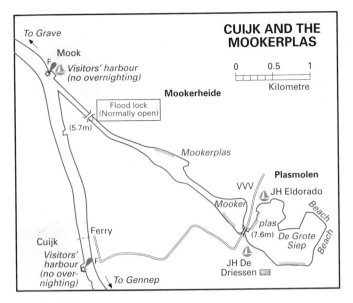

castle stood on the west bank where the neo-gothic church now stands. The old tower adjoining it was part of a 14th-century church and prison, and now houses Museum Ceuclum, a well-presented display of Roman finds from the surrounding area. These include many day-to-day artefacts as well as some of the 400 steel-tipped piles which supported the brick-built bridge. As well as the exhibits you can also climb the tower and enjoy a good view of the Maas valley across to the ice-age ridge of the Mookerheide. Also close by are a small sculpture garden and the Amerika museum, dedicated to the original cultures of North, Mid and South America. In the 19th century Cuijk was the location of several tanneries and the high street still seems to host more than the usual number of shoe shops as well as a good selection of shops for regular supplies. A busy market is held in front of the new town hall on Tuesdays from 1100.

CUIJK

Where to stop

The small visitors' harbour at Cuijk is only permitted for daytime stays and even the inside berths are affected by wash. However, a short stop at this interesting town is well worthwhile and beyond the unpromising-looking motorway bridge the old town is close at hand. For a longer stay there are several mooring opportunities in the Kraaijenbergse Plassen to the north of the town. WV De Kraaijenbergse Plassen has a large site in the first lake, to starboard on entering after the open-standing flood lock, beyond a 7.6m bridge. If you continue under a further (8.7m) bridge you come to a further lake where free lakeside bow-to moorings are possible on the south side, although noise from the nearby motorway bridge is quite noticeable. Further still WSC 't Loo has space for boats up to 12m as part of its extensive campsite complex.

What to see

Cuijk (pronounced 'cowk') was another important Roman settlement and in 400AD was the location of the first and only bridge across the Maas. A large

MOOK AND THE MOOKERPLAS

Where to stop

The small visitors' harbour is protected by a wave break but is again unsuitable for overnight stays, although it is close to the small village. Just a couple of café-restaurants are available in the centre which has a busy crossroads running through it. Just south is the entrance to the Mookerplas, the most northerly of the Limburg lakes. Beyond the first fixed bridge (5.7m) there are lakeside bow-to moorings and anchoring possibilities, and beyond the second bridge (7.6m) two yacht harbours with all facilities. On the west bank is the friendly cooperative yacht harbour De Driesen which has unmetered water and 10A electricity, as well as a popular terrace restaurant. On the opposite bank, JH Eldorado is a more commercial marina with every conceivable amenity but electricity is coin-operated and the berths more expensive.

What to see

Mook (pronounced 'moke') and the Mookerheide were the site of the 1574 battle in which William of Orange and his legion of freedom fighters defeated the Spanish. Today the surrounding woodland is part of a national forestry area which is a favourite haunt for Nordic walkers, cyclists and joggers. You can enjoy a view over the Maas valley from the Heumens Schans, a fortified remnant of those battle-scarred days. A more recent battle is commemorated in the Mook war cemetery on Groesbeekseweg, last resting place of parachutists of the 82nd US Airborne Division who landed in the village in September 1944. A small VVV office is on the Plasmolen (east) side and the ferry to Cuijk is an easy bike ride away.

Restaurant tip

The Loopplank at De Driesen has a good value daily special or you can walk or cycle to Plasmolen where you can enjoy the facilities of De Grote Siep day beach as well as a visit to another of the Pannekoekenbakker chain of pancake houses.

Enjoy a bird's eye view of the town from the top of the old tower

The Maaspoort gives access onto café society in Grave

HEUMEN

The small yacht club at Heumen is very close to the motorway and not recommended for visitors. The sleepy village centre has one grocers if you are in dire need of stores.

GRAVE

Where to stop

Free visitors' moorings are situated close to the Maaspoort just upstream of the lock and the yacht harbour entrance. These are convenient for daytime visits as a fee is chargeable at the yacht harbour after 1300. At WVS De Stuw there are well-specified new box moorings laid out for visitors near the entrance to the harbour, with unmetered 6A electricity and water included in the mooring fee. Harbourmasters duties are fulfilled voluntarily by members so you can find a space and expect a visit around 1900. On site facilities include pump-out and mast crane.

What to see

The strategic position of Grave (pronounced 'khrarfa') meant it was frequently besieged and it became one of the most fought over towns in the Netherlands. In more recent times, the canons that stand on the city wall have mainly been used to warn of floods. The market square lies between the St Elizabeth church and the old town hall, and a market is held here on Friday mornings. Every first Sunday in July a musical festival is held with numerous acts and performers in venues all around the town.

RAVENSTEIN

WV Windkracht is a small harbour on the edge of the village in a quiet spot overlooked by a popular terrace restaurant. There is limited space for boats up to 15m with the usual basic facilities. The fortifications date from the 14th century when the local duke fell out with his opposite number on the Gelderland side of the river. The stage-mill De Nijverheid stands on the site of a former wooden mill and is open to the public on Friday afternoons. The 30m high structure is built on top of a bastion of the town wall and you can enjoy a good view over the town from the top. In the town centre you can visit the museum of glass and enamel art on Marktstraat, where you will also find a small market on Friday afternoons. The history of the city and its monumental buildings are described in the walking tour available (in English) from the VVV office in the mill.

MAASBOMMEL

Gravel extraction along a disused arm of the river has created a large lake complex for water sports and recreation. The first harbour to port on entering is WV De Gouden Ham which has all usual facilities and plenty of space for visitors, but you will find free lakeside moorings for daytime stops and several other harbours to choose from. The amenities in the pretty village are limited to one grocers and a small selection of café-restaurants. An information centre is near the lake entrance where you will also find a foot/cycle ferry, which runs in summer across to Appeltern. If you are a keen gardener you will not want to miss the Tuinen van Appeltern, Europe's largest model garden park with more than 180 separate themed exhibits.

LITH

There are free visitors' pontoons just downstream of the ferry where daytime only stops are permitted. The pretty market square is lined with lime trees and there are a choice of cafés, restaurants and shops. Lith (pronounced 'lit') is best known for the large weir and lock complex, which provides a fish ladder, mainly used these days by young eel. East of the lock in the disused arm of the river there is a bunkerstation on the way to the large water sports centre of Jan De Groot at Lithoijen where there is plenty of space and all facilities. West of Lith there is a lakeside marina in the Lithse Ham, another gravel pit turned recreation area.

HEEREWARDEN

The watersports and camping centre at WSV Heerewaarden is a good place to stop for a visit to the Great Rivers Visitor Centre on Langestraat. The small educational centre concentrates on river fishing and local wildlife and from the tower in the garden you can see both the Maas and the Waal.

ALEM

Once part of Brabant province, this tiny village is now in Gelderland and the disused arm of the river is home to JH De Maas, accessed via the Kanaal van Sint Andries lock, where wi-fi is available.

KERKDRIEL

Several marinas are located in the gravel pits on the outskirts of the village. Marina De Brink is owner-managed and offers a comprehensive service including solarium, restaurant and heart defibrillator. Water is coin-operated (€0.50/100 ltrs) but 16A electricity is included and the marina can provide detailed information on local amenities. The moorings are opposite the entrance to the mere and as well as bikes, canoes and pedaloes can be borrowed for use on the quiet lakes. Fuel and a small chandlers are available at the bunker boat just north of the lake entrance, and a further chandlers at the neighbouring Van Gent marina. On the second lake, Restaurant De Oude Klipper is recommended for a slightly more upmarket experience.

HEDEL

Just west of the 's-Hertogenbosch road bridge, two small harbours are situated in a gravel pit on the north bank. WSV 't Stik is to port and takes boats up to 12m, whilst at the far end to starboard JH Hedel can take boats up to 18m. The small town has the usual shopping facilities and the historical museum on Voorstraat has a collection of coin seals from when they had their own mint.

AMMERZODEN

JH Ammerzoden has adequate facilities for an overnight stop including on site restaurant. The nearby 14th century moated Kasteel Ammersoyen is partly used as the town hall and for temporary exhibitions, and the great hall, ladies apartments and tower rooms are open to visitors.

Cruising in the Southeast Netherlands

It is hoped that this more detailed summary of the waterways of the Southeast Netherlands will encourage English speaking yachtsmen to cruise the area more extensively rather than just use it as a through route from Belgium. For those already cruising along the Volkerak an excursion along the Mark and Dintel navigation is possible for mast-up yachtsmen as far as Dinteloord, but motor boaters could consider cruising further and enjoying Oudenbosch, for example, a charming and hospitable town worth visiting.

For those on longer cruises, the route southeast through 's-Hertogenbosch along the Zuid-Willemsvaart and Kanal Wessem-Nederweert will take you to the heart of the lovely Maasplassen in the Maasbracht area where it is well worth relaxing in Roermond or Stevensweert and enjoying the amenity before cruising back down the Maas with the current of this river navigation in your favour.

This whole area, now documented here in English for the first time, will come as a surprise to even those long-term visitors dedicated to the Dutch waterways and gives genuine credence to the truism that 'the more you know, the more you know you don't know'!

Glossary

The Dutch waterways can seem rather impenetrable at first, with many of the names seemingly unpronounceable and every word a yard long. This glossary is designed to familiarise you with some common terms which are regularly used in relation to the waterways or in day to day life.

aanlegplaats / ligplaats	mooring place
afval / restafval	rubbish
ANWB	association for tourism
bakboord	port (side)
bediening	service (opening) times
benzine	petrol
betalen	pay
betonning	buoyage
bezet	busy
boei/ton	buoy
beweegbare brug (BB)	moveable/opening bridge
bezoekers	visitors
binnen (haven)	inner (harbour)
breedte	breadth/beam
bromfiets/brommer	moped
brug (bruggen)	bridge (bridges)
brug/sluis geld	bridge/Lock toll
buiten (haven)	outer (harbour)
diepgang	draught
diepte	depth
diesel	diesel
doorvaarthoogte	headroom/air draught
douche	shower
draaibrug	swing bridge
fiets / fietspad / fietsverhuur	bicycle / cycle path / cycle hire
gat / geul / vaarwater	navigational channel
geen (eg ligplaats)	no (mooring)
gesloten	closed
haven (kantoor)	harbour (office)
hefbrug	bridge raised vertically
jachthaven (JH)	yacht harbour
jachtwerf	boatyard
liggeld verplicht na.....	mooring fee payable after... (time)
marifoon	VHF radio
meldsteiger	reporting pontoon
melden bij havenkantoor/ havenmeester	report to the harbour office / harbour master
nieuwe (haven)	new (harbour)
markt	market place
ondiep	shallow
ophaalbrug	bridge raised by an overhead lever
oude markt	old market place
reparatie (haven)	repair (harbour)
singel/gracht	(moat) canal
sluis (sluizen)	lock (locks)
spoorbrug	railway bridge
stroom	current/electricity
stuurboord	starboard (side)
touw	rope
vast brug (VB)	fixed bridge (non-opening)
vast gedeelte	fixed part (e.g. of an opening bridge)
veer / veerpont	ferry / floating bridge
verboden	forbidden
verboden aan te meren/ verboden afmeren	no mooring
vissershaven	fishing harbour
vrij	free
VVV	tourist office
waarschuwing	warning
wasserette / wassalon	launderette
waterstand	water level
winkels	shops
winkelponton	shopping pontoon
WSV / WV (Watersport Vereniging) / VVW (Vereniging Voor Watersport)	water sport (yacht) club

Communication Essentials

ja	yes
nee	no
alstublieft	please
dankuwel	thank you

Greetings

Goedemorgen	Good morning
Goedemiddag	Good afternoon
Goedenavond	Good evening
Hallo	Hello
Dag	Hello and bye
Tot ziens	Till I see you
Dooi!	Byee!

Questions

wat	what
wanneer	when
waar	where
hoe	how
waarom	why

Directions

noord (N)	north
zuid (Z)	south
oost (O)	east
west (W)	west

Days (normally written without capitals)

maandag (ma)	Monday
dinsdag (di)	Tuesday
woensdag (wo)	Wednesday
donderdag (do)	Thursday
vrijdag (vr)	Friday
zaterdag (zat)	Saturday
zondag (zd)	Sunday
feestdag (fd)	holiday
vandaag	today
gisteren	yesterday
morgen	tomorrow

Months (also written without capitals)

januari	January
februari	February
maart	March
avril	April
mei	May
juni	June
juli	July
augustus	August
september	September
oktober	October
november	November
december	December

Numbers (1–10)

een	one
twee	two
drie	three
vier	four
vijf	five
zes	six
zeven	seven
acht	eight
negen	nine
tien	ten

Weather forecast (Weersverwachting)

zon	sun
regen	rain
neerslag	precipitation
bewolkt	cloudy
half bewolkt	partly cloudy
mooi	good/nice
matige	moderate
slecht	poor
veranderlijk	changeable
buien	showers
onweer	thunder
kans op	chance of

Pronunciation

Throughout the book the symbol 'kh' has been used in the pronunciation hints to represent the sound of the Dutch letter g, which is similar to the 'ch' sound in the Scottish word 'loch', pronounced with as much emphasis as you can manage.

'd'	at the end of a word normally sounds like	't'
'en'	at the end of a word normally sounds like	'er'
'e'	at the end of a word normally sounds like	'er'
'w'	often sounds like	'v'
'v'	often sounds like	'f'

Common vowel sounds which will help you to pronounce words correctly are:

'aa'	eg in Aalsmeer sounds like 'ar' as in market
'ee'	eg in Sneek sounds like 'a' as in plate
'eu'	eg in Terneuzen sounds like 'oo' as in too
'ij'	eg in Nijmegen sounds like 'I' or sometimes as in the number 5 (vijf) sounds like 'ay' as in tray
'oo'	eg in Hindeloopen (and stroopwafel) sounds like 'oa' as in boat
'oe'	eg in Hoek van Holland sounds like 'oo' as in hook
'ou'	eg in Oude Maas sounds like 'ow' as in house
'ui'	eg in IJmuiden sounds like 'ow' as in house

Food & Dining

aardappels (gebakken)	potatoes (fried)
aardbeien	strawberries
appelgebak	dutch apple pie
appelsap	apple juice
asperges	asparagus
belegde broodjes	filled rolls
belegen kaas	matured cheese
biefstuk	rumpsteak
biefstuk van de haas / tournedos	fillet steak
bitterballen	breaded meat balls
brood	bread
broodje	bread roll
dagschotel	dish of the day
ei (eieren)	egg (eggs)
forel (zalm forel)	trout (sea trout)
frites/patat	chips
gambas	large prawns
garnalen	shrimps
gebak	tart/pie
gebakken	fried
gerookte	smoked
gesneden	sliced (for bread)
groenten	vegetables
haring / nieuwe haring	herring / fresh salted herring
jonge / licht belegen	semi-matured cheese
kaas	cheese
kabeljauw	cod
kalkoen	turkey
kersen	cherries
kip (filet)	chicken (fillet)
knoflook	garlic
kreeft	lobster
lepel	spoon
loempia	spring roll
mes	knife
mosselen	mussels
ontbijt	breakfast
paling	eel
rekening	bill
rundvlees	beef
rundergehakt	minced beef braising
runderlap	braising steak
salade/sla	salad
schelpdieren (or zeevis)	seafood
schelvis	haddock
schol	plaice
sinaasappel	orange
slagroom	(sweetened) whipped cream
spek	bacon
suiker	sugar
tong	sole
tonijn	tuna
uitsmijter	fried eggs on bread (often with ham or cheese)
varkensvlees	pork
varkenshaas	pork loin
varkenskotelet	pork chop
vlaai	flan/tart/pie
vlees	meat
vork	fork
zalm	salmon
zeebaars	sea bass
zeeduivel	monkfish
zoet	sweet
zout	salt

Getting to know your ANWB Wateralmanak 2

Services for leisure boats in the Netherlands

Explanation of facilities section

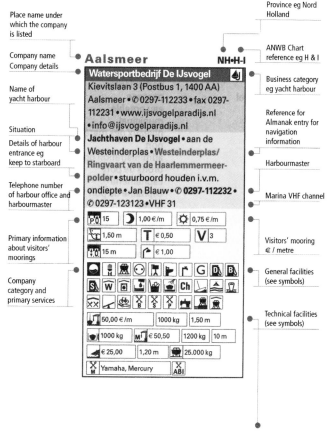

Province eg Nord Holland

ANWB Chart reference eg H & I

Business category eg yacht harbour

Reference for Almanak entry for navigation information

Harbourmaster

Marina VHF channel

Visitors' mooring € / metre

General facilities (see symbols)

Technical facilities (see symbols)

Place name under which the company is listed

Company name Company details

Name of yacht harbour

Situation

Details of harbour entrance eg keep to starboard

Telephone number of harbour office and harbourmaster

Primary information about visitors' moorings

Company category and primary services

For the technical facilities of hoist, boat lift, trailer slipway, and boat slipway, the cost, the maximum capacity and the maximum depth are given.
For the mast crane, the maximum length of the mast is indicated.

For engine repair businesses that do not work on all makes of engines the specific makes worked on are given.

Before making use of technical facilities, it is advisable to seek a quote from the business.

The introductory pages of the Almanak include English translations of the Abbreviations (Afkortingen: page 19-21), Keywords (Trefwoorden: page 22-23) and Explanation of Symbols (page 29). Studying these will help the reader to understand the Almanak entries. (Page numbers refer to 2007 edition).

The main body of the *Wateralmanak* is divided into three alphabetical sections, which are indexed with blue tabs on the edge of the pages.

The first section is **Navigational information for Dutch waterways and places**. Each waterway and place is listed alphabetically with its relevant details. This section is indexed at the back of the book in the section marked 'Wateren/plaatsen' and an example of one of these sections is given on the next page.

The second section is **Facilities for leisure boaters in the Netherlands** (see illustration). This section lists all marinas and other nautical business, alphabetically by place name, and describes the facilities available at each one using the common symbols. This section is indexed at the back of the book in the section marked 'Voorzieningen'.

The third section is **Water tourism information for Belgian places and waterways**. This is more restricted coverage of the main Flemish Belgian areas which might be visited and is also indexed under 'Wateren/plaatsen'.

At the back of the book there are tide tables for Harlingen, Hook of Holland and Vlissingen, and time differences for other nearby places as secondary ports, as well as other useful navigational information. There are two further indices, marked 'Naam kunstwerken' which lists all bridges, locks etc by name; and marked 'Nummer kunstwerken' which lists the same information but referenced by the numbers used on the ANWB charts.

Remember when using the alphabetical indexes that in Dutch 'IJ' is a single letter listed with the 'Ys' and pronounced as 'I', or sometimes 'ay' as in 'tray'.

24

An example of an entry in the first section on waterways and places

Name of waterway

The first sentence gives an overview of the waterway and its length. e.g. *From the Westerschelde at Vlissingen via Middelburg to the Veerse Meer at Veere. Length 14.5km. The canal can be transited with a fixed mast.*

ANWB chart

Waterway authority

Maximum speed

Maximum draught

Water level: Canal water level = Normal Amsterdam level + 0.9m
(Note: NAP stands for Normal Amsterdam Peil (water level) and is a datum to which many bridge heights and water depths are given)

VHF: Channel

Locks

gehele jaar – whole year
dagelijks – daily

Bridges
beweegbare – opening
bediening – service
gratis – free
ma. t/m zat. – Mon – Sat
6–22h – 6am–10pm
zo. en fd. – Sundays and Holidays
spitsuursluitingen – rush hour closures
draaibrug – swing bridge

Bridge name

Times of rush-hour closures

Air draught when closed

Convoy times given for northerly direction from Keersluisbrug starting at 5 minutes past, and in southerly direction from Stationsbrug starting at 41 minutes past

Services: *See under 'Arnemuiden', 'Middelburg', 'Veere' and 'Vlissingen'.* This refers to the second alphabetical section of marinas and nautical businesses.

Kanaal door Walcheren

Van de Westerschelde bij Vlissingen langs Middelburg naar het Veerse Meer bij Veere. Lengte 14,5 km. Het kanaal kan met staande mast bevaren worden.

ANWB Waterkaart(en)/Atlas(sen): Atlas Z.

Vaarwegbeheerder: Provincie Zeeland, Directie I &V, Abdij 6, Postbus 524, 4330 AM Middelburg, tel. (0118) 63 15 26/63 15 43.

Maximumsnelheid: Tot 20 m^2 natte doorsnede 15 km/h; 20 tot 30 m^2 12 km/h; 30 m^2 of meer 8 km/h.

Maximumdiepgang: Tussen de binnenkeersluis in Vlissingen en het Zijkanaal naar Arnemuiden 4,50 m; tussen het Zijkanaal naar Arnemuiden en Veere 3,70 m. Zie ook onder 'Bruggen'.

Waterstand: KP = NAP + 0,90 m. Er treden peilvariaties op van NAP + 0,70 m tot NAP + 1,10 m.

Marifoon: Sluizen te Vlissingen en Veere, kan. 18, Sloebrug in Vlissin-

---

gen, brug in Souburg, Schroe- en Stationsbrug in Middelburg, alsmede de Arnebruggen naar Arnemuiden, kan. 22.

Sluizen:
– Sluizen Vlissingen **(880)** in de toegang tot de binnenhaven en het Verbindingskanaal in Vlissingen, bediening te allen tijde, zie 'Vlissingen'. De binnenkeersluis (met ophaalburg) in Vlissingen, tussen het Verbindingskanaal en het Kanaal door Walcheren, staat open (tel. (0118) 41 23 72).
– Kleine en grote sluis in Veere **(871)**. Bediening: (gratis)

dagelijks	(gehele jaar)	5.30-23 h

Bruggen: De 5 beweegbare bruggen worden op afstand bediend vanaf het sluiscentrum te Vlissingen. Bediening (gratis):

ma. t/m zat.	(gehele jaar)	6-22 h
zo. en fd.	(15 juni-16 sept.)	9-21 h
	(16 sept.-15 juni)	10-19 h

– Keersluisbrug **(bb, 879)**(H 1,50 m) kent voor alle dagen twee bloktijden per uur waarin niet bediend wordt, resp. van .14 tot .22 h en van .44 tot .52 h. Verder wordt de brug in de periode van 1 april t/m 15 okt. van ma. t/m vr. van 8-20 h éénmaal per uur om .22 h bediend, of bij een aanbod van 5 of meer recreatievaartuigen, met uitzondering van de feestdagen.

K – Sloebrug **(bb, 878)**(H 5 m) wordt aansluitend op of vooruitlopend op de Keersluisbrug bediend.
– Souburg-draaibrug **(bb, 877)**(H 1,50 m) kent voor alle dagen twee bloktijden per uur waarin niet bediend wordt, van 6.23-6.28, 6.45-6.50, 7.23-7.28 h en daarna elk uur van .23 tot .29 h en van .49 tot .56 h. Clustering/konvooivaart, waarbij recreatievaart vanuit Vlissingen en vanuit Middelburg zoveel mogelijk gelijktijdig de brug passeert.
– Schroebrug **(bb, 876)**(H 0,60 m) te Middelburg wordt dagelijks onafgebroken bediend volgens schema. Verder wordt in de periode van 1 april tot 15 okt. van ma. t/m vr. van 8-20 h éénmaal per uur om .56 h bediend, of bij een aanbod van 5 of meer recreatievaartuigen. Verder zijn er op werkdagen spitsuursluitingen bij alleen recreatievaart, van

---

Verder zijn de Keersluisbrug en de Stationsbrug een belangrijke schakel in het regionale busnet. Als de aard en het aantal schepen het bij deze beide bruggen toelaat, wordt de brug pas 5 min na de officiële bloktijd geopend. De beide draaibruggen hebben naast de hoofddoorvaartopening ook een nevenopening. De nevenopening is alleen geschikt voor recreatievaart. Voor een zo efficiënt mogelijk gebruik van de beide doorvaartopeningen wordt de recreatievaart geregeld met elektrische en vaste richtingborden (BPR, bord D3a). Bij de vaste borden geldt 'de groene scheepvaartseinen bepalen de te gebruiken opening'. Dit kan dus toch de bakboordopening zijn.
Verder wordt er gestreefd naar konvooivaart, waarbij in noordelijke richting bij de Keersluisbrug wordt gestart om .05 h en in zuidelijke

---

richting bij de Stationsbrug om .41 h.

Voorzieningen: Zie onder 'Arnemuiden', 'Middelburg', 'Veere' en 'Vlissingen',.

Index

Although in the Dutch alphabet 'IJ' is a single letter listed with the 'Y's, in this book words beginning with 'IJ' (eg IJmuiden) have been indexed under 'I' for the convenience of English-speaking readers.